WEST OF THE AMERICAN DREAM

NUMBER FOURTEEN

TARLETON STATE UNIVERSITY

SOUTHWESTERN STUDIES IN

THE HUMANITIES

William T. Pilkington, Series Editor

WEST OF THE AMERICAN DREAM

AN ENCOUNTER WITH TEXAS

PAUL CHRISTENSEN

TEXAS A&M UNIVERSITY PRESS

COLLEGE STATION

Library of Congress Cataloging-in-Publication Data

Christensen, Paul, 1943–
  West of the American dream : an encounter with Texas /
Paul Christensen.—1st ed.
        p. cm. — (Tarleton State University southwestern
studies in the humanities ; no. 14) Includes
bibliographical references and index.
    ISBN 0-89096-753-9 (alk. paper)
  1. American poetry—Texas—History and criticism.
2. Christensen, Paul, 1943-—Homes and haunts—
Texas.   3. American poetry—20th century—History
and criticism.   4. Poets, American—20th century—
Biography.   5. English teachers—Texas—Biography.
6. Texas—In literature. 7. Texas—Civilization.
8. Sánchez, Ricardo, 1941–   9. Gordone, Charles.
10. Miller, Vassar.   I. Title. II. Series.
  PS266.T4 C47 2001
  811´.5099764—dc21
2001000225

CONTENTS

ILLUSTRATIONS

PREFACE

This is a book about Texas as seen by one man passing through its immense terrain. It is told personally, through my eyes, through my perceptions and imagination. I cannot make it all seem like fact, since much of it is the work of gradual understanding—a process that began in impressions and lingered on as memory, then dreams, to become mortared into shape by fact and connection.

Such processes are the land's own—with its great table of prairie and plain made from the crumbling of the Rocky Mountains. Wind erodes the crests grain by grain, and the dust spills down on the back of the Pacific winds to build up a soil over what was once bare sea floor, basalt, and granite rock. I believe the key to understanding Texas, the key to knowing any place, is to find the connection between land and the human nature formed by it. To know land is to know the self. Myths are the simplest form of that knowledge; perhaps mores and customs are glimpses into that relation. In Texas, the process of self-knowing gained from land-sense has only just begun. A long interlude of heroism and self-congratulation by conquering whites has delayed the process of self-recognition through humble study of the local world. We have only just begun.

The religions that abound here in all their many forms, most of them sharing the great taproot of Christian vision, have subtly refused to know the soul that amasses its character in craggy mountains, bitter creeks, vast empty reaches of semiarid land, and all the wonders of the weather. That imposing dimension of the nonhuman has been refused a voice. Though I have met ranchers and dryland farmers who speak of the land and weather as if they were difficult partners, living things to contend with to make a life, I have also met town folk who have no idea where they live or what part the epic landscape and its history play in their lives. The character of the average citizen—Anglo, Latino, African American—involves some sort of defiant humanism that makes the land a stranger. Which means we do not really have a treaty between the insect world, the wind world, the storm worlds of heat and northers, and our notion of self. The native world still possesses the tatters of a vision in which human beings occupy a part of some nurturing system of energies. We do not have the puzzle figured out, the pieces put into place. That will come, but at what price and at what level of humility and openness will it happen?

I have begun a journey inward toward the land and myself in this book. I realize now that my adult life has been textured by the place where I actually live as I work, pay bills, do my chores around the house, raise a family, and maintain my professional life. There is a real land beneath and around me, supporting what I do even when I do it without consciousness of its presence or powers. The weather is for many people the only reminder that nature is out there, with forces it can unleash upon sprawls of houses built recklessly in flood plains and in Tornado Alley; weather is all there is for many people living in apartment complexes and in air-conditioned houses. The rest of nature is the abstract, uneventful flatness of land one glimpses through the windows of a speeding car. The horse inhabits that world, as do the cattle nodding off under trees as the day grows hot. A few birds, a few turtles and snakes, make up the sum of what people think of as nature lying out there.

Even those who want to be aware of their dependency on the rest of life point away from themselves when they talk of an ecosystem. It remains somewhere beyond the windows and walls of the house in which we might be conversing—a place you point to, as if it began hazily in the grass and was swept away into creeks and under the trembling shadows of the elms and cedars, going west and north of us until real nature suddenly established itself. But not here among the carpets and chairs, where there is only the human dimension to be concerned about. But let an earth tremor rock a few dishes and cups in the cabinet, or crack a wall, and suddenly the boundary between us and it vanishes.

It should tell us that any boundary we may imagine is only a dream as we plunder the far side for our momentary advantage. That dream is fading as I write this preface. The "Battle in Seattle" in the winter of 1999 was an awakening to the realization that what we are now plundering may well be our own future. That was the cry in the streets as the World Trade Organization met in Seattle to plan strategy for the global economy. The youth were back with their banners and placards, and the barricades went up out of an old fear of public unrest.

This past June of 2000 I was in the little town of Millau, the "Seattle on the Tarn," in the beautiful hilly terrain of the Midi-Pyrenees of France, where a replica of Ronald McDonald was being hoisted in effigy by a group protesting the spread of American junk food into Europe. Others cried out against the WTO, genetic modification of plants and animals, and the threat of a uniform, corporate-managed world culture of consumers all eating the same simple wafer of modified beef and drinking the same sugary soft drinks.

Millau is the place where the French government tried to build a new army post twenty years ago, and it was José Bové, the sheep farmer, the new Lech Walesa of Europe, who protested by seizing a farm in the government's way and daring them to evict him and by having the villagers buy up all the available land and deed it to friends in little square-meter lots—a move that would have tied up the government for half a century processing each claim to eminent domain. Millau, now Prague, and then somewhere else—a smoldering fire beginning to break into open flames.

This book was written in the throes of a movement aborning in the minds of idealists and ecoactivists and ordinary people like myself, who care about what happens when technology becomes its own end and purpose.

It was conceived at the end of a long process in which Texas came to birth—as the land of heroes embodying all the dreams of immigrant America, ordinary figures who became rich, powerful, lords of the land, conquerors over others, millionaires and billionaires. But a new age now questions the fundamentals of western individualism, the very philosophy that made Texas important to American and world culture. Here lay perfect and limitless freedom to be what you wanted to be—the cradle of boundless self-expansion imitating the land's own unbounded expanses. Nature was there to be plundered for personal greatness. Altering the land bore no immediate or perceived consequences for the future; no one had to pay the bill after nature played the tune. Such questions were not to be asked in a place of bounty and infinitude, so the heroes—oil men, ranchers of the caliber of Charles Goodnight, business leaders like Ross Perot, visionaries like Trammell Crow—came and carved out their empires from the passive land. That was twentieth-century Texas; the new millennium is beginning to squirm under the old covenant of self-enrichment; the bills are coming due with exhausted aquifers, lower water tables in the once fertile plateaus of east Texas; the air is no longer wholesome and pure, as it was when the bluestem grew tall here. And now the oil patches have started to go dry. The infinite cupboards of nature are now looking half full, even a bit bare to the hands accustomed to reaching in for personal enrichment.

The age of heroic self-realization is coming to an end on a planet crowded with life, demanding its meager share of what remains. Everything has its limit, and we are reaching our own in North America. All this redounds upon the meaning of Texas as nature's treasure trove and upon my own imagination as I look around at the land that once inspired epic individuality. It now forces us to question the dreams we dreamt.

No wonder that I have looked long and hard in this book for the poets who offer a vision of nature sense and of responsibility to more than one's own self. The poetry of self-reflection is no longer tolerable in an age glutted with self-indulgence. We need narratives of participation and of reciprocity, stories that lay down the terms of a new morality of environmental sensitivity. We need poets who can show us how to live more thrifty and less invasive lives, so that the land we love can be bequeathed to distant generations in a usable form. We need a poetry of moral passion and delight, of land-love and understanding of the needs of others. We need a poetry that gives us a large, generous, religious vision of where we fit into the folds and creases of a complex terrain with a long prehuman history. We do not need to know the intimate journal-like details of consumer poets who thrive on finding material equivalents of their own transparent souls. We need poets who can annihilate self-interest and embrace strangers and unfamiliar worlds. We need new Whitmans to come into America to pick up the dialog he set in motion between self and world. If the poets can work it out, we will have a myth of self that we can build on in our daily lives, in our functions as users of the land. We need our poets to give us heroes who do not take, but give; who do not conquer the land, but make it thrive and allow it to recover its fertile diversity.

When I left Philadelphia after completing my graduate studies, I was leaving a known and comfortable urban world where all my habits and desires were circumscribed by human ingenuity. I lived within an artificial construct, where the brick factories, rail yards, smokestacks formed a palisade against the primal world. But when I came west, I experienced what many travelers have felt after crossing the Mississippi and encountering un-bounded land and overhanging sky: a sense of the real magnitude of nature.

Perhaps even then I knew that I must enter the West with a change of heart. I open this book by thinking about others, those who lived at the bottom of society, the misfits, the discarded, the unwanted. Perhaps it was my initiation into Texas society that made me take an earnest interest in how the other half survived, what they wore, what they looked like, how they spoke and eked out an existence on the fringes. I begin this memoir with my first bearings in a strange new country and then turn my attention to those who lived around me. This move west was like a second birth, a new life commencing at the age of thirty. I could look at things I did not understand and simply absorb them like a child learning colors, textures, the alphabet.

I know that at some point I moved beyond these first encounters to enter the world I had come for—the literary environment. As a poet, my mind was preoccupied with craft and my own development as a writer—looking for images, metaphors, the native symbols buried in the imagination of the people. I felt a sense of mission even at the first turn leaving Philadelphia—the desire to slip out of one body of information into another to explore some edge of America I did not know before. Texas was a new mind, a new relation to America. So I came as a student of poetry, and my ears were large.

Thus, the third chapter of this book takes an abrupt turn to a poetry reading, something I knew a great deal about having read my work in halls, bars, classrooms countless times with a few other bards and to a scattering of listeners.

This book is the only one I know of where the ritual of a public reading is dismantled and analyzed part for part, including the manners and customs of the poets, their appearance, their loneliness and isolation from the general public. I recount it for you as if you had never attended such an event and would like to know what occurs in these bright halls with so many empty chairs available. It is a combination of town hall, union rally, religious service, church supper, Sunday sermon, and Bible reading, and many other fragments of ordinary public ritual—with the poets baring their feelings and souls to strangers. It is my introduction into the local art scene, and it throws open the door into Texas poetry, my primary subject herein.

Chapter 4 is an exploration of the origins of modern poetry in the state and of the crucial role women played in shaping poetry as a voice of conscience over the slaughter of Indians and bison, the ruthless aggression expressed against all forms of otherness, to make Texas into familiar white homeland. Chapter 5 is about the two cultures of Texas in the first half of the twentieth century, with women meeting and conceiving the bases of a regional literature at their reading clubs, and men establishing a work culture in which art and leisure played an incidental role. The separation of the sexes slowed the evolution of the arts, and only after the victory of World War II did men vigorously lay claim to literature and dismiss women's writing as the "pink tea" school of belles lettres. But women were the architects of literary expression, and the poem was already spoken for. It would not be until the 1970s that men and women both would create the regional lyric of the present era.

Chapter 6, "A Photo Album," is a pause in my literary journalism to catch up with my own personal journal—in this case, a series of brief portraits of figures who came into my life and who embodied the very qualities of Texas life the poets were attempting to translate into verse. This is the first half of *West of the American Dream,* a journey through Texas and its writers, with a few historic sketches to account for the odd twists and turns in the making of poetry in the region.

I say region because the term "Texas" is neither static nor absolute, but spills out its cultural and philosophical energies over its own boundaries. As the geographer D. W. Meinig noted in *Imperial Texas: An Interpretative Essay in Cultural Geography* (1969), there are forces dispersing culture along trade routes much as the wind carries seeds and pollens, and these forces have spread Texas well into the High Plains of New Mexico, up into Colorado, and south along the Rio Grande Valley. Texas is a shimmering, mobile, historically altering shape that absorbs fringes into itself and holds them like a gravity field. Even the non-Texas authors I sometimes mention, such as Mary Austin, Willa Cather, or Peter Wild, are part of this Texas force field, if only in a book or two. The Southwest has several great cities, but one of its anchoring powers is this mercurial shape we call Texas, with its myths and cultural energies illuminating the ground around it.

In the chapter called "The Imagination," I make the case that a long history of denial about the value or function of imagination has been reversed in the twentieth century, centered in the movements of modernism and its post–World War II sequel, postmodernism. Together, these whirlpools of experiment pulled off one of the great reformations of western life—a return to the recognition of nature as a conscious force in human life. While the effects of this revolution did not reach mass culture until recently, poets in Paris, London, Berlin, Vienna, Mexico City, Barcelona, New York, and Chicago were aware that a new literature affecting the relation between "I and thou" had been invented. No longer could the world be simply an "it" in the esthetic equations of painting, poetry, sculpture, and dance; now there was what the poet Robert Duncan called "participation mystique," a new dialog between imagination and the earth. A return of the mythic imagination meant that writers had reopened nature as an extension of human consciousness—a soul to talk to, appeal to, implore, and to lose oneself in as invention turned toward the nonhuman. It was in the final stage of postmodernism that I came to Texas, in 1974, to begin my own introspective encounter with the state.

The two chapters that follow, "How to Read a Poem" and "Democratic Vistas," are broad views of what Texas poetry achieved in the period following World War II to the present and the figures who helped shape the course of contemporary writing—friends, acquaintances, a few close collaborators. I recall some of my experiences while hosting the radio program "Poetry Southwest," which ran from 1977 to 1987 on KAMU-FM and put me in contact with many of the important writers active regionally as well as nationally.

The next three chapters are larger, more detailed portraits of writers who make up a kind of gallery of the extremes of literary experience in Texas: a founding spirit, Vassar Miller; an inspiring dramatist and teacher, Charles Gordone; and one of the great voices of Chicano life, Ricardo Sánchez, all of them great presences while they lived and forces in the lives of writers now.

Finally, in "The Simple Bitter Sap," my title taken from a poem by Walt McDonald, I give my own view of what is missing and what needs to be done to bring Texas poetry not only to maturity and fulfillment, but to make it powerful enough to draw the audience it deserves. That readership, still skimpy and inattentive, needs to be called to the temple, as it were, to learn about the new spirit of participation and interaction between human dwellers and their natural home. I am impatient with the mediocre subjectivity of much Texas poetry and want the great awakening of mind that has liberated other regions to happen here.

Someone once told me I owed Texas a book about itself. I have held forth on the subject at many podiums and shown considerable relish for my opinions, good and bad, about the writers and their work. Now it is time to give a general reckoning of what has been done and what needs to be done. We are close to the time when our writers will join a great national colloquium on the identity of Americans, in this age of reappraisals of our national vision. We are called upon to give our voice to America from the Southwest, and this book is both the history of our poetic labors and my own personal urging that poets come of age.

As usual a book of this kind is not written alone; it is inspired by many helpful friends and colleagues. I am grateful to Lloyd Lyman, former director of Texas A&M University Press, for proposing the idea of this book many years ago, and to Noel Parsons, former editor-in-chief of the Press, for encouraging me to complete the project.

But many other figures loom in the background as muses, authorities, and guides to the state's literary history. Foremost are my dear friends, the poets Paul Foreman and Bob Bonazzi. I hail these writers, publishers, pioneers, and lyric geniuses, who broke ground when the times were changing, for their courage, their boldness, and surely their stubborn natures against all odds. Many nights were spent in close reading of the poets and in debates that exhausted all the wine and cigarettes and left us cheerful but spent as the sun came up. I listened as much as I bent their ears, for nothing can substitute for being here year in and out, doing the work, tightening the belt went grants were scarce and promises had been made to hopeful young writers with good manuscripts. The state was this implacable boulder, and these were the men who put their shoulder to it, shaking it off dead center toward something new.

But good talk was a feast with a long table, and prominent among the invited were such poets as James Hoggard, the voice of North Texas, and Miguel Gonzalez-Gerth, editor of *Texas Quarterly* in its final years at the University of Texas at Austin, one of the great quarterlies of the region; present also was Dave Oliphant, editor of Prickly Pear Press and one of the important chroniclers of Austin literary life. At the head of the table was Willard Spiegelman, editor of *Southwest Review,* whose meadowy pages were given to me to fill with Texas ink when I had something good to say. Also present at the table were Paul Ruffin, my friend Joseph Colin Murphey, and Richard Hauer Costa, editor of *Quartet,* another fine magazine brought down from New York and made into a sensitive instrument of the work here.

Tom Zigal is at the other end of the table, former editor of *Pawn Review*, where much of the best work we did in the 1980s was recorded and sent out to the hinterlands. And Bryce Milligan, formerly the literary director of the Guadalupe Arts Center and now publisher of Wings Press, where the new work from San Antonio is being put between covers. I include among the guests of the table John Campion and James Cody, both involved in the literary daily life and both good poets; John Herndon is dining among us as well, with his wife Susi Wong, designer of many of our books. Down the row I also see Leslie Ullman, the poet and director of the bilingual Creative Writing Program at the University of Texas at El Paso, and beside her the poets Janet McCann and Sybil Estess. And down in the corner, Ewing Campbell and James Hannah, fiction writers who smelled the bacon and came inside. And beside them, I perceive Dale Smith and his wife, Hoa Nguyen, editors of *Skanky Possum*, the exciting new Austin quarterly that has gotten us going again. Another who helped out with good advice and books is my friend and colleague, Marco Portales.

The feast of writers here contributed to the making of this book; their ideas, their idle chat on a summer afternoon, their dark thoughts over the wine, their anger and disappointment, even their bitterness, inform this memoir and help me to grasp this ineffable region. But so too did my students help me toward articulating the ghost of thoughts in my head. They were curious, the way all good Texas people are, about themselves and what made them, what slanted their vision to this peculiar world of sun and grass.

This book does not come into the world friendless and without relations. An antecedent book of essays I have admired and which influenced me greatly is Dave Oliphant's *On a High Horse* (1983), which canvassed the new wave of poetry in Texas and in Central America after postmodernism; a new book has also cleared the way for my own, Tom Pilkington's *State of Mind: Texas Literature and Culture* (1998), which makes a fine, intelligent assessment of Texas prose in all its forms, from sports journalism to the newest fiction.

I dedicate this book to the memory of Joe Gilstrap, friend, neighbor, plumber for most of the years I have lived in Texas, and a man who was the very picture of youth and innocence in the state, and the Laocoön of his age, wrapped in the coils of addictive drugs. He took his life as I was finishing this book, just when I began to look for him to show him my portrait of him with his shovel in the earth.

CHAPTER 1
FIRST THINGS

This story of a twenty-five-year encounter with Texas begins with an anecdote from Philadelphia. I was packing up my rental house in Powellton Village, a little nineteenth-century enclave of townhouses and row houses on the edge of west Philadelphia, near enough to walk to the University of Pennsylvania where I was finishing up my doctoral studies. I was headed for my first teaching job, at Texas A&M University, in an obscure little town called College Station, somewhere on the dry, slightly undulating Coastal Plains of east-central Texas, as my atlas informed me. It was 1974, the torturous year of the Watergate hearings and the famous Nixon farewell wave on the steps of his helicopter. He was leaving home, and so was I. Both of us were going west to unknown futures.

When I had brought around our big yellow Ryder truck and assembled friends to help me lug down fifty cases of books and all the odds and ends of student life, mostly bricks and planks, chipped dishes, a few cumbersome chairs, and a bed frame, my neighbor Bob Ross came by to see me. He stood on the porch while my wife and I eddied around him with cartons of old 33 records and piles of bedclothes. He stood smirking to himself, pretending not to be amused at my self-importance. A journey lay ahead, and I was the star of this enormous decision.

"So you took the job," he said, as I passed by.

"Yes, I'm going to Texas."

He leaned closer to me. He had coffee on his breath, expensive coffee from some little shop on Walnut Street. He was an assistant professor, but he had been let go and was looking for a job again. "It's a dead end," he said. "Don't go."

"But I want to. I mean, I think I want to," I said. It was always my weakness to let my indecisive nature reveal itself.

"It will take you nowhere," he said. He was not one to give opinions freely. I figured he had been at his kitchen window a long time watching me come and go with boxes. It must have pained him to think how ignorant I was—heading off to Texas with dreams of the good life, a few years there, then back east to Princeton, maybe Harvard. I knew nothing about Texas; he knew a little more, but not much. Out of his fine, thin-lipped mouth came all the historic prejudices against the last state of the South, the borderlands.

"I'm still going to do it," I said. "Maybe I'll last a year and be back. Don't let them rent the place out until I call, okay?"

He went away after hugging me farewell, but Bob had put a seed of doubt deep in my soul. I put on a forced gaiety after that and whooped up the troops with my singing and dancing around, pulling up the heaviest loads and pretending to waltz my way to the truck. But that seed of doubt would trouble me all the way across country. It would trouble me all the way to now. But I also knew that trouble meant adventure, risk-taking, maybe something momentous and new that would alter my life. So we got up into the cab of the truck and steered it around a corner, as Spring Garden Street, our home for four busy years, suddenly, irreversibly became a memory.

How many others in America have bid farewell to friends and the familiar world and set off as we did, to parts unknown? Of course, there are no more Indian raids on the settlements, no swollen rivers to ford with a lead horse and a prayer. We were not going off the map into the mud and the endless prairies, hoping to see an old shoe on the trail to guide us. There were no abandoned pump organs or books along the way, thrown off the back of wagons to lighten the load the last few hundred miles. No wooden crosses and stones to mark the graves of children who had fallen and been crushed or who had caught a fever and died. No horse skulls; no snakes coiled at the water holes, ready to strike a naked foot. No more captivity yarns where the wives are taken off by raiding parties to live in tipi villages the rest of their lives. No more Cynthia Parkers.

We were taking freeways all the way, almost door to door. With maps, diners to stop at, motels for the night. Easy, swift travel, with none of the old-style perils. Only car wrecks and the tedium that might make us doze at the wheel. But I wasn't going only for a job. I had a theory that inland America possessed myths and secrets no regular history book or conventional poem had yet told about. I was going off as a kind of intellectual pioneer. For the past four years I had been studying poets who had looked for the myths of American life, in particular the poet Charles Olson, about whom I was writing a dissertation. It opened my eyes to the notion that land is not static or godless but an active ingredient in human identity, human consciousness. What Olson had discovered as myth in New England I wanted to find in Texas. That was my plan, my ambition—apart from teaching literature. I wanted to find the myths that created the sense of being Texan, and the assumptions that created a spirit of place called the Southwest.

What did it mean to live west of the Mississippi, in some sense west of the American dream? What lay beyond the woodlands and the familiar South, the stretches of America that seemed to fray at the Mississippi Valley and become some new order of land and spirit west of it? That was my question as I started off. I was certain that beyond the older American dream of a man and his castle, every one an assured place in the sun, was some other reality where the dream shifted. After Louisiana, you ran out of Europe's ambitions and headed in a direction where nature took on new and epic proportions in life. That was my intuition. I hoped to be able one day to prove that nature rose up in a larger way and became a more imposing, influential force out west. The West meant something like a lower and wider sky, more ground, more forces to counter with, and thus a renewed sense of the power of the earth to inspire as much as to thwart ambition.

Whatever we were heading for, it meant something like an adversary of giant proportions and a new wiliness needed to go around or deal with it. Everyman a coyote—perhaps that is what lies west of the American dream. The great dust storms, the droughts, Tornado Alley, the vast timeless deserts and mesas, the Great Plains, the Gulf Stream, all these were portions of a giant's body, parts of a natural god's fury. Humans were dwarfed no matter how rich they became, or how many head of cattle they counted in their herds. A cowboy was a world mythic figure largely because he was someone who had given in a little to the natural world and become an aspect of it, no longer just a creature of the city or of ordinary life. He had entered into this other reality of Nature large and become a minion, a servant of the herds and the rainstorms. He had adapted backward and downward toward nature's laws, and that made him a new hero of the industrial age. Natural man.

Maybe that was what it meant to go west of Louisiana, west of Euro-America, west of Anglo tradition and law, and finally, west of the past. To live in Texas was something like cutting into the future, probing a post-Anglo world of Indians, Mexican Americans, African American cowboys and farmers, the world of mixed races and dryland dwellers, iguana sellers and cactus grinders, basket weavers and armadillo hunters. A land of the javelina and the fat, melting sun of an August afternoon. The land of moonrises that bleached the whole desert like a bedsheet, and of rain storms that would make Noah shake. It was a land of lunar craters and Salvador Dalí dreamscapes, and of old Aztec *brujas* and desert *curanderas*. All that lay beyond the primary culture of eastern and southern America.

The land west of Philly turned deep bluish green. The trees were tall, dense, with little black creeks easing along over their roots. By Tennessee, the grass shifted to emerald, and the fields were small, elegant forms of geometry, with plow lines running ruler straight to old wooden fences. The earth was a celebration of late summer energy. By the time we reached Arkansas, the south had frayed out to its slightly browning edges.

I still didn't know if I was happy or just bewildered by this abrupt end of my eastern-rooted life. It was exhilarating to be on the move again, saying good-by to student poverty and the ramshackle sort of life I had been living for years. But this westering edge of the old South was beginning to fade into shacks and tumble-down barns, and old houses steeped in their memories. The big shaggy oaks bore the heat and drought of centuries in their gnarled branches, one of which usually held up the tatters of a tire swing or some rickety steps climbing to a long-abandoned tree house. Dusty paths going off to swim holes, here and there remains of an outhouse, tilted precariously over a creek bank.

Dead end? Taking me nowhere?

At Texarkana, we were to take our first turn from an inexorably westering route over ten states. We turned left, to go down the eastern edge of Texas. It was near three o'clock of a Saturday afternoon, late August sunlight. Heat was up, dry winds blowing against us through open windows. My wife had been this way before, years ago with an old boyfriend in a convertible Ferrari, whirling out to California on a holiday. She knew the country, but didn't much like it. She gazed about, happy to be going somewhere after teaching high school in Philly the last four years to put food on our table. She liked the idea of renting a house through the newspaper, not knowing what it would be like. Or where. We eased up to the junction where we were to turn, and the sun cast very long rays over the open ground.

It was that openness of land that entered my imagination like no other landscape had done before. And I had seen quite a few dramatic landscapes in my time. I was the son of a foreign service officer and had been plucked from my suburban slumbers in Virginia at the tender age of twelve to be whisked first to France and then down into the heart of Beirut, Lebanon. A few years later, I found myself at a boarding school in the mountains of Baguio, in northern Luzon, the main Philippine island, alone for the first time in my life. I ate off dishes served by a headhunting tribe of the hill forests and even danced with them behind the kitchen a few times when the proctors weren't looking. Then I lived in a planter's villa in the center of Saigon, in a time just before open war broke out in the jungles of central Vietnam. I had seen a lot, and much of it lines my imagination as a writer. But this was different.

It was a sight that greeted many migrating families over the last century and a half. My father's family had come this way as well, to homestead in Union County, New Mexico, in 1910. My grandfather, a stern, hard-eyed Illinois machinist descended from Norwegian stock, had gone in with a partner to "prove up" a claim on a half section, a government-issued tract of land exactly one-half mile in size, or 320 acres. They stuck it out through four hard winters and sank some roots in that wild short-grass prairieland, which is the extension of the Texas Panhandle not only in landscape but in culture. A lot of others sold out long before my grandfather went back to his job at the Federal Arsenal in Rock Island. By that time, he had seen the last remnants of Indian tribes, befriended the itinerant Mexican shepherds, raised the highest kafir corn and milo maize, and become noted for the quality of his pinto beans. He got his deed, passed it on to his son, who in turn passed it down to my brother and me. I still own the land, though I haven't seen it in forty years.

On the only hill around that farmstead, my three-year-old father ran to catch the moon in his arms. He was a budding poet already, not quite like the medieval Chinese poet, Li Po, who drowned trying to embrace the moon in a river after a night of hard drinking. My father thought he could catch it because no moon had ever been so close to earth, he said. It was in reaching distance. The sky over the grasslands was low, very low. It had strange magical powers and exerted its gleaming influence on all the life below.

The stars at night
Are big and bright—
Deep in the heart of Texas!

When the family returned to Illinois, it was only after a transformation of the soul. The prairies had marked their thinking in ways too deep to understand. They had weathered an ordeal and come out of it harder, more resilient, but also wary of an angry god. Only a god of anger could so arrange the wind to make it collapse adobe walls and rip off roofs, and send sheds spinning on their ends. A good hard storm could freeze the cattle to the ground and turn a flock of sheep into ghost sculptures. They came back wiser, less idealistic about the world. Perhaps that is the heritage of all pioneers—they lose their power to dream fragile worlds. They tuck in and dig at the resisting ground of whatever ambition they happen to have. That was my father, a practical man whose emotions had gone deep inside, like the sap in a winter tree. He was unknowable, and seldom spoke about his feelings. He had the demeanor of someone who felt any expression of self was an exposure, an unnecessary vulnerability. That was his father's way, too. That was the code of silence among many Texans I have known.

A few years ago, I sat watching my aged, white-haired father eating his supper and surprised him with a question I had meant to ask for a long time.

"Did you love your father?" I asked.

He put his fork down and turned his short, stout hands under his chin. He thought about it. He pursed his lips to tell a story. He has a rich, deep baritone that carries even in a whisper. "There was a family over toward Staunton, about five miles off, we sometimes went to see, just to have a little company. We went there and I played with the boy, who was older by a year. I had made a toy rifle out of a stick I found and he wanted it. I wouldn't give it to him, so he went in to my father and said I had beat him with it. My father came out and didn't say a word. He took off his belt and whipped me with it until I was full of welts on my back and legs. He broke the stick and threw it over the fence and went inside." My father paused a moment. "I didn't have any use for him after that."

I didn't have any use for him! As if use were the highest virtue. Not loyalty, not care, or desire, or even love, but *use!* That was prairie logic. A man abuses your faith or trust and you don't use him after that. So they parted company, and my father grew up early, with a few lumps on his chin. The Depression came along and slowed his education, but from what my father told me, there were no handouts from his dad. In one brief moment of an afternoon love could die, replaced by something like cordiality or acquaintance. He could put the whole history of a relation in a few words, saying almost nothing, almost everything. What room was there for a luxurious language of the heart in such country, from such experience? These were Norwegians, and the world knows this group of human beings is among the most taciturn and aloof on the planet. But this quickness to cut ties was something else again, and it told me how thin and perishable was a love of language *out there* in that mystical wide land I was heading toward.

Strangely enough, my father was a poet in college, a rather good if conventional one. A "rimer," I would call it later. But also a translator who loved the rather wilted eloquence of Lamartine and some Baudelaire (my father had a sensuous side he tried to conceal), but not Rimbaud, not the daring experimenters. He loved the security of the nineteenth-century mind, which tucked in all its corners and embellished the interiors, making poetry into crowded Victorian parlors of oversized, ornate furniture. He was practical, even spare in his ways, and yet lush, overblown in his sense of art. He would have known and understood the need of pioneers to build a house with a large decorative parlor and gingerbread trim, with massive sofas and a piano, lots of lace in the windows, a wife in stiff crinolines and shawls, her hair a foot high on her head, twisted into elaborate sculptures. He would have known that this kind of gaudy refinement was a stay against the wilderness all around. You did it to save your life, you accepted the female art of softening the interiors of things because the hardness was so pervasive outside. And he would have liked Mirabeau Lamar's "The Daughter of Mendoza" the same way, for its desire to escape from mere survival into this vision of the tawny beloved Victorian beauty:

> O lend to me, sweet nightingale,
>   Your music by the fountains!
> And lend to me your cadences,
>   O river of the mountains!
> That I may sing my gay brunette,
> A diamond spark in coral set—
>   The daughter of Mendoza.

It was his mother he loved, the young Swedish-American woman who had thrown her pan over a rattlesnake in the barn and chopped the critter in two with an ax. My aunt told this and other stories about the New Mexico venture in a little book called *Pioneer Homesteaders in Union County*,

New Mexico: 1910 to 1914. She identified herself as Olive Desire Christensen Slocum, a name that seems to telescope out of a land of olive groves into longing, to the high north of Norway to the lower north of her husband's English roots. And then, then to New Mexico, because this is America, where the roots to earth are severed and you drift as you will, or as the wind carries you. Palos Heights, a suburb of Chicago where she spent much of her later life, was nothing to this memory of the prairies, the hardpan earth, the mule she rode to school, the plowing of the cornfields, the pinto bean sacks in the barn used as barter at the stores in Des Moines. That was life, and the suburbs were something in another key of existence much less exciting to her.

Homesteaders' wagons must have halted on this rise where I slowed down in my truck, just as the highways parted. The pioneers went west, I was going south, down toward the Gulf. They must have camped here and stared out at the vague horizons, perhaps a lone cloud dropping rain on some speck of the endless backdrop. Here was an American myth as large as the Rockies, the Mississippi, or any whale. I could feel its mystery all about me.

Open country, rough and rolling, but the southern edge of the Great Plains. It lay there copper and silver from the last sunlight, smoldering still. It was silent land, with the wind hardly moving the stiff grass. To the left were woodlands, far to the right the Chihuahua and Sonora Deserts, the Rocky Mountains, and the Pacific. Below us was the Gulf Coast, where the Gulf Stream churned its way around the curve of coast and out over the Florida Keys on its way east. It would seem we had come to the mystical heart of the continent, bounded by different cultures and by vast natural forces.

The ranches were out there, in the distance, small brown dwellings surrounded by wisps of fence drawn like spider web over the fading earth. You felt the weight of so much sky curving over you, blue and star-flecked at the center, black and gold at the edges. A few hawks were still above us, watching for moles, gophers, a careless jackrabbit out for a late supper.

The mind reels helplessly, out of words against this Zen riddle of space. There are no contours, no convenient corners when you stare out into the void of this kind of land. It shimmers, it moves without moving. Your compasses do not work here. Nothing inside you can define what your eyes see. There is only the blankness, more vacant than sea blankness. At least in the sea there are waves, troughs, wakes to tell you that you move, that you have a path to make. But here, with the land beginning to slow and widen, and become the purest sense of inertia your body has ever known, you feel that space turn inside you, moving you into what might be a nausea of the great nothing before you. There is no milestone, no orienting tree or cleft of rock, only the immensity. And what strikes fear at such a vision is that your life becomes stripped of its days, its measurableness. There is the vastness and you are here at its edge, and death is on the line somewhere. The line keeps moving as you advance, and it leads you nowhere. It takes you to more of itself. How does one cope with this immeasurable sense of the future, where your own life would be a mere stake in the ground, an invisible bit of whiteness no larger than a deer's tail?

Moby Dick keeps entering my mind as I recall all this. The great whale, the novel that turns a whale into the first American myth. In his famous chapter "The Whiteness of the Whale," Melville comes close to defining that feeling one has looking into the Great Plains from its southern terminus. But he says it about whiteness: "Is it that by its indefiniteness it shadows forth the heartless voids and immensities of the universe, and thus stabs us from behind with the thought of annihilation, when beholding the white depths of the milky way? Or is it, that as in essence whiteness is not so much a color as the visible absence of color, and at the same time the concrete of all colors, is it for these reasons that there is such a dumb blankness, full of meaning, in a wide landscape of snows—a colorless, all-color atheism from which we shrink?"

I was grateful for the pines that went along my side of the truck. They were the last fringes of forest before the land opened into the great corridor of level prairie extending all the way into northwest Canada. I could look into the early night sky and see cabins behind those trees, and small towns blinking along some winding river. It was still a part of America I understood, the dense world of trees and hills, where towns were natural things tucked in among the braided limbs. If I craned my neck I could see out the west window all that unstructured reality and realize we had come to the great hinge of experience. This is where the very notion of nature altered its identity and swung off into something that was not only the end of arboreal America, but the end of European consciousness as well.

The western mind was born of trees and close shelters, where the sun disappeared into a maze of black limbs each night and rose on the brow of some neighboring hill. It was a world small enough to minister to the human ego, to nurture dreams of conquest. One America grew up from Maine to Louisiana, an extension of Europe's mind. No transition necessary. Simply build a few log shelters, name your streets after English villages, and go about reconstructing an Old World in the New. Even the Caddo Indians who lived in this part of east Texas were familiar people to the first settlers; they had already established complex social hierarchies, towns, a sophisticated agriculture, and trade with other tribes. They too were of the arboreal world and offered no resistance to the westward movement. The Caddo seemed to say to those brave Anglos about to enter the infinite flat world, "Go ahead. Be my guest. But don't ask me along."

That was the end of a certain world. Beyond lay nature's prime meridian, the 98th longitude, the biological dividing line of east and west America. Walter Prescott Webb has made us all aware of this biological divide in America in *The Great Plains* (1931), where he tacitly argues the considerable notion that nature has its own mind and will in the Southwest. The power of that book moved Anglo thinking closer to the Indian world by just such a vision. Two hundred miles ahead of us was that strange, invisible barrier where flowers, bees, grasshoppers, crows, and spores all seemed to know it was their edge as well. This side of the 98th was the Atlantic world, and a foot or two west of the 98th meridian was the beginning of the Pacific world. The Rockies were a buffer zone, a kind of ramp over which the Pacific westerlies had to soar and then dissipate, drying out the Plains that slanted down to the Mississippi Valley. Nature knew, and obeyed the line almost as well as the Caddo did at their thin edge of the east Texas treeline.

The moment my wife and I had crossed the Mississippi at Memphis, we were going upland slightly, imperceptibly. We were climbing a tilting ramp of earth some fifteen hundred miles wide that was the dispersal of granite, basalt, sandstone, and minerals swept off the slopes of the Rockies by wind and rain. The earth here was mostly alkaline, bitter soils with salt residues, shallow rivers, not the humus culture trees require. It was dry land, with only creeks offering suitable habitat for short, stumpy oaks, willows, the exogenous yaupon and mesquite. This was the lying-down Rockies, the dismantled mountains, watered by streams and erratic storms, and combed by nearly constant winds.

When Charles Goodnight, the "father of the Panhandle," established the vast JA ranch in Palo Duro Canyon in 1875, named after its principal owner John Adair, an Anglo-Irish aristocrat, the canyon was still populated with

Comanches and great herds of buffalo. Goodnight had gone down into the moist depressions of the desert floor where springs oozed from the canyon walls and a few small lakes offered watering for his herds. Beyond, up on the higher ground, was a prairie soil that had not been disturbed for thousands of years. It was there from the origin, pure aerated earth dunged by buffalo and antelope, never exposed or ruptured by a plow. It was opened the first time in the late nineteenth century by settlers, and went dry and blew away the moment you tried to plant in it. It was reserved for bluestem, a nourishing form of "buffalo grass," and other long-rooted grasses and was essentially stubborn, primal, one-minded about what it knew to grow. The land broke down under the first plows. In the southern High Plains, the dust storms blew all through the 1930s as a result of the plow and overgrazing. Ten thousand years of soil culture stopped by the drag of a prairie plow. Perhaps that is the basis on which the local hubris formed. You could stop nature here with a knife, or an inch of lead. You could stop it, but you would not necessarily survive doing it. The lessons of nature were hard earned in this flat land, and every hamlet and farm we passed in our yellow truck was like a parable from the Old Testament, tales about suffering, loss, warfare, racism, power-grabbing, bonding, weeping, death, and the grim will to survive against all odds. We moved along our little forest edge like lost children, awed and innocent.

Night crept over us as we went south and worked our way west toward the Brazos Valley. When we arrived in Bryan late at night, the town seemed dreamy to us. Perhaps it was tired eyes and road fatigue, but the little houses, the dark side streets, the glow of porch lights all gave the town a quaint, storybook character. When we awoke, the sun bleached away all the dreaminess of the night before. The August light was blinding, and all the houses were painted white. We shielded our eyes as we drove around looking for a house on Dellwood Street, a curious name in such a burnt little prairie town. But there at the end of a narrow paved street, a little bungalow with green shutters, a sagging garage, and wilted yard. Inside, the living room floor tilted to one corner, and thick muggy air assailed us the moment we entered. A loud air conditioner rattled in the dining room and could hardly push the cold out into the adjoining rooms. Beneath the house, we soon discovered, was a muddy pond from a rain the week before.

The backyard was defined by two wobbly fences, each with a mangy dog staring through, beginning to growl. Along the north fence was a row of dead bean vines, each curled up as though it had died in a fire. Drought had drawn up the earth into knots of pottery-hard clay, with deep cracks zig-zagging all through the brown grass. Someone had labored and given up growing a few peas and beans; the sun had won another small victory over human beings.

My wife and I unpacked and went about furnishing the empty house with perhaps more industry than it required. But we were avoiding each other's eyes for now. Who wanted to start a debate the week before classes began, and with all our money already spent making the move? Right now the elms along the Schuylkill River in Philadelphia would be turning golden; cool winds would be blowing in from the east at night, making it blanket weather. It was time for hiking in the Poconos, for taking picnics out along the Delaware, or up into New Hope, where the hills were covered with dense, blue grass and late-summer flowers. Here, the land was gray and beige colored; only a few sharp weed stalks survived the summer drought. The shell of a dead armadillo lay in the street outside, its head crushed. It seemed to represent some aspect of summer I did not want to ponder just then.

The sky was weak blue, with the sun like a raging furnace at the center of it. You could only squint when you went out to the truck, and you hurried back into tepid air conditioning from the dining room. The bedroom had turned into a kiln by four in the afternoon. Our sheets were hot to the touch. Fortunately, our door led directly into the dining room, so with a few turns of the knobs up to maximum cool and fan, we got the air to circulate. We would sleep, at least.

When evening came down, it was still hot. We sat out on the front step with the Ryder truck crowding our small front yard. We had still to unload our Land Rover, which I had filled with boxes and driven into the Ryder truck. It was cheaper to carry it inside than to tow it behind. Ours was a working-class neighborhood, divided between Hispanic and Anglo. The neighbor had managed to keep alive some flowers in a window box, and a little hackberry tree was adorned with a clump of prickly pear cactus. They kept the curtains shut and seemed to know how to stay cool in this weather. Our windows were all open now, except for the bedroom and dining room. We had eaten lightly and now sipped on cool white wine.

Something about heat intrigues you the moment you get used to it. It makes life want to come out, to share. The sounds of neighbors talking behind hedges, inside screened porches, on front steps made it all feel like an older, forgotten America of porch culture. It was good to hear so many voices, such distant laughter up and down the streets. The beers were popped and greeted with a quiet *gracias* or thanks; the talk would rise and fall like a breeze in the trees. The suburbs lay elsewhere and were quieter, less intimate. We had seen them on our cruise around town; ranch houses facing the street, garage doors left open, as if to boast about all the lawnmowers, bikes, storage cartons piled up inside. The decks were behind the house where you could not see any social life. Out front you heard the sigh and drag of the lawn sprinklers, the constant furry hum of compressors hidden by shrubs. These were white neighborhoods. They were no different anywhere in the country, and all of them flickered with TV light and walled out strangers. We crept along, fearful of arousing any suspicions from late-night walkers. We just wanted to see if there was any difference to the middle class out west. There wasn't.

Here it was different. The street was potholed and trees were half dead. A few houses could use a paint job and a new roof. No garages, just carports. A big semi tractor waited for a trailer tomorrow to be hauled up to Oklahoma or over to Colorado. A bread truck was parked down the road. Kids played out until very late and did not come in until a voice grew dark and angry. Whitman's America, the workers idling after a long hot day.

Who could have foretold the great battles for possession of the land would end in this friendly, if not intimate truce? The Indians were gone, the buffalo nearly erased from the earth. The surviving parties to a century of bloody conflict were the *norteños* over here and the Anglos over there. Each side had to compromise, to yield something of their ways to get along. An Anglo here was different from a midwesterner or an easterner. They probably would not get along too well if you tried to mix them up at a party. Accents would be wrong; diets would be too different. The clothing would tell if you came from rain and woodlands or from hot, cloudless prairie. People here liked their windows big, their outside near. Back east, the houses were shut tight and coal fumes lingered in the rooms through summer. You never forgot the furnace below, or the winter vestibule with its inner glass door, all the galoshes and overcoats hung up just inside the front door.

Here, no sign of winter anywhere. Only the hard-pan earth, the sagging fences, cicadas droning away by early morning. The slow tempo of afternoon grinding to a halt by five, when the sun melted everything from roof

profound sense of order that placed the white Europeans over everything else. Brazos County is the continuing saga of three groups burdened with traditions and visions that resist mingling. A fourth lingers in the mind as the absent American Indian. The boundaries between races have softened considerably since the turn of the century, but the resistance to merge has found other ways of expressing itself. Subtle, quiet, tacit ways that go along under the political correctness, the humaneness that desires to be fair and equal.

Even a newcomer senses the hierarchical order of the races in Bryan. The lowlands gather together the African American and Mexican American poor, where the creeks rise and the ground is boggy. The life in these little creek hollows is dense and opaque; a few *pulquerías* and sugar shacks make up the night life, where the tequila and gin flow freely on weekend nights. The houses are a hodgepodge of shanties, shacks, cabins, and the salvaged hulls of old wooden mansions partly dismantled and moved out of their old neighborhoods. To stroll among the narrow streets in the heart of the poor town is to enter a kind of *art brut* second world, where the roofs bend crazily, the porches are either tilting or broken off; stove pipes jut at all angles from walls and windows, and ponds stand choked with car hulks and rusting appliances. Everything is in decay, but the human spirit is vibrant, strong, erotic. Here nature has the upper hand, and it is not rare to find some boy dangling a long black snake or fat snapping turtle on the end of his fishing pole, walking home to show his mother. The smells are of barbecue and fried chicken, roasting potatoes and beer. The music deep in the trees, under the owl hoots and frog *rivets,* is slow earthy soul at one end, weeping *ranchero* at the other.

When you come up out of these bottoms into the daylight, you must first pass the cemetery where all the departed gentry lie in state. Big monuments, smoky willows and oaks, a few yew trees, lots of gravel paths for the funeral corteges. Judges, lawyers, doctors, the town managers are all sequestered here, at the north edge of Bryan. The road beyond leads to higher realms, and almost immediately you skirt the highway suburbs, built since World War II for returning veterans and a new, populous blue-collar class of workers. Bryan is the county seat, with an old downtown of western storefronts, a hotel (under renovation), an intersection with three long-dead banks, one of which introduced the first night depository window in the nation. It is obscured by a Coke vending machine. Where old general stores did their business you find antique shops—full of Texas Victorian chairs and settles, the usual assortment of ottomans and crocheted fire screens, copper bed warmers. This is old country, with a few white mansions here and there reflecting the faded prosperity of some of the Brazos Valley cotton families. Fraternities took them over. The Southern Pacific comes down through town blasting diesel horns all hours of the night and day, making the dogs howl.

Toward the university you have the professional suburbs, with their manicured yards, ranch houses with long roofs and lots of garage at one end. The drive will have two, maybe three cars; a high cedar fence separates one yard from the neighbor's. A riding mower sits in the drive; bikes lean against the side door. A look of comfort, security; the rooms dark behind their windows. It is an eastern style of life, a grudging accommodation to plains living—with many of the habits of the Northeast carried to Texas, made possible by central heat and air, microwaves, and other luxuries. The wind blowing over the salt grass does not enter into the rooms of such a house, but goes over the roof and looks for openings elsewhere. The interiors are soft, with long sofas, polished tile floors, lots of humming appliances, long corridors with bedrooms going off. A life lived in spite of the weather, the conditions of a south, low-lying terrain.

I am neither a historian nor a geographer, but those are the two eyes with which one sees in Texas. The two are really one, a conversion of the natural and human worlds. Whatever I know about Texas is mainly what I have read. Having no other kinship but a land claim in New Mexico, I was, you could say, the product of mere hearsay and book learning. But if you live in this region a while, a good long while, and possess curiosity and a modesty to ask questions of those who are native, you come to know Texas a little. You develop a personal understanding of it, which is like having a foot or so of the old prairie sod in your head, growing in your imagination.

And it is that inner grass on which I graze as a poet, a writer. It was many years before I could write about Texas, but even in my first tentative short stories, I felt a deepening relation to the land, even the land I did not know. The northern openings to the Great Plains above Dallas, over the Red River, that Indian boundary of the 1880s. I could feel its presence, and know it was up there, and that I was living at the southern terminus of the buffalo ranges. I was on some lump of shelving where the "coastal dark prairie" bit into, crumbled beneath first the "Fayette Prairie" and then the "Black

Prairie." The land came up at this point above the old Gulf shoreline, and the ground cover told you that. You could smell the difference going northwest, rising out of a moist, slightly stagnant air that seemed to remember its years underwater over past aeons. The land around the Fayette Prairie is lighter, more airy and diverse with wild flowers; the land below, where Bryan, my little town, and College Station, the sister town and home of Texas A&M, are situated, has the sea in it, a logy saltwater passiveness where things come up gray, twiggy, more stubborn.

Nonetheless, it was the ground I lived in, where I started a second life. And it has nourished me both as a poet and prose writer. Poems came rapidly after my first few years teaching, poems about wind, the hard sheeted rains that blew up from the Gulf and over from Mexico. The blue northers that shook down laundry and rolled trash cans into the streets, and began as long beards of rain falling slanted into the sunlight, and then came down black and furious with thunderheads and great curtains of lightning, and left behind the bright, cold air of true winter. All this poured into my diaries and journals, and my lyric poems. Weather, and then the seasons, the two seasons of coastal Texas—winter and summer. And winter was furtive, uncertain, a two-month show of snow flurries and heavy rumbles of wind and then quiet again, thawing. Winter was one long procession of fronts and then came a vast opening of the year from May to November in which the heat built its solid walls around the middle of the state, making everything go limp and fall asleep, from dogs to human beings, insects to rosebushes.

How it was that a poet could find so much information in weather changes, especially these monotonous phases of a bipolar year of heat and cold, I don't know. I spent the better part of my early life here trying to see what was really out there, and not just see it through eastern eyes and memories. That was tough, and I am still practicing. My short stories, which came grudgingly, were about the conflicts and passions of what I imagined to be the rigors of contemporary ranch life. I cobbled together more borrowed experience from friends, from stories my students told me, from my own rambles around the hinterlands of Brazos County. After a while, I grew more confident, and began to penetrate the outer skin of Texas rural life. I began to see how my characters were both me and some curious alloy of land, weather, and the human beings who lived in it. I was becoming adept at a certain level of perception, which meant I could also begin to read Texas literature and understand the information that went between the lines, in all the pauses of the dialog. That was what began to make such a book as this feasible to write—a way of organizing the perceptions that befell over twenty-five years a life thrown out of its eastern orbit into a vortex of riddles and paradoxes.

As a writer, a poet, a speculator in the traffic of history and geography, I will have more to say about my wanderings in Texas, the writers I met, the friends I keep, the land I have come to love and venerate. The actual process of learning day by day gets lost in a memoir such as this; one simplifies in retrospect, sorting the ideas from all the daily chaff. To my book-informed imagination, I see Texas as a kind of fulcrum of North America, a place where opposites converged, tried to fuse, separated into unstable alloys and shifting hierarchies. The very question of American identity seems to be hidden here on this arid land, on this anvil of the American soul.

The founding of the nation came in two phases: a southwestern founding from Spain, a northeast founding from England. Add the Africans, the French, the Germans, the Italians, the Scandinavians here and there, the eastern Europeans, the Arabs, the Asians, and you have the rest of the crazy quilt of American diversity. But in the East, you have the concentration of western Europe, a culture that had already passed through the Reformation, the Enlightenment, the French Revolution, and the Industrial Revolution. It made for a certain urban, Protestant, egalitarian culture that obscured the authenticity of New World things—their unique biological identity. The hills were not English hills or French hills, or German hills, but curiously American hills. Even the painters denied what their eyes saw and painted Vermont and New Hampshire as if they were the English Cotswolds or the Scottish glens. The river valleys, the Hudson, the Charles, were translated by the brush into the River Wye and the Thames, the Loire and the Seine, the Rhine River. The very essence of northeastern America was that it was indistinguishable from western European topography and could thus be renamed to stand for it. No problem.

But as you headed west of the then-called Middle Border, you came upon the Indian mounds of Ohio and Indiana, and the more intricate water-clocks and star-map pools of other mound builders in Tennessee and Alabama. You knew there was some different dynamic at work, some human interpretation of a purer, more frankly American world. It could not be denied. The naming shifted perceptibly toward Indian soul-names, place-names that bore some spiritual significance of the resident gods. You had come upon aboriginal America, the outback of non-Europeanized human nature. And yet the Deep South prided itself on creating a Nouvelle France, a Nueva España from these humid woodlands. Perhaps they did achieve a second Europe here as well. But the effort to transform was less complete.

The southern novelists have shown how an ur-American wilderness lingered on as the South's unconscious. It came up through the roots, through the tobacco leaves, the palm fronds, the bougainvillea and kudzu. It was the beginning of American eros, a land of explosive violence, irrationality, and deep currents of sexual passion. Hart Crane, William Faulkner, Tennessee Williams, Flannery O'Connor, and Toni Morrison would all discover its latent primordial character in the twentieth century; Wallace Stevens would make Florida the realm of imagination, by which he implied that New England was the pole of reason and mere practicality.

The sheer plushness of southern nature was the gateway to a purer sense of America. It had to do with some exotic energies not available at the southern ends of Europe—not in Sicily or in Andalusia. Something more than arid or sunny landscapes, but a place combining a long evolution of blood sacrifice and what the French call *le negre dans le cœur,* the darker passions of the heart. This mythic South was a delta of native bloods and traditions, where a separate founding of America occurred long before European settlement. Now that founding takes on greater latitude as new theories of "multiple entry" into primordial America gather force. An ancient world came to tropical America from different paths, not only by a land bridge over the Aleutian Straits, a trickle of human life following the bison herds down into both Americas, but perhaps by sea as well. If so, there are multiple layers of history to be rediscovered, which will vastly expand the official histories of Mexico. That is the key to Mexican identity: a sense that a deep native history preceded the European invasions and that this secret and largely destroyed history, older than Greece or Rome, represents a Jungian universe of myths and legends. The contemporary southwestern imagination now draws upon this unarticulated past as a source of images and dreams from which new writing will come.

When I consider the makeup of our street, what I see is that on the one side white blue-collar workers represent a complicated modern self evolved from various European roots into not just an American but a Texas-American. We are seeing a convergence of multiplicity into something singular and communalized called an Anglo. The word "Texan" is the

complement to that identity, and a wealth of ideology swims below the surface of the terms "Texas" and "Anglo"—for by Texas one means a place
where a racial battle was fought and won by whites, and Anglo implies that
victor represents the westward push of Protestant religion into alien terrain
once held by Catholics and indigenous pantheists. To my left, occupying the
eastern part of Dellwood Street, then, is a row of houses occupied by a group
of neighbors linked by racial and religious history. Their identity as Europeans is worn away, and a new, politically rich communal self has taken its
place.

On the west side are houses whose porches are shadowed by four-
o'clock and whose occupants are mainly (except for us) from south of the
Rio Grande. Their identity is not converging but dispersing outward again
from what was earlier a simple sense of just "Mexican." That implied
Catholic, some combination of Indian and Spanish blood, poverty, a peasant origin, and traces of an earlier pantheism associated with American
Indians. Now, with the Chicano movement at a very mature stage of articulation, the word "Mexican" is beginning to unravel into a labyrinth of
native histories, including Olmec, Toltec, Totonac, Mayan, Aztec, as well as
a host of other tribal histories—all of which contribute to the idea of Mexico without exhausting its possible meanings. One side of the street has
formed its identity into a very positive moral and ideological argument; the
other is undergoing the profound historical process of redefining and mul-
tiplying its identity into some fabulous but not yet fully stated set of relations to paleo-America.

We parked our car somewhere on the potholes between the two sides and
lived our rather fragile academic life between their boundaries.

And because I have lived so long in other countries, I rather liked my position as foreigner among them. I could hear arguments from both sides
and sagely nod and smile without committing myself to the validity of either one. I envied both sides their fabulous histories and knew that they expressed their claims to the past in myriad subtle, half-conscious ways. The
Anglo was not only claimant to a land won by blood and will but was also
the carrier of the South's history and had undergone the transformation of
the Civil War and Reconstruction, and the reemergence of the South in a
new form in the twentieth century. A relation to the African American, formerly the slave labor of the region, added a whole new sediment of irony
and detachment different from the rest of American consciousness. This

too was carried perhaps a little too lightly in the head of the average Anglo here. But the expression of such complex regionalism seemed to require no effort at all—parades down Main Street, celebrations of San Jacinto Day and Easter, devotion to the high school football teams and to Texas A&M's Aggies were metaphors and symbols of identity I would not know how to read for decades. Here was a hieroglyphics of regional speech told in hats, blue jeans, boots, bandannas, slurred speech, spitting, haircuts, the Confederate flag, pickup trucks, dances like the "Cotton-eyed Joe," prison rodeos, precision drill teams, military preps, barbecue, conservative politics, church suppers and Sunday school, and all the other Anglo tics and customs.

It was American patriotism and race pride filtered through southern history and something else, the western dimension of life beyond the forest belt, in that grander, stranger mode of nature where desert and plains met, swirled, baked, and became post-European. That was the sieve through which Anglo-Texas strained its identity down to something unique, lime-sour, practical, and boisterous. It was almost as if the race had encountered its last victory over otherness and was still brimming with the joy of it all, and now made a civilization based less on universal human values than on the myth of racial conquest. The Anglo's vision is not yet mature but is based largely on the power of insistence, perseverance, and luck, principles of a victorious people who believe in their good fortune. The moral attitude is one of taking from nature without necessarily having to give back—which is also the mind of the warrior, the victor.

On the other side of the street, a more condensed, refracted, tacit mode of cultural projection—to me, at least. I could not decipher much behavior on first contact. The smiles, the demurrals, the modest ways in which compliments were deflected, all that seemed like some Hispanic rendition of Tío Tom. In time, I realized our neighbors were crossing a mine field to befriend us. Anything could go wrong and did, eventually. Already we were strained by our differences, social and ethnic, and there were also the eyes of the street on our little trips back and forth between houses.

We were unaware how fragile our relationship was, but as I went to school each day and saw how distant relations were among the races, I soon learned. Whites made up the vast majority of students and professors; grounds keepers, maids, cafeteria workers, and maintenance crews were all drawn from the Hispanic and black labor pool. It was apartheid in a mild, but persistent form. In twenty-five years, the only change I have seen is the employment of more women of color in traditionally male jobs like tractor mowing, gardening, repair work. Slowly, imperceptibly, the student body has darkened a little, and the faculty is now somewhat more balanced with women and African Americans.

Central Texas, centered on the old Austin land grant, but considerably expanded since then to encompass the land between the Trinity and Colorado Rivers, is also the most racially diverse area of the state. But the geographer D. W. Meinig saw all this back in 1969. In his book *Imperial Texas,* he wrote that "Central Texas has persisted as the great area of diversity. In this varied physical arena of woods and prairies, hills and plains, rich river bottoms and thin-soiled cuestas, there is more human variety than anywhere else in Texas: Anglos of every background, Negroes, Hispanos, and all of the European groups. Proportions and distinctions have changed over the years (the Hispanos are more important and widespread today than ever before, for example, while differences between Anglos and Europeans have certainly faded) but all the historic elements remain discernible" (108). If any sort of fusion or integration of race and culture is to occur, it will happen here. It hasn't yet, and there is already a long history of tension and inequality to complicate new efforts at unifying the region, but at least the major players are all "in place," Anglo Texans, Mexican Texans, and African Texans.

But because 1974 was still part of the *ancien régime,* it meant our friendship with Maria and Jose would collapse from the pressures around us. One day we were invited over for a cup of coffee. It was late afternoon in October, still hot but with longer nights to cool us down. We sat in their tiny living room, with Jose fighting off drowsiness. He had come from a rougher life, and his body was played out. He sat up with his eyes wide, clutching the faded ends of his armchair. To break through the tired chat I tried a new word on them. I asked if they were *chicanos.* Looking back on it, I see what a gaffe I committed, but I was all smiles, ready to explore the word.

They both froze at the sound of the word. It meant something sharp, piercing, the worst of all possible words, perhaps. They had spent their lives trudging north toward some state of invisibility in the Anglo bastions of central Texas. Now I used a word that came up from the border, where anger and political resentment were brewing a whole new racial conflict with Anglo authority. It was the undoing of all their sacrifice and hard work. The little house with its curtains, green shutters, the car in the carport, the little scrap of green grass were all threatened, singed by the word.

They concluded with a nod that I was learning too fast and was now prying into their secrets. I could almost feel an old garden gate shutting between us. From then on, we were polite, but no longer friends. Cathy and Maria talked now and then and exchanged a plate of this or that. But our visits to one another were over. We were just neighbors, and when we moved away a few months later, Maria became our babysitter once in a while, someone who occasionally sold us a pack of tamales. Jose was on dialysis, a very sick man; when Maria retired from school they moved into a country house. We let the last strings fray. The racial divide had finally parted us, and I regretted it. I could have learned a great deal from Maria; she was a clear window into the other side of Texas.

What was Texas? *A dead end?* A beginning? It was the end of the South, not quite the beginning of the West, but its threshold. It was something in between the directions, a place secreted within the ambiguity of zones, regions; it bore a different character from either South or West and meant something only nature could account for. It was flat country with shallow rivers draining into the Gulf; it was Comanche territory once, after they drove the Apaches south of their old hunting grounds. It was Spanish colony and Mexican province. It was a terrain where Anglos came one by one until their numbers were sufficient to take it over for themselves. It was slippery ground and looked for foreign alliances before it petitioned to become a state. It seceded and joined the CSA and came back to the Union keeping its original constitution intact. It retains the broadest charter for self-rule of any state and continues to think of itself as sovereign, a "Republic" of the mind. It is in many ways the purest form of America, with its races separated, its ground spacious, its resources giving it power into the far future.

It is also a fulcrum of national politics and commerce. It is like the nation in having no firm, deeply rooted capital of mind and heart. Like the nation, there is no one city that dominates, but rather, three—Dallas, Houston, San Antonio, with Austin serving as its Washington, D.C., and still playing a minor role in managing the energies of the state. All the races are here, the religions, the forces to shape America in the twenty-first century. Increasingly, California and New York represent not national interests but coastal ones; Texas begins to manifest a certain national personality in its political life, and now in its commercial power.

So what is it? Where does one go to burrow in and discover its elusive soul? A sociologist would say, "Count the people, their jobs and lives." A philosopher might explore the values written into laws and morality; a geographer would elaborate on the topographical factors that divide Texas into regions and microclimates, each with its own culture. I am none of these. I am a poet with a strong curiosity about human beings. I would get at the hidden soul of Texas my own way, through its myths and fantasies, its dreams and illusions, even its tacit, repressed knowledge of things too alien to the group soul to be spoken aloud or written down. I would get the smell of the state's breath, so to speak, by watching, listening, looking around, and eventually enter its inner life by reading the poets. In this most neglected art of the region are certain truths and insights the other arts seem reluctant to utter.

CHAPTER 2
OF UNDERWORLDS

Is there an underworld in Texas? A place where the exiled live, work, pursue their pleasures? I asked myself that question, because that is the way one gets to know a foreign country. Go to the dark corners of a city like Beirut, walk the alleys and sniff the hole-in-the-wall restaurants, see what lives behind the broken shutters of a tenement building. Enter a dark hall and stand listening to the noises, the muffled cries, the shouts on the third floor. Eye the kids, the old women as they labor up the stone steps to some one-room flat with a chipped sink, laundry hanging from the water pipes. Then you know something about the rejected, the parts left out of the social philosophy. It tells you something of what to expect about the elite, those who live in the sun, and how they got there.

So where does one find an underworld in a town like Bryan, Texas? By January of my first year teaching, I had bought an old house—a large, Victorian townhouse with porches, broad brick columns, steep roofs, and lots and lots of rooms to wander in. It was part of Bryan's downtown, built for a man named Edge who owned a dry goods store on Main Street. The old store still bore the name of Edge's, though it had become a clothing store by 1975. Around town lived other Edges, a once prosperous family. This house was the last of the great houses of Sims Street, on high ground, facing east, with the bedroom windows opening to the south to catch the Gulf breeze all summer long. The other mansions burned down or were razed after World War II and had been replaced by rows of modest bungalows.

We were around the corner from Main and Bryan Streets, the original town grid. City Hall was down the road, along with the fire station, police headquarters, and the courthouse. So we strolled a lot, and one of our strolls took us down to the Bryan Mission, a red brick shelter for the downtrodden, the out-of-luck, the drunks and vagabonds of the region. A night desk clerk took in drifters after hours; a dormitory housed the regulars, who paid their keep by working at a recycling plant or the second-hand store. It was a Baptist rescue mission, with a minister in residence, who gave services in the chapel under the dorm.

Such places have a certain smell to them, whether they are in Philly, San Francisco, Chicago, or Bryan—the smell of old shoes, talcum powder, rotting roof beams, rain standing in the alleys, cafeteria soup, old men in washed-out pants and shirts. The man in charge of things was named Earl, a flat-faced, balding sixty-year-old of Norwegian descent with a firm handshake and polite manners. He liked professors, and when he greeted me and learned I was "at the college," meaning Texas A&M, he sized me up carefully and pronounced me a friend. I did not know it at the time, but that was a high honor and something to count on for the next several decades. I still go down to see Earl once in a while. He runs a tight little ship with his wayward inmates; he keeps things in line. He kicks out the bad eggs and sometimes refuses the drunks who come in off the freight trains. You have to be clean, he says, to get into his house.

And the guys out front, sitting in the sun during their noon rest, are clean. They roll their own cigarettes from Bugle bags; they tilt back their wooden chairs and rest their heads against the searing hot brick wall. They wear white, like the Texas prisoners over in Huntsville, white pants and shirt, black belt and shoes. They get such outfits if they work the kitchen or some other "uniformed job" around the place. The others wear civvies, the stuff that comes in from the donation boxes. Clean but broken men, each with a gaping wound in the psyche or the heart. They come from broken homes, abusive homes, or from orphanages and prisons. They've been wrapped around a bottle of bourbon or cheap red wine or beer most of their adult lives, and are jumpy, uncertain creatures now—livers hard, eyes red, hands shaky.

Each a kind of rag doll or abandoned puppet, I thought, looking them over on our first visit. Some walked off in the middle of the afternoon to come back a year from now, Earl told me. The others stayed on, starting out young and staying until old. He had been there thirty years, but he would not say why. That's his story. He had "some trouble," he said; I found out they all said that to you. One tall thin man with wispy blond hair came to do yard work for me later on. He pulled a rake with all the enthusiasm of a man in deep sleep. He worked his jaw, dozed over the rake, and then fell to with a burst of speed and got up little piles of leaves. He wanted water to drink, but more than anything, a chance to talk. So I listened to him, and what came from his small mouth and loose yellow teeth was a Homeric odyssey of one man on the freights, with every town and lake and hill clear in his memory. He knew everything about the topography from here to California and back to Maine. He was an idiot savant, I think, with an encyclopedic recall of everything he ever saw. And a lyric genius for describing snowfall in Kansas City from an eastbound coal freight, or the sunrise over Salt Lake as seen from a boxcar heading down to Phoenix.

He got "rail fever" every now and then, he said, as we sat on my back patio having iced tea together. That was about three times a year; he went off to see his mother, he said, in Topeka; he had an itch to see winter up north, and a longing for autumn in New Hampshire. The yard bosses were gone, he said; you didn't have to fear being caught, unless you were hanging off the side coming into a restricted rail yard. Otherwise, you got on, made up your bedroll, bammered down for the night's run, got up early and jumped out for coffee and a ham sandwich, and hopped on again if the town wasn't right. Then you wore out and came back to Bryan and to Earl's kitchen. You picked up a broom the next day and sat out on the chairs after lunch.

Everyone had a story; everyone had scars on the cheek or the wrists, where barbed wire caught in a run from a work farm. Everyone had a faded tattoo or crossed eyes, a tic or hard blink, a stutter or a long look. Someone had hit them too hard as babies or beat them in the barn and run them off at sixteen or younger. They didn't make it. They fell off the path and landed in rehabs and joints and got flushed down the gutters of Texas society into the mission, the last stop before hard time in a maximum security ward. Some were nuts left on the sidewalk when the asylums were closed. Others were smart but crooked, accident prone, weak willed, hopeless, suicidal. They were the leftovers of the social pyramid, the dough you trimmed from the pie shell and balled up in a corner, until some use could be found.

Earl got the ball of dough and made minions and janitors out of it. He had a low opinion of most of them. "Lazy," he said. Earl had finished high school in Illinois, and he venerated higher education as if it were the next step beyond religion. He was bright, observant, a wide reader of books and newspapers. He kept up with politics and social affairs and had a long list of names to send cards to at Christmas and Easter. I have my own, signed "with love, Earl."

The men of the mission lived close to a world of fable. Their bodies were closer to the animal world of instinct than to human reason. They lived partly by dreaming and took reality as this unchangeable, often adverse state of things from which fantasy delivered you. Liquor was one way out of the world; drugs were another. But the nodding lunchtime dreamer also escaped from his woes and sat quietly in his tilted-back chair winging his way inward. The fable world was all about, a carnival reality of deformed bodies and amputated limbs. A young raffish sort of black man, with a leg missing from an accident on the freights, went about the streets swinging on crutches. He was like a praying mantis with his thin sticks and his swaying body. He had a handsome face and looked you hard in the eye when he asked you for money, then swung off with his quarter or fifty cents to get a drink, or a pack of smokes, as he called them. He was part of that half-dream half-waking twilight that pervaded the mission.

So were the women part of the Rabelaisian underworld, the ones who came there to work in the kitchen or in the back rooms; one or two were grotesquely fat and could barely move. Their limbs seemed inflated with helium, and their girths stretched the loosest possible dress they could find among the bales. They dragged along on worn sneakers, ankles the size of oak roots, and legs fanning outward under a ragged hem like the limbs of a sea creature. They too enriched the archetypal twilight.

A block or two away was an actual subterranean vent where you might find a human face or two bobbing out of the thick darkness. Behind the little western-front stores of Main Street was a block of land that angled down steeply to a dry creek over which the stores had been erected, supported by cement piers. The ground ran down under them and left enough height that a man could stand up underneath. It was cool down there below the floors of the little shops, but muddy and raw with old timbers and crates, rats, and the occasional black snake. At night, it was a place to convene friends with a bottle of jack and some smokes. No fires, though; they attracted the cops, who patrolled in a cruiser once each night, occasionally flashing a search beam down among the rubble and cans, and the darting human heads that were momentarily bleached white. Walking by on a late summer night, with the streetlights to guide you, you would see faces there, ghostly eyes peering out from their little Hades at possible trouble. They were not dangerous or hostile men, just winos and misfits, men like Huck Finn's liquor-soaked pap lolling in his hogshead in Hannibal, Missouri. The same dead-end lives languished here, in a vale of pure impenetrable dark and privacy, where they could cruise some obscure mental coast only booze could take you to. They would stand up if they recognized us, and allow us to observe them in their heavy woolen overcoats and navy jackets on a sultry, burning night, each with a bottle in a paper bag, a butt glowing in their fingers, like a file of prairie dogs peering out from a desert burrow.

The mission was the drying-out place, a small-town purgatory you went to to get right, as the men put it. "You has to get right," they would say, imitating the voice of the minister, and slicing a hand into a palm for emphasis. "Right" was a peculiar mantra to them, a word that compressed all the morality of town into a syllable. Their thinking was numb and brutal, born of endless repetition of a few ideas—shouted down at them through miles of habit, fear, disorientation, stubbornness, and primal sleep. They repeated their lessons to anyone who stopped to say good day. "Right," they said. Got to get right. But all this seeming logic occurred in a kind of medieval tapestry of unicorns, serpents, angry gods, devils, and angels. Just three doors from the dormitory entrance was an old honky-tonk serving beer and bourbon all through the day and night. A wooden overhang bent down like a broken hat brim onto the street, behind which were swing doors leeching out smoke and beer fumes that drifted up the street into the noses of the lost. "You got to get right," but the booze came wafting out of a dark, cool room where a few crones sat hunched up on bar stools, their glass of amber working all afternoon with replenished ice cubes and an endless cigarette in the ashtray. A jukebox gave out the nasal twangs of Willie Nelson, a siren to the old cowboys. It was a world in which the devil sunned himself on a toadstool in the very garden where the angels tried to whisper good counsel to the wayward pilgrims gathered there.

This was the old frontier Texas, now turned psychological in the minds of its abandoned. The old way of being—in a simple space without irony or subtlety. It was a humorous world always bordering on violence, or seething hatred. The nerves were bare in such men, even if the will was broken or weak. The fist was easily thrown, and Earl was on the spot telling the bad ones to pack up and "git!" You had the feeling that manners and customs in the evening were those of the bunkhouse, the frontier, the wilderness shacks of the old prospectors. You spoke little, didn't mess with the next man, and kept your goods in a locked box. You knew everyone came from the same checkered world of youth and you chose not to hear about it. In the morning, the dinner bell rang early, and the day began exactly as did the day before, and the day before that. A cowboy's world, based on cooperation, self-effacement, rote learning, with a tough foreman in Earl, and a rancher in the role of minister.

The men bore that stance and look of Remington's cowpokes, good thin men with hardened arms and legs who would have gladly taken off on a horse into the emptiest horizon and done the work. In society, they had been elbowed out—too slow, too alone, too diffident or moody, of no practical worth in urbanized Texas. This was a museum of old cowboys, hung up on the hooks now because the present had moved on. They were the bats of the Texas underworld, quiet, sleepy, taciturn men with amber fingers from chain smoking, and loose, inarticulate mouths.

The mission thrift shop operated like a general store on the edge of the frontier. Piled high in bins were old clothes, shoes, socks, underwear, ties, dress shirts, leather jackets, all tangled up in each other's arms and legs. A few women went through the stuff with patience, a baby on the hip, another sucking a dirty bottle at her leg, a third negotiating a wagon out from under a ton of furniture, with the sofa above leaning precariously over the child's head. This was the store for newly arrived immigrants from the Rio Grande Valley, or farther south. They spoke no English, had little wads of dollar bills clutched in a palm, and were completely at home shopping for the family wardrobe in this pile. It resembled the *mercado* of the village, where used clothing merchants came once a week to offer America's discarded fashions. An old grandmother sorted through dozens of socks looking for a mate, while her husband stood by with a can of Coke, sipping now and then. He had on a straw hat slouched down over his dark forehead. He would rather be out in his *milpa* planting the spring corn than standing by idly while his wife shopped.

I thought I was the only professor to brave these depths, but I found two or three other profs milling about looking for the odd table or lamp, or some piece of machinery they might fix up. One was a sort of hippie grown up, wearing sandals and sporting a ponytail, looking for kitsch, he told me. He was a philosopher in love with the detritus of the industrial age, the junk and lava lamps, the Elvis dolls, the kitchen gadgets that never worked. He collected them. He had a justification to be here. I did not explain my own presence, just smiled. Another prof was retired, a landlord now trying to furnish his apartments on the cheap. A third just kind of faded away when I looked at him. So we milled about with the bottom dogs and the outcasts, the newly arrived, each with a dollar or two to spend.

The colors of the underclass seemed to run through a rainbow of wounded hues, purples, mauves, dingy yellows, faded reds, scab browns, sticky, soiled white things with old paint stains. How to react before a big lumpy suit with giant shoulder pads sewn in, huge pants with thick, linty cuffs and pockets with holes in them, the seat shiny, the inseam worn thin by fat legs trudging to work for years upon years? These pants held up to a young, dark-skinned field worker speaking luxurious lightning Spanish to his friends. He laughed, gold teeth flashing in the noon sunlight. He threw back the pants and humorously dismissed the Anglo world with a grunt. No matter the suit came from the last war, or the one before. Thick, woolen, ugly brown, with all the sadness of a salesman's last days in Chicago or Detroit, thrown into a charity box outside some church and taking on a second life of wandering among the clothing bins of the underworld until arriving here in a bale of other rags and carpet scraps and old fitted sheets with patches. Now for sale again, $1.99.

Shoes in a corner, lots of them, each with a big toe box for some guy with bunions, boots worn down at an odd angle, sneakers with the sides ripped open; high heels with old Jane Russell toe holes. The styles my mother wore when I was a kid, red shoes with high blocky heels, low mules with a bit of silver sprinkled into the cloth, housewife slippers, and shower slops without the thongs. The whole array of footwear walked-out, kicked-out, used-up but for another month of wear by someone looking for a job, not above daubing the front with a bit of shoe wax to make a good impression. The crab world of scavenging the last morsel of value from a consumer nation's waterfall of discards. The mission was a graveyard of excess and indulgence, a mountain of partially consumed things that came down the social hill to this shadowy vale, where the human mice crawled about, sorting things, and the crabs scuttled over the bones.

The faces here seemed never to venture out beyond the immediate precincts of the store. You didn't see them on campus, in the big department stores at the mall, on the sidewalks in the white parts of town. These were the grotesques of the underworld: oddly shaped faces, flat skulls, bruised or close-set eyes, heavy arms and legs moving along from aisle to aisle, patient, dogged, the inertia of mass life and poverty. But also something vigorous and indestructible under the grim, colorless surface of each body. It was the last of the peasant world, I suspect. Hands that seemed to know by touch whether something was still useful; the fingers gripped knowingly, sensitively, as if the objects were still carrots, potatoes, turnips, and peppers.

You knew that this very kind of flesh and spirit had settled Texas earlier; this was still pioneer blood, ready to break sod, fight the weather, inch along under the hailstorms and Indian raids, an indomitable hardness equal to the adversities of the land. The goods were tawdry, cheap, easily broken or worn down, and yet these hands, so patient and masterful, held them carefully, as if they were worthy of respect. Brown hands, short fingers with chipped nails. How like the objects they touched were these human beings, no longer of this time, but discarded or unwanted. What they knew and how they read the world were out of fashion; they might save the world in the next famine or drought or war, but for now, with peace and prosperity all about us, they were of no practical use. They lingered at the edge of the light, at the bottommost layer of society.

Once outside again, in the Land Rover, we breathed deeply, relieved to have a place in the contemporary world. Maybe we were fulfilling Mao's demand for all good Chinese white-collar workers to know the life of the peasant once in their careers; we were dutifully dropping down out of our academic ledge to the peasant world, to be reminded who carried our privileged existence on their backs. We were humbled a little by what we saw. Neither Cathy nor I had much to say. We would come back, often, to furnish our big rambling house with cheap but well made out-of-fashion furniture, and I would sometimes find a pair of shoes that were old Brooks Brothers or Florsheim, that could pass muster at work.

Bryan was no different from any other small town in the country, in the sense that shopping was now the major form of social life. The store replaced the old meeting house; you saw your neighbors here, you found the community, such as it was, milling about, buying or simply looking. This is how we gathered now. If you wanted to know who lived in the Brazos Valley, you didn't go to City Hall or even church, you went shopping. Students told me the grocery store was a great place to pick up dates. You stopped a potential mate and asked where he or she found the tomato sauce. That got you talking. You made your move after that, maybe invited your new friend home to supper, to try out a new recipe. Love in the market. The rest of us pushed carts and eyed the humanity. With a cart you didn't have to make excuses, you could stare with impunity.

One night, late, after my customary bedtime, I found myself wandering the aisles at two in the morning. I had discovered we were out of coffee and went looking for an all-night supermarket. The Safeway was lit up, and there were cars in the parking lot. When I went in, I found myself among workers coming off the night shift at the aluminum door factory and the fertilizer plant. Young couples with sallow complexions and dirty clothes, slogging along with a baby in a plastic seat, propped up with a bottle. The food piled in the cart was mostly boxes of cereal and dry potato mix, quick foods made by stirring in water or milk. Cheap flank steaks and bags of chicken legs, ice cream and instant coffee. The women didn't cook from scratch anymore; no time, I guess. The guys, thin and lost in their blue jeans, didn't get fat on the starch and lard diet. They drank beer, would get paunches later on. Right now they were trim and healthy, with Lucky Strikes in their shirt pockets and cans of Skoal in their back jeans pocket. But the wives were heavy and still very young, breathing hard just to stoop for the box of Tide on the lower shelf. They had tired faces, baggy eyes, a harried look at twenty-five. They were aging fast. No one else was up at this hour, except me, from the white-collar world. I imagined that these were the people who dropped out of high school or barely finished, got started as garage mechanics and then drifted. Now they stamped out aluminum sheet panels for storm doors all afternoon and night, drowned out by the banging of machinery and the clang of metal dropping onto carts and conveyor belts.

These were the couples who lined the Dellwoods of Bryan: hard-working, earnest couples whose lives were defined by night shifts and babies, bills and a hard drunk now and then. I figured that they didn't go to church or vote or listen to political speeches. Their TV consisted of soaps and comedies at night, and once in a great while they went to the movies. I thought they probably read the local rag for the ads and seldom if ever read the editorials. Their lives were extremely mechanical, and yet, they had friends, they laughed over the same things, their nights off were shared with a few neighbors in the backyard, over the burger grill, with beer on ice and football on the tube. It wasn't a bad life, when they got to play and relax; at work you didn't have to think, just pay attention and not get hurt.

As an artist once told me, the hardest thing to learn as a painter is to look without thinking. To see through and by the eye, and not through the mind. The mind foretold, or associated, or thought it saw—without going blank first to record what is really there. How to compose without thinking, letting the ear dictate. The same is true with poetry—how to form words as sounds first, with sense second. The poem as bird song, animal chant, not ideas. Was I looking without thinking now, I wondered, pushing my cart around the endless aisles of canned and frozen goods?

If I noticed anything, it was the hands again. How firm, large, dirty, and precise were these ends of the arms among the hard-working class. The hand was everything, as if nearly all of consciousness had drained down the arm bones into the finger joints, until a man with good hands could do almost anything needed without trial and error. I hired my neighbor, a young erratic guy with a cocaine problem, to do some digging around my water pipes. He took the shovel away from me after I had been kicking the blade into the hard clay a few times, and he began to ply the blade with the expertise of a surgeon. He knew how to jerk, twist, and then scoop with such elegant motions that the hole quickly appeared, and he was not tired. He bent into it, spoke in that slurring, side-mouthed way of men at work, and got a trench going in no time. Little motions that reduced the effort, quick, efficient, almost magical calculations of how to apply the blade to the resisting ground.

I was gripped by his mastery; I hated digging because I didn't do it right. I had no consciousness in that part of me, so I was blind, groping, struggling, often cursing under my breath to get a little earth up and fling it, usually halfway on my shoes, or into the hole again. I watched him light up another cigarette, hang it from his lip, and go back to the work, head tilted, eye squinting from the smoke curling up, talking along, telling me stories about his family, using the rhythm of digging to talk by.

His mind was like a bare untilled field, hardly anything of interest there aside from some television shows he watched, a few jokes he heard on the *Tonight Show*. Idle hours without too much analysis or reverie. Nothing complex or ironic, or idealistic. He took life as it was, but his shovel seemed like a pen in his hand, and he was writing some sort of lyric statement in the earth he pulled up and flung in short, majestic little curves.

It was the hands touching a box of frozen peas, letting them drop into the basket, pushing the basket with curved, callused fingers that could tell the difference between three-eighths and five-sixteenths and keep nailing. The eye was simple, not trained to discern complex fields and foregrounds, but sure and eagle-hard at telling where the nailer went under the shiplap, and to know precisely how to sink a ten-penny nail into a three-inch center, four whacks, the last deeper by a half note and she was home. The nails held in the mouth, pounded into the wood with a heartbeat rhythm and a clunk on the fourth whack. Such beauty in a human body, such coordination of movements and rhythms. The woman's hands were powerful, too, and touched with soft, precise motions. She ran cloth under a commercial sewing machine at some warehouse with tube lights and a noisy ventilator fan up on crates, pulling out sweat and hot steam-iron air through the large side door of a corrugated tin wall, with the railroad tracks as the only view. Long rows of women working under dingy little machine lights, pulling fabric along to make tarps and tents at some speed where the hands possess all the consciousness of the body.

Such hands gave new meaning to the words cowhand, farmhand. It meant you wanted a man whose entire being had seeped down into his fingers. You wanted tough, muscular, accurate hands. You didn't want a poet to do the fencing for you, or the branding. You had no use of writers or thinkers, or dreamers of other worlds. You wanted someone who willingly let all there was of mind go down into the hands, perhaps the feet. Sometimes the back, as well. A strong back and a weak mind—there was the formula for certain kinds of work. And it was virtuous work, a prowess at tasks for which there was given little credit or prestige. Why, I don't know. But you could almost feel the moment that manual skill lost all its honor in America—about the close of World War II, when vets were given the G. I. Bill and a nearly free ticket to college. A whole generation of ordinary Americans suddenly raised their sights to the next class, the next income bracket, and just as suddenly dismissed the world of manual dexterity.

Even the carpenter and the shoe repairer were left behind, in a new darkening limbo of mere labor. Service was the new way, an ability to read, write, and analyze became the future form of work. The heart of consciousness was rising out of the hands back into the eyes, into the face, the mind. Perhaps that explains how glutted was the market for things that were only for use, not to be repaired or renovated. The idea of the car as something to tinker with would be ending soon—too many sealed boxes and computer chips, not enough bolts to undo. The hand was going idle, but for now, in this bottom world of Texas, the hand was still king. I could admire all the forms of hands I saw in the Wal-Mart store, at the hardware counter, old thick fingers with blackened nails holding something with that lightness that told you these hands could think before the eyes. Beautiful peasant hands, thick as carrots, half-curled, brown with wrinkles, and yet full of sensors and precision.

I had wandered into Texas during the great transition from one world of labor to another, the next higher realm of technology and paperwork. All about me were the ruins of manual labor, a world gone to seed. It was still inhabited by a majority of the Texans I walked among, and yet they were slipping away. I did not know it at the time; it was a transition so vast and pervasive, it could not be abstracted into an idea. It was simply there, a palpable sense that something was going away, and attached to it were nearly all the values and emotions that bound Texas as a region, a sensibility. Perhaps I knew it, and did not choose to acknowledge what it meant.

My sympathies were clearly on the side of the losers after my first year in Texas. I must have known that we were experiencing a kind of social Titanic, the manual working world listing and sinking below the level of the social consciousness. There was no funeral over it. Only one book seemed to have grasped the significance of the moment, John Graves's *Goodbye to a River* (1960). On its surface, Graves bids farewell to an undammed Brazos River on the eve of its being manipulated, ending a certain way of life along both banks. But it is also a farewell to an era in Texas, a time of family business and farms, an economy of small means that was about to fade. No one picked up on it at that time; it was almost too early to say that Texas was rounding a historical corner. But soon after, the book was hailed as a classic, and critics praised it for its prescience without specifying exactly what it was foretelling. The truth is, any book that suddenly grows larger than its subject is a flash point, a sudden illumination of murky historic patterns. And Graves had done that at the very edge of a process—the social descent of the working classes.

Perhaps nostalgia and sentimentality over what made a Texan different, hard work and willingness to get in the dirt and shove, kept anyone from saying more. But hadn't the writers known, and were they not saying so in a fashion? There was farewell in the air, a brooding sense that something had been altered for good, some irreversible turn had taken place since the Vietnam War and the rise of the Sun Belt that made the old family ranch a thing of fragile beauty, highly perishable in the urban era. The night owls were all shopping after their factory shifts, and the day people were hard at it in the two-story offices of the strip malls and little complexes around town. People kept drifting in from the country, until almost everyone had walked away from the old ways. They were now standing about in the air-conditioned vacancy of the modern work world, where hands were clean and delicate, used to typewriter keys and phone pads, and tuning knobs.

Perhaps my call to Texas came at the signal that more would need to be educated, the classrooms of the university would soon become the focal point of a generation. The look of rural Texas beyond the perimeters of the towns was drab, perhaps more drab than ever before. Not poverty or drought this time, but social indifference, a lost sympathy for the farm, the natural world. Perhaps that is why so much fiction of the time was given over to farewells to country living. Larry McMurtry's famous grouse over rural subjects in contemporary Texas novels misunderstood the mood of writers. His essay, "Ever a Bridegroom," delivered at the Fort Worth Art Museum in September, 1981, dismayed the audience, which heard that rural life was unworthy of a mature regional literature and that authors must now focus exclusively on urban, middle-class society, according to its leading purveyor, a decidedly nostalgic fabulist himself. Perhaps McMurtry meant "No more tears, ladies and gentlemen. Get on with it." Or maybe he felt that the cheap sort of romance that lingered over film and television and the regional novel was too much, a worrisome excess. (How McMurtry intended the title of his essay, I cannot say—the familiar phrase is "ever a bridesmaid." But the title is his main regret about the essay, a slip of the fingers, he admits in his postscript to its reprinting in *Range Wars;* and nobody ever called him on it, he also noted.)

In truth, writers were not prepared to accept the inevitable misfortune of the working class. It was out of business, something that had occurred to other regional working classes twenty and thirty years before. Television, for those who had watched it carefully, could pick up the subtle lament over the end of manual labor and the beginnings of a new, more artificial life in the cities. Sitcoms were, by definition, a genre that grappled with the transition to higher forms of labor on the East Coast; they examined the stresses of moving into suburbs, the pitfalls of a career husband's long hours at work; the brittle social mores that were developing to replace the simpler, more manually intensive lives of housewives before World War II. So much of the new life was associated with comfort, convenience, automated households, leisure, and the delicacy of having to live with more time on one's hands. Over it all was smeared a thick paste of domestic idealism, of course. But the pathos was nonetheless visible in *The Honeymooners, The Dick Van Dyke Show, The Bob Newhart Show, The Mary Tyler Moore Show, I Dream of Genie, The Beverly Hillbillies.* Jackie Gleason's comedies were older in vision, rooted in tenement immigrant life; the others in my list reflect the future, the transformation to life in the sprawling suburban belts of Chicago, New York, and L. A. What remained of the lower class came through in cop shows, *Barney Miller, N.Y.P.D. Blue, Hill Street Blues,* where the manual laboring class came in for interrogation and booking, still smart, witty, full of animal cunning, but stripped of any social prestige.

At the same time that we watched such stories in our living rooms, the newspapers began talking about a new world somewhere over the seas—a Third World, which seemed to distill the concept of manual labor as a thing unique to other lands, a special purgatory of nations where people still tilled land with a team of oxen or a donkey, drove a pony cart to the village market, walked to school, if there was a school, and made parts to fit old American cars left in their country from decades past. Suddenly we had a place with which to transfer the very notion of manualism, and to deed it to our inferiors, the backward nations outside the west, the old colonial outposts. So the thought of working with one's hands became, in a flash of a few headlines, something utterly foreign. And that foreignness translated itself to our own minorities at home. Now manual labor could and was done by those outside the white race, who were tacitly, if not officially, deemed inferior by virtue of origin, race, or poverty.

That was the situation of my own surroundings in Texas at about the time of my arrival, the mid-1970s, a world of work that had become attached psychologically to foreign desperation. Those who were required to perform manual tasks, below the level of skilled work—such as electricians or plumbers—were part of some other cultural continuum that the nation had pulled free of. Texas was a culture still based on rural, manual labor values but was fast defining itself as a futurist culture of space travel, computer technology, agrobiz, and global commerce.

So one lived in two worlds at once—the world of the arts and literature that still dwelled on the older values of the farm and ranch, the sodbuster's achievement against wilderness, and a new culture without a literary consciousness, the world of finance and technology. Only a few writers had looked that way, mainly television script writers, who could put on melodramas about the rich that were highly successful, if not in Texas specifically, then nationally and internationally. Notable among these was the film *Giant*, based on Edna Ferber's novel, with its hero Bick Benedict grappling with the easy fortunes made from oil against a vision of the rural past when raising cattle was a moral way to make one's living. He is essentially lost in the process, reemerging as someone who largely gives up his rural heritage to accept his new power. The classic sitcom/melodrama is, of course, *Dallas*, which also transformed the myth of the ranch into something new: the ranch as headquarters for operating a corporate empire of land and oil deals run by a ruthless CEO like J. R. Ewing. That transition from one Texas vision to another succeeded, but at the cost of dissolving the regionalism of the new story. It was now a national story of power and lust that could be set in almost any populous state and feel at home.

The thesis that art should now turn to the subject of corporate and urban Texas carried with it the threat that there was no region in such tales—only the national story of class separation and personal enrichment, often at the cost of losing one's regional attachments and character. J. R. Ewing is less the Texan who makes it big than he is the amoral tycoon of Dreiser's stripe. The writers were not so eager to take up McMurtry's demand, since it meant giving up one of the important claims of the Texas writer, that his or her work was an examination of an opaque, closely guarded privacy of place, which the imagination would now reveal after a century of formation.

The faces of the late-night supermarket denizens were like those in Brueghel's paintings of medieval peasants—slack, inexpressive, or making exaggerated expressions of humor or grief. If consciousness has gone to the hands, the face remained neutral, drained. Something I have noted over the years is this carelessness with the face, so unlike the faces in the world I live in—where even the slightest raising of an eyebrow can mean a dozen things, most of them disturbing. Our word *supercilious* refers to the hairs above the eye, in the eyebrow, the *cilia*, which when raised mean either sarcasm or condescension, dangerous looks in the bureaucratic realm. But in the face of a Texas laborer, you find very rubbery expressions of humor, broad winks, clucks of the tongue, pouted lips to create simpler, less subtle messages of feeling. The face is blunter at this level, with fewer ways to suggest what one means—as if meaning were reduced to short, clear, aggressive sentences—anger, a pair of white, close-set lips, hard breath; joy, wide-open mouth, eyes squinting; lust, lips partly opened, eyes half shut and staring. Those are looks that beg for no second meanings or delayed intentions. Everything is in the moment, and on the surface—where action will soon follow. But I cannot help feeling that when we are in the presence of some-one who toils in this society, we think the absence of facial language a sign of dullness. It isn't. The face is not used the same way; the compensation for working hard is to have omniscient hands, and inactive faces.

I think that all of this analysis of working-class people is anathema to the average American, who clings to the belief that we live in a classless society. Such comparisons in behavior between those who toil with their hands over those who work with their heads are greeted with scorn as arrogant conde-scension. That may be, but the result of such timid idealism over the last several decades has been to ignore the manual laboring classes as if they did not exist, except for comic purposes in television sitcoms. Our literature has long ago turned its back on these classes, the dirt or truck farmers, the fac-tory stiffs, the drudges of the institutions. We live in a mediated world where only the higher wage earners receive ink and attention—as consumers. The wealthy are left out like the drudging poor, and only the middle is targeted with klieg lights and celluloid. But how can you know a region, a sense of place, if you don't look at everyone? And everything?

The moment you move out of the Wal-Mart and Safeway late-night world into the regular working-hours daylight, you leave behind the ani-mated, skilled hands of the lower realms. You find yourself among well-groomed, slimmer, more self-conscious people, whose faces have a thou-sand small ways of communicating emotion. At the other end of state route 6, the highway cutting through the towns of Bryan and College Sta-tion, lies the upper world, centered on the university. Here you found an abundance of people who enjoyed the status of belonging to the commu-nity, of ruling over it and setting its standards. The business students were noticeably attractive, well dressed in suits and dresses, walking with leather briefcases on the way to class. They drove new cars and carried themselves apart and were headed for careers in the towers of Dallas and Houston. These were the future managers of the state, and each knew it—groomed, refined, handsome, Anglo, and already managerial in bearing.

No other group of students fit the young executive profile so well. The engineers were increasingly foreigners from the Pacific rim; the agriculture students were serious, hard-working, and rural Texans, dressed in riding jeans that crinkled at their knees and dragged behind at the heel, with yoked western shirts and cowboy hats. The girls wore similar clothes, with roper boots, low-heeled creamy leather boots that you could easily walk in. They also headed for the West Campus, to the meat science labs and genetics departments, the soil crop hothouses, the barns. The scientists and liberal arts majors were nerdy, bespectacled types, out of step with the mainstream of students. For most students, the social ideal was someone who was neither intellectual nor practical, but physically appealing, gregarious, a joiner in groups and work teams, someone whose intelligence was for use, not for inventing utopias or asking hypothetical questions.

Texas was still making itself, building its institutions and power bases. It wanted men and women who could talk, think, inspire others, but who were neither so independent of mind as to be loners or doubters. It wanted loyalty and willingness among its managerial ranks, and you could tell already from the young on campus who would pull the big levers and who would not.

Standing in an elevator in the university's Rudder Tower one day, I was surrounded by eight or nine executives on their way to a meeting with someone high up in the administration. I was the shortest man there, shorter by a foot. The rest towered over me like loblolly pines. Slender men in good, tight-fitting suits; no three-piece power suits, just good, light woolen suits of gray and thin invisible striped patterns, jacket unbuttoned, dazzling white shirt and silk tie inside, new leather belt with brass buckle. Good shoes with long plain fronts and thin laces, almost brand new. They stood eyeing one another, getting information through blinks and half nods. I missed the import of these signs; maybe they were asking who the little guy was, I don't know.

Their faces possessed all the consciousness there is in a human body. It had floated up out of the legs and hands into the mouth and eyes, and into those large, deeply creased thinking organs behind. Supple, thin-lipped mouths, used to nibbling and chewing slowly, sipping wine. Mouths that gauged the listener, spoke strategically, had little calculated pauses here and there, a scratching, back-of-the-mouth timbre that connoted authority, poise, secure knowledge, self-possession. Any one of these guys could have talked me out of the deed to my New Mexico land in a minute, just by staring at me, uttering a few tingling syllables, holding up a Mont Blanc pen for me to sign the agreement. I would have shivered, grabbed the pen, and scrawled my name. These were the masters of the paper and fax world, men who measured everything with a glimpse and tailored their logic to the subtlest distinctions and nuances.

This was the business sense for which Texas is justly famous. Such men were the refinement of the old cattlemen of the past—hard dealers and tightwads who ran huge herds and operated on wide profit margins. They never told you their worth or how they operated, they just did their thing and got immensely rich. These were the sons and grandsons of that model, and they could sit quietly and hear almost any babble and nonsense and make sense of it, not give away any emotion or vulnerability. They sat in conference rooms at long varnished tables and parried their way through complicated negotiations, never raising a voice or letting things drift. The pen tapped on the note pad, the strategy formed, and the meeting closed with both sides feeling good—but with one side clearly winning, and the other taking the hindmost.

I did not know the town's business class well, but I could observe that it had its inner circles and outer limits, and that some were at the very center of social life and others, while rich and enterprising, even generous with their money, didn't mix. Two kinds of businessmen came to Bryan: those who had native roots sunk down five or six generations in cotton and cattle, and those who came in lured by the expansion of the university and all the research opportunities such a thriving academic institution made possible. They came from Houston and the Northeast, and they didn't rock any boats when they came. They assimilated quickly and moved from strip mall to main mall, buying up little interests and consolidating their hold on some niche of the marketplace.

As usual, I found myself somewhere in the middle between these two societies, neither of the one or the other, but having some access to both worlds. I would never be appointed a trustee to a bank or have a seat on the arts commission, which required more credentials and standing than I would ever possess. But neither would I be hounded by the police or suffer the humiliation of having to drift from job to job. I floated between the extremes, a kind of will-o'-the-wisp. That is the writer's place in life, I think. The fewer the strings or attachments, the more the mind and imagination are free to roam, question, probe, draw conclusions, and cancel them out again. I had not mastered either sphere, but I was beginning to see that however different the manual laboring class and the managerial class might seem at first, there were important similarities undergirding them, putting them together as a single thing in central Texas.

Both worlds revolved on a need to belong, a demand for social cohesion and mutual identity. Where the little dance clubs and yard parties of north Bryan brought together laborers and their families, football and the country club, the churches sprinkled through all the neighborhoods brought together the upper world, gave a feeling of sodality, mutual support. The funerals of the managerial class were always occasions for the peers to come out and see themselves assembled, united, woven together by common ground, faith, tradition.

If I saw an obituary of some length in the paper with a studio photo of the departed, I made haste to attend the funeral, just to see who was who in my town. And when I arrived, I found myself among the legal profession, the medical class, the administrative world, always a combination of people who dressed and spoke alike, who were elegantly casual and yet part of some world that selected its members by a few unbending principles. When the legal profession turned out to bury a judge one year long ago, I found myself among the prosecutors and public defenders, the law and order of the town, with its soft laughter and good manners, its dark suits and shiny sedans. It was a class that bore a physical uniformity—height, slenderness, fair complexions, a manner of speaking that was both educated and subtly regionalized with a drawl, a sweetness of tone and laughter. This was the community's elite, the power brokers and shakers of the two towns, and their smell and posture and color revealed what the social vision aimed for and achieved. It was a type of human being who had escaped from the toils of mere earth, from the degradation of having to use muscles and reflexes to wield the heavy tools by which the lower world earned its keep. All that was removed from the group, like so many burdens that allowed them to stand straight as reeds. A few gardened and played softball with the kids, but there was the elegant gesture of cleaning the long-fingered hands when touching an implement or handling the smudged ball in the yard. A kind of dusting of the earth from those immaculate sensors. They walked in ways that told you all physical exertion had been excused from their lives, except for the workout at the gym, or a game of tennis. Otherwise, this was the leisure class, at home in marble and brass, long gleaming tables, offices where the world came to you in the form of documents that you read and filed, or wrote your notes on, and returned empowered by your signature.

The class in power would necessarily turn back to an ennobling past and its myths of the original Anglo self against wilderness. If it had left the earth behind, it would want to be reinforced in its now more artificial realm by a literature that kept alive the origins of this class. Hence, the demand for an art of heroic self-appraisal and a celebration of the adversities by which the winning class had achieved its victories. The harder the fight for land and economic well-being in the novels and films about the Anglo conquest, the better the story.

Correspondingly, an art of sympathy and consolation for the displaced and rejected from the social order would be perceived as laying guilt at the same doorstep. A shrewd publisher would think twice about turning from the one literary tradition to the other, even at the risk of glutting the market with romances and modern gestes. And that is precisely what happened at around the time I arrived in the state—a literary landscape dominated by the very generic romance that McMurtry dismissed as antediluvian and hopelessly provincial, with a struggling alternative press at the other end of Texas' Fleet Street—offering the consolatory vision of the rejected, but with little help from the donors or the big arts groups. The little presses went begging, hat in hand, and found themselves, in the words of David Yates, the publisher of the literary tabloid *Cedar Rock,* counting on grants as "found money," good for one splash. You could not plan ahead, you only seized the day with your check for two thousand or three thousand dollars, did the book, flogged it to death at the readings, where an impoverished, scant audience kept its distance from your book display. The nay-sayers, for some of these minor presses ended up taking the adversarial route, were kept to the side.

McMurtry, for all his speech-making against the romancers, ended up serving the middle class of readers with more of same—large, three-decker Victorian sagas on the last of the cowboys and the old times. He couldn't help himself; the myth of the conquerors must be refreshed every few years to keep the story alive. The little presses would have their day, though few would believe it back in 1974—a time when almost the only publishable story was the marginal Texan and how he or she got there. That is the present, a kind of torrent of old furies and corrections pouring over the reader's head.

CHAPTER 3
POETRY READINGS

No sooner had I gotten used to my surroundings in Texas than I began to sense among the writers I talked to a feeling of being ignored, misunderstood, of being cut off from any readership beyond a few friends and pleasantly indifferent listeners. The literary ache to communicate is as painful as any other ache—and as hard to soothe away as the pain of a lost love or a phantom limb. Some of the writers I know were prematurely aged from having tried and failed to reach out with their words. You knew who was a writer in Austin by the look of a hollow, pained face, a shabby appearance at a hall where poetry or fiction readings were in progress. Someone gaunt and stoop-shouldered would be in the back of the hall talking quietly to old friends, with a dog-eared manuscript under one arm or peeping out of an old shoulder bag.

I have attended many readings over my twenty-five years in the state, and I don't remember enjoying many of them, only a few. Someone decides to get up the money to host a "literary festival," as they are called, and rents a theater or borrows the floor space from a bookstore or bar for the afternoon. Flyers go out to an old list of addresses, and posters are tacked to lamp posts and doors. A few minutes before the event, the chairs are still mostly empty and the poets assigned to read are standing about casting shy glances at the door to see if more people are coming. When the time is ten or fifteen minutes west of the hour, a person gets up to the microphone and introduces the first reader with an anecdote, a few details about his or her books, then looks about the largely empty hall and calls up the poet.

The reader mounts the steps with manuscript in hand and begins shuffling through the loose pages, occasionally looking up to smile. Finally, with the microphone adjusted an inch from his beard, he clears his throat, pushes back a mop of dark hair, draws a breath, and gives you every expectation he will begin reading. But he changes his mind, goes looking for another poem. The audience, thinly scattered over a few of the eight or ten rows of chairs, waits patiently, or whispers while the poet looks for his opening poem. A few more stragglers enter the hall and sit down. They are friends and the poet waves to them, smirks at his awkward situation on stage, and goes digging for the poem that will start the evening.

Finally the poem is read, a simple lyric written in colloquial speech with all the obvious romantic clichés pruned out of it. No Texas poet would allow him or herself to commit the fatal error of gushing over flowers or landscapes. There are subtler ways of importing the mystery of nature into the language. The imperative of poetry now is to speak like the man or woman in the street, in short plain phrases, occasionally swerving into a more figurative language near the end, where there is supposed to be a moment of revelation or an expansion of feeling. Often there is no such expansion, only an unpredictable closure and then silence. Sometimes there is spontaneous clapping, other times people just shift in their chairs and cough, waiting for the next poem.

And the poems come one after another, each one a still life or an anecdote in the poet's life, bits of a mosaic of a fragmented existence bordering on the same world country and western music describes: divorces, infidelities, trailer trash, and alienation. The inventory of experience is narrow, confined to daily dilemmas and missed opportunities. Hardly anything the poet reports from his own life differs much from the lives of the audience; everyone is a writer who has come to hear him, and does not find anything objectionable or falsified. But neither is there a power to interpret things or illuminate the common condition. A few phrases seem shapely or worded well, but the tenor of the poem is about urban living, with its routines, artificiality, remoteness from any sense of heroic past.

The poetry has one message in common—that the materialism on which Texas individuality is predicated is not enough. There is a dark gap between what money buys and work earns in the way of privileges and what the self desires as meaning and belonging. So the poems illuminate the little narrow crust of hungers and dissatisfactions in a loose, rambling sort of speech that lilts here and there and comes to a halt. The audience is patient, but a few hands pick at worn sneakers or torn places in blue jeans, or merely fidget over a paperback or manuscript.

The poems roll on for another thirty minutes and a new poet is called up. She comes to the podium prepared with a thin sheaf of papers. Almost at once she is reading, eyes down on the manuscript, voice soft and nearly inaudible. She seems oblivious to the audience she now faces, as she takes us for a tour of her apartment, her job at the copy center near the UT campus, and then home again to a supper of tossed salad and black beans, and then into her mind as she tells us the problems she had growing up, finding her way in the world. The picture is not grim, but it does show us what it feels like to be cut off from the mainstream, doing things that most people don't put up with. The roaches, the high rent, the car under a lonely street light where a rapist might be waiting, a job without a future, and the corner desk with its old floppy-disk computer and borrowed printer.

The audience is listening, but it is not under any spell from this realism and confession. The injunction to admit no magic into the poetry is observed page after page. There is only the real world to contend with, and each of the poets who reads is not happy with it, has not made his or her peace with it. The poems are an unsystematic, lyrical critique of America's hardness. The lives reported on seem always on the distant edge of things, cobbling together the minimum needs of existence. There is no comforting or consoling bohemia to turn to; others in the lineup report mostly on their loneliness, their time spent in quiet rooms writing as the traffic drifts by on the interstate, or the neighbors turn up loud stereos a moment and then turn them down again.

After ninety minutes or so of readings, the back rows are empty. There is talk in the lobby and out on the street, and the front row contains the last dozen faithful, who probably are waiting to take one of the readers home to a party. The attention is no longer focused. The few who do pay attention are waiting to read their own work. But there will be no "open mike" tonight, the organizer tells them, and the last few listeners get up and make a noisy retreat. The final poet is left with two friends waiting for him at the door, and there is no applause when he folds his manuscript and puts it into his backpack. There is only the large array of chairs, some of them crooked now, the rest pristine, unused.

The poem in Texas is a descendant of New England literature; it was in Boston that the American lyric took shape from English and French models. A process ensued in which aristocratic speech and florid manners in the European tradition were whittled down to a more common mode of New World speech. That took several centuries to perfect, and when done, Robert Frost deepened the American voice and emptied into lyric all the wisdom and caution of New England experience. It was a limited sort of voice that Frost gave America—dark, preoccupied with living in adversity and unfairness, divorced from any consolations of nature. New England's stony soil and hard winters made nature seem hostile, not nurturing. The New World was more a paradise of moral ordeals and tests of loyalty than it was a garden of delights. Few times does Frost say anything good about the natural world around him; it is mainly a place where old men dread the coming on of night and old women argue for a little kindness when their hired men die on their property. It was a place where roads wander off into yellow woods, each one indefinite and perilous, and often ending in isolation. Edwin Arlington Robinson offered no better; he sketched in the miserable hidden lives of people from Tilbury, with the accent on "bury," and his heroes preferred drinking wormwood to wine, or to putting a "bullet in his head."

For an essentially optimistic people, Americans preferred their literature to dwell on what William Dean Howells once prescribed as "the more smiling aspects of American life." The naturalists and the pessimists of New England had darkened Wordsworth's natural love into something like a mythological war between human beings and a wild continent. Poetry was born in an era of Indian wars and seemed to culminate in its Atlantic phase at the time when the great buffalo herds were being exterminated. It was born in blood and destruction while an epic struggle was being waged to transform wilderness into something more familiar, an English landscape. The poem in America clung to an English song style and added homely touches from the New World here and there. But the real American character, when broken into at the range of its deeper feelings, seemed to be brooding and pessimistic, not at all sure that the New World would ever be "home."

While Americans chose the brighter examples of Frost's poetry as their favorites, the main thrust of his poetry, as Richard Poirier showed in an insightful study of Frost's vision, is essentially fatalistic. That part was obscured, much as the Victorians bedimmed the presence of a similarly tragic vision in their own poets of the late nineteenth century. It was a selective awareness on the part of Frost's readers, and he did not object. He took his money and awards and, toward the end of his life, cultivated his new "cracker-barrel" philosopher image. This was a much lesser poet who could claim the love of American readers. They had accepted a partial and somewhat diluted Frost, whose very name should warn you what sort of poetry you would get from this man.

But that was the poetry that became the American style. Frost had nailed it. Not Whitman, whose spiritualism and pantheistic vision were too foreign, too intellectual to be embraced. The American reception for Whitman was restricted to one or two poems, the rather silly lyric effusion "O Captain, My Captain!" and the more dignified "When Lilacs Last in the Dooryard Bloom'd." Both were riming and comforting sorts of poems far from the verbal brilliance and abandon of "Song of Myself," with its love of "squaws" and runaway slaves and rough sex. That was the Atlantic miracle, the possession of European song and its transformation into Americanese. It set the mode for lyric thereafter, and it traveled inland with the pioneers toward the Middle Border, and then veered south and southwest. When the poem arrived in Texas, it had lost some of its sophistication and become a bit of doggerel in the worst hands.

The anthologists were hard pressed to find words to describe the body of Texas poetry without insulting the state. "Little need be said of the early poetry written in Texas," wrote Leonidas Payne, a professor at the University of Texas, in *A Survey of Texas Literature,* published in 1928. "Like the poetry of our national colonial period, it is almost devoid of artistic merit," Payne wrote. The early poetry was "extremely sentimental and moralistic" and echoed "the thought and style which we have come to call Victorianism." The poetry after 1865 "did not produce any notable original literature. But there was, nevertheless, a vast amount of mediocre poetry" (17, 43).

Things had not improved much by 1940, when the WPA compilation *Texas: A Guide to the Lone Star State* was published. It listed only two books of Texas poetry worth reading, Hilton Ross Greer's *Voices of the Southwest* and its sequel, *New Voices of the Southwest,* coedited by Florence Elberta Barnes, and of these voices, only about a third belonged to Texas poets. J. Frank Dobie wrote the WPA guide's sketch on Texas literature and mentions cowboy songs but only those collected by John Lomax. Greer's preface to *New Voices* labors for a way of saying what Leonidas Payne put a little too bluntly: "If at times [southwestern poets] are too conscious of their experiments in form, of their regionalism, or of their non-regionalism, it is to be remembered that the Southwest, as a whole, in a literary way is young, and that self-conscious zest and enthusiasm are the characteristics of youth" (*New Voices,* 30).

But Payne may have put his finger on the problem with Texas poetry when he noted that it was patriotic, sentimental, and defensive about local values and opinions around the time of the state's founding, and later, during and after the Civil War. Poetry is a naked art; it exposes the inner self. If there were misgivings or guilt feelings about how the state came to own its land, or how it extended the slave belt of the South, such things were not easily talked about. And the poetry could only repress the information by being dull, or falsely romantic. You can almost feel that concealment in the language of Greer's anthology—with lines like these by William E. Bard, from "Desert Dusk":

> The sun, half-loath to quit day's parted husk,
> Goes down, lingering on the yucca-tips. . . . (*New Voices*, 47)

And again, from Mary S. Fitzgerald's "Spring in East Texas":

> Today I stood with aching throat
> In sunny meadows, starred with gold,
> Where daisies open drowsy eyes
> When burnished buttercups unfold. (94)

The strategy is to talk about "something else," the land, or the weather, and not drift into dangerous feelings. Though as I wrote several years ago in an essay, "The Buried Life: Texas Women Poets, 1920–1960," "The meek and orderly landscape seen through the eyes of amateur female painters, writers, and essayists characterized their own repressive lives. Things were portrayed as being in their place, performing their assigned tasks as flowers, beasts, hills, and desert—and thus supportive of the well-run, male-dominated social order where few ambiguities of life were tolerated or permitted to retain their savage aspect" (*Texas Women Writers*, 288).

Both men and women elevated discourse in a literal sense, elevated it above their own real thoughts and attitudes. No one can think of landscape in such terms *all the time,* or heighten every tidbit of thought into ecstatic lyricism. It suggested camouflage, a pompousness concealing certain rather plain truths. You know that such poets put down their pens and went out into the street to speak normally, in the drawl or twang of the region, using the common tongue to express themselves. Why was poetry so stiff, so forced with eloquence and predictable sentiment in a land where action was more valued than words and where plain speech was the sign of sincerity?

Poetry would surely have failed to reach down into an audience's inner life, even though Greer reported that "verse-making in Texas has become almost an epidemic" in the 1930s (*New Voices,* 29). He even called it a "poetry movement in Texas," a term that often means a whole society had been jolted enough to suddenly change styles and unload a lot of impacted feeling. The Depression was on, surely a source of emotion and powerful stories; so was the Southern literary renaissance, with a lot of the major poets of the country teaching as close by as Baton Rouge. Carl Sandburg was making Chicago famous, and Robinson Jeffers was putting Big Sur on the literary map. Eliot made St. Louis and Boston centers of literature. Texas *wanted* to be part of this national outpouring, and the books were mounting up. But years later, after the poetry epidemic of the 1930s and 1940s had subsided, the estimate on Texas poetry was that it was still mediocre, hardly worth the trouble of preserving but for a few genuine talents, like William Barney and Vassar Miller, and one or two others. Big storm, little rain.

Let's go back to the hall where the poets were reading, but only for a minute. Look around at the figures sitting there. What makes them different from the people who do not go to poetry readings? I mean the ones who are at the mall shopping, or in the movie theater, at home reading *Texas Monthly* while the barbecue pit heats up. Perhaps the clothes they wear tell us something. The rough jeans and sandals, the worn-out cowboy boots and soiled shoulder bags, all that stuff seems like it was salvaged from life on the prairies. They are dressed in a sort of nostalgic symbolism of the frontier. Some wear beaded leather jackets and have tied feathers to their hat brims. They have crossed Indian symbols with western cowboy symbols; the rest go about looking like farmers down on their luck. The beards are out of old nineteenth-century daguerreotypes, and the women wear full-length skirts, or just baggy shorts and bib overalls, or old thrift shop hand-me-downs. Cock an eye at this crowd of poets and you get the feeling they have all impersonated aspects of the Texas past. They inhabit a space that goes back to a time when the regional character was just forming. And what they import into that past is an attitude of tolerance, openness to the Indian, the Mexican, and to wild nature. Listen closely to the poems and you will see a kind of revisionist fever in the poetry—the dreary spectacle of a life at the margin is also embedded with a dream lore of wanting to relive the origins of the region—to correct the errors committed, perhaps to save the bison and the longhorn, the wild plum trees, the vast savannas and unfenced prairies.

The poets have reinvented the past and now live partly in its imaginary country. But not as purveyors of a continuing Texas mythology of the cowboy heroes and Indian fighters. Their sense of revision includes celebrations of the unsung pioneer wife, sympathetic renderings of the Mexican peasant, lyric poems about wild country and its indigenous human cultures, animals, and plants. The contemporary urban setting of much of the poetry is the symbolic landscape of an erroneous victory. Here are some examples chosen quite at random from Billy Bob Hill's anthology, *Texas in Poetry: A 150-Year Anthology*. The first is from Martin S. Shockley's "Armadillo":

> Ambling across aeons to my backyard
> she pokes her little snout into my mind,
> ancient cousin from my dismal past.
>
> .   .   .   .
>
> Cornered beneath my juniper, she digs,
> and in a moment burrows out of sight.
> I grasp her scaly tail and pull;
> she holds in tight;
> I have to dig her up.
> Trailing zoology, she ambles off.
>
> I tool-using primate, hold with my spade
> dominion over armadillos. (181)

From Pat Stodghill comes "Rattlesnake Roundup":

> Seeking fresh air
> they crawl out of the den
> curving slowly, hibernation stiff . . .
> crooked brown scaly ribbons,
> diamond etched,
> wrinkling over the rough rocks.
> Their spade heads rise,
> eyes staring, forked tongues flickering.
>
> .   .   .   .
>
> Bringing innate fear, the people come,
> armed with legends . . .

mystic powers of evil, sex, fertility, rain, immortality . . .
to sit on the hard benches under the lights and girders
at the Nolan County Coliseum,
to stare back at alien eyes. . . . (180)

And finally, Naomi Shihab Nye's "The Endurance of Poth, Texas":

. . . I want towns like Poth
and Panna Maria and Skidmore to continue forever in the flush,
red-cheeked, in love with all the small comings and goings of
cotton trucks, haylifts, peaches, squash, the cheerleader's
sleek ankles, the young farmer's nicked ear. Because if they
don't, what about us in the cities, those gray silhouettes off on
the horizon? We're doomed. (170)

In another anthology, *Inheritance of Light* (1996), edited by Ray Gonzalez, a typical poem runs along the same thematic lines, like this one from
William Barney, called "Once more in Los Ebanos," with its closing stanza
stating the general argument of Texas poetry:

If all the rest of the clock
ceases to tick, in Los Ebanos
Time will go on. There will be laundry
to put out; from somewhere men will come
wanting to cross the muddy water.
The ferry is halfway to Mexico now. (150)

Miles Wilson makes the counter argument in a poem called "Slash Burning," with the emphasis on the ravening present:

It goes like this—
forty acres, give or take,
of bedlam. A derangement of land
called clear-cut. (159)

In another poem by Wilson, "Keeping Track," the attitude toward technological Texas is Orwellian:

I have not forgotten the long, tiled halls
which wait for us in official buildings,
the metallic breath of circuitry seeping

out of cool rooms, the secretary
who knows what is going to happen. (160)

Among my own poems in the Gonzalez book is "The Motel," with a typical theme of escape from the alien present:

. . . as we approach the
    emptiness in which it
        takes its life

exhausted, our eyes pressed
    inward from the monotonous
        journey south

eager to sleep, to push
    away the limits of thinking
        and surrender
to awake in another country
    under the soft night,
        where love is possible (170)

"To awake in another country" is a line taken from the Argentine writer Jorge Luis Borges, who wrote "to sleep is to wake in another country." The core of the poem lies in the line "to push / away the limits of thinking and surrender." But surrender to what? The image of a country south of the border, perhaps Mexico, perhaps only a fantasized subtropical place behind or repressed within the idea of modern Texas.

Poetry represents the vision of a lost utopia, a racial and animal paradise displaced by history and betrayed by industrialization and urban culture. The poem need only record daily life, down to its most banal minutiae, to illustrate that modern city life is brutal, even tragic. We can begin to understand the colloquial speech, the bland unromantic rhetoric from which this poetry is constructed. To romanticize would be to separate oneself from the ordinary citizen and thus complain only from a heightened, rarefied sensibility of the poet. So the poem must be as ordinary as margarine, as blunt as diner coffee and Campbell's soup. The tacit argument of poetry is that the poet is the generic citizen, so that what he or she reports is Everyman's condition.

Then the poem's gritty or mundane reality has a kind of sociological truth to it, which should make it reach out and shake a few emotions loose in an audience. But it doesn't. And the reason that no one comes to a poetry reading is that the poets are making arguments that unravel the myths on which state pride is based.

No one wants to have his confidence altered or dismantled, so that the job where you get all your money, the office where you have power, the home that gives you pride, the spouse and kids over which there is an untested and consoling sense of authority—all this falls under the scrutiny of the dystopian visions of poetry, which hungers after an imaginary, highly revised past where things could have taken another tack.

The tack of an imaginary history is not always spelled out—though the best Texas poets are clear on how they would redesign time and event. They would reverse the flow of history beginning with southerners creeping over the black prairies into central Texas, setting up small claims, going along with Austin and his Three Hundred, plowing up the wilderness and transforming it into ranches and oil fields. Mexico would not try to colonize the province of Coahuila, but let it go back to the Comanches. The land would welcome back its former tenants, the bison and javelina, rattlesnake and armadillo. The southern plains would be sprinkled with turkey pear and hogplum, devil's claw, and purple sage. The arroyos would run red with ocher-dark rains, and the banks hedged with knock-away and seepwillow. The running creeks would be shaded by cottonwoods and the green-flowering mustard tree. The Brazos would flow undammed from mouth to delta, winding through yaupon brakes and darkened by flocks of grackles and bobwhite quail. The wood rat would thrive here, among raccoons and moles, ground squirrels and the lizards.

Somewhere along this historic dream a few sensible Anglos would wander in and live among the Indians, and learn their ways. A sharing of cultures would allow a few small settlements to get started; maybe a fence here and there would block off the wild prairie from the cornfields and orchards. It would be understood that you didn't build on or fence in the buffalo grounds, and that horses were something that you didn't always get to keep. You let a few go wild. When parties of Comanche came to barter, you would smoke with them, trade skins and seeds, and offer the use of your corrals for their own herd of ponies. You would accept their right to worship buffalo gods and weather deities, and you wouldn't invade their hunting grounds or defile any aspect of their culture.

You would attempt to learn their language, and use their signs, their greetings. You would come to their defense should the federal troops come in to bully them north. In contests of horsemanship you might compete and hope your son or daughter would learn their skills well enough to give them a good fight. Maybe one of your children would marry one of theirs, and you would enter the tribal blood. Something of your ways would leech into theirs, so that towns would not seem so alien or imposing on their liberties. The more sedentary members of the Indian nations might settle there with you, and become farmers, storekeepers. There might even be conversions, but only at their suggestion. A town here, a tipi village there. The land still mostly wilderness, and only a few settlers encouraged to enter such land where the laws of nature were above human intention.

In William Carlos Williams's knotty, vinegar-laced history of America, *In the American Grain,* he says there is something like fate in how Cortez walked in unopposed and conquered a warrior nation of Aztecs with little trouble. Nothing could stop the Europeans from coming; the Aztecs fell on the one side, the Plains Indians fell on the other. It was fate, written into the wind and the soil. Little by little, according to the utopian rehistory of Texas, the distinctions between Indian and Anglo would dissolve, and a real Southwest of mixed heritage, mixed religion, mixed uses of the land would emerge. It would occur along so slow a helix that it would grow like nature, and become nature. The social system would be as thorny and tough as cactus and mesquite. It would root deep in the semiarid plains and flower a little here and there, but without the bristling steel and glass artificiality of New York and Chicago. It would be the other America, the rough and natural America where myths of wilderness would remain active and inexhaustible.

That was supposed to be the fate of the Southwest—it was a collection of ancient myths of what is pure nature, and what kind of human being does such nature feed and shelter? The Southwest was supposed to be the heartland of the New World, where all forms of heroism and mystery were to be preserved, left intact as the rawness at the core of the New World American. The fact that oil seeped up from the ground in black pools and called for entrepreneurs to take it, to form an oil economy, is that force of fate Williams talked about. Nothing could stop it. It came and offered its vast powers to those who would fight for it, conquer it, exploit it, and shape an industrial empire around it.

The taking of Mexico was the other force of will. Nothing could keep the Anglos from coming from all points east and south into this raw, cheap land. Some squatted on it, others bought false claims and moved on. Some dug in and thrived until Indians destroyed them, or sold out when the depressions leveled the local economies. Nothing could keep back the forces that would wrest the land from Mexico and cement it into the Union. *But what if?* What would it be like now if it had stayed under Mexican rule longer, and then atrophied from its grasp, to be neutral, a land without masters or builders, or exploiters? What then?

There lie the dreams of Texas poetry. If railroads hadn't come, *what if?* If the sheep farmers and cattle ranchers had not fenced off the plains and stopped a bison cycle of ten thousand years, *what if?* If oil had not been discovered, which means if Ford hadn't made the Tin Lizzie Everyman's conveyance, *what if?* If the Indians had met a different settler, gentler, more easygoing, of a different fiber from the Celtic sort who came empowered with long histories of individual rights and a fierce defense of their faith and way of life, *what if?* Then the heart of America would possess something like a natural Eden of mixed races and wild symbiosis with nature.

But no one has tried to make a full articulation of this tacit utopianism in poetry. It is easier, less taxing on the ears, to make poetry a diary of personal daily life, where the plodding, gloomy routines of a fallen paradise are indirectly the argument, and so much more accessible to casual readers. Merely take your stroll through downtown alienated Austin, or the glass canyons of Dallas, or the vast wastelands of working-class Houston, and you have proven by inversion that the old utopia would have been better. Such diaristic poetry as is written by the majority of poets is so conventionalized in content and attitude that you would violate a norm to depart from it and theorize aloud, picture the utopia in direct terms. The implication is enough; that is the main practice of poets. All such language about dreary apartments, sirens in the night, lost lovers, and dull jobs is the dystopian pastoralism of the region. Dwight Fullingham's "A Soothing Gloom" comes to mind as the model poem of Texas:

On a day such as this, a day as restful as the
Shadow of a hackberry tree, twilight
Descends over confusion and an anger that

Softens finally into the peach
Glow of a study lamp.

Books. Their deckle edges
Invite handling, like the gold
Coins of friendship.
Youth. Its noble hopes have been played out
Amid servile fires.

The large desires begin to vanish, and in their
Place: a quieter time, a time subdivided into
The smaller moods of life. The late sun
Strikes a minor tone of whispered
Prattle and silent agitation.

Driven back into the soothing gloom, I
Resist meditation's ancient spell, refusing to
Take my cue from the muses' striking hour.

Tonight the moon wanes below the horizon, revealing
No silver token of its ever
Coming again. (*Inheritance of Light*, 176–77)

The logic of the poem requires that everything be rooted in a self, a personal life of daily, simple events. That is the first convention. And it means to bridge the private life of the poet to the familiar life of nearly everyone. The consolation of books is set against the despair of some larger, but only suggested tragedy—a "confusion and anger," a spent youth giving into "servile fires." One must "resist meditation's ancient spell," by which I read the desire to dwell on the sorrows of a paradise lost. To return to the revisioning of history in order to rewrite Paradise back into imaginary life is no longer as compelling as it once was, when we were all younger. It is at this hour, with the sun lowering and the solitude of night coming on, that the "muses" strike—calling forth images of a fabulous past.

Poetry has no audience beyond its own practitioners because this myth runs counter to the prevailing social philosophy of Texas. The individual pursuit of happiness and fulfillment, on which much of the regional culture is based, has nothing to do with a pastoral Eden of wilderness and sympathetic Indians. That Eden features a group soul passing through all human life and natural surroundings, which is squarely up against the idea that we each have a small soul that drives our will and desires. The contemporary individual seeks his or her success through a regimen of initiative, perseverance, willingness to delay rewards, a passion for work, and a well-honed competitive spirit. The modern city inspires the desire to overcome its ambiguity and alienation by succeeding. If the city seems at times a little sordid and impersonal, bogged down in criminality and corruption, and rife with a new kind of urban savagery among the poor and homeless, then it comports with the idea that a city is an arena of work and struggle, a place where egos clash and wills collide. The city is ugly because the struggle of modern existence is mainly about wits and reflexes and quick decisions in the pursuit of self-interest. The very squalor and brittleness inspire a desire to make it, to get the rare rewards of money and prestige that will allow you to inhabit a correspondingly soft and dimly lit retreat in the suburbs, where you can restore yourself from the savage struggle to rise to the top.

The luxury sedan, the shower and shave, the clean suit or dress, the briefcase of calfskin leather—all these are shields and insulation from the bleached reality of urban industrial life. You have your comforts, you go into battle in an air-conditioned office, in board rooms and corridors, and the rest of the city, with all its despair and isolation, are merely the landscape of a ruthless but essentially open-ended social system. You make it, you enjoy; you fail, you take your lumps. That occupies so much of the mind and physical exertions of the average city worker that there is no time, and no desire to inquire into made-up histories or the despondency of poets for a relation to earth and to otherness. It doesn't connect.

Poetry does not venerate what people are doing; it questions and rejects such lives, or weighs them in a scale against an idealized past. But is poetry alone in this project to vivify a sense of the past? Popular culture in general seems to swirl around the same themes as the poetry—most country and western songs delve into the same vision of an implied fall from an older world, where the average working-class man or woman is now suffering insecurity, unemployment, divorce, infidelity, poverty, and all the other ills of a society that seems to have abandoned its concern for the underclasses. The whole body of cowboy movies is preoccupied with working-class visions, and with a sense that the frontier was better than city life today. The urban cowboy is a complex image of rural man dropped into the urban landscape where he disintegrates for lack of a sense of belonging or being. Drugstore cowboys are idlers in the city, pastoral rejects who find themselves surrounded by alien forms of labor. They are men whose only relation is to animals and land, weather and hardship. The office is no place for them. The cowboys of Larry McMurtry's sagas are forever bidding farewell to a heroic era, reluctantly departing from its last vestiges on the working ranches of modern Texas. Everyone is saying good-bye in western novels and films, and clinging to the image of that past by affecting to remain cowboys and ranchers. The cowboy is corrupted into meanness by urban life; the TV serial *Dallas* shows us how corrupt ranch life becomes when the cattle are gone and only the outward semblance of old Texas remains, while the bosses do their mischief in the big city.

But the myths of film and music are not altogether the myths of the past represented by poets. The heroic cowboy is also meshed with the idea of the Indian fighter, trailblazer, domesticator of the wilderness, which is where the poets walk away. The broad features of popular mythology in Texas appeal to an unskilled labor force feeling increasingly shut out of the social hierarchy as business refines its practices and includes only highly trained programmers and specialists. The city is a symbolic landscape of the powerful and the skilled against a two-story wasteland of the unskilled and powerless. The Old West appeals because it turned on the ranch hand, the cowpoke, the pioneer farm wife, the ordinary. That was their finest hour, and their past is celebrated in the film world. They are given flattering portraits of their capacities and traditions.

The poetry does not simplify the myth of the past as a working-class pioneer cultural experience; it is more interested in the past as a philosophical Eden, as a quarrel with the religious and commercial forces that voided nature and transformed it into resources, potential wealth. What nature really represents is not just wilderness but some aspect of being human that has been disconnected from instinct and mystery. Nature represents the freedom of organic life to enjoy its desires, to indulge in the purity of existence, as against the channeling of all energy toward self-interest, social advancement. The poet who laments the fallen past is trying to deal with a sense of being cut off from his or her own pleasures—denied their uses and access by a demand for intensive and continuous labor.

The poet is not interested in the heroism of work, as laid out in popular cultural narratives; there is some idealizing of pioneer ranch life, and of the old fathers wise in the lore of woods and hunting. A little of that, but most of the poets are college-educated urban people who do not have any direct links to a working rural past. They are using that natural past as a screen on which to project a personal grievance against a labor-centered new social order, where they feel their work dehumanizes them or robs them of their autonomy and self-pleasure. They do not want to slave for advancement or material rewards; suburban luxury is not that attractive to the majority of them. If they had choices, they would follow Pat Little Dog out to the ar-royos and live in a kind of hogan with lots of cats and dogs.

The poets' appearance becomes transparent when we realize their cloth-ing and hairstyles cobble together bits and pieces of their visionary argu-ment against the alienation of work. The blue jeans connect them to the prairie pioneers; their sandals and beards, their lack of makeup are aspects of a group that refuses to compete for a niche in the office world, where ap-pearances are everything. They deliberately breach the conventions of the successful careerist. Their shoulder bags and rumpled briefcases are signs that they belong to an urban fringe–dwelling class that recycles the dis-carded goods of the wage earners. They may well be wage earners them-selves by day, but at night and in the company of fellow bards, they assume this other persona of the disenchanted urban critic.

Their self-indulgence, which takes the form of reading, enjoying food, sex, idleness, sensual pleasures, is an expression of their desire to expand consciousness into the body, to make it part of the feeling apparatus as against the rational organizational human who represses pleasure to maxi-mize working efficiency. The poetry has a serious sociological critique of labor and compartmentalized existence, which it filters through one large metaphor called the natural past. That heroic and unrealized past of wilder-ness and racial harmony is essentially the opposition to whatever we mean by the modern city, with its rigorous hierarchies and money values. And because this poetry is relentless in its expression of that opposing view, it of-fers a difficult, perhaps intolerable message of bodily desires and hungers the larger audience must turn its back on. The audience will not listen— perhaps because this poetry is a warning, a seed of doubt, some sort of prophecy against the consumers' own most cherished wants.

The empty hall with its few poet stragglers is not the child of the Six-ties Movement. This is not some lingering ghost of hippie idealism. As far back as the 1920s, when the vast majority of poets were women publishing their poems as column filler in small-town newspapers across the state, you will find clear, sometimes strident lyrics on the violation of the land and a deeply felt pathos for the slaughter of Indians and wildlife. I wrote my essay on Texas women poets when I was teaching in Kuala Lumpur, Malaysia, for the year; I had done my research but needed more examples of what I was calling then a woman's anger in Texas. I asked my friend Chuck Taylor to root around in the poetry archives, and he wrote back that he had found an abundance of material to back me up. It was an eye-opener to him that the body of women's poetry back then, supposedly sentimental and mushy, a drab sort of garden verse, turned out to have teeth and a sharp tongue against the male regime of wholesale slaughter of coyote, bear, snake, raptor birds, gophers, prairie dogs, anything that impeded the closing of the plains for the purpose of cattle herding. The women minced their words at times, but some of them were outspoken, clearly angry and resentful in terms that Annette Kolodny explores in *The Lay of the Land* (1975) and *The Land before Her* (1984), where earth is the metaphor for the female body, and abuse to the ecosystem is a kind of rape or cruelty felt in themselves.

The rape image applies especially to the oil boom, as in Eda Vine's poem "Oil Land," where she describes the penetration of the earth as a kind of forced sex:

Wherever oil—time's hoarded treasure—lies,
Skeleton forests of tall derricks stand
Gaunt as half-starved ground from which they rise.

. . . .

And far into the pallid sand's deep hold
The twisting drill pierces to liquid gold.

. . . .

Gas pockets flare like bivouacs at night
In growing numbers, until man has rent
And gashed the soil in a Titanic fight
That sucks its substance bare, and leaves it spent. (*A Book of the Year*, 15)

More rape imagery occurs in another representative type of women's poem, the violation of innocent nature, in "White Heron," by Lois Vaughan McClain, modeled on Sarah Orne Jewett's short story, "A White Heron," on the same theme:

A shot rends the air!
The white heron has fallen!
Wings that have soared are forever still;
Blood-stained and crumpled the rare lovely creature
That but a fluttering breath-space ago
Was a wisp of white cloud
That the wind was pursuing. (*Texas Women Writers,* 290–91)

If this were virgin land, as Henry Nash Smith argued, the female writer associated the vulnerability of earth with her own being. What happened to the land happened to her. This connection would build up a literary resentment for decades to come, culminating in the women's movements in Austin, where that anger has been focused, honed into a poetics, a movement. Men associated the land with their own nature, and saw in it the source of their courage. To adulterate by urbanization was to weaken the contact between natural rawness and masculinity, hence the enshrining of the frontier as a male domain. Both sexes derived deep psychological meaning from the idea of wild Texas. It was so important as a concept that once it began to disappear by the 1920s, it was time to formulate the myth of wild nature in written form. That was the achievement of the Old Three, as John Graves called J. Frank Dobie, Walter Prescott Webb, and Roy Bedichek in an essay collected in *The Texas Literary Tradition* (1983).

J. Frank Dobie's prolific canon is an adulation of maleness through wilderness myths and history. His prose gushes with eloquence over the masculine mystique, but it can sometimes be as spare and direct as Hemingway's. He was Hemingway's contemporary, and he celebrated the cattleman and the trailblazer the way Hemingway venerated the soldier and hunter. Cecil Robinson, who wrote the classic history of southwestern literature, *Mexico and the Hispanic Southwest in American Literature* (1977), cited this telling quote from Dobie's introduction to *Coronado's Children* (1930): "These tales are not creations of mine. They belong to the soil and the people of the soil. Like all things that *belong,* they have their roots deep in the place of their being, deep too in the past" (xvii). Note the dual relation of a people, to the soil and to the past. They are really one, a depth of local nature and a time of openness. That is the enshrining moment, the mythical sphere on which the psyche of the region feeds for strength and courage even now. "In a Texas which has been declared ruined by oil money and Cadillac culture," Robinson observed, Dobie has influenced a younger generation of writers, McMurtry at their forefront, to continue the mythological process of relating humans and their habitat at the psychological level (*Mexico and the Hispanic Southwest*, 339).

Walter Prescott Webb achieved almost as much with his panoramic studies of the Texas landscape in *The Great Frontier* (1952) and *The Great Plains* (1931). The titles repeat the mythological word "great," and the greatness of Texas lies in these foundations of frontier and epic landscape. Another important mythic study is *The Texas Rangers: A Century of Frontier Defense* (1935). All three and others, including *Divided We Stand: The Crisis of a Frontierless Democracy* (1937), study the geography of a myth, as does Roy Bedichek's *Adventures with a Texas Naturalist* (1947). The word adventure gives to this seminal work the nuance of a quest, which Webb appropriated in a posthumously published work, *History as High Adventure* (1969).

The foundations of Texas mythology were not in the cowboy songs, but rather, in these documentary and critical works by the Old Three, all or nearly all of them written during the Great Depression or shortly after. While other parts of the nation were collapsing under the weight of its cities and industrial economy, the Southwest beckoned as an untamed province, where the ordeal of courage imposed upon its human settlers made them heroes and epic victors. That relation, while adamantly male in its vision, was coinciding with women writers' vision of a land that was violated, transformed, weakened into submission. The sexes were not communicating at the same level, but both were laying the groundwork for the writing to come.

So powerful was the hold of the Old Three upon younger writers that McMurtry could no longer work under its monopoly and cried out against it in his famous address to the Fort Worth Museum of Art in 1981, "Ever a Bridegroom: Reflections on the Failure of Texas Literature," which the *Texas Observer* published soon after. Writing in the *New York Times Book Review*, A. C. Greene's interpretation of McMurtry's earlier essay, "Southwestern Literature?" included in the latter man's book of essays, *In a Narrow Grave* (1968), is that McMurtry was trying "to purge Texas letters of the myth of Dobie and his fellow Austin writers." McMurtry, as one critic argues in an essay in *Myth and Voice of Texas Writers* (1991), was tired of the influence of Dobie and company and of a "frontier myth that is a vapid, hollow illusion that is in the final analysis more destructive than useful" (16).

Evidently the Depression-era logic of a heroic myth of land and male psyche no longer persuaded writers of an urbanized Texas. The "Bridegroom" essay, as Don Graham saw it, argued for a "turn to contemporary cities for material, not backward to the past in a nostalgic, retrograde recycling of worn-out tales and jaded myths" (*Myth and Voice*, 15).

But Graham was trying to deal with the fact that McMurtry's *Lonesome Dove* repudiated his own attack on this very myth by returning to it! Evidently, Texas fiction depended on the myth far more than McMurtry had realized. It was the mother lode of storytelling in Texas, and one departed from it at one's peril. Masculine courage required certain rituals and beliefs, and at their center was the settling of the Texas wilderness, the wresting of the province away from Mexico, and its ranch and oil history.

Popular culture embraced the masculine vision of a triumph over wilderness, and popular culture had now transformed that triumph into a working-class myth, as I suggested earlier. The movie-going public would find in westerns a reassuring heroic fable; television would supply other narrative strains of the myth all through the Cold War. The crisis of masculinity that came with the defeat in Vietnam ended the tradition, or rerouted it through the *Rocky* and *Rambo* sagas, and through other heroic narratives like the *Star Wars* trilogy and the Vietnam War films. The cowboy myth was pushed aside until McMurtry reworked it, and others were soon at work writing new novels and film scripts on the last of the cowboy heroes.

Poetry was alone in its rejection of the myth of Anglo triumph over wilderness; perhaps the women of the 1930s had laid the framework for a female vision that was stronger than Dobie's influence. The themes of violation of the land and of the raw, unviolated land as a source of human strength evolved unimpeded over the decades, and spread out in all directions in the post-Vietnam era. Defeat had weakened male mythology in all its forms, and women were enjoying a period of political and cultural liberation that fed directly into the language of poetry. Males who were opposed to American imperialism and to war in general could join women in developing an opposing view of the mythical past—as a metaphor of the body and as an extension of the soul and the unconscious.

The empty hall with its scattering of bards, male and female, was a sign that a polarized myth was in the room—being exercised in verse language that chronicled an innocent array of details about the dislocations of a poet's life in the city. Underneath the mild surface was a troubling second text on the region that questioned more than a myth; it raised questions about unbridled commerce, the rights of minorities, the waste of resources for profit. Poetry could be dangerous in the wrong hands, or merely obnoxious and unwelcome in the hands of average writers.

CHAPTER 4
I AND THOU

If Texas poetry began with a feminine grasp of the relation between body and landscape, it was perhaps the only place where such a perspective found voice in the region—a female voice, collaboratively developed by both men and women. The Depression had something to do with the flowering of the woman's voice in the region. The Depression called into doubt the very elements of self-reliance, initiative, perseverance in America—it was like a defeat in war. The men were challenged to the roots of their philosophy of aggressive self-interest. Things had occurred that made ordinary men fail, in spite of their profound willingness to compete. Forces greater than individuals acted against self-interest and removed the circumstances by which social advancement could occur. The purely male myth of heroes and sodbusters, Indian fighters and rebels against Mexico goaded a second myth into being through poetry—the female vision of a symbiotic relation between humanity and the environment.

The South's defeat in the Civil War had produced a similar resurgence of female independence and provoked an outpouring of feminist novels, poems, essays, and political activism that did not abate until the outbreak of World War I. The men of the South were scrutinized and found wanting in sensitivity and tolerance of female ways. Kate Chopin's *The Awakening* (1899) was perhaps the culmination of the entire post–Civil War reassessment of the southern chivalric code. And in general, more women than men were sympathetic to the plight of blacks and found themselves cautious advocates of civil rights and other social causes dealing with equality. The discourse on southern men ran from *Uncle Tom's Cabin* (1852) to *Gone with the Wind* (1936). The post–World War II literary resurgence was a woman's movement on paper, stating the sympathies of white Anglo women for Plains Indian cultures, the natural landscape of the open plains, and the plight of the animals being hunted to extinction as the price of settlement.

And you find the counter culture of women writers emerging in odd places, as in Davis Foute Eagleton's grade-school textbook, the *Texas Literature Reader,* published in Dallas in 1916, which includes Fannie Baker Darden's poem "Yokonah," in which an Indian chief appears to a white woman during a rainstorm and asks her

> Dost thou think, thou foolish pale face,
>> Thou are wiser in thy pride
> Than my mighty band of warriors
>> When we trod these prairies wide? (52)

Evidently, the "pale face" is not at all averse to sympathizing with this ghost of the Indian past, a frequent theme of women's poetry from then on. Wiped out without a trace, the ghost is not complaining so much as reminding the living that what was wasted in the name of land greed and aggression against the alien leaves the land poorer. And there seems tacit agreement with these remarks, if silence can be taken for assent here.

What is curious by half is that young readers were expected to file this sort of information about slaughter into the same memory that read boisterous tales of state patriotism and white victory speeches, without reflecting on the possible contradictions or paradoxes of that mix of sentiment. But read on they did, and this book, like others of its period, is remarkable for its variety and sophistication compared to today's simplistic grade-school readers with their political correctness and self-censorship.

For that matter, John L. McCarly's anthology of Panhandle poets, *Wind in the Cottonwoods* (1936), the second in a series of local anthologies (the first, also by McCarly, was called *Prairie Nights and Yucca* (1934), includes Marile Lockhart's poem "The Legend of Palo Duro Canyon," which narrates the suicide of a young Comanche girl, Winona, after being told to give up her lover, a Spanish soldier, to marry a fellow Comanche. The poem takes her side of the matter and seems to welcome Winona into the fold of women whose love life was thwarted by pig-headed fathers. Race here seems to be no issue.

Even more stridently pro-Indian is Anna J. Hardwicke Pennybacker's grade-school text, *A History of Texas: For Schools* (1912), where she writes, "Every disturbance was charged to the red men. The agents investigated the charges, and declared that in a few cases the Comanches had been guilty, but that the Brazos Colony was entirely free from blame, and that the majority of the acts of violence [in 1858] had been committed by unscrupulous white men, who felt safe in so doing, as they could rely on popular prejudice to lay all crimes upon the citizens. The citizens heeded nothing said by the agents, but demanded the removal of the Indians from Texas, and threatened violence if their demands were not granted" (235). To soften these remarks, at the risk of being illogical, she comments in her notes, "It must seem cruel to the young student, when he reads how the Indians were driven from place to place, and hunted down like beasts, but he must remember the provocation his Texan ancestors had. In those dark days no mother on our broad Western prairies ever rocked her babe to sleep at eventide without the fear that the morning would find it torn from her arms and murdered by the red men" (331).

I was not fully aware of these things when I wrote my essay for *Texas Women Writers,* nor were the others who contributed essays. None of us saw the immensity of the groundswell pouring from women's imaginations; the remythologizing of Texas and southwestern culture was going on from the earliest writing of the twentieth century. It was a renaissance of women's voices, a tide of quiet, insistent whispers and innuendo, and some cranky assaults upon male dominance. That was everywhere and was an unacknowledged tradition of their coming into print. Contemporary readers did not make much of the questions being raised in the poetry, or the fiction. It was safer to say if women were doing the writing, then the tradition was both provincial and second rate, another mediocre attempt by Texas to put itself into the national literary forum.

But the groundwork of a second mythic system was achieved in the early, modest lyrics by Texas women. The themes they developed addressed the Indian slaughters, the decimation of natural life, and the transformation of the land into cities and oil fields. The garden was a metaphor of the gentle human self watered by a solicitous and nurturing female spirit. What happened to the primrose was a slight upon the female body; what gouged the earth for money was a rape of the land and of woman. Lexie Dean Robertson, the first native-born Texan to be named poet laureate of Texas (1939–41), and an inner circle of very skilled women launched into this theme of oil and aggression and were very nearly outrageous in their criticism. But that was the Thirties, the Angry Decade, and while the women sawed on their fiddles in Texas, a lot of others were taking on Wall Street and the trusts in much louder language. It all seemed part of a larger reassessment of runaway capitalism, and not so much a mythic retelling of the Southwest fable. But the latter is truer of the body of writing that we critics surveyed in this estimable, this all too rare attempt to get at women's imaginations in *Texas Women Writers.*

So Texas was one of those pockets of America where a counter philosophy received a little rain, began to sprout and send up more shoots. The greening of Texas could be said to have begun with these marginal commentaries on the land and how it reflected human behavior and morality. Dorothy Scarborough's *The Wind* (1925) advanced the female vision of a cruelly adverse terrain set against human desire, which in turn reflected upon a social world in which women were discovering their consciousness of having suffered—not so much at nature's hand, as at the hands of their own husbands and fathers.

The idea of the Southwest was a man's invention; it represented a battlefield of ideas, philosophies, and racial conflicts. The plains were a place where Europe, that is, the western Protestant extremity of Europe terminating in the British Isles, was to be tested against indigenous pagans and Spanish Catholics. Religious wars had been fought in Europe from as early as the Crusades of the twelfth and thirteenth centuries, to the Reformation, the Hundred Years' War, and the Industrial Revolution.

Catholic cultures formed the southern rims of Europe and represented a stubborn, ancient, rooted agricultural way of life, resistant to any fundamental change of that relation to earth. Scratch deep enough into Catholic theology and you find pantheism still living in its roots. The Greek pantheon had crept into Catholic thought heavily disguised; the saints and the miracle workers were not too far removed from all those heavenly helpers Greeks called upon in times of crisis.

The very forms of worship with idols, candles, incense, and promises are as old as Sumeria and the Neolithic age. The very lushness of nature suggested the work of many southern gods pushing up the buds and fruits of a year with only a mild interlude of winter. It was the north, with its snow and ice, its bleak half-year of bald ground, that seemed to suggest a more abstract god not always vigilant toward things on earth. The north of Europe, like the north of any large country or continent, was the place where human meddling seemed more than a preoccupation, but a manifestation of a cold-weather mind, a winter imagination. The linguists tell us speech is more clipped, less elided or drawled in cold latitudes, and they have grouped those languages of northern speakers into cold-climate tongues, as against the warm-weather speech of languorous southerners, who drawl, slide, melt, and water speech, and with it, their willingness to submit to nature's rules. Nature was good the farther south you tended, feeding you, sheltering you with lots of shade, slaking thirst with sweetwater creeks and rivers. The north accepted struggle as the predicate of human life; the south found nature motherly and nurturing, as well as smothering and cloying. The south tended to deify the organic world; the north was suspicious of its cruel intentions and tried to master it.

Women were removed from the religions of the north little by little; the Reformation had diminished the role of Mary at the heart of Christianity. The Counter-Reformation put her back on the heavenly throne, but only after Catholicism in general was weakened, split from the rest of Christianity. Northern Europe became the great Protestant belt of industry, and a culture of male authority, whereas southern Europe continued to venerate a host of female saints and mothers and remained faithful to Rome. Women did not rule in the market or in politics in the south, but they ruled their households and husbands, and dominated the culture through food ways and healing, the powers of persuasion. The north was a region of the mind as much as it was a latitude or climatic zone. Unlike Rome, whose heart was occupied by the Vatican City, the northern metropolis put commerce at its heart, the banking houses which were built to resemble the old cathedrals. Slowly a ring of factories made up the outer perimeters, and the roads no longer led to the cathedral but to the centers of civic power—the great commercial towers, the political offices.

A northern European city dominated nature with its human artifice; it was a place of rationalized labor and production. The rich ruled by their wits and resources, not merely by inheritance. By the early nineteenth century, a city came into the folklore of the south as the place where one's roots, heritage, good or bad name dissolved into ambiguity. The city was the zone of rootless life, where you could escape into the dark alleys and be anything, or anyone. The village was the place of memory where your face was your character and family name. In the city, you detached yourself from all village memory and became a thief, a prostitute, a street laborer, a busker, or an opportunist who climbed up the ranks to wealth and power. A village held you back, rooted you in the strict unchanging hierarchies based on nature's cycles. The city was a place of dissolution in which seasons, night and day, good and evil, blended together and lost their reality. That is the grudge at the heart of Texas literature, a deep suspicion that the city was a northern form of power cutting at the very strings by which southwestern man took his strength and character.

How that figures into the literature of the modern era is interesting, but not really our main subject. Southern literature is composed of fables and hallucinations, eerie stories of miracles and apparitions, all based upon the idea that nature is alive and full of ghosts, spells, sprites, and devils. Northern realism sprang up as an extension of the new inductive sciences and promised to record the literal germs on the surface of city life. The new urban vision in fiction dissected, analyzed, literalized everything, and sorted out men and women according to certain broad categories of good and bad. At a very crude angle one might say that the American South dwelled in the powers of nature, while the North explored the limits of human control and expanded the reach of the city. That the North should have conquered the South meant the city would triumph over the savannas, over the plantation economy, over cotton and ranching. The future was Dallas, Houston, and Austin, and the past was the small family ranch and its covenant with nature. As David Teague remarks in a revisionist look at southwestern art, *The Southwest in American Literature and Art* (1997), "For the most part during the 1890s, that is all the desert was to Anglo America—the backdrop for human undertakings" (64). The paintings on the subject had no detail, no perception of the natural events that went on behind the heroic epic unfolding in the Anglo conquest. Remington was the measure of that artistic perspective, as against the desert paintings of Georgia O'Keeffe forty years later, in which no human beings are present, only the desert bones and flowers are in the foreground.

When we come back to the arguments of poetry in Texas, I cannot help but believe that what I am hearing in the language is a lamentation over the loss of the southern philosophy of nature. Women felt it sharply in their own struggle to keep alive a sense of the wildness of things. The vast amount of garden poetry they wrote is a celebration of that natural world that is shrinking away. Flip the pages of Greer and Barnes's *New Voices of the Southwest* and you will find that almost any poem you read supports this theme of lamentation, this loss of a comforting connection to natural will. Here is Berta Hart Nance's "Sea-Wind on the Prairies":

When wild geese mutter from the smoky sky,
And tawny leaves drift slowly to the ground,
The sea-wind leaves the waves; its piercing cry
Upon the prairie slopes begins to sound
And how it mourns along the dim ravine,
Where gray wolf-shadows darken and are gone,
And how the tortured mesquites twist and lean,
While, like an angry tide, the wind beats on! (159)

Alice Corbin's "Red Earth":

After the roar, after the fierce modern times
Of rivets and hammers and trams,

.   .   .   .

Here is the desert of silence
Blinking and blinding the sun—
An old, old woman who mumbles her beads
And crumbles to stone. (75)

"Red Earth" makes the connection between land and body we have been
finding in a lot of women's poetry, but it also links land to the spirit of Mexico, an old Catholic *mujer* saying her rosary. In another poem, "In the
Desert," Corbin nails the relation of desert to Mexico when she writes,

Beyond, on the bare hillsides,
Yellow and red gashes and bleached white paths
Give foothold to the burros,
To the black-shawled Mexican girls
Who go for water. (*New Voices,* 75)

The land in this poetry is not so much "ours" as it is "theirs," a Mexican
earth related profoundly to the women. Some of the poets in this anthology
lament the passing of the Indians, and relate the earth to them as well. If that
is the case, the women are quietly associating the spirit of the land with
those who once owned and have lost it to Anglos. This is a nature of mystery especially because it belonged to an Otherness of females and ancient
New World traditions. It is only partly one's own now that it is settled.

But a second text in these poems of the 1930s seems to be saying that any grievances women may have with the male regime of modern Texas can be stated through an allegiance to the mystery of the soil—both as one's own body, and as the stolen or appropriated property of native women, as seen in Corbin's "El Rito de Santa Fe":

> This valley is not ours, nor these mountains,
> Nor the names we give them—they belong,
> They, and this sweep of sun-washed air,
> Desert and hill and crumbling earth,
> To those who have lain here long years
> And felt the soak of the sun
> Through the red sand and crumbling rock,
> Till even their bones were part of the sun-steeped valley;
> How many years we know not, nor what names
> They gave to antelope, wolf, or bison,
> To prairie dog or coyote
> To this hill where we stand,
> Or the moon over your shoulder. (*New Voices*, 76)

Jean Milne Gower has a poem in *New Voices of the Southwest*, "Cliff Dwellers," which takes the now familiar trope of the womanly land in the form of a mesa, the Mesa Verde of the poem, where the Mesa Verde "lifted her stone wings, / Soft fledged with piñon and juniper / To mother" the cliff-dwellers (106). Red earth bore kinship to red skin, an Indian cosmos. In Marie Grimes's "Necessity," you get the sense a woman walks into the Texas outback and is restored spiritually, metaphysically by her surroundings, which belong to a deep sense of racial, religious Otherness in her midst. The North, she says, is fine, but the Texas landscape is deeper, fuller in nurture:

> How should I walk a mincing round of days,
>   When every heart-beat lifts a voice to speak
> Of redbuds bursting in a rosy haze
>   Along the windings of a Texas creek,
> Or fix my fate where there was never heard
> The insistence of a moon-mad mocking bird? (112)

Jeannie Pendleton Hall takes on the persona of landscape in "Yucca by the Road-Side":

Spite of all the loud new ways,
    Here my spiky leaves grow thick,
And from out their green I raise
    Holy, white, my candlestick. (113)

My spiky leaves, *my* candlestick.

Increasingly, this poetry bids farewell to a familiar northern landscape of cities as masculine country and relates the Texas landscape to a female self, as Margaret Bell Houston puts it in "Song from the Traffic":

(Manhattan—Manhattan—I walk your streets today,
But I see the Texas prairies bloom a thousand miles away!)

.   .   .   .

(It's raining in the barren parks, but on the prairie-side,
The road is shining in the sun for him who cares to ride!) (121)

Siddie Joe Johnson, who grew up in Corpus Christi, wrote "The Land I Know":

These are the songs I sing of the land I know—
Tall, cool songs going down to the Southern Gulf—
Maybe no better songs than my brothers sing—
Maybe no better land than my brothers go—
But always my song and my land, and, so, beloved.

    This is the dream I've made
    In the yellow heat and the thin
    Mesquite-tree shade.

These are the bones I worry—
Coyote call and cactus bloom
And *agarita* berry.

.   .   .   .

The oleander hedges
Bloomed red as a young girl's mouth.
"Another song—and the singer, the same—
But one who has loved the South." (129–30)

What these poems seem to claim is that poetry is a discourse on the land as the domain of the southern imagination, an organic world of nurture related to primal native traditions and folkways. To disturb it is to interrupt the flow of female energies and identification. If we go back to Webb's *The Great Plains,* there is at the outset an argument that what entered the Southern Plains was essentially a northern European folk born of the forest belts and utterly unfamiliar with the openness of the new terrain. The 98th meridian, that famous boundary Webb marked as the plumb line running down a little to the west of Austin, was a wall of nature dividing Atlantic plant and animal life from a Pacific biota. And the forest belt along east Texas was the last of European familiarity to the settlers coming west. To enter this virgin land was to break a sod that had been untouched since its inception around eleven thousand years ago—as the scree or debris apron of the Rockies. It was a body, mystical in origin, belonging to a kind of New World inland paradise—a harsh, inhospitable Eden to the uninitiated human being, but an inexhaustible garden of nurture to bison and pronghorn sheep, to the Plains tribes that moved with the herds and ate at their fringes.

The women poets seem to have regarded this separation of zones in Texas as a way of demarcating their own identity against an eastern, an Atlantic Anglo culture. And to build cities in Texas, to transform the land in the oil boom, as Lexie Dean Robertson's poems describe it, is to violate a female precinct of nature. It constituted an epic rape, and the poems come close to saying so. Since, as Webb argues, the High Plains seem to have blocked the South's farther expansion to the west and allowed northerners to penetrate more rapidly, based upon their different forms of agriculture and industry, then the Plains area not only decided the outcome of the Civil War, as he suggests, but brought in an alien form of land use and city-building from northern European traditions. The conquest of the land seems to have been a new victory over Rome and of southern female traditions.

In 1866, a year after the close of the Civil War, a pious Methodist woman named Martha White McWhirter had a "second blessing" at her dishpan one hot August morning and decided there and then to remove herself from her husband and set up a small commune of women and children in Belton, Texas. The group became known as the Sanctificationists and created a fund from the sale of eggs and butter to help other women denied money by their husbands to run households or pay for medical expenses. Other women prayed for sanctification and began divorcing their husbands to join the commune, which set up a hotel, a laundry, and other services.

Beltonians were at first indifferent to these events, but "the town split wide open," writes Eleanor James, a historian with the Bell County Historical Society, in *Women in Early Texas* (1994), "as woman after woman left home and husband, taking with her the daughters and even the small boys; for these were wives, mothers and aunts from the best families in town and from the leading churches." Finally, "a posse of husbands clattered up the stone walk to the McWhirter porch, called out that they wanted their wives, and sent one intentionally mis-aimed bullet through the paneled door, just to frighten them" (185).

When two Scottish carpenters, brothers, showed up in Belton and asked to be admitted to the movement (they had been members of a similar group in Scotland), it "was too much for the Belton men; however outrageous they considered the acts of the women, they were, after all, ladies and they could not be fought." But men betrayed their own sex by asking to become part of such an order, or were deemed foxes in the hen house. The two brothers were beaten in the street and sent away. When they refused to go, they were "tried for lunacy, . . . and whisked away to the asylum in Austin. Obviously sane, the men were kept at the asylum only overnight" (186). The sexes had polarized both here and elsewhere in the era of land rushes, gold fever, and the closing frontier.

However that may be, Anglo women writers were now exploring a sense of nature based upon gender and pastoral values, and men were using nature as the test of their abilities to conquer wilderness and adversity. Traditions and separate mythical systems representing male and female values sprang up accordingly and radiated outward into the whole of Texas society by the end of the Depression era. The voice of women would fall silent, however, at the outset of World War II. Military victory brought about rapid commercial expansion and the development of the major cities, which closed a literature of natural sympathies. The conclusion of war was a victory more grand than had been any other—and opened a new era that gave the male vision its apotheosis of power, the Atomic Age and the Cold War.

The reading clubs, run mainly by women, would not attract new members from the next generation; they would linger on as library committees, women's clubs, and auxiliaries and take on a certain quaintness of a bygone era. The Poetry Society of Texas would continue issuing its yearbooks and awards, but the real flurry of literary activity had subsided by the 1950s, and practical affairs ruled. Texas was growing, and a subtle, pervasive vindication of male values and ways characterized the state's cultural life. Women were entering the universities in considerable numbers, and farming was dying. The small towns were losing their young to the cities, and corporations were moving their subsidiaries and headquarters to the Sun Belt. While the Texas economy remained vertically integrated around oil and the beef industry, it was being forced to diversify into space technology, computers, and a host of service industries looking for lower operating costs.

Urban Texas meant that the older ecological vision of poetry would have to find a new direction. In fact, if the Sixties had not come along to revive those vanishing interests in the old ways and in wilderness, the poetic voices of the 1930s and 1940s might have gone the way of the reading clubs. Instead, a new generation began to voice renewed interest in Indian culture, ecology, and the deeper Texas past. How the new generation grafted its language and attitudes onto the roots of earlier women's poetry is not entirely clear.

It happened, and it underscored the still not apparent fact that the main tradition of poetry in Texas belonged to women. Men were only a Greek chorus to the great solo female artists. They laid down the framework of what poetry should talk about and how it should approach the problems of northern urbanism and southern pastoralism, of the land as body, and of the past as spiritual lore. All that would fall into the hands of the Vietnam/Watergate generation and fire a renaissance of prolific writing.

But the connection between older women's poetry and the younger poets was a mysterious phenomenon of postwar academic Texas. It must have been a matter of teachers of southwestern literature going back to writers of the 1930s and assigning readings. Dobie's *Guide to Life and Literature of the Southwest* first appeared from Southern Methodist University Press in 1943 and was revised and expanded in 1952, about the time one would have wanted to see this book come into the classroom. Poets began entering the classroom to teach their art and to look at the odds and ends of an unacknowledged tradition. They opened the eyes of students to the midcentury poetry boom on both coasts and stimulated a new wave of writing based in Austin, only tangentially affecting Houston and Dallas, San Antonio and El Paso. But the new poets were taking their art seriously and feeling their way along the paths marked by the Depression generation.

But even Dobie was pessimistic about the literary front in his time. He lists only twelve books of fiction and remarks in his preface to the 1952 edition of the *Guide* that "actualities in the Southwest seemed to have stifled fictional creation." A spate of minor classics had been awarded prizes by the Texas Institute of Letters throughout the 1940s, and a body of literature had grown out of the war, but not much in the way of poetry. No one could have foreseen the emergence of Vassar Miller by 1956, who would shortly become the foremost poet of Texas and a national figure of great prominence thereafter.

Miller, of whom I will say more in a later chapter, should not be regarded as the exception, the genius in isolation, in Texas. No great writer is ever the exception of a time or place, but rather its measure, its limit of excellence. A writer of great amplitude rises on the wave of every other writer's work, and reaches out beyond him or her to the higher or highest point of vision. Miller was no different. She had been reading her contemporaries and paid special attention, as I will note again, to the poetry of Edwin Arlington Robinson, a cranky, dark-tinged ironist on Maine life and a superb craftsman of a few lyric forms. She would base her own work on this poet's lean, compressed style of colloquial formalism and bring it to a very high polish. But she disappointed critic-poets like Dave Oliphant later on when they found few or no regional references in her work.

Was she really Texan in her poetry, Oliphant asked aloud in his reviews of her books. The answer was, yes and no. In *Heart's Invention: On the Poetry of Vassar Miller*, a 1988 book of essays edited by Steven Ford Brown and devoted to analyzing and weighing Miller's output, nine of us wrestled with the value of her work and what it meant, and I don't think—looking back on this effort—we came anywhere near answering the question. She was over our heads. I rather think she was over her own head. Larry McMurtry wrote the preface and was both gushing and self-deflating, saying nothing to add to his singular praise of her work in his manifesto a decade before, "Ever a Bridegroom."

What we could not see back in 1988 was the fact that Miller was coming out of the dominant female tradition of poetry and had absorbed its themes and perspectives so deeply as to incinerate them in her imagination and make them completely her own. I thought, as did a few others, that she was the southwestern counterpart of the Confessional women poets, Sylvia Plath and Anne Sexton. That was only partly true, of a truth too trivial to matter. She was not confessing anything much, certainly not the anomie and suicidal despair of those two. She was not part of the same Cold War feminist collapse of spirit that was the work of Confessional women poets.

She was in a different relation to region altogether. No, what hindsight tells me now is that Vassar Miller took the condition of her cerebral palsy and made it the sick body of the conquered desert and plains of industrial Texas. Her debility was the land's, and her aches and pains, her loneliness were the wounded landscape. While others a little younger than she lamented the spread of the cities and the wasting away of the land in direct terms, Miller was recording it through her wasting flesh. It was at once the tragic theme of violation and a personal lyric of great pathos and urgency.

She did not preach ecological gospel; she didn't have to. Her self was the land's extension all in one—and we readers knew she was getting to the relation but we did not know how. We only knew by instinct that she was right to talk of her terrible ordeal of failing muscle and bone, her loss little by little of vital independence. She was the only possible voice of the prosperous postwar years. But others talked about her religion, her pious Christian views. And I don't think they were right, or quite right. The reaching out to a Christian God was equally to a male authority, a great masculine power from which she begged forgiveness and love. The male regime was consolidated in this plea to an aloof, distant, often unyielding God in her prayers—which crystallized the relation to region that women had been sketching in poetry since the 1920s.

No one else had thought to write from the position of the victim before; that was how we were fooled into thinking Miller was another Confessionalist, just another one. But if she could become the land, through human illness, she could read the will of the desert, of the various prairies and plateaus of the state. She could say how it felt to be plundered and drained, and left depleted, unspirited, mere "backdrop" to human events. Her work represents the cost of certain philosophical and religious attitudes brought in by settlers, who transformed in order to exploit.

How the land reacted was echoed in Miller's inventory of her own sinking physical self—a readout of lowered water tables, desertification, salinization of the cotton bottoms, pesticides poured on grain crops, and the sucking dry of the oil lands. The use or abuse of Texas had been the province of soil scientists and wildlife managers, and game wardens and fisheries experts; but Miller seemed to capture the pathos of the land in her plaintive, personal lyrics more poignantly and tellingly than any extension service pamphlet ever could.

Miller broke through the formal barriers other women would not cross—that is, she was wounded enough to write from a crippled, suffering source. The poetry before her had been protected—a woman was strong, from a secure household, from a position of Anglo superiority, which subtly undercut her sympathy for something weakening or wounded. She wasn't there, wasn't *there in spirit* to tell us how it hurts. You had to be Indian to know, or black or a Hispanic farmer down on his tenant luck to know. She knew. And by breaking the code of the perfect soul weeping at others' misfortunes, by slipping into the victim's body, she could write from the land's own soul.

Somehow, Miller's books seem related to the making of *The Diary of Anne Frank* (1945), written by one who also wrote her sufferings from within the victim's body. That drew to a bead the whole of the Holocaust experience. The nearness of the Other in the America of the late 1950s was beginning to fascinate and draw writers—who wanted to know more personally what the suffering meant. Miller was first, but note how John Howard Griffin took the same path when he entered into the identity of a black man in his journal, *Black Like Me* (1961), which illuminated the condition of the African American southerner in the racist Deep South as had no other sociological research. It was the same gesture! The same identification with the Other. And another writer, Chester Seltzer, also stepped to the edge when he became, more or less, the Hispanic drifter Amado Muro. I was on to him back in the late 1980s when I wrote an essay called "From Cowboys to Curanderas: The Cycle of Texas Literature," which appeared in the *Southwest Review* in 1988. I knew he had achieved something as fundamental as the poetry of Miller but couldn't say exactly how—it was deep, frightening, racially brilliant of him, but the key was missing.

The key to breaking into the reality of the Southwest was to cross over the racial and natural divide and voice from the side of Otherness what pain and debility the region experienced. It was only a matter of time before the actual native writers would take up their pens and begin writing from their own perspective; after that, *le déluge!* In the meantime, there were the new writers coming of age when I arrived in the state in 1974, a time in which the white world took its deepest shocks since the Civil War. Not only had the Vietnam War been a loss, but we now suffered through the ordeal of the Watergate investigation and President Nixon's resignation. The aftershocks were deep and had already entered into and blighted a generation's idealism—my own. What I saw were white writers beginning to express themselves from a weakened position in the social hierarchy. They were not so sure of their footing anymore, unhappy with the authorities that ruled their lives, and disenchanted with their own lives. They were feeling the wounds that Miller had already staked out as a landscape as big as Texas.

The Vietnam generation was raised and injected with an enormous sense of guilt and violation from the geopolitical sphere. They brought it home to Texas and into the new poetry beginning to be collected into chapbooks, alternative press books, and a spate of interesting, if tentative, anthologies coming out around the time I was unpacking my suitcases. Two movements were dovetailing at that moment, 1974: a post-Vietnam release of emotion and the rise of the women's movement. They were connected, of course; a defeat at war always liberated the women from a certain quietude and passivity. This time, however, a slump in the economy did not absorb the returning veterans, and there were no victory parades to greet them or to monumentalize a victory. Instead, tales of horror and drug abuse, massacres and waste came back through the news media, which seemed to encourage domestic criticism of government, then business, and finally, education—as wards of the same gender that had lost the war.

The anthologies were trying to trace the new emotions of the era, this opening of male wounds and a strengthening resolve of women to speak out, to contend, to invade the provinces where males had had their temples. It was all coming down, those barriers—soon enough a new black movement would rise, to be followed swiftly by the Chicano movement, and gay rights. The shakeup was just starting as I looked around the towns in my little niche of the Brazos Valley. Did I know what was afoot at the time? Only partly. I had a partial knowledge of the forces at play—having watched most of the Watergate hearings on my little Sony TV in Philadelphia, while I should have been writing my dissertation. Then, in Houston, in 1975, I attended the opening of the PEN Center, with Susan Sontag and a host of other dignitaries of the New York literary world sitting above us at a long table, willing to respond to our questions.

I had just been hugged by Grace Paley, who was conducting yoga exercises for the women at the back of the hall. Ishmael Reed was nearby, watching me approach an open microphone to ask a question. I remember saying that NOW (the National Organization for Women) was having its conference across town, and here we were meeting as writers. Would the feminist movement affect the way we write and think? Is there a female way of seeing that is different from the state of writing now? A style, a grammar, or usage that would be coming into our consciousness later? No one wanted to answer the question. Each demurred and I stepped away. But Reed gave me a bear hug and said I was a kamikaze pilot like himself. He then asked how much ad space did one have to purchase to get a book reviewed in the *New York Times,* and iced the hall.

Reading over Dave Oliphant's 1973 gathering of new poets, *The New Breed,* on the eve of a long, agonizing period of literary brush fires and gender wars, I see little prophecy in the poems. No anticipation of the crises to mark our time. But quietly, in some of the poems, are the themes of the 1930s—the self as nature, the body as landscape, filtered through male imagery, since the majority of the poets here are men. Robert Burlingame comes close to identifying the main thrust of new Texas poetry in "She Knew the Names," which opens

> Like an Indian she knew the names
> of all the grasses and could explain the code
> inside every bud.
> And if any insect blitzed through her garden,
> she knew whether to spare him or spray him stiff. (65)

Burlingame remarks in his note that he holds "strong feelings of the desert, especially its plants and rocks. I live in the desert's heat and light. . . . If I ever work out an esthetic concept of my own, it will be in the blaze of the desert, in its silence" (64). His poem makes the deeper identification of woman and Other in the phrase "like an Indian." That phrase touched the edge of something about to happen. Another poet, Tomás Rivera, makes a clear identification of woman as the land in "In the Sun":

> A new day.
> I will lie down in a field
> with a bright red sun smooth as a scythe
> rising in my eyes.
> I will close my eyes and dream, a floating woman,
> of my own blue hair

streaming behind me
in the shallow water of your bed.
You will reach out and touch me like a standing sheaf of
wheat.

You will wake me. (146)

Robert Joe Stout also makes the identification of woman and wild land
in "I Awaken Her from Reading":

Above the lamp above the bed
    I saw a sparrow
    flutter, spread
    tipped wings,
        its shadow
    on her book,
      her eyes
    on lives within the words
    her life a shadow
    out beyond the light.

I willed the bird away
She whirled
to look, her face
a folding-in of feathers,
                  head
stretched forth
in song. (175)

Peter Wild's note to his section of poems observes that "as a resident of
the American Southwest, a region of the Anglo, Mexican and American Indian, I often hold conflicting sympathies and allegiances" (188). Indeed,
that statement would seem to be applicable to all twenty-five poets in the
collection, of which only two are women. Oliphant's preface states his intention to bring together poets who speak forcefully of their regional identity, although a good handful of the poets say the landscape has no palpable
influence on their work. All good poetry, he remarks, bears the stamp of
place in it, suggesting that a sense of place is a more reliable hallmark of

quality than universality of vision. Good poets spring from the soil, he says, without quite penetrating to the heart of that idea—ultimately, identification of self with nature. That view may have been ahead of its time in 1973, but Oliphant is close when he writes that "these poets remain faithful to a literary tradition which draws on the Spanish contribution to the region, the stoic character of its people accustomed to the land's undependable ways, and through closeness of earth and sky a sense of the nearness of man to a larger scheme of things. Far from the famous braggadocio associated with Texans, it is this latter aspect of the poet-state relationship which inspires a poetry well aware of man's smallness in the presence of natural and cultural wonders" (14).

Travois, the other anthology to appear around the time of my arrival in the state, was edited by Paul Foreman and Joanie Whitebird, from a much wider canvass of the state's poetry. I remember the poster announcing *Travois*'s call for manuscripts hanging in the hallway of the English Department at Texas A&M, and I remember being curious to know what the word *travois* meant. I did not respond with some poems; I was too new to the local scene. It was 1975, and the anthology came out a year later. *Travois* is a French word for a sling used by Plains Indians to carry kids, tipis, food supplies, and made with the poles used for holding up the tipi, dragged over the ground on runners by dogs, later by horses. There is not the intensive thematic control visible in *The New Breed; Travois* wanted to publish any new work that passed a general test of competence for the editors by poets born or raised in Texas and by the émigrés, as everyone called the out-of-staters. Foreman wrote the introduction, in which he casts the new poetry renaissance in terms of landscape and harvest: "The groundswell of writing and publishing in Texas has something of the nature of winter oats, the blades breaking the ground even where there's yet frost. And there's harvest in Edinburg, Lubbock, El Paso, Dallas, San Antonio, Houston, Austin, Texas City, Stephenville, Stratford, and all over the state."

Even without the theme pincers Oliphant applied, this book provides a unified vision—drawn from 156 poets in as many pages of text and graphic art. The poets come from all corners, some in exile, like Foreman himself, others from small towns and rail stops—a real cross section of the Texas outback. About a third of the poets are women, many of them the major or minor stars of today's literature: Naomi Shihab Nye, Pattiann Rogers, Susan

Bright, Eleanor Crockett, and so on. And they are all the daughters of the older generation—chanting a faith in nature that is more pointed and political than ever before. The anthem of recent women's poetry may have been written by Susan Bright in "Junction Stream":

i feel engines
    shake the land
building building
    housing tracks bridges
building building
  marketplaces expressways
        longwords
in autumn
    mallards stop here
waterholds
    the sky together
waterholds
    a man together
met a social scientist
    How does it work?
        i asked
can you stop it
    no he said (18)

The assault on the landscape is drawn from a larger fable of invaders into a natural world for purposes of war. The Vietnam conflict was over only a year before, and the weight of that experience is everywhere in *Travois*. The fable of a large technological power scorching the rainforests with Agent Orange and descending onto villages with hordes of whirring helicopters is ingrained in the imagination. The imagery of war is sucked into the women's fable of the leveling of the Southwest—and the poets are by turns subtle, overt, or strike out angrily without targets. The terms of this new fable make women into vulnerable land and men into marauders and slayers, though always with a sense of man "in general." The anger is mythic, fabulous, a dimension of the imaginary world in which ghostly images from television and one's own nightmares take the place of specific references.

Pattiann Rogers puts her relation to men thus:

I can make gardens,
Grab weeds by the throat,
Ease them body and roots from the soil

. . . .

But you are covered
With poses and protestations that will not loosen. . . . (131)

Images of Asian slaughter proliferate in what might otherwise be tribute poems and laments, as in Jane P. Moreland's "Two Faces":

"Another birthday,"
the caption says,
"for the last survivor of the massacre
near Winnemucca, Nevada, 1911."
Another birthday
for the blood-drenched, screaming infant
found strapped to her dead mother's back.

Both faces smile,
but there is in both
a wrinkle at the eyes, a darkness,
the deep memory: when warm flesh beneath her went cold. (132)

Violette Newton's "The Alien Prisoner" works up a captivity yarn of a woman stolen by Comanches and later rescued by white soldiers. She has learned Comanche ways and finds her white rescuers total strangers—another veiled reference to the war and those who had crossed over to the side of the victims. It ends, "She caught her fingers in her braided hair / and wondered what they meant when they said, 'kin'" (134).

Terry Morrison has a short, untitled poem that nails the identification of woman with whatever grows out there on the prairies and along the arroyos:

the morning rises like a woman
how like a woman to her dress
it lays the night aside

so morning makes covenant with woman
just as woman makes covenant with the world

so you are woman
piled with the softness of magnolia petals
and the white roundings of their tongues
while leaving the flower to its tree (147)

Compare Morrison's poem with Jennifer Hurst's, which throws into the equation of woman and landscape a grouse against commerce, steel-and-glass commerce of the cities, in favor of village barter:

(I'll trade you a poem for a chicken)
perhaps
and I am hoping for the day soon
there will be once again a time of trading
and not buying
a time of sharing the gifts of our hands
remembering that open hands are never empty
and so
perhaps
and i am hoping you will agree so that
we may begin this day
the fruits of my land
for the fruits of yours. (148)

Healing from war may be the half-disclosed theme of Diane Jones Reynolds's poem, "April":

Underground beginnings congregate.
Early grief has been deposed.
A green conspiracy is afoot. (84)

And Rosemary Catacalos has a sense of woman as compounded of nature and Other and victim, all in the same fertile metaphor of a female cornucopia somewhere south of the border, in "And Where are the Women Poets?":

this woman is no moon
what you see, she owns
and more;
pain, fruit, visions
push between her legs
into the mexican streets . . . (85)

Lynn Novak closes her poem, "Litany," with "oh earth mother my mother my mother" (90), and Leslie Palmer asks, "I got to feel like a peach tree in spring" (92). Evalyn Hartmann sees herself as another child of the ancient Indian world in "Olmec," where she describes herself as

an infant in the world
but i . . . , i
am a jaguar
my soul stalks the earth
it will be as strong as the jaguar soul
my feet will be as swift
my teeth as sharp
i will bravely learn to cross the rivers
i will find rest within the caves
[i] . . . , i too
will be forever. (125)

The Vietnam War lies behind *Travois* like a black sun, emitting its guilt and gloom, and a polarity between I and Thou. Women saw themselves in the murky palimpsest of history—as the conquered Indios, the defeated of 1836, the slaughtered Indians, as the exterminated wildlife of the Southwest, and now as the dead peasants of Vietnam, against an inviolable military and commercial male elite. Their response was to rework the fable of the innocent and abused land and make it bristle with political hints and glimmers, and to slip their own souls into the war losses.

The men in *Travois* were not exactly flagellating penitents, but there is a poignancy in their lyrics of nature—Jim Cody aligns himself with the wild rivers and the deep southwestern past; James Hoggard has a crusty rural voice, with all his sympathies put on the side of what is lost or spoiled. Oliphant is the memoirist, like Foreman, for an earlier, more innocent Texas. On and on, the men make a choral background to the Niobes of Texas, offering their own rites of purification for sins committed in their name or by their brothers. It is a strange book, as if the travois in question were loaded with the cultural burdens and sins of a place being sung away on these lyric rhythms. Anyone thumbing these pages back in 1976 might have thought the poems superficially romantic or just quaint, but they are like thin skin stretched over a wound that grows deeper in the flesh as histories of one kind and another coalesced, festered together.

And there *is* something quaint, undeveloped about the poetry. Though it took on more of history into its formulas, and enriched the identity between land and self, that relation was still largely unexamined, naïve. The land was an "it," a great Thou in Martin Buber's theological sense, a vast Other enveloping with its immense soul, as against an ego, a sensitivity, a meek awareness encrusted with a few western ideas about self and individuality. Women were distrustful of this unitary and isolated notion of a self, cut off from some invisible but profound umbilicus to the Great Mother. Almost by instinct, women poets reshaped the relation and put flesh on this invisible cord. They characterized their sex as communal, sharing a common bond of historic slights and lack of privilege, and likened their status to what happens to nature under the blade of men.

And yet, other poetry in the country had moved on—exploring a kind of metapsychology of self in which obscure corners of self were given voice and a place in the poem, often an antiphonal place within a stanza offset from the main flow of the poem. This multivocal surface of poetry was beginning to display a sense that self was not purely of one sex or another, just like nature. The male voice was a condition, an aspect, but so was the female side of self, with its own italicized choral replies. An argument moved down a wider avenue of print, splitting off into quarrels among different nuclei of self—each with a tongue and a kind of language. Jung had commented on the dream as a kind of stage play with all the characters and properties representing parts of the same self. Now the poem was catching up to the idea by laying out fields of print in which different aspects of self were acting out one's consciousness.

By extension, so was nature receiving a new perception as being not one thing or gender, but a panoply of distinct forces in creative play. The constructive side was always in the embrace of death and destruction, the yin and yang of cosmic creation. Things get more complex as Gary Snyder begins to argue, in *The Back Country* (1968), that the deeper one goes into dreaming and instinct, the more one returns to actual wilderness. We carry the lost America in our imaginations, and it is connected to what the poet and anthologist Jerome Rothenberg has called the collective imagination of the past. We were once all one and only now begin to realize what we have lost by the notion of the single soul—all its consoling tendrils to the world snipped to give it autonomy.

Still, it was my feeling at the end of the 1970s that we were pushing the pendulum too far toward a pan-feminist vision and beginning to bash the male end of culture too hard. The poets were beginning to weep in their poems over their male anguish and guilt and to attempt to erase their whiteness by sympathizing too eagerly with any cause that seemed to cry victim to male cruelty. Those were embarrassing years, and with the 1980s we entered the age of the theory revolution. I began reading the new theories of literature with interest, but when the jargon began to congeal and the dismantling of history and literature accelerated, I became dubious, then withdrew altogether from the frenzy. The next twenty years saw a torrent of anger, rejection, reassessment of any version of the past, and a present that was like war-torn rubble. The era was marked by soggy, indifferent lyricism on the national scene and by desperate attempts to love the woman called nature by a lot of southwestern men.

It was a confusing time for everyone; it liberated many who would not otherwise find print, and that is to the good. I cheered the coming on of Pattiann Rogers, Sandra Lynn, the meteoric rise of Sandra Cisneros, Harryette Mullen, Rosemary Catacalos, Naomi Shihab Nye, Betty Adcock, and the more modest successes of Pat Little Dog, Susan Bright, Susan Wood, and a host of newcomers. But the poor males were not doing so well; a few writers found their niche as formalists, like R. S. Gwynn. Others kept the old themes and worked them with high polish, like Walt McDonald, Dave Oliphant, and James Hoggard. Others continued to write from traditions beyond Texas, like Thom Whitbread, Bob Bonazzi, William Burford.

The latter two, in particular, draw upon French symbolism and the sophisticated lyricism of Wallace Stevens and Hart Crane to construct a new kind of voice in Texas—the self-negating presence in which imagination has no centralizing ego to evaluate or dominate the perceived world. Bonazzi's poetry is by turns riddlesome and playful, asking difficult, unanswerable questions about silence and emptiness that correct a long-held belief in the sovereignty of self in Texas. His poems in *Living the Borrowed Life, Fictive Music,* and *Perpetual Texts* move poetry in the direction of Vassar Miller's—toward a spirituality that is at once religious without a church, and esthetic without a particular bias or ideological position.

And the old hands were still at work, among them William Barney and Foreman, Joseph Colin Murphey, and Alfred Huffstickler. Huffstickler, the old man of Austin, a bard whose poems are to be found in almost every small journal in America, is that curious figure in white hair and old clothes who ambles along the streets of Hyde Park in Austin, being greeted by those who know and certainly cherished by those who value the lean, taut language of the best of local lyricism. I was among the newcomers, and wrote myself into Texas little by little—adopting the local themes as I came upon them from the women, and from some of the more daring male poets. A lot of writers fell silent at this time, wary of the shift of ground and not at all certain they believed what they read from others.

Some few poets took the high road of writing directly on myth itself, like John Campion, whose *Tongue Stones* (1990) won the Violet Crown Award from the Austin Writers' League that year and who plows into mythological ground with unflinching courage. This thick tome of a book moves among the *chakras* of Tantric yoga, through the constellations, the creation myth of the Mayan *Popol Vuh*, the Christian *via negativa,* the cosmic symbolism explored in Giorgio de Santillana's *Hamlet's Mill.* It is a tour de force of postmodern encyclopedism, and yet its heady mix of allusion and cryptic note taking are too much, a great cloud of autumn leaf-smoke and voodoo, and it did little to budge the old male paradigm from its central place in literature. The women were working more modestly at pushing the rock, and their sprouts and green laughter were beginning to make a difference.

What we needed and still need is a breakthrough poetry that will hail the transcendent sexual balance of nature and creativity, and cease carping at scapegoats for all our woes. The new vision should be cause for rejoicing, a sense of the great forces of the planet as being entwined, reciprocal, symbiotic beyond our wildest dreams of heaven. With that liberating scheme to base our ethics and behavior on, we might move poetry beyond the meager sentimentalism of nature too much lyric is stuck in—even now. The males have bought the vision that they are a one-dimensional gender, when in fact we are all of us great murky universes of contradiction and humor that no concept can measure fully. The women are blended as much of maleness as the men are of womanly virtues—and when that gets said, perhaps the new literature will come up to the common sense of the lowliest Plains Indian lore. Then we can really move in the direction toward generosity and forgiveness.

But the combined forces of women, and the outpouring of Hispanic and African American poetry created a kind of literary village on the banks of the Colorado River, something new in the mind. Some brilliance and alternative thinking has come out of it, and it was sorely needed. These writers remembered the fragments of their ethnic stories, their family life, their food and beliefs. It seeded poetry with new stories and faces, and their voices taught us some new rhythms and a sprinkling of black slang and some good border lingo.

The vision espoused by these writers was a direct outgrowth of what the women of the 1930s were saying, only now the tones were richer, deeper, and the self more complicated. What happened to the wild rivers and open plains had also consumed the liberties of marginal people. The return of their voices was almost like a sudden springing back of ancient forests onto desert ground. It was a great watering of tears that had sprouted up these voices, some of them ghostly and echoing of old beliefs. The words of Ricardo Sánchez, with all its barrio anger, the sweeter tongues of Nephtalí De León and Carmen Tafolla, added to the plaintive lyrics of Rosemary Catacalos and Ahmos Zu-Bolton, and of Pattiann Rogers's lush garden chants—all this was a second flowering of the Southwest. And a good start.

The Lone Star state has been spawning generations of visionaries who pine for lost connections to the woods and prairies and to an Indian dimension rudely severed by the forefathers. In the state that has contributed a powerful myth of the wandering hero, self-sufficient and self-driven, the poets are reaching out for company.

The 1990s ended with half a myth built, its rafters jutting up without roof shingles, the floors gaping with holes, the walls not yet set with windows. But a house all the same, a house of the spirits for the making of a second, perhaps substantial vision of how life is to be lived in the next century here in Texas.

CHAPTER 5
"GOOD-BY, YOU BIG LUMMAX, I'M GLAD YOU BACKED OUT"

A cowboy was one of my first students at Texas A&M University. His name was Taylor, which he changed to Jim Welch after consulting an astrologer about his bad luck. He had a drinking problem, had run through a lot of women in his time. Now he lived alone in a trailer house on the edge of Bryan, working at night as a disk jockey for a country music radio station. He had a deep rich baritone, was lanky, handsome in a craggy boozed-out way. His mouth was tired, thick, his teeth slightly protruding, so that his lower lip pushed out into a kind of whiskey-laced pout. He had sad, swimmy eyes that were lightly bloodshot and roamed around as he talked. He hunched over to be confidential, and his breath smelled of leather and tobacco. His speech was the kind you heard after your fifth drink at the bar—slow, drawled, resinous as an old saddle, and creaking like a barn door.

A young black girl sat near him, and when he drawled out one of his rambling comments in our freshman essay course, she would visibly wince. She seemed to loathe him. He represented something that stung her like nettles. She was a good writer, with the darting eyes of a fox. She did not seem to trust me, and she seemed uncomfortable in an otherwise all-white class. She was a Texan, too, but from some little rural town where the races were strictly divided. Now, because of her wits and her shrewdness with words, she was here, studying business or management, listening to the voice that represented some sort of male domain blocking her advancement. She kept her own counsel, got an A from me, and shuddered all through the months as Jim Welch cleared his throat, stretched out his six-foot-two frame, boots crossed, and began one of his seat-of-the-pants lectures to me.

I kidded him about my being a greenhorn, an easterner, a dude who didn't know which end of the horse ate the oats. He would laugh and tip back his dirty white Stetson, pull on his leather belt, and crook one boot under until he could get down to face me eye to eye. Then he would give me some breathy explanation about horsemanship, or ranching, or the nature of short-grass country, like the ground around us. Once, on a Saturday afternoon, as my wife and I were cleaning the house, we heard galloping nearby—real galloping of horse hooves—and figured it was a carriage that sometimes went down our street. But when we looked out the screen door we saw a palomino tied up to the cedar tree out front, already nibbling the grass. Jim walked up with his spurs jingling, done up in a fancy cowboy outfit with black pants and a yoked shirt of black and white check. He wore a black Stetson with the string untied. He came in and sat down like Kid Shelleen in *Cat Ballou,* making one of those Lee Marvin pouts of his.

We were thrilled.

Jim played the cowboy perfectly. He had the stare, the lurch, the gangly arms, the long thin legs, the enormous feet bound up in ostrich skin Tony Lama boots. He was the real thing, we thought, made by the sun and the prairies, and an angry God. He talked of weather as if he had herded the clouds—and looked off with that squint that made you recall every western movie you had ever seen. Then he told us he was from Illinois. He said it matter-of-factly, as if being from elsewhere was no slight upon his assumed character.

He was an airplane pilot and flew charters and had come down to Texas one day and loved it so much, he couldn't leave. He put aside his piloting for a while and drove a truck. Then he bought a few acres of scrub oak, fenced in a part of it, bought three horses from a neighbor, and began his new life. He renounced his Illinois past, threw away his only suit and a few ordinary shirts, and transformed himself into the Marlboro Man. He smoked unfiltered Pall Mall cigarettes, had a can of Skoal in his jeans pocket, and smiled with the roots of his teeth lined with snuff stains. When he satisfied himself he was the real thing, he got a job on the radio talking cowpoke jargon. He was good. I tuned him in sometimes and listened to his patter—it was humorous, clever, maybe a little too studied for a real cowboy. The old wranglers spoke with lots of "well, sirs" and ers, ahs, and long pauses. Jim was slick, and silver-tongued.

But no one doubted his sincerity, not even the black girl who sat near him and shivered whenever he raised his hand. We all believed that Jim Welch had become the myth, had put it on like clothes and a hat. But was the myth inside him? Did he see the world through the eyes of the cowboy? Was he perpetually young, hard-edged, careless with women? Did he have some bond to the horse and the land that could save him from loneliness?

His drinking finally caught up with him, and old Jim Welch slowed down at the age of forty. He had graying temples, and his nose had begun to droop a little. His throat was corded with veins and little cross-hatched wrinkles that would not tan. His liver must have gotten tired of those two-six-pack nights in front of the tube. One day he couldn't quite keep it all going; the symbolism was beginning to kill him. He went to an evangelist and got found, and came back sober, with a Bible next to him on the seat of his truck. He quit the radio job and went back to piloting, and every Sunday he was at church until late in the evening. Some of his swagger had worn off and he was leaving for California.

Jim Welch was a mildly clever man, but he was also a kind of marionette, a self-strung puppet. What lured him into the role of the cowboy was a magnet buried deep in the southwestern landscape, with a field of gravity that reached all the way into the origins of civilization. He couldn't know it, but he was being drawn to one of the great archetypes of manhood—lightly fleshed in the brimmed hats, high boots, and denim of the twentieth century. When he put on the clothes and drawled his first bit of ranch-speak, he must have felt a tug deep in his spine. He had found himself in a culture wholly consumed with masculinity. Or was it?

Whatever the cowboy is, he is not just a creature who came on stage around 1870 and exited when barbed wire, "nesters," and rail spurs into the ranch towns eliminated the need for trail drives. The cowboy is rooted in but transcends Texas; it is an archetype with antecedents in the *vaqueros* of Mexico and the *gauchos* of Spain; a version of *gaucho,* called a *gardien,* can be found in the Camargue of southern France, where the white ponies have been used in sheep herding for centuries. The steppes herders were legendary a thousand years ago and may have been around for another several thousand years before.

If the movies shaped him into the loner, the soloist of the prairies, that is only one side of the cowboy. There is the shaman side, too, and a complexity of perfected nerves for quick defense, immense riding skills, an ability to psyche out the herd to anticipate when a stampede might be coming. A good cowboy understood his horse better than his wife or friends; he knew trail lore and weather and had a certain inner consolation that allowed him to dissolve into organized groups and play a role, but also to saddle up with little emotion and head off again, into nothing. This was a way of life and work that seemed to gather up a lot of male propensities and focus them into a single type.

One day, Jim pulled up to the house with his horse trailer and asked me to go riding with him. I had told him of my one experience on a horse at a rental farm in Virginia, where a friend and I hired two bitter old nags and went up a dusty trail. We were warned not to let either horse look back to the barn or we would lose them. My friend was talking when his horse craned her neck, stared at home, and then did a kind of 180 and galloped wildly toward a high wooden fence. Just before colliding with it the beast turned and my friend was hurled off the saddle and slammed headfirst into a wall of pine. He was knocked out and woke up with a bloody nose and sore neck. My horse had come after, but I had so checked her reins that she could barely see the path. We came in a distant second. I saw the anger of a horse, and felt the alien power of its will. It was as if we had wandered into a world of insulted animals that took their revenge on poor duffers like us.

We drove into farm country and Jim pulled up onto a shoulder and took down his ponies. The little palomino was his, the fat gray one was mine. He had saddled her up already, and he held the stirrup for me. A narrow swatch of ground followed a fence up a hill, and our ponies got into single file. Jim gave a cluck and his old paint started to run. Mine followed at a lope, but I knew nothing about riding and bobbed on her back, halting her progress. She tried running faster, but I was turning sideways and one foot had come loose from the stirrup. Jim saw my trouble and slowed, then came back.

"Rake her ribs good, she'll catch up," he said, thinking I couldn't find the controls to speed up.

"She's fine," I said, keeping my head down.

"Nah, just growl and give her a kick, she'll pick up, you'll see."

We went on a while, and now my pony sensed I was a nerd. She stopped to browse. We stood there while Jim went over the hill, then came back at a furious gallop. He slowed with a great show of skill, the hooves of his palomino digging in and sliding to a halt in front of us. We packed up; he gave me a look that said it was no use.

He had a bigger horse, he told me on the drive back to Bryan. A big brown stallion, he said, eighteen hands. An old boy, a bit-chewer and an unpredictable scalawag. Once, when the horse balked at a cattle guard and wouldn't enter the field, he dug his spurs into the animal's sides and the horse bucked him. He almost came off, then he sat tighter, kicked harder, and the horse nearly turned itself over. Jim held on like a bull rider. Then the two stood there in hot sun, both sweating, both refusing to give in. Finally, in a rage, Jim came down with his two fists onto the horse's head and the animal fainted. They landed in a heap on the gravel. He still kept his seat, and slowly, very slowly, the animal came to and found his legs, got up, and loped into the field. He had been mastered, finally. He never balked again.

"The trouble with you is you aren't in the horse's mind yet," Jim told me. "You don't think for it, you think apart from it. You got to be its will, its desire to do something. When it sees what you want to do, it goes along. That's what a horse is—a creature wanting to think, and you do it for him."

He cantered around the yard on his pony to demonstrate how close he was to horse thought; she stopped, turned, went forward, backed up. She nodded when he loosened the reins, then she walked up to the cedar bough and he tied her up. She stood there staring at nothing until he petted her and whispered, then she bent down to graze. It made me think of the Lippizaner stallions in that ornate old theater in Vienna where the animals waltzed and pranced on their hind legs as a rider curled up in the saddle, flicking his reins a little to tell the animal what to do. All that desire to master lay in a thousand such images of uniformed riders with their docile beasts. It was a peculiar male desire, though women have always ridden well and can perform amazing feats of dressage. Still it is a man's thing, a male dream to have a beast respond to every flexion of knees and fingers.

The centaur was Greek shorthand for a certain ideal of warrior—a man whose lower body is horse and whose torso and head are human. They were warriors in a crude sense: powerful, musky, capable of bravery but also of rape and destruction. Because they were merged creatures, one did not master the other, but lived side by side. A knight of the Middle Ages stood for something more—a cold, human mastery over the beast within and beneath one's legs. And not until a man could ride well, lance well, was he sent off in the romances to do battle with a dragon, that monster of uncontrolled lust and anger. When he conquered such an animal, in the name of St. George, the dragon slayer, he conquered himself; his reward was a young virgin, the very one the dragon was guarding in the woods. The romances understood perfectly how males must conquer instinct and impulse before achieving adulthood; the dragon story illustrated the male ordeal of growing up.

The earliest art we know of, according to Michael Rice's study of bull cults in the ancient world, *The Power of the Bull* (1998), are depictions of ur-cowboys trying to communicate with huge four-legged beasts: "From late Upper Paleolithic times to the end of antiquity the bull is always honoured as a divine creature, as the manifestation of a god or as the witness of a god's presence. For more than 15,000 years therefore this creature has seized the god-making imagination of men throughout the great band of territory which sweeps from the Atlantic to the borders of India, and south into Africa" (5).

The earliest art contains images of bull leapers, men whose one skill involved tossing themselves onto the backs of immense bulls, some of them aurochs eight feet tall at the shoulders, and flipping back down onto their feet again. These were the original rodeo clowns, and the act has not changed much ever since. A man was drawn to this four-legged fury and momentum from a primordial identification with its masculine mystique. The animal seemed to have no head, only power and a desire to fight. To tease such an animal was a way of claiming its might; it was, as Rice argues, a god of men. And the horse was the way to make one equal to a bull, especially the buffalo of the Plains. The herding of fierce bulls among the long-horn stocks was another instance of a kind of possession or mastery over the bull. And a horse became an inseparable extension of how one could tap into a deep secret about the male psyche. J. Frank Dobie's interest in the cattlemen of the Southwest is nearly a veneration of the kind of man who could make money at breeding, droving; it was not just business acumen Dobie admired, it was horse sense, an ability to read the bull's mind. Imputed to a cattleman more than to a cowboy, a mere functionary of ranch management, was this larger masculinity that ruled over the world of bulls and cows.

The cattleman's ability to manage large herds and breed stock was a kind of magic few men possessed or had the courage to cultivate. Goodnight stands as one of the giants of the cattle world, a man who raised over three hundred thousand cattle and after thirty years in the business, lost only twenty-six thousand of them to natural disaster or illness. Of the twelve million head of cattle driven to Dodge and other railheads from 1870 to 1890, Goodnight had had a good part of this stock under his own management. The cattleman, and his cowboys, entered into a world that had never been managed on this scale before, and somehow, by intuition and sheer pluck, took complete possession of a system they had invented in the saddle. Therein lies part of the myth of the Plains.

Another part of the myth is space, the kind of infinite space that the Plains laid out. This vast tract was partly old sea floor, glacial moraines, mountain scree, and alkali wastelands. The Rocky Mountain upthrust created what Jay Peck calls in, in his essay "The Destruction of the North American Bison," a vast "rain shadow" that starved out a primordial forest and drove it back to the east Texas arboreal frontier. The decaying forest seeded the bare ground with enough nutrients to develop a grass culture "thought to have come from central Asia by way of the Bering land bridge" (*Ecotropic Works,* 36).

To enter into the Plains was to be diminished to a flea or a gnat; you were not quite human anymore. You were a bug among endless horizons. When the poet Charles Olson said in *Call Me Ishmael* that he "took SPACE to be the first fact of America" (1), he was thinking of the Plains but also of the Pacific Ocean, where Captain Ahab wandered, a kind of water cowboy, looking for his white bull whale. The first painters of the Plains saw the landscape as an ocean, not fields of grass running off into oblivion. So the cowboy was someone who had the tenacity not to be scared off by endlessness, by sheer immensity. But it bothered almost every other nineteenth-century traveler who ventured into the grasslands. Certainly Francis Parkman was daunted and hated the "savages" he met there, and the tedious repetition of landscape for weeks on end. The prairie schooner was well named as a kind of grass ship.

Almost every creature that inhabited this terrain was equipped to navigate its endless unremarkable expanses; the hare seemed especially adapted to it, with a fine sense of smell. So was the rattlesnake, which could burrow from the heat or from unseemly vibrations of heavier animals. The deer were remarkable for their ability to send signals by lifting their white tails, their scuts, a kind of phosphorescent fur that sent a light flash many miles and alerted straggling herds of deer to stampede to safety. The idea of semaphore came from watching deer send their alarums out to others at great distances. The Plains Indians used smoke signals to communicate over the infinitude of grass. Hawks and other raptor birds took readings of the sun to find their way home again. And a man alone on horseback had to memorize swales and shale banks and arroyos and scrub oaks, the way a Bedouin might fix the order of dunes and a few palms during desert crossings. The cowboy came last, on the eve of the iron horse and then cars; he was the last man to cross the expanse with only his nose for guide, and a few landmarks. He joined the great tradition of outback riders, from aborigines to veldt riders, to steppes horsemen, to the Comanche and Apache hunting parties; he was the last dryland sailor.

If you think of it, Plains ecology begins with buffalo herds that were self-managed; a few human predators tagged along and picked off the sick, the elderly, or the young, but were no more in control of its progress than were the wolves who also thinned out the weak. Disease was rare, and the rigors of migration along its feeding cycle from late winter to late fall meant that only the strong survived and mated. When captive herds were raised, the domesticated buffalo was prone to many infections and illnesses, the price of confinement and conservation of the weaker strains.

The herd knew no authority outside its own shifting leadership; it shaped everything around it, a fact that fascinated Goodnight, who became an authority on the species and helped to found the American Bison Society in New York. Goodnight not only aided in preserving the lower Plains buffalo, but befriended many of the Plains Indians who hunted it. In a way, everyone who came into contact with the buffalo became immersed in what some writers now call "buffalo culture." One could not help but learn the lore of the herds, their feeding ways, calving rituals, their migrations and stampedes. A common garment of the Plains was the buffalo robe; tipis were covered in buffalo hides; the fringed and beaded shirts chiefs and other dignitaries wore were made from buffalo hide rather than deerskin. A woman's skills were rooted in buffalo flesh and skin, and the old men were delegated the task of boiling up the tallow and glue used in making arrows and bows. The Plains world was buffalo-centered, and for good reason: it was the principal food for any human being living in its semiarid ecosystem. The Comanches went deepest in their immersion into buffalo culture, but the longhorn and the modern English breeds have also created their own herd cultures and influenced Anglo ways of life. From buffalo culture to hamburgers and fries is a long leap, but the cultural influence of the grazing animal remains undiminished.

The cowboy is someone who descended part of the way into animal culture and lived in that between-zone of beast and civilization. Not quite a centaur, perhaps, but someone who knew the ways of beef cattle well enough to anticipate their every move, and to participate in the rituals of roundup, branding, polling, and droving until animal and human being were nearly one. That relation was new in America, and it transferred the role of the Plains Indians to the victorious Anglo rancher.

No other line of work was quite so drenched in ungulate symbiosis as this—and it rubbed off in curious ways. A man was no longer fit for mere city life if he lived on the ranches; he always came back to the bunkhouse and preferred his horse and saddle, his night under the stars, and his songs on the trail drives. He had followed the example of the Comanche, who came down into the Plains from a sedentary mountain life five centuries before to become an extension of the bison world. Comanches and cowboys were alike, however much they were opposed. Many Indians were among the cowboy work pools, as were Mexicans, the *comancheros* who traded with Indians and whites, former slaves, and all the mixed-race youth of Plains migratory life.

It was John Lomax who first published "Home on the Range" in the 1910 edition of his book *Cowboy Songs;* it was sung to him by a retired African American chuck wagon cook. *Musica ranchera* and the *corridos* (ballads) are Mexican cowboy songs; the majority of trail songs came down through song traditions of the Deep South, with lines going back to the "Come All Ye's" of Ireland. In other words, the cowboy songs were working-class songs shared by black, white, brown, and red cowboys. It did not matter who had the song, so long as it was singable on the trail or around the campfire, and someone could add a new stanza to it to keep it fresh.

There are stories of how the herds were lulled through windstorms and cold nights by such songs. Many of the songs were sung directly to the herd—to keep the herd moving, and to ease the suffering of the "drags," calves dragging swollen bellies along the trail because they had been weaned too early and were eating grass before their rumen had formed.

What does it mean to ride a horse well, I asked my friend Welch. He thought about it, and gave me a blunt answer. "You know who's boss."

But if you assert complete dominance over the animal, have you not cowed it into mere mechanical obedience? Will it still possess its own initiative and daring if a rider is totally in control? He didn't know. He hadn't thought about it. The answer lies in how a man is trained for military duty, I think. He is walked to death and shouted at, and broken of his original independence, or his narcissism. While that is being done, he is also learning to march in unison with all the other men, how to turn tight corners, how to clean his bunk and locker, and mop barracks floors. All this is diminishing his will and making him obey his superiors; at the same time, he is being exercised, run, and taught aggression. So there is some reserve of strength and anger in him that is not removed. He is partly mastered, and partly liberated. He learns how to ease forth the emotion to kill on order, but also to suck back cowardice and go forward into danger when ordered. Something of that balance must lie in the mastery of horses, knowledge of how much to master, and how much to leave to the horse. If that is so, then a man is also learning what not to indulge in himself by way of lust or anger, and what to channel into fierce competition and skill.

Once a man learned how to ride, he became part of a team on the ranches and followed the precise orders of his foreman. He was not his own man in ranch work, but lived and ate and worked collectively. He followed the herd, he understood herd logic and herd culture. He was more fit for droving than for anything else, though many cowboys had once been soldiers. John Lomax tells us a little more about the cowboys in a note to a revised edition of his *Cowboy Songs:*

> These boys in their twenties, who could ride and rope and shoot and sing, came mainly from the Southern states. They brought the gallantry, the grace, and the song heritage of their English ancestors. Their own rough songs often took the form and manner of English ballads. . . . We cannot trace all the influences, but we do know that the aftermath of the Civil War sent to Texas many a young Virginia aristocrat; many sons of Alabama, Mississippi, and Georgia planters; many a coon hunter from Kentucky; roving and restless young blades from all over the South (and from everywhere else). From such a group, given a taste for killing from the Civil War, in which Southern feeling and sentiments predominated, came the Texas cowboy and the cowboy songs. (xviii)

In his essay on the destruction of the bison, Jay Peck puts the migration of Civil War vets into the Plains more stridently: "The Anglo arrival in force following the American Civil War severely affected all natural and cultural processes in the region, to say the least. Honed in the fratricidal firestorm of the early 1860s—its parent population numbed by single-battle five-digit body count—the American military brought not colonization and conversion to the plains and the southwest (as the Spanish had), but through scorched earth and holocaust, brought the pure economic efficiency of devastation. In the later years of the war, Sherman had learned that it was more efficient to deny an enemy his essential resources than to meet him in bloody battle" (*Ecotropic Works*, 43–44).

Writing the new southwestern histories in the 1990s has involved many reassessments of the significance of the cowboy. The editors of one such study, *Under an Open Sky: Rethinking America's Western Past*, sketch in the meaning of the all-male encampments of the ranches:

> Inside particular communities, gender boundaries helped define regional self-identity. To take just one example, in certain commodity frontiers of the nineteenth-century West—especially those involving minerals, livestock, and lumber—a disproportionate number of immigrants were male. This simple fact bore a host of implications for received notions of gender. Lonely frontier men might so exaggerate their longing for the "feminine ideal" that their actions when meeting a woman became a caricature of nineteenth-century ideologies of domesticity. The few women who lived in such areas—many of whom were nonwhite—found that traditionally unremunerated women's work suddenly had a market and could earn a money wage. Restaurants, boardinghouses, laundries, and brothels all represented an extension of the market into the domestic sphere. All prospered from unbalanced frontier sex ratios. In much the same way, men without women found themselves having to take on roles that would never ordinarily have been theirs, so that male gender identities also had to undergo subtle shifts in frontier circumstances. As with ethnicity and class, the gender boundaries that emerged in such places helped shape new regional selves that were distinct from each other and from their common ancestors. (22)

The cowboy songs that came of sexually segregated life explored some predictable themes: loneliness, longing for the girl left behind, regrets over past sins, and some solace from companions. These songs laid the basis for much of country and western music now, with its Irish violins, lilting waltz rhythms and polkas, and a plaintive lyric over love lost. It was a body of male song, depicting work conditions and the monotony of the trail drives. There is, perhaps, in the yodels and trills, the crooning in falsetto, a desire to supply the missing female by voice, if not by image.

But there is also the theme of deep bonds among the men, sometimes verging on homosexual love, but never quite. The implication is there, latent and rich, as in this "salty dog" song collected by Lomax:

Eph Kate was a cow-punchin' boy:
To throw a steer was his only joy;
He could rope and tie a maverick
In the wink of an eye and make it stick.

Refrain:
Baby, won't you come and be my salty dog?
Eph, baby, come and be my salty dog;
I love you true, indeed I do.
Oh, Eph, babe, won't you come and be my salty dog? (*Cowboy Songs,* 110)

No doubt the deprivations of cowboy life made the rousting and gambling on payday a kind of liberation, a plunge to oblivion. There are numerous songs about the spendthrifts at the end of the drive, wasting their wages on booze and dancing girls. But the songs also trace out the theme of the grasping bar room Lous in the prairie towns, and with it the darker suspicion that all women were sirens and soul snatchers:

Now, I've got no use for the women
A true one may seldom be found.
They use a man for his money;
When it's gone they turn him down.

They're all alike at the bottom;
Selfish and grasping for all,
They'll stay with a man while he's winning,
And laugh in his face at his fall. (301–302)

Putting down the women was not the main theme, for sure; everyone wanted his "gal" in town, but there were enough songs to say that once a cowboy was married and pushing a plow, he longed for his other life. Often he took his leave, as in "Lone Driftin' Riders," which tells of Red Conkin's attempts to settle down:

He married Dolores from old Mexico
And turned to dry-farming, but the durned crops wouldn't grow;

He rode off one mornin' and left Dolores flat,
And said, "I'm a cowboy, I've had enough of that."

There is young Skeeter Bill, he's known far and wide,
He courted poor Sally to make her his bride;
But the call of the trail herds rang sweet in his ears,
So he rode off that spring and left Sally in tears.

. . . .

So girls, all come listen and don't ask me why.
Beware of the cowboys that go driftin' by,
They'll love and caress you, they'll win you somehow,
Then ride off and leave you if you ever cry. (308)

Things get darker still in "The Llano Estacado," when a woman asks a cowboy to ride to far-off Mustang Spring and bring a flask of its water to her. He dies trying to, and the closing stanza shows how hard a woman's heart can be:

That night, at the presidio
Beneath the torchlight's wavy glow,
She danced and never thought of him;
The victim of a woman's whim,
Lying with face upturned and grim
On the Llano Estacado. (315)

In "The Texian Boys," the origins of which go back to the days of the Texas Republic, according to Lomax's note, a familiar warning is delivered to the women to stay away from cowboys. The song was sung on the "beef trail" between Texas and Louisiana, and it opens,

Come all you Louisiana girls and listen to my noise.
If you happen to go West, don't marry those Texian boys;
For if you do, your fortune will be
Cold johnnycake and venison, that's all you'll see—
That's all you will see.

. . . .

Hello, girls, listen to my voice,
Don't you ever marry no good-for-nothing boys,
If you do, your doom will be,

Hoecake, hominy, and sassafras tea—
And sassafras tea. (339–41)

"Sweet Betsy from Pike" tells a love story with a twist at the end, when a dance with a miner makes Betsy's lover-turned-husband jealous enough to divorce her:

Long Ike and sweet Betsy got married of course,
But Ike getting jealous obtained a divorce;
And Betsy, well satisfied, said with a shout,
"Good-by, you big lummax [*sic*], I'm glad you backed out." (391)

These songs and other frontier ballads skimmed the essence of frontier working life. Bret Harte and Mark Twain put into prose parallel versions of these stories of men in isolation from women and society. What happens, as these sketches of Plains working life reveal, is that men are pushed to the limit of their gender and exhibit all the clichés of violence, gun-slinging, boozing, and showing off that feminists have groused about ever since. But these were men who had dropped out of urban society in the South, or come down from bankrupt farms in the Midwest (the Middle Border), or who were the *métis* and assimilated Indians from deracinated tribes, or were fugitives from slavery, or emancipated blacks looking for a niche. The collection of men who became so fiercely bonded in the work of cattle herding formed enclaves in which the male spirit seemed hammered flat on an anvil, driven to an extremity of sexual differentiation.

The same was true of the militias that formed to protect the cattlemen of the border, forerunners of the Texas Rangers. The separation of the sexes caused men and women to polarize their identities, and to establish different cultures for themselves. It was not so much a breakdown of community that we see in late-nineteenth-century Texas, but a process of secreting cultural codes for each gender that eventually split community into different languages and cultures. How different these cultures became is the subject of much research now, with a bead on the question of how women created their own world.

At the same time white women were organizing to support female education and cultural programs, black women were also forming societies to promote much the same thing for themselves. Jacqueline Jones Royster offers a fascinating glimpse into how black women were launching their own lyceums and "societies" in her book, *Traces of a Stream: Literacy and Social Change among African American Women,* beginning with the Young Ladies' Lyceum at Oberlin College in Ohio: "In the early 1850s . . . the Young Ladies' Lyceum (renamed the Aelioian Society in 1861), was organized to rival [the men's organization, the Oberlin Lyceum]. Both groups read various works (as the club titles indicate), wrote essays and poetry, and spent their meetings reading essays and poems aloud, listening to musical performances, discussing the issues of the day, and occasionally even debating the issues of the day" (191).

While the majority of members of the Aelioian Society were white, African American women were invited to join soon after. The topics raised at their discussions included such issues as "that women should enter the medical profession" and "that a slaveholder can be a Christian" (191).

One such study, a dissertation soon to become a book, is Betty Wiesepape's "Literary Societies and Writing Clubs in Texas: 1890–1940: Their Role in the Development of Regional Literature," which looks at literary organizations, most of them dominated by women, that sprang up around the closing of the American frontier and continued well into our own time. She studies four writing clubs in the larger towns where records were preserved, but her broader outlook includes clubs of various kinds that began as early as the 1850s across the protected parts of Texas. Educated and articulate women found themselves at a frontier that was more conservative, orthodox, and repressive than where they had come from. Already, women had developed a tradition of protest that took many forms—from poetry to editorials in local newspapers all across the settled areas of the United States. Protest poetry in particular formed a rich body of work that allowed women to voice their concerns over slavery, abolition, the abuse of Indians, the atrocities of the Civil War, and the like.

To cope with the cultural deprivation they found in Texas, they formed groups with rigorous admissions criteria—a bona fide education and writing talent—in which to share writing and ideas, to organize libraries, arts commissions, and schools, and to encourage younger writers. Men attended some of these groups, but women ran them, established the contests, and launched the careers of numerous poets, some of whom, like Grace Noll Crowell and Fania Kruger, would develop national reputations. But by the late 1930s, when men began to take over the literary establishment, "scholars and literati" alike began to denigrate the "pink tea poets," as

J. Frank Dobie is alleged to have called them. According to Wiesepape, "The stereotypical image generally associated with them is one of middle-aged women dressed in hats and gloves, assembling to drink tea, to read kitchen poetry, to partake of dainty refreshments, and to show off the latest fashions" (4).

A 1999 article in the *Dallas Morning News* quoted Wilma Turner, president of PEO, a national women's organization, saying that "a number of women's organizations began shortly after the Civil War" and that most of these organizations were in fact "study groups." The Association of American University Women was founded in 1881 and grew enormously over the next few decades. This movement and others like it fueled the local reading clubs of Texas. Even those clubs that were described as "all male," Wiesepape notes, "were actually composed of individuals of both genders, and in most clubs, females outnumbered males" ("Literary Societies and Writing Clubs," 6). In 1897 there were 21 clubs registered with the Texas Federation of Women's Clubs; four years later there were 132, and by 1941, there were 1,200 clubs, according to Wiesepape's count. She also notes that 85 percent of all the libraries in Texas were organized by the Federated Women's Clubs of Texas, which "influenced the founding of the Texas Arts and Humanities Commission, urged that art and music be taught in public schools, established art scholarships, and arranged for a traveling art gallery" (15).

Such clubs have a history going back to the Reformation in Europe and were originally underground cells for various heretical cults and dissidents. That side of things may have carried over into the Texas reading clubs, where women doubtless exercised some of their griefs about male society and bent to the work of making a feminist universe for themselves. But their primary role was to encourage women to write, and as I have stated here and in my own essay in *Texas Women Writers,* under a thin veneer of decorous verses is a lively, contentious voice of protest against an era of Indian and animal slaughter, land waste, and racism.

The reading clubs were places where women constructed an identity for themselves, a process the editors of *Under an Open Sky* call pioneer "self-shaping." Poetry was their primary mode of expression, since few outsiders would think to inspect the words or sentiments of poetry, which in nineteenth-century America was one remove from common prayer. Conventional poetry was moralistic and high-minded, but the more spirited and independent-minded poets examined their anger and resentment and enjoyed support and female bonding from the reading club where they shared their work.

Jacqueline Jones Royster pushes her thesis about such organizations a bit further, and in a direction I find very interesting—what she will call "ethos formation" as women band together to become social activists as well as advocates of mutual improvement among black women and some black men eager enough to join women in their common goals. She remarks,

> After the Civil War, cooperative activity escalated. A slate of organizations in both the North and the South included groups of women who participated in the woman suffrage movement, in order to gain the vote for women; in temperance reform, which used an anti-drinking springboard to refocus attention on issues of home and family and on community development; and in the literary clubs and benevolent organizations of various sorts in which the women were already experienced. By the post-Reconstruction era, African American women had accumulated a long, rich experience of community activism. They were leaders, with skills learned from experience and expertise garnered in running different types of community organizations and engaging in different types of social reform. Most consistent, across these networks of clubs, African American women acquired and refined skills as writers and orators that were unique for their day. (*Traces of a Stream*, 210)

In other words, there is a case to be made that women from all racial and ethnic groups were involved in "ethos formation" during a time when frontiers were giving way to early urbanism, and when men were engaged chiefly in eliminating the last Indian resistance to the settlements and fending off rivals to their cattle interests and the spread of grain cultivation over the open plains. While the men fought their battles, women laid down a common consciousness of gender to promote their own interests and many of the values that would later construct the community life of the early twentieth century.

The clubs were a groundswell of female opinion on everything going on in Texas. According to Elizabeth Long, a sociologist doing research on seventy-four reading clubs in Houston, the club phenomenon drew in almost everyone in the community, including ethnic minorities of all races, although the majority of members came from the white middle class. Of the seventy-four clubs Long studied, forty-three were all women, twenty-eight were all men, and the rest were mixed. By 1921, the Texas Poetry Society was formed with the help of Therese Lindsey. A renaissance of poetry flourished briefly in Texas but was derailed by the Depression, when many critics and historians dismissed the women's literary movements around the country as "divisive," marginal, less compelling than workers' issues—hence, ignored ("Literary Societies and Writing Clubs," 48). The clubs were important to women writers from then until the outbreak of World War II, when men claimed the literary movement with an outpouring of fiction and memoirs.

While it may be true to say, with the editors of *Texas Women Writers,* that women writers ignored the primary myths of Texas and shaped "a tradition of their own," as the book's subtitle would have it, the claim is slightly misleading: "Much of what Texas women have written for almost two centuries reflects their insights into those areas of Texas life ignored by the true believers in the Texas Mystique, epitomized by J. Frank Dobie and his admirers. Except in occasional witty satire, the state's women writers have valued individuality over stereotype, and unlike many men authors in the state, women have ignored the prevalent image of the state as a masculine domain, dominated by cowboys, rednecks and rich businessmen" (45).

Women were not so much making their own path as making *the* path for poetry; by the time my generation came of age, there was no other tradition. Men had not seriously shaped or determined the forms or the content of Texas poetry; their art form was the cowboy song and stories of rites of passage for young men. Even so distinguished a poet as William Barney launched himself through the Texas Poetry Society and the local clubs, the female-dominated writing clubs of Fort Worth. And what he wrote, as I shall have occasion to say a little later, follows the general theme of the land as body, the land as the extension of the sensitive self.

And I am not all that sure that women favored individuality over stereotype, a curiously loaded generalization that values any sort of individuality over typing. The land was typed as female, as a flesh daily wounded by exploitation and greed; the land was the raped woman, the victimized woman, the offended woman. To pollute, to dam, to tame, to harvest, to clear-cut were all forms of rapine and pillage, and women were writing against them all. The fact that something personal was attached to mere land—vast as it was—is the principal gain of women's poetry of the first fifty or sixty years of Texas writing. But there is hardly the sophisticated, elaborate sense of self that our *Texas Women Writers* editors want to secure for women's writing. Types were just as valid and necessary—the wounded woman in all her forms, both real and figurative—as were fully individualized portraits.

The elaboration of an esthetic and a vision of the land in Texas fell mainly to the women of the frontier era, who established a systematic, pervasive literary network for shaping consciousness about the state of nature, the price of settlement, and the inequalities of a male regime directing commerce and politics. This sensitivity to male conduct, with all its freight of injustices and peccadilloes, forms not only the literary culture of Texas at its outset but also the unconscious culture of the region, a term I borrow from the Argentine American composer Lalo Schiffrin. Poetry is, after all, only an archipelago in the sea, a partial manifestation of what lies under water, all the mountain ranges and volcanic chains of psychic life that remain obscure or out of the reach of language. What women discussed, how they sifted through their own willingness to obey, to help, to endorse the work of men from what they would not do or encourage, that is a great sea of unrecorded thought which the poetry is unable or unwilling to fully trace. But what poetry may not tell us is that women controlled far more of town life than we might assume.

When you walk down the main street of a small Texas town these days and peer into an antique store window, as I often like to do in my own town of Bryan, you behold something of a stage set, a curious kind of theater that is a view into the lives of Texas families a century ago. And what you discover there is that women had their say almost completely in what one sat on, where one ate, with what plates and flatware one dined, where one took his or her leisure, through what curtains the light came in, and by what lanterns and hurricane lamps one read the Bible or the newspaper. All this filtered through female intelligence and bore the judgments, the tastes of women. Women monitored each other and had subtle, strictly enforced standards by which to keep each other up to date, and in line. The women legislated from the center out, and men abided their authority more than we know.

The antique stores are female museums. You can observe the taste of women for tiger oak rockers, fire screens, hand-painted chandeliers, fainting couches, Indian-head sofas, rag quilts, brass firedogs, bed warmers, embroidered shades, linen tatting, a spidery world of elaborations and intricate needlework, a scrawl of female signatures written over every surface, and insinuated into the most neutral of objects—even a transom window with its stained glass figures of fruit and blossoms. It's all female, with hardly a nod to men's tastes or requirements. The men are represented by shaving mugs, spittoons, a worked saddle, some pistols with scrimshaw handles, a few canes and mustache curlers, maybe a barber's chair and boot trees. That is his little corner of the world. You could put his things into a large box, but you couldn't move a woman's world in a week—she has her universe spread out too far, too deep to be removed easily.

Texas, after my first ten years or so, was revealing an irony that rocked me back on my own heels and made me laugh out loud. Texas, that mythical place of cowboys and oil and cattle barons, was as thin as pond ice—a veneer of symbols and heroic fables. What was clear is that under it, and all around it, is a woman's culture, rooted firmly, and long ago articulated through a grassroots literary movement powered by endless reading clubs, library auxiliaries, church groups, discussion circles, Sanctificationists, sewing bees, socials, charity organizations, welcome wagons, and all the rest.

Texas is a feminine culture, simple as that. And over it, pasted onto it like so many animal cartoons on a crib, are images of men vaunting their prowess and political power. *But why?* Texas women are not the frilly belles of the Deep South. I rather think they are still belles but long purged of their frills and complacency by the trek west and the rigors of frontier life. They came with a sophisticated cultural awareness and set up shop the moment they arrived. They did not wait, or fall silent because Indians raided the outpost settlements. The clubs were going right after the Civil War, we are told; yes, and the clubs were formed by women who had witnessed the defeat of their southern husbands. Now, in Texas, women were not so easily daunted by masculine power. They were far less idealistic or optimistic than some of their poetry would have you believe; they were romantics with a new psychology that linked them to the earth on which men stood. And how a man stood or acted on such female earth mattered greatly, so they wrote it down, they argued it. They insisted on their own premises and ways of being. And because men were busy elsewhere, the poetry accumulated uncontested.

And the men were busy trying to restore lost pride and dignity from the defeat of the Civil War. The victory over Mexico was an important and powerful myth of Anglo male superiority that the Civil War canceled out. If we allow that the cowboy was the product of a southern evacuation of youth, streaming over the Sabine River after the South's collapse, accompanied by free blacks, we might say that the hopes of men rested on youths creating a new mythology of men who, though defeated in war, could break the wild spirit of mustangs, shoot down savages, and claim a wilderness. The women did not participate in this masculine mythology of the Plains; they were establishing their own myths and self-images. Their very clothes were emblazoned with animal figures; their names were drawn from flowers; their kitchen gardens told you they were cultivators of herbs and vegetables. They manifested too many sides of the ecosystem to ignore their claims to the land.

If the cowboy caught on with the wider world, that was how Texas projected a victorious male image to the outside. But within, among the houses and daily affairs of Texas, the state was female. And any poet who might want to participate in the tradition of regional poetry had but one way to proceed—to regard the land as a woman of sensitive feelings and flesh, and to revere the female's continuity with the red-tailed hawk and the coyote.

And that poet would also have to put up with a widespread rejection of his or her art by the average Texan, who had long ago dismissed poetry as marginal, sissified, part of some alien vision having little to do with the hard realities of southwestern life. The bleachers of the Friday night football game are always full; the stands at the rodeos are crammed with spectators; the monster-truck rallies command sell-out crowds, and the demo derbies are always packing them in. These are male rituals and command undying respect and enthusiasm, even patriotic fervor. They are theaters of conquest and victory through which Texas men nurture their self-esteem.

But the fine arts go begging for listeners, and the reading halls are empty these days. Behind the arts lies an indestructible association between a denied gender and its dissident history. To have rejected the attempt of the southern male to reconstruct himself through a new myth of prowess, as many women writers have done, is to have betrayed Texas, and poetry was perceived—at least by some—as a betrayer's art.

Long ago, the red of clay
  And my crumbly, shelving rock—
These I saw, and, far away
  Shaggy bison-hump and hock,

And the velvet backs of deer,
  And the rabbit's tearing pace,

(Bulging eye and streaming ear,)
    And the Indian's stealthy grace.

Yet, though now no horses shy
    At a skull half-hid in grass,
And the sleek black highways lie
    Where the dim trail used to pass,

Cactus, Caliban of plants,
    Still disports with twisted limb;
Butterflies about him dance,
    Making golden sport of him.

Redbuds dress as for a ball,
    When the March winds hush and warm
I upon my crumbling wall
    Lend to June my silver charm.

Spite of all the loud new ways
    Here my spiky leaves grow thick,
And from out their green I raise,
    Holy, white, my candlestick. (Jeannie Pendleton Hall, "Yucca by the
      Road-Side," *New Voices*, 113)

I am the trees of a forest swayed one way only;
I am the trees of a forest lonely, lonely;
I am bent by the dark winds, I sway
To the earth of my roots, I am bent one way;
I am a forest of chevronly trees—
I am bent double, the seven seas
Moan in the monsoon of my tossing;
I am the trees of a forest crossing
My rain-stripped branches in disarray;
I am black with rain, I am hurled one way:
I am rooted and torn, I am bent askew—
Following you, following you. (Margaret Tod Ritter, "Storm Chant," 175)

CHAPTER 6
A PHOTO ALBUM

Over the twenty-five years I have lived in Texas, I've met a lot of Texans, native born, émigré, short-termers, derelicts down at the local Baptist mission, drunks, prisoners, rich folk, and the dirt-poor blacks who eke out
desperate lives in the lowland stretches of the city. I've met the variety, or
almost the whole spectrum, from politicians to paupers and homeless
couples passing a jug in the city park. As a professor I may have taught as
many as five thousand or six thousand young Texans, heard their stories,
their outrageous excuses for missing classes and tests, and consoled them
on the deaths of grandparents and parents, siblings, and lovers. I have had
a good vantage point from which to study the garden of Texas varietals
growing old, being reared, getting married, and parenting their own young.
It follows I should have accumulated some strong memories of the characters I have come across over this span of years, and some of their portraits
are included here.

FRANK SALVATO:
RETIRED SHOE FACTORY FOREMAN, SALVAGE MAN

Frank came into my life very early on, almost the moment I had bought
the old, spacious house on a corner near downtown Bryan, two blocks west
of Main Street. There were many mansions on this street, owned by the better merchants, but only mine had survived urban renewal after World War
II. Ours was built in 1916 by the owner of a dry goods store, who gave himself a splendid wooden barn of a house in which to raise a big family. The
building was fronted by square pillars of beige brick, with a massive archi-
trave spread over them and a sleeping porch beneath. The yard was a good
half acre in size, with a small outbuilding to the north of it serving as an
apartment. It stood on the grounds of a once splendid kitchen garden, of

which there are a few pictures in our file. The railroad track goes by a block beyond, shaking the piers beneath the house and waking sleepers at all hours.

I had some building projects, and the man to see about used lumber and gingerbread trim is Frank Salvato. I found him tearing down a house one winter day in 1976, accompanied by a sway-backed character with a pint of whiskey in his coat pocket. They were stripping nails out of boards and piling them up near a rusty truck. Frank was a tall man with an elegant long nose and a very large face, heavy white brows, a mouth that fell into a cold sneer and brightened easily at the approach of a potential customer. His voice was high-pitched on certain syllables and almost whining in the middle register, and slow, southern, very drawled at the tail end of his sentences. He seemed to sing a little of his speech and then forget the melody.

When I got to know him better, I found out his parents had come over from Sicily at the end of the nineteenth century, lured to the Brazos Valley after the first farmers had pretty well used up the soil for cash crops. A few droughts and some market crashes drove the farmers out, leaving long tracts of river land vacant and waiting for hot-climate peasants to take over. So they came, and the path to America led first to New Orleans, where many got down to stay, including my mother's family; others came to Texas to plant cotton, milo, and sorghum.

Bryan had a large concentration of Sicilian immigrants, and they built several Catholic churches in the area. They put out St. Anthony altars on his feast day. A St. Anthony altar requires a person to give thanks for prayers granted by loading up a few trestle tables with cakes, cookies, puff pastries, and pies and to put a notice in the newspaper that all this fare was free to any comers. The altars were stripped by midmorning. The local convenience stores sold canned olives, grated cheese packs, cans of peeled tomatoes, and boxes of pasta to the surviving links of the old Sicilian quarter. But like all such ethnic differences that come to Texas, these played out and went underground. The tolerance for discrepancy of manner or custom was not deep, and Sicilians, like the Czechs of nearby Caldwell and the small hamlets in the farm country, learned to moderate their habits and keep things in the community.

Frank was a modified Sicilian, with the bearing of an aristocrat. He was a tall man, well built in the chest, with good sturdy legs that he adorned with very fancy boots polished by the old black man at the barber shop. Frank was a romantic with an eye for the women; he took the measure of my wife early and enjoyed his long visits on the porch, and his early morning glass of whiskey from our larder. He chewed gum to cover his breath when he went home for coffee at ten or eleven in the morning.

He hadn't come up in the world very far in his long life, but he made a living as a floor boss at the shoe factory, where soles were cut out of sheets of rubber and sent on to other assembly plants to the east. There were die-cutting machines on the floor and packers at one end, and Frank, tall and stately, and cool tempered, would roam about making sure the women worked at speed without chatting or looking around. The shoe soles came off the loading dock in great quantities, and the grim corrugated iron buildings that sprawled a block or two into a field kept a few hundred families in groceries and utility money, but worked them hard. Their union was weak, and I can recall several times when an ACLU lawyer came along to defend someone with carpal tunnel syndrome or some other disability from the tedious labor.

Frank was a fair man, with an iron will. I think the women who worked there both liked and feared him. He had the bearing of a complete man of the West, with his beautiful boots, his long trousers held up with a fancy leather belt, and his long, soft-featured face and drooping eyes. The voice seemed to ask for one's indulgence; the eyes were Sicilian and shrewd and saw everything at a glance. The mind worked percentages the moment his mouth opened; he was selling something, cutting a deal, and giving you the hindmost of any object he had to share.

Frank was that part of the male psyche that goes into business; he had few close friends, but a wide field of acquaintances, clients, and a shady border leading down into the local underworld. I knew that border briefly when Frank offered to make money available to me at a moment's notice, when I was up against some tall bills of my own. He said he could find the cash, up to ten thousand dollars, in a few hours, and I could pay it back on a flexible plan.

"How much interest?" I inquired offhandedly.

"Not too bad," he said, looking over my shoulder at the pecan tree in my yard. "About 40 percent. Got to pay back when it's needed, of course."

"You mean, like the whole thing?" I asked.

"Could be," he said. "Business is business."

I knew then that the money was from a source in Houston, and the links of that cash were to the casinos in Nevada or the money launderers in Miami, or maybe the sharks in Brooklyn. It was real mafia money, and Frank, wily old coyote that he was, managed to deal and not get crushed by this ominous force in town. But his money mainly came from investing in coffee joints in town, a club where the girls were not always waitresses, and the little niche he had found tearing down old garages, stores, and rotting houses. The lumber was piled up in his own place at the western edge of town where the road goes off to Austin. He had mountains of lumber there and pieces of old roof, lots of trim, iron work, bricks, cinder block. The house he was perpetually building was rough and unjoined at windows and doors and almost buried under the loot he carted off from his salvage jobs. His wife was a beaten woman with a broken, haranguing voice. It was unpleasant to go there looking for him when I needed wood.

Frank would emerge from his junkyard estate dressed in a blazing white shirt, dark trousers, a white Stetson perched on his handsome white head, with his boots brilliant as a night sky. He was an imposing man, and the whole town knew him. If he were walking, the toots from passing cars made a staccato rhythm, and Frank, loping with that curious sideways shift of men in boots, would keep his fingers partly flexed in a salute to all the tooters. He didn't always look up, unless he recognized the horn or the car. Some people were more important than others.

Since I dealt with him often, I was among the ones who got him to pull on his hat brim when he saw me. We would chat a while on the sidewalk, or he would give me a lift in his truck to the work site. We would sit about while he pulled nails or spoke in his soft, high notes to the man in an old tweed coat, whom he called "the wino." The wino, since I never knew his actual name, was a smart old critter in his own right, and he worked hard under Frank. He was a thin specter of a man eaten up from many decades of bad booze and sleep on park benches, or in the alleys. His teeth were gone, and his chin was full of turkey wattles and moles. But he was articulate and funny, and liked to break off a chat when the three of us were together.

The wind would howl out of the north, the sky would darken to slate, and there we would all stand with our pants legs beating in the wind, talking about the new governor, or the highway construction linking us to Houston. The time spent jawing was not discounted from the wino's wages, I was told. It was all part of the slow pace of work and the languorous rhythms of life in Bryan. The wino would return to his claw hammering and sorting of planks, while I eyed the lumber piled up so far. Frank would be watching me and estimating what I could be taken for in the next deal. There were a lot of pauses in our talk while I picked up a piece of shiplap and ran my finger down the cracks in it. Frank would say it was solid, and I would cluck my tongue and throw the board down.

I could sense the moment when a deal should be cut. I would look at my watch and begin to make excuses for leaving. I had business in town, or my wife needed to go shopping. This tensed up Frank's cheeks a little, and he would pick up the discarded board, turn it over, admit the cracks were serious but that the board had value still. I agreed, reluctantly, and would make my way to the curb, but slowly. Frank would come along behind with the board and ask what it was worth. I would hum a little tune to myself and hear a price, about twice what I wanted to pay. It would be shaved in a moment, and I would shave it further. When it got down to a dollar a piece, for fifty boards, delivered to my driveway, hands shot out of our pockets and we gave each other an appreciative small grin. I was off by twenty cents, maybe thirty; Frank always won.

This ritual occurred often, as I built porches and a little deck on the apartment house, added a wing to another building I had bought from Frank and put in the backyard. The precise manner of our bargaining always withheld the greed, the high stakes of the game. We chatted all the while, and money, while it was at the heart of our meeting, came up in spasms at the very end. This is how business is done in Texas, whatever the commodity. Oil, cattle herds, real estate, office towers, old boards are sold by men who divide the transaction between mannerly discourse on other subjects, a price here and there sprinkled into the pauses, and a shrewd game of logic and bluff in which the one always wins, the other loses contentedly.

Frank knew all the ruses of the Texas businessman. He was a product of their world, and he had the loner's grace, steel, and courage to cut through friendship and find the greed point, the root of desire, and tease it with whispered prices, inducements, the very devil himself hung from his tongue. He knew that in this hard land one wanted something and if the means were in his pocket, there was a way to sell it. He would not fail if he could play the game of desire, withholding, and finally gratification. It was an art, like teasing a rattlesnake into a bag or getting some wayward, skittery steer to come along to the herd. The businessman in Texas had to have a keen animal sense, to know how the primitive heart really works. And in

Frank's expertise with a board, he could play me for all my vanities, my weaknesses; he exposed the flaws of my character, got me to show my whole soul on my face, and made me thankful after I had been exposed.

How much Frank was worth was anyone's guess. He wore good threads, nice hand-made boots, always a fine thirty-X Stetson, had his big mug shaved at the best barbershop, and his hair trimmed by the guy who clipped all the ranchers' hair. So he was doing fine, and he ate out at his joints a lot, had female company in the off hours. He knew money, and the darker powers of the community, and somehow jumped before he got struck. Some didn't know how agile he was, or wily. But the wino did, and I certainly was an adept student. If he had been born in Mexico, or taken there early on, he might have come up in the Sonora desert as a *brujo*. There was magic in him, and some primordial instinct honed by five thousand years of market sense in Sicily that inspired him. He had a witch doctor's grasp of psychology, and no one, high or low, was beyond his perceptive ranges.

As an outcast, for his immigrant credentials and religion put him on the margins of Bryan society, he did well. If there is poetry in business, Frank was a minor craftsman of the art. He knew the language, the metaphors, the forms, and he had the slippery ease of the practitioner, the friendly charm, the openness that had rooms behind it, and dark places hidden from anyone. His wife hardly knew what went on in the greater world that he strolled through. Few if any of his circle could say where his money and interests all lay. They knew parts of Frank the way I did. The whole Frank belonged to one man, under his Stetson and inside his boots. And it was the peculiar strength of this male psyche that he kept his own affairs apart from himself as well. There were secrets about Frank that even Frank didn't know.

When I had an old porch to replace a few years ago, I went over to my neighbor, a carpenter, to ask where I might find some used lumber. I was out of touch; I had been in Europe a good while and was back again, looking for a bargain. He came out to the front yard and rubbed his forehead a while. He was at a loss. The modern profession of carpentry required new materials; the used market was a thing of the past.

"The old guy who used to sell is dead," he said. "His widow might have some stuff left if you want to ask about it. I forget his name, though."

"Frank, Frank Salvato?" I asked.

"Yeah, that's it. Died about four months ago."

I was saddened by this fact. A little part of the spirit of the town has departed. It left me feeling a bit more of a stranger after all these years. Frank was a dusty window into the world of higher business. He was a portal of sorts and showed me the skills and the craft of selling at the humbler layers. He gave me a sense of what is required to be rich in Texas, the immense intellect and skill and luck that goes together into a miraculous equation for some men, and the cold, bloodless strategy that is sometimes needed to pull off the really big deals, the epic whirlwinds that occur in those Houston towers and quiet little suites in Dallas. I would never know this world intimately or directly, but its modest representative at the other end of the market, selling splintered boards from old Victorian hulks, gave me a glimpse into its mysteries.

MARY FERGUSON: HOUSEWIFE, WIDOW, AND POET

Somebody told Mary Ferguson to look me up. My reputation as a poet, editor, publisher, and sometime private coach to poets had spread beyond the four or five people who had bought my services. I was now being passed among an outer belt of writers after having taught in Texas for some ten or twelve years. So she called me up one day and spoke for half an hour about her interests in poetry, her desire to put a book of poems together, and to publish it. Would I help?

I listened to the list of her accomplishments, and the poets under whom she had studied at one time or another: Cynthia Macdonald, Richard Eberhard, James Dickey, Vassar Miller, and now me. It was a good group, partly northern, mainly southern. She had grown up in the little town of Brenham and now lived in Temple. Between times, she had known a man named Slim, who was the love of her life, a big tall Texas man whom she idolized and wrote love poems to in the years following his death. When I saw a sheaf of her poems, some were unfocused or frameless, or underwritten, others were mushy, sentimental pieces, but a few hard nuggets caught the voice of a Texas woman with uncanny grace and precision. She had the gist of the story of the prairie female down, and I took her on.

A poem about her father, "For a Boy Named Will," made me think I was on the right track in my early notebooks about the raising of Texas girls. It is a beautifully understated summary of a girl's perceptions of her father:

It was not much of a birthright:
the blood-sucker land
that grew wild plum and typhoid
as certain as the spring floods
that paralyzed the Delta.
He buried mother, father
and his young wife, Claudia,
in that Mississippi give and take
before he climbed the hills
to find my Texas mother.
In his brown eyes, the fires
of the Old South sparkled; in his voice,
the river's low and lazy laugh:
a legacy as enchanting as his own
"hocus-pocus in my pocket," ⸺
and a glory to his girls. (*When We Speak of Mysteries*, 5)

The language is under strict restraint; the storytelling is just under the surface. The details all point to struggle and male passage, and the ultimate, though qualified, success of a man coming into his own. The words "legacy" and "glory" play a strategic role in the poem's theme. This is the anthem of many women in Texas, honoring the myth of their fathers and lacing the story of the myth's enactment in the terms of death, harrowing, and near-failure.

"Brenham is a small town," she writes in one poem, "Humpty Dumpty," full of "organdy girls / and boys in white linen." And in another poem about girlhood, "I Was Seven," she writes of the night the Ku Klux Klan came to the black church to give a donation, after which she hears the preacher "praising God / and the K.K.K." The little book she rewrote under my wary eye, *When We Speak of Mysteries*, is a set of cameos catching the Texas girl and woman in profile; they are not deep takes on the psychic travel of such females, but the freeze frames capture all the emotion of certain crucial turns in her life.

There is one in the collection, her first and only book so far as I know, called "Masterpiece," which comes close to idolatry, a shameless candor and delight in her love for Slim:

When I walked into the Accademia
and saw David

it was breathless déjà vu:
A bridge, I sat ecstatic
on the side of the bathtub
watching my husband
shave. (20)

Corny, unless you know the brambles and sagebrush gaps between the sexes in the Sun Belt, and the shivers that run through the base of the spine for love to occur, for a woman to unravel her privacy long enough to speak this way.

The armadillo is not the only creature of the desert wrapped in Reichian armor to keep its juices from vaporizing in the heat. The female is one who, though passionate and honest, will not likely show her weaknesses to a lover. She will prefer to pal around, to joke, to have some hard words now and then for his failings, to conceal the sentiments that spring up in the spare, terse language of this little lyric. There are others, several more in fact, that betray the heart in this book.

When I met her face to face for the first time, Mary Louise Ferguson presented herself with a few self-effacing remarks and some off-putting praise for me. That's a good sign; it meant "Be honest with me, or I'll keep lying to you all day." I came down flat and observed her mouth for a while. Her teeth were turned around a bit, putting out her lower lip, as if she were on the verge of tears. But the upper lip was humorous, and her eyes, loose and tired (I took her to be about sixty-five or so), had laser sharpness in them. She was another keen assessor of the human organism, and she was counting up my flaws. She liked what she saw, which made her smile appreciatively. I was grateful to have passed her test. And she was a very sharp weigher of men; she had known some powerhouses, including her husband, whose image she carried within her the way a priest is never without his chalice.

Her voice had a lazy, sidling quality about it; she was in no hurry to finish sentences but let them disappear into a new paragraph much on the same subject, but with the attention shifted. You had to pay close attention; she was bright and informed, and knew far more than she let on. This is always the female way in conversation with men, a coyness masking a close scrutiny. In my case, though a near stranger, she was testing me for a long time, then gave in a little, softened the edge of her voice, spoke more toward her teeth, and I felt intimacy suddenly. She was speaking directly now, no tricks.

Let us see: soft skin, a slight sagging of the cheeks, some crepiness of neck, a few creases under her eyes, the nose straight and slender, rather dignified. A ring or two, some flash on her hands, a wristwatch, if I recall right. And a fairly sturdy short body, a height of about five feet, five inches or so. Another generation, fed on starch and fruit, and one or two nights of meat. The mouth bore that curious double standard of tears and laughter, and her emotions bore the same intricate web as well. She was keeping back sorrow, though it dimmed her eyes once to talk about Slim. He was irreplaceable, but mind, there was a man in her life who loved her well, and fully. She appreciated it, but the mark of her soul was made by the first man, and nothing would mark it like that again.

She seemed pared down to me, not one for chatter or frilly images. She complained about other poets overwriting, falsely adorning their poems with clichés and silliness. Okay. I understood that. She had got beyond the amateurish gush. She had learned from other poets to get down to the gist and shut up. She hated filler; she complained that some of her poems went on past the point. My job was to figure out how to compress the poems and leave a thin skin around the ideas, or the key images. When I showed her I could do that, she warmed to our collaboration. A second kind of trust emerged.

If you enter a woman's imagination this way, something like a doctor-patient relation develops. It can be encumbering, and sometimes ends in unwanted or unprovoked passion in younger women. It can happen between men. It is a dangerous business to assist someone in the articulation of their secrets. You become party to inner events and a sort of healer in the process. You find the banter and reject it; it is like a command for depth, truth. The soul of your apprentice responds with relief; someone, some stranger, cares what I say and wants it plain. The process can suddenly swing both parties over an abyss, clutching at one another.

I was grateful Mary had been over the depths before and would not flinch. She did not reach out; she thanked me cordially, but her words were genuine. I was given some rare glimpses into her emotional life, and she was not embarrassed. It comforted her. She was a serious writer, and learning the craft made her bold; she had already made her writing self into a third person, which meant you could criticize and it would not sting the other Mary. That was important; most writers cannot separate the poem from the poet, and they can't grow if they become stumped writing it. We had some clear space between the woman who lived and the poet who remembered. The memories got better, and we whittled and sawed and pruned, polled? Some of the poems began to ring with a certain density. They were right.

So on we went, like two hikers with a flashlight exploring a dark trail together. It was curious how Mary sometimes spoke of her other self as if it were a daughter, a neighbor. Of course she knew this was a version of herself, and she would fill in sometimes with what the poem could not say— and I would get her to put a few more words into the poem, to tie up loose ends. Then she would laugh at how I managed to get her to go back into the Mary in the poem—to relive a little. Sometimes the poem was sealed for her, an odorless enclosure where the other Mary had said once something that could not be revised. It was there, buried in the wood, like a nail in a tree.

The book was formed out of moments of self-appraisal, when she grasped herself. We made these moments the core of the poetry, and surrounded them with lesser epiphanies—about growing older, about love becoming a kind of habit, a comforting old shoe of emotion. I meant for the book to be a winding path that led inward to a point where life became clarified in a few short statements. Then you would go out again into mere woods, mere dirt and undergrowth again—as in real life. I pulled a line from one of her poems and told her that was the title, *When We Speak of Mysteries.* She gave me a look, as if to say, "But what does it mean?" I thought it hinted of the lowered voice, the unexpected intimacy and strangeness of when one does mention a mystery—the self? The heart? But there was a pun embedded in the words as well; mystery is from a Greek root, *myein,* meaning "to keep silent." To speak violated a certain secret or trust with oneself. That was the thrust of her poems—letting one in on the vital secrets of a woman, but only so far. Delicately. I could not tell her that—but I knew that a Texas woman kept her feelings to herself, unless driven to explain or share. She was used to being private and would more often tease or distract than be confronted with how she really felt.

Her book was close to that sense of actual womanly emotion—of having to pry into memory to find certain emotions carefully hidden away. Her poems were of the "silent voice" kind, thoughts to herself never spoken to Slim. She felt them, but did she ever say them *to him?* Doubtful. She was writing unconsciously in the tradition of other Texas women, who wrote for each other but not for men. Not directly for men. The gap between the genders was too great to expect that one's emotional outpourings would be received well. So these poems, like so many other love poems written by women, were internalized voices—still secret though now put down on paper.

We put them together as a core of revelations surrounded by lesser lyrics about childhood, about her daily life, a few trips abroad, with two men who made up "the soul's society" in her life. They were not perfect beings; she reserved judgments on both of them, but with the other departed, she allowed him to grow in her imagination and become something else—an idealized version of her father, perhaps. He represented a version of the mythical Texan, a masculine power she could now adore without qualification, which she couldn't do while he was alive. She was nurse to these hard leathery egos, and a supportive actress to their high mythological theater. She willingly suppressed a part of her own independence to be there, as in "The Good Sport":

Watching the door
of the Pro Shop
for you to come out
grinning
waving your winnings
I wondered how many
hours days years
I have waited
bearing three babies
swearing to leave
listening
for the drone of a plane
a car in the driveway
a boat at the dock
a horse in the stable
bringing the hunter
grumpy and gruff
to be fed
and bedded
and pled with
to come home early tonight
all because you were the only one

you bastard
who could turn me on (19)

This is not every woman's desire, or idea of a life; but it puts into perspective the conditions of Texas marriage for a lot of them. And it insinuates a hidden control, a will that operates in liminal ways to hold on to a mate. She implies, covertly, that it is she who controls the marriage, and the male, slightly buffoonish, awkward, childish, is coming back to a relation in which the wife is parent.

She might have something in this, for part of the mystique of the married woman is that she must contend with the boy in her heroic husband. He keeps part of his youth because the male myth focuses its interest on the young man at the edge of adult life, not the older man looking back. Inside every Texas he-man is the boy first, manifested in a thousand ways, but mainly in his cowboy gear, the symbols of eternal youth. And this poem, like a few others, implies that in marriage a young woman suddenly must age herself into motherhood as part of the maintenance of the occasionally foolish ego she lives with.

Son and father both vie a little for ultimate allegiance from the wife. I saw a little of that in Mary's own son, who struck me as unfinished, a figure without strong outline in the face or the will. He may have suffered the power of his father too long, and now drifted a little. He was intelligent, but reluctant. He showed himself a little passive when we met; he had a novel about crime in high places. Apparently he knew a lot about the art market and antiques and poured his thriller plot into the character of an art dealer and some sort of spy antagonist. It was movie stuff, but it was leaden prose. I was given the task of cleaning it up.

I did not do a great job, and I was at a loss as to how to enter into this more treacherous relation. The son repulsed me, gave me a line not to cross. I did what I could with the text, which brought it up to a point where the flimsiness of the plot was more naked. Good prose always reveals the shakiness of the structure in novels. I gave it back and pocketed my two hundred dollars. Mary was pleased I had tried, but there was the maternal dimension showing to a glare. The son often loses out to a strong mother, and this one was tough by half. She loved her boy, now thirty-five or so, but he was not going to come up to the heroic status of Slim. That was a murky part of her life, and she didn't write about. She suffered it.

JOE WILLIAMS: LABORER, HERMIT, NATURALIST

Imagine a smallish man, red-haired, someone headed in the general direction of Harpo Marx, from an old family in central Texas. There were three brothers, the oldest a lanky, handsome man with a voice so flat it quacked when he spoke. They were working-class boys, but all three had gone to college. Joe came out and began a slow drift into the marginal world of single, unemployed men. He hung around the family house, and no one pushed him out again. So he stayed on. He had some troubled relations with girls and lost interest.

For a time, he went around sitting quietly in friends' living rooms without too much to say. He went off to fish by himself and would spend a weekend out on the Navasota River banks, sleeping rough, fishing, whittling poles, and trapping small animals with little homemade traps. He did a lot of thinking out there, alone in the tall cane brakes, with the highway nearby rumbling with cars headed down to Houston. The little muskrats and moles scampered near his campsite; he tracked the prints of a big raccoon, and what appeared to be wild pig tracks. The chicken hawks and ringtails perched on the limbs of a few cottonwoods hanging over the river.

I had a print shop with a rickety potbelly stove roaring with crate wood and sticks. It barely kept the room warm. My breath smoked as I set type for a few book projects I had going. I had started Cedarshouse Press in 1977, and occasionally I would go out to the studio, as I called it, and work on one or two of the books I had promised. I would hear a knock on the door and Joe would come in with grass seed in his hair, a rumpled jacket, worn-out blue jeans, and work shoes. He would scout out a place to sit and curl up. A few words would pass between us, but with Joe it was not necessary to keep up any persiflage. He preferred to think and study the flames through the stove lid.

In time, I would hear a little phrase or two from him, or he would unfold a piece of paper on which he had written a poem. He would read this to me in a quavering soft voice. It wouldn't be much, a little connection between a hawk's flight and the turn in the river, or stars in the night forming a rose or some other emblem. It was hermit thinking, and he wrote it down in a dry manner, no images or flash, just the bare thought. He had a mind of winter, all spare blackened branches, one or two birds in them.

I didn't know it then, but he was one of those boys who didn't flower properly, and the myth rejected him. He hadn't come up to the rites. A short, slightly built man with odd ways, he was fated to tumble into space. No one seemed to care; he had a few male friends who found him eccentric and harmless and looked after him a little. But he sought out the ones whom he thought might like his monkish lyrics. I was one, and told him so. I thought he was a tattered version of Thoreau, and he made me feel a little like Emerson receiving him in his rustic clothes, with the smell of the autumn woods on him.

Sometimes he would tilt his head a bit and mouth some curious little adage he had made up. "Nothing lives until it kills." Or "A bird is a lizard with curiosity." Sometimes the words didn't quite phrase, and he would laugh to himself and rewrite in silence. He smoked unfiltered Camel cigarettes and put the ashes in his cuff. He would study my movements and wear that entranced expression of his on his homely mouth, his eyes, blue under the thatch of red hair, sleepy and frozen at times. He seemed to go completely blank as if a peculiar empty spate of blood had coursed over his brain. It pleased him to go void at times, and he would come out of it with a shudder. Sometimes he would stand up out of a long silence, pat his pockets for his cigarettes, and bolt from the room. I might not see him again for a month.

He was a study in negatives, oppositions. He had nothing in common with his big brother, who had the tough, lean flesh of a ranch kid. He was lucky with girls where Joe was hapless. He had a surly mouth and said funny things out of it; he wasn't bright or deep, just wry and observant of the things around him. You could see that beer, sex, and smoking cigarettes had all become the core essentials of his manhood. But Joe had no interest in the mythology; he had wandered back into the natural world again, curious to know where the life force came from. And he seemed to find the answer in the private lives of crickets, geckos, grackles, and starlings. He knew their nests and burrows, and would tease out some little varmint with the end of a pointed stick. Or feed some little hairy creature bits of pecan meal and tempt it out of its hole.

This kind of life is hardly possible any more; the land used to be full of such vagabonds traveling with a kit bag and a bedroll, but that was thirty years ago. Joe was one of a kind, a river hermit, who came and went from town almost at will. He would stop in at his family house and eat, shave, and shower, and then go off fresh and clean into the woods again. Or come over to my house.

Later years told on his isolation, though. He began to weaken, and to go deeper into his various trance states. We all noticed it and talked about it. His speech became muddled. There were chemical changes going on inside him that might be dangerous. I hardly knew him and rarely saw him, so I could only speculate about it. But once, in midsummer, on a scorching hot weekend Joe seemed to have had a final scrape with the female world. Someone let him down hard, and he went off into the woods and threw himself onto a mound of leaves. It covered a fire ant mound. He had slashed his wrists and fallen into a deep hemorrhaging sleep. The fire ants stung him all over his body, trying to kill him, I suppose. Someone found him in the evening and dragged him off the mound to a hospital. He had a few hours of life still in him, but he recovered. They had poured a bottle of antitoxin into him and given him a pint or two of new blood.

He roused, and he found himself incarcerated in the local mental ward. Joe had passed from ordinary isolation into a mind tunnel. It seemed to re-arrange him physically; his arms and legs were very loose, like a mauled doll's. He had a funny, dissociated laugh that fell like water out of his mouth. His eyes were no longer disciplined; they seemed to sweep around like a drunken lighthouse beam. But his mercurial, pixieish nature had grown richer. He was a ruby now, deep and translucent with oddity, and I found him a walking, breathing haiku poem on some imponderable relation in nature. He had become a mystic, and would pluck the threads of his blue jeans by the hour chuckling over a joke in his head.

Finally, he was around no more. Someone took care of him at last, fearful he might just burrow in with the muskrats and gnomes. Rumors come back now and then that he is in Galveston, or El Paso, or working on a ranch upstate. But the truth is more bland; he is wandering in his private universe, and I suspect his feet know all about linoleum and public mental wards.

He is a gingerbread man someone molded in the wrong tin. They had made a poet and a dreamer, instead of the usual lanky hero type. He ran away with his raisin buttons and his big sugar smile and the world around him scratched its head. He didn't fit in; he was the most outcast man I had ever known. He seemed to have fallen more off the earth than did the beggars and gypsies; he was hanging by some old cypress root at the end of the world, picking his nose, laughing quietly to himself.

CHARLES GRIESSER: ELECTRICIAN, STORYTELLER

It has always been my principle to spend as little as possible on repairs to houses. If I cannot do something myself, I'll get a friend to help me. If that fails, I go to the phone book and look for the smallest ad, preferably a line in the white pages. I want an honest man, and it is my experience that anyone with a skill to ply corrupts himself by the time he is thirty. After that, price gouging, parts switching, excessive labor charges are the rule. A man who has worked his whole life in the construction trades has no conscience; if he does, he is one in a thousand.

Charles Griesser was one in a million. He was an honest man, a very good one. Not generous, not foolish, not emotional; just good. And I called him one fine morning in the spring of the year to ask if he would look at my wiring problems and give me an estimate. The house I had bought was condemned the moment I signed the deed papers. That was the deal with City Hall. They would not put up the red tags condemning the dwelling because of electrical problems until the bank dumped the property on some greenhorn like myself. By the time I had driven from the lawyer's office to the house with my new door key, the red tags were fluttering like the flags over a car lot.

The old wire was jute and pillar, a 1920s version of electricity. The jute was eaten away by rats, and the pillars, little porcelain knobs, were slanting this way and that across the attic and down the walls. They were a mess. Someone had stuck pennies into the fuse box and burned a big hole in the wood. I had not studied these things when I bought the house; I was thinking of the spacious rooms, the high ceilings with coffered beams, the sleeping porch and brick pillars. I was dreaming when I should have been adding up my costs.

So Charles Griesser moseyed over in his black 1948 Ford pickup and got down onto the sidewalk with the steadiness of a drunk sailor. He staggered and held up a palsied arm to his forehead to get the light off his cataracts. He found the house all right, and then me studying him with alarm. We shook hands, and the palsied limb began to shake and fan the air. He grabbed it with his good arm and steadied it. We went into the house and I gave him a guided tour of attic space, service wall, and all the lighting fixtures, outlet boxes, and so on. He wrote down a few notes, and the scrawl he made came from his trembling hand. It looked like a seismograph report on the 1985 Mexico City earthquake.

He said little; he mumbled a little and sucked on the loose denture plate in his upper jaw. He was stoop-shouldered and his legs, while still good, were slow to find the earth. He had balance problems along with incipient arthritis (he wore a copper bracelet on his left arm), and various other ailments that an eighty-year-old would find conventional.

I gave up all thought of hiring him; he was physically incapable of mounting a ladder or threading wires through tiny little junction boxes. I was amused at his willingness to study the matter, however incongruous the situation. We went out to the front yard again, and he studied the house with his shielded eyes. He just looked up and down with a look of astonishment at all that wood and brick before him.

"Well," I asked dubiously, "do you think you can do this work?"

"Do it?" he croaked. "I did it the first time, son."

"The first time? When was that?"

"Back in 1928," he said matter-of-factly. "Guess I can do it again. I know where all the mice are hiding."

He showed up a few days later with boxes of wire, outlets, plugs, screw caps, ladders, a tool apron, soldering gun, a permit for rewiring the house. He was very professional; he had his notes and he began to draw out wire and snip it, telling me which circuit it was for. It was all very fast work; he took his wages by the hour, and when needed, he would bring in an assistant. I volunteered, and he accepted. So for three weeks of hard, intricate labor, we rewired a three-story house of forty-six hundred square feet, all the rooms, halls, crannies, kitchen pantries from top to bottom. It was done, and they were tasks no ordinary human being could possibly manage on his own. But he did—with coat hangers, a few words of encouragement, and a miracle or two.

And all the while he told me the history of Bryan, in a slow, denture-rattling speech with a lot of country twang in it. He was not bumptious or raw; he was very sharp-witted, and clear. And if he had not been forced to work as a young man, he would have gone to the college, he said, and become an electrical engineer. But it was his religious heritage never to complain, and to accept his lot with joy and forbearing, which he did. He had lived in the town for almost seventy years and knew every water hole, fishing spot, hunting thicket there was, from Sulphur Springs to the "Navasot bottoms," as he called them.

He got his rum arm from being electrocuted at the country club one rainy day, when the juice was hot in the wrong circuit. He jumped like St. Vitus, he said, and burned out the nerves in his upper arm. He did it twice, in fact, a second time about two years later, and permanently ruined his co-ordination. But he could still pick up a little screwdriver and guide the ground screw into a junction box directly over his head, while eight rungs up a wooden, wavering ladder. He was a master craftsman.

"Well, sir," is how he started each morning of stories, with his big hand hung down to receive the next wire plug or box as needed. I would be at the foot of the ladder with all the supplies at the ready. "Well, sir," came as happy words to me. It meant another foray into the 1930s with scenes out of the old rail depot, where the bums came in on the boxcars and jumped down by the score to make for the porches marked by other hoboes before them. He remembered everything of interest, and he told each story in the rhythm of his work, squeezing a word when he pulled the wires tight with his needle-nosed pliers, or gasping in long strokes as we fed wire into the ceiling.

"Well, sir," he said one afternoon after lunch, as the work resumed. "There was an old colored man worked at the water tower over by the tracks. You know, the old one they just tore down."

I knew the one.

"Anyhow, this old colored man was pretty good with his tools, and he kept the job longer than most. Folks got used to havin' him round, you might say. Well, summer come and it was a dry one, it was hot as a beetle's back in a smokehouse. No one went out much, least ways not in the afternoons. Got up past a hundred each day for thirty days or better." He gave a lunge at the chandelier, hauling it up by the chain to attach to the post he had just screwed in. We were working in the dining room at the time.

"And?" I said by way of continuation.

"And I mean to say, there was no more water in the ground. Came time to start using the water tank, which we did. I was asked to go around and get the valve open 'cause the old man wasn't to be found. He'd gone off, we guessed. So I cranked the thing open and got the water into the pipe and we lived off that for most of August, maybe September, I can't rightly say. But it was a long toot on the water tank. Don't happen often, but seems those summers forty years ago were hotter. I did actually wonder what became of the old colored man, but you got the trains comin' by every three hours or so, and for a poor man it's hard not to grab on and go north for a little rest. Pass me that solder gun, will ya?"

"This town ain't mean spirited. But it has its ways. And some of those ways means a colored man don't mix with the white folks. Know what I mean? We got real color lines in this town, and used to be a lot harder than it is now. People have gotten a little softer in their attitudes, but back then, it was not a good idea for a colored to be found in the white neighborhoods after a certain hour. If the police didn't pick 'em up, the vigilantes would. It was a town that liked the color of its own skin, you might say. And didn't want to mix anyone with anything. The coloreds went to their own school, and had their own churches. I'm not what you call a racist, but I didn't go lookin' to break the rules, either. I need my solder roll, thanks.

"Spanish folks are a little like that, but not as much as the coloreds. They stayed put. I don't like the look of it much, it isn't my idea of a Christian life to take after anybody for the color of their hide. But there was a lot of nigger hate, and I didn't go up against it much. I was on too many boards to make a fuss. I just went my own way, and treated coloreds as well as I knew how. It got ugly from time to time.

"That particular summer was an ugly time. When it's hot, people get sore easy. And I recall some fires in the colored part of town. There was a lot of accusations in the paper, and someone had a photograph of a man in a white cape leaving a fire in his big old sedan. I knew who it was. But I kept to my own business. It was a hot, long summer and there was always trouble somewhere in town.

"When we finally had some rain, it was late September, and I got some boys to go to the tower with me to shut off the pipes. The tower looked pretty rusty by now, so I asked the mayor for some money to clean it up and paint it. We got up to the top one day and I pried off the lid to go into it after we had drained the tank, and there, floating on the bottom, was the skeleton of that old black man! He had fallen in. We had been drinking his tea all summer!"

So much for prejudice, I suppose. Perhaps it mollified the old rubes to have integrated their diet if not their lives. I was happy for the old man; he had got his revenge.

We talked about the old dynasties in town, the lawyers and judges and the upper crust, whom he knew only as a tradesman changing out ceiling fans and putting in circuits. But he was a clever soul, and he didn't miss any details. He saw the spoils of the professions all over these mansions and preferred his own honest life as a humble fixit man. And he fixed everything. His work shed was a museum of old motors and ancient revolving fans; he tinkered, and had an excellent engineering mind. He seemed to intuit the ills of machinery, and with a deft turn of a brush or a little jiggering of the switches, he had some old relic of the deep past whirling back to menial life again.

His wife was from West Texas, the treeless plains directly under the universe. She had come east to marry Charles and said her elbows hurt banging into so many trees around here. Like a lot of other west Texans, she felt that trees were eyesores, and green grass was a nuisance. But she had lived here for sixty-five years and had gotten used to the organic world sprouting up each spring. She was a solid Christian lady and a sinner in her imagination. She loved an off-color joke or a sip of wine, but always on the sly and accompanied by heavy winks. "So you bought a Cadillac," she said to me after we had showed up in a brown Sedan de Ville we had bought at the used-car lot. "Know what we call them back home? The 'kind-we-like!'" she said with peals of laughter.

Charles was the moralist, intelligent and fair-minded in most things; he believed ardently in the Baptist vision of a suffering life without luxuries, amenities, only the narrow path and a hand for your weaker brethren.

The big yellow house where they had lived all their adult lives was in a Hispanic neighborhood slowly going to seed. Migrant workers were moving in, and the old families were selling off and going into nursing homes. Charles and Ellie-Mae hung on, living in their high-ceilinged musty rooms, with the old cactus table and rattan rockers, yarn rugs on the floor, and dark framed etchings of the Texas landscape hanging on wires from the wooden wall. The rooms smelled of gas stoves, and food left out. They were old people now, and a bit forgetful. But the jars of preserves and pickled vegetables were still put up on the old shelving, and there was evidence everywhere of the simplicity of an honest life. I loved them both.

Once, in a moment of warm friendship among the four of us, he invited us to church the next Sunday. I declined with a few fumbled words, and the matter was dropped. I learned later that this is the final reserve of a Texan: the invitation to his church takes down the last boundary to real friendship. We were being asked to join the larger family of the First Baptist Church of Bryan, where Charles and Ellie-Mae were congregants of fifty years or more. To be asked in by an elder was as good as a passport, an introduction to the mayor and chief of police, a guarantee of fair treatment by your brethren.

I didn't know.

PAUL FOREMAN: POET AND PROSPECTOR

I had heard about Paul Foreman the moment I arrived in Texas. He was living in Los Angeles at the time, and was cofounder, with Jim Cody, of TAWTE (Texas Artists Writers and Thinkers in Exile), a group of Texans who kept up with each other while living outside the Republic. *TAWTE*, the magazine they published, bore the following statement to potential contributors: "Submissions are welcome from any writer, artist, or thinker, who lives in Texas, grew up here, or has sojourned here long enough to have had their hearts captured by a little hunk of the lone star state." Such writers also contributed to Foreman's journal, *Hyperion*, and eventually showed up in books he published under the Thorp Springs imprint, named after the town on the upper Brazos where he grew up.

Paul Foreman was bright and curious as a boy, and did not quite buy the masculine mystique; he was more interested in reading than he was in football. A teacher at Granbury, where his family had moved, took an interest in him, and her book collection was open to him, the only such book collection in town. So he got to fill up a prodigious memory that seemed to store details with almost photographic recall. Even now he can quote from a long life of bookworming, and he carries around an amazing almanac of book facts, author lives, the minutiae of publishing history in Texas and elsewhere. He knows great swatches of history and geography, but like all such polymaths and autodidacts, he may know more than he can synthesize into arguments or visions.

Once, coming back from a long weekend in Monterrey, Mexico, Paul and I drifted into late-night conversation, both of us tired. He mentioned the beauty of the young Mexican girls, how they radiated a seductive magnetism no mortal could resist. He went on in raptures over the pulchritude south of the border, rambling like a man too long on the trail. I listened and shared his enthusiasm, but I was driving and said little. When he had finished, I asked if he had noticed that such ravishing young beauties were also *madres* and *mujeres grandes* a year or two after the honeymoon? Had he reckoned the other side of womanhood in his romantic dreams? No, he said. Or, he said nothing at all. We drove on thinking about it—how lovely the orchid, how powerful her scent—and how much more powerful her authority and presence a little of the way into marriage. Then I asked him if he

PAUL FOREMAN AND PAUL CHRISTENSEN. Photograph © John Christian

had noticed how in Protestant countries like our own that women stayed small, if they could manage it. No answer.

"Well, Paul," I said, "a woman's body is not altogether her own to use. Catholic countries encourage women to become the mothering authority of the house, and largeness is part of the role she plays. A man stays small, like an adult son. Here, a woman is encouraged to remain slight, and plays the daughter to a man, who is more often a bit fat, with a pot belly by forty— a father with a pregnant look about him. That's the religious difference between men and women on both sides of the border." He smiled to himself. Paul could tell me everything there was to know about the towns, the history, the political parties of Mexico, but I could tell him what those facts added up to on the personal level. We smiled like a couple of collaborators in some shady enterprise.

His reputation hung like a thin cirrus cloud over Texas when I came. He had put out his bulletin to the world that he was coming home when he announced publication of *Travois* in 1975. As I say, I saw the poster in the halls of my department when I started work but chose not to send anything off. I was too new, didn't see myself as anything but a guy from Philly who just happened to be teaching in Texas. But no sooner had Paul come home to Austin than he began to attract writers to his table, and to the bookstore he started up. Thorp Springs had been going for a few years and already had a reputation as a good press.

Among the early publications of Thorp Springs Press was his own *Redwing Blackbird* (1973), originally published by Philip Caputo's San Francisco small press, Headstone, and then distributed and reprinted three times by Thorp Springs. Paul was involved with the Bay Area poets, a group of writers still writing out of the ferment of the San Francisco Renaissance. Berkeley was a lively center of activity for much of the West Coast avant garde, and one of its main thrusts was what we now call the Green Revolution, a hearty interest in the life of the old-stand forests of northern California and the coasts of Oregon and Washington. Poets were still following the lead of Gary Snyder in those years and taking on the corporate paper giants and their logging interests. Foreman learned a powerful lesson from all these calls to protect natural resources and wilderness; he could turn it onto his own state and write from his own experience of growing up on the banks of the upper Brazos. These emotions were poured into the poetry he was writing in the early 1970s.

I am not the first to say that Foreman's first book, *Redwing Blackbird,* has not only enjoyed staying power over the last twenty-seven years; it is simply a well-crafted, solid little collection. It touches on major themes that would overtake us in the ensuing decades; his "Old Buffalo" anticipates the great revival of interest in that once nearly extinct animal, now thriving at a population of well over three hundred thousand. His homage to Ezra Pound is right on and tells us the real axis of growth in poetry has occurred along the Whitman/Pound/Oppen/Olson/Snyder line of poets—to the present day in Texas. This was the tradition that renewed our contact with the natural world, and Paul's opening section, "The Woods," declares that fact in simple, forceful language. His closing section, "Home," touches everyone with its respect for roots and his marvelous, I would almost say classic, tribute to his own river, the poem "Brazos de Dios."

He came back to get the literary scene active again and told everyone to come around. Brazos Books was housed in an old field-stone building just off Sixth Street, with a small art gallery beneath, the Bois d'Arc Gallery. The intellectuals showed up, the artists drifted in. Paul set himself up in a swivel chair in one corner, and the books were arranged on shelves across the white walls. A basement apartment was rented to a local artist. It was a homey place, with a wood stove hissing away, and Paul holding forth on any subject one cared to raise. He was a wise old sage at the age of forty, and looked the part: his face was round, soft featured, with droopy eyes and a voluminous underchin beginning to hang down onto his shirt collar. His chest was large, his thighs full in loose-fitting corduroy trousers. He attired himself on the cheap, buying his plaid shirts and wool pants from thrift shop clothing bins. His shoes, a pair of old hiking boots, gave you the impression Paul had just come in from the woods. Never once in a score of years have I seen him wear cowboy boots or blue jeans, or even a western shirt.

Paul is a collection of odd paradoxes. He is a country boy from north Texas who had schooled himself in Chinese literature, the pre-Socratic philosophers, the world of Ezra Pound, and the vast universe of fiction, which he knew or seemed to know firsthand. He could quote you passages from Heine, one of the greats in his pantheon of poets, Rilke, and his favorite philosopher, Heraclitus. He read Plato for pleasure, and sprinkled in references to the dialogues at almost any juncture of a conversation. He was old Texas, but he had spent his early adulthood in California taking courses at Pepperdine, then Berkeley. He sat in on the poetry course taught by Josephine Miles and managed to hear or study under Berkeley's best. By the time he came back he counted among his friends the poet Czeslaw Milosz, Miles, masters of Chinese literature, and many of the writers of the Bay Area, whom he had befriended through his press and magazines, or supported one way or another. He especially liked Julia Vinograd, famous in Berkeley as a street poet, who recited her work from a stepladder on any street corner and sold books out of her backpack. She made a living that way.

He had stories about all the writers, both in California and in the old guard of Texas. George Sessions Perry was near the top of his list, particularly the novels *Hold Autumn in Your Hand* (1941) and *Walls Rise Up* (1959). He told me once, with a look of confidentiality, that Dobie was not much of a writer, and was a poor man on facts. This, in Paul's mind, was sufficient to dismiss him for good. The politics of the man did not bother him; there was something too wise or old Texas about Paul to worry about the cast of a man's shadow. He weighed a writer by the use of his information. He was friends with Larry McMurtry, and with William Barney, with whom he shared a love of the north Texas country.

Paul was poor, but he was also generous and treated you to a lunch faster than you could treat him. He never visited without a gift of a rare book or a limited edition of a new book of poems. He asked for little in return, except perhaps a good conversation. If you bought books at his bookstore, you found a few extras thrown in while you were talking to someone else. I remember Kenneth Rexroth, the old man behind the San Francisco Renaissance, writing about the death of Paul Goodman, saying that if Goodman had been born in another country, he would be world famous. I think the same might be true of Paul Foreman; if he had been born elsewhere in the country, Massachusetts or Maine, or California, he would be very well known today. But in Texas, he is a small press man with a few admirers and cronies.

His father was a hunter and fisherman and knew the crafts of the pioneer; he could shoot and field dress a young deer, jerk the meat, cook up the legs and tan the skin, work the hide into a leather pouch or some other useful article. He knew all about the migration of birds, the ways of trees in winter and summer, how to catch fish in a murky river, which birds were edible and which mushrooms could kill you. All this lore got passed down in one form or another to his sons, who went out with him into the nearby woods. There was a sturdy pride in knowing forest and prairie lore; Paul took his knowledge of the landscape very seriously. Later, when he turned to prospecting, it opened the earth to him. He read it like a good book, from surface minerals down to the mantle. It was a great pleasure to go off on a drive up country with him and have him lecture on the history of the land as we roared through. Sometimes we would get down and study a creek bed, pick up a few bits of chert or marl, examine them for clues—and go off again.

When John Graves wrote *Goodbye to a River,* he was describing Foreman's childhood world on the upper Brazos. Graves knew the life there, the families, and wrote with keen insight on what river people were about to lose forever. A certain kind of Texas was dying out, never to return. It was still a Huck Finn world of small, sleepy farms, a few villages scattered about the hills, a life condensed enough to put into a roomy pocket of your overalls. If it went, it meant that a certain root back to the pioneer mind would also be severed, the root connecting Paul to his own past.

Paul, too, felt the change when he returned to Thorp Springs, where he was born and lived his first few years, to see how the town had fared in his absence. It had grown, modernized; it had put out more roads into the hinterland. It was not the same. The river was not the same, either. When Paul's father died, something else had been chipped away out of the origins of Texas. The state was getting smaller.

Paul did not argue, he asked; he did not step on feet with his knowledge, he opened subjects and followed their trails book by author until his listener grew pale at the avalanche of facts and passages tumbling from his mouth. When Paul saw that his listener had had enough, he would switch to another subject, rabbit hunting, perhaps, and the types of rabbits, their different natural predators in the woods, the proper means of dressing such creatures, and he would throw in some local recipes from Brazos culture and his dad's culinary skills. A willing listener would fidget by now and look longingly at the windows and the stupid, happy, silent world at large, and wish himself in it. The humbling and drubbing one received in a friendly, breezy, happy sort of way at Brazos Books left a man limp and palsied.

The writers came into the bookstore hoping to find him in residence. Al Goldbarth came frequently to chat about poetry; so did Larry McMurtry, and Robert Bonazzi, Tom Zigal, the younger scribes like John Campion and John Herndon, older bards like Barney and Joseph Colin Murphey. Dave Oliphant, when he wasn't feuding over literary issues, came in to chat or graze on the book spines. Rosemary Catacalos, Sandra Cisneros, Naomi Shihab Nye made visits when they came to town on reading chores; Susan Bright held forth there at Paul's weekly poetry readings, as did Pat Ellis Taylor, now Pat Little Dog, and Chuck Taylor, Ricardo Sánchez, the Peruvian poet Julio Ortega and his then-wife, poet Cecilia Bustamante. It was a microcosm of the intelligentsia, and Paul's wife, Foster, a student of Asian art whom he met and married at Berkeley, filled in any gaps Paul left on the subject of eastern cultures.

A little later in our friendship, I met his brother, Don. I rubbed my eyes at our introduction; he had just come down from a mountain range in California after prospecting with a pick and a mule for several years. Don had written one short ballad about the bear he wrestled outside his cabin one morning. He recited it from memory in his fringed leather shirt and worn-out jeans, flat-heeled boots, worrying a loose tooth in his mouth that made him draw breath from the corners of his mouth like a snake's hiss.

He spoke in the thick, worn-down syllables of a man who has lived the better part of his life among rocks and streams and the cold winter wind of high country. He had a few nuggets of gold in his pocket, and his nose had become a kind of tapir's snout; he could smell yellow metal in a rain storm, he could feel where the seams lay under his thin boot soles. He knew ore, and he had gold fever. He was a man out of the deep Texas past, and he cared for nothing in the modern age. He made his wallets and seed pouches and his tobacco bag out of the rodents he caught in the creek near the bookstore. He handed out coins and food to the bums who still lingered in the neighborhood from harder days. The Sally Hilton had not opened yet, and Don was king of the hoboes.

When Don died of heart disease, Paul had been without a steady income for many years, ever since he left the police force in L.A. in 1976 or so. He had tried a few enterprises like the gallery and bookstore, but these only brought in pocket money. Times were hard in the Foreman house. But one night Don appeared in spirit at the foot of Paul's bed and gave him the white nuggets he had found in the Feather River at the base of an old caldera in California. He imparted his gold fever to him, and Paul's life was changed.

Paul woke, grabbed up the minerals on his bookshelf, studied them a long while, and began a high-speed self-education in mineralogy, geology, hard-rock mining, and the art of assay. In a year's time, and after haranguing friends until their ears fell off, Paul emerged from his chrysalis a formidable geologist and expert on caldera mineral deposits. He knew all about volcanic necks and vents and magma concentrations, and where the platinum groups were and how various igneous rocks in a river bottom could lead you to buried treasure upstream.

He became one of Coronado's children, and joined the dusty trail up the mountains. He was known in the trade as a good field geologist. He once confided to me that he found geology professors wanting in basics, and unable to keep up. New methods of laboratory analysis coming out of South Africa were revolutionizing hard-rock mining, he said, and anyone in the platinum-finding business had better know where to send for "good numbers." To date I don't think any of the big mining companies has taken the bait of one his assays, though he has mapped, gridded, sampled, and explained the land he holds for his backers until it must be transparent to mining outfits. Some of the narratives prepared by professional mineral men are quite stunning—as exercises in cryptic prose, with a few glimpses into epic earth history.

Mining may never make Paul rich, but he vowed that his money would be shared with friends, and some devoted to his press, where it would enjoy the prestige of a high office-tower address in Austin. Lovely, sun-filled words to the ears of his circle, including mine. It was not important how much money came into his pockets. He deserves whatever he gets; he worked for it. He wore out many pairs of boots stalking after the white gold. He hired his own son, his friends, his remaining brother—hoping all could benefit from his windfall. But the bloom is off the rose, as they say. The dream is faded. It may still happen that a sale will rocket him into the towers of Austin. But if it doesn't, gold fever opened the doors of his perception.

He knows the land from underneath; that is the gift his brother gave him. He has an eye for reading the simple ground, which is the final education of a poet. He cannot walk a trail in the woods without perceiving in the glint of a stone something of the mysterious origins of that ground. He will stop, pull out his loupe, squint at a little sliver of quartz, and begin one of his prose poems on the nature of earth under our soles.

Paul is writing again, translating Heraclitus, drifting back to his poetry books. Among the people I know, he looms largest—as a generous spirit with an unsatisfied longing to reach down to the very spirit of earth—which seems so adamant and distant to the rest of us.

CHAPTER 7
THE IMAGINATION

Imagination in its true meaning is the faculty that perceives images, or as Wordsworth would have it, partly constructs and partly receives them out of life. Things swirl, and the new physics shows us a world of subatomic particles entering into and dissolving out of myriad temporary constructs that we summarize as reality. But the "world" is a house of many colors and fluid changes and does not stay the same. So where does the sense of permanence or repetition come from? Or is it an illusion, like solid matter and fixed forms? This is the crux of twentieth-century thought, and on it rest many of the assumptions we make about imagination and the possibility of expression. And Texas is party to the debates.

An English philosopher, Alfred North Whitehead, may have advanced the argument for imagination in a book called *Process and Reality* (1929), which reached the eyes of many poets by midcentury. In it, Whitehead imagines a universe that is fluid, with particles sifting and building and turning back to sand again. But there are forces at work, like the idea of "color," which is a quality of things and not itself part of the flux of matter. It transcends the continuous shuffle of matter into and out of forms. Color is like form, a thing apart and yet present in the making of any "thing" we might perceive. So color and "form," whatever that is, are catalysts or agents that enter into any given mass when it is forming itself into things. These properties of color and form he called the "eternal occasions," and their place in the creation of objects is accompanied by a sort of "will to cohere," not Whitehead's phrase but a poet's contribution to the discussion, the poet Charles Olson.

What Whitehead and the postmodern poets, most of them in the Northeast and in California, have been urging as a vision of matter is that it is *alive* and *wants to create its own objects*. Whitehead became lyrical at the close of his long, metaphysical exploration of the concepts of matter and change, and he concluded that we are merely passing through one of many eras of the life of the universe; this one, he said, was the electromagnetic age, but it is just a ring in the tree. There will be others of a different kind of energy and formal character. Then he became an old pagan theologian when he cast about for a metaphor to describe the longings of the universe for form. He said it is a little like the many primal origin myths in the world that tell of a spirit suddenly waking from its meditative slumbers and realizing it is disembodied. It creates matter and longs to enter it, to become something manifest and changeful.

The universe, Whitehead speculated, is the materialization of a god, a god putting on the clothes of matter until fully manifest in the total harmony of all subparticles. That is the will of the small and the energy driving it; it is looking for its ultimate shapelessness. Matter is thus *becoming a body* and, at a higher level, *becoming the body of God*. This exotic theologizing may seem a long way off from any discussion of imagination. But not so.

The imagination as used by writers of the deep past was the faculty of mind in which gods are perceived in nature. To use this faculty effectively one must have a theology that leaves god in the ferns and the robin's song, and in the wind rattling the pine cones at sunset. Nature must not be pasteurized of its *daimons* and sprites; it must have its voices and its purposes that lie beyond human will or use. It must have its own separate soul of which the human community is but a small, lacy extension. The world must be mysterious and difficult, and possess its own mind and will, which human beings partly decipher through symbols, intuitions, visions, nightmares, dreams, and visitations.

All that has vanished, and the imagination that once functioned as a tool of the theologians and wizards has been reduced to almost nothing in the modern era. Hence the importance or the intrigue Whitehead caused when he speculated on the nature of matter as being a kind of raiment or shining robe beginning to hang from the shoulders of some spirit longing to show itself. That sort of theorizing is not part of modern physics, but Whitehead's credentials were impeccable. He had cowritten one of the great mathematical treatises of the twentieth century, *Principia Mathematica* (1925), with Bertrand Russell, and was, according to the criteria of American and English science, a reliable source. But it was poets who read *Process and Reality* and saw the implications for a turn toward vision again, and a reinvestment of "reality," that is, nature, with a divine purpose other than, or apart from, human agency or interests.

The poets saw the return of the ancient use of imagination as augury and theology, as the third eye in the forehead for seeing gods and spirits moving in the tremble of the leaves, or in the flutters of wind over the lake. The imagination had a chance to be put back into business, and the movements in art across the twentieth century have been a steady plod forward toward resurrecting the full functions of imagination as the reasoning power by which spiritual questions are answered. As Fritjof Capra argues in *The Tao of Physics: An Exploration of the Parallels between Modern Physics and Eastern Mysticism* (1991), the roots of physics "are to be found in the first period of Greek philosophy in the sixth century B.C., in a culture where science, philosophy and religion were not separated. . . . The Milesians were called 'hylozoists,' or 'those who think matter is alive,' by the later Greeks, because they saw no distinction between animate and inanimate, spirit and matter. In fact, they did not even have a word for matter, since they saw all forms of existence as manifestations of the 'physis,' endowed with life and spirituality. Thus Thales declared all things to be full of gods and Anaximander saw the universe as a kind of organism which was supported by the 'pneuma,' the cosmic breath, in the same way as the human body is supported by air" (20).

The religious urges of poetry and painting and music are now fully evident in modern art, and the more theoretical branches of physics, chemistry, biology, ecology are all turning toward the riddles of their subjects and adding yeast to the theological ferment of the arts.

The twentieth century was unwelcome to many people for the very reason that it reverses so much of what is held to be truth and right reason. Capra again: "It is fascinating to see that twentieth-century science, which originated in the Cartesian split, and in the mechanistic world-view, and which indeed only became possible because of such a view, now overcomes this fragmentation and leads back to the idea of unity expressed in the early Greek and Eastern philosophies" (23). Consider the long background of western thinking leading up to the present, which has been a process of discarding polytheism and animism, once the essential forms of western thinking, from the notion of consciousness, reason, and the concept of mind. The old pagan religions mixed everything up; body bore the powers of mind all through it, and nature was a great shimmer of spiritual energies fussing and discoursing and meddling and creating, and destroying all at once. The gods were perhaps mere metaphors for scientific categories and natural laws, but the term "god" conveys the right mix of both pure science and the mystery of nature's "will." The cosmos was a continuous dynamic of spiritual and physical forces, but the great drive of western power was to break down this order of cosmos and split everything up into spirit and matter. It gave the human being a more privileged place as the source of spirit or mind, and a liberty to manipulate, exploit, control the events of nature.

In the classical literature of Greece and Rome, there is a steady pressure to end the reign of the gods. They are being made increasingly abstract and intellectual; as Jane Ellen Harrison shows in her various studies of Greek theology, from *Themis: A Study of the Social Origins of Greek Religion* (1912), to other seminal studies, the original earth gods are slowly pushed up into the sky, which is really the metaphor of the human mind. The gods leave the body in Greek culture to become psychological gods; the theology of Greece and then Rome is fast becoming the anatomy of human character with a god for every mood and part of brain. The body and the landscape are no longer given the power to "think," or to show forth the presence of spiritual life. The imagination is slowly withering in the process. David Miller, a Jungian therapist, signaled the twentieth-century theological renaissance in *The New Polytheism: Rebirth of the Gods and Goddesses* (2nd ed., 1981), as did James Hillman, a leading Jungian analyst, in his provocative *Healing Fiction* (1983), his comparative study of depth psychology under Freud, Jung, and Adler. It is his contention that the disappearance of polytheism under Christianity created the dilemma of an unexplored, unarticulated inner life that has occasioned, in his estimate, two millennia of neurosis and psychosis requiring a vast spectrum of quack therapies. The gods, he says, were voices of the body and told of illness coming, of conflicts unresolved, and were the healing daimons that Christian fathers turned against as the demons. Here is Hillman's take on demonology:

> The denial of daimons and their exorcism has been part and parcel of Christian psychology, leaving the Western psyche few means but the hallucinations of insanity for recognizing daimonic reality. By refusing even the possibility of more than one voice—except the voice of the devil—all *daimones* became demonic and anti-Christian in their message, and in their very multiplicity. . . . Today we call the internal policing of the psyche by an *inspectio* become inspector general 'mind control.' Here we be-

gin to see the staggering consequences of denial of the daimons: it leaves
the psyche bereft of all persons but the ego, the controller who becomes
super-ego. No spontaneous fantasy, image, or feeling may be independent of this unified ego. Every psychic happening becomes 'mine.' Know
Thyself shifts to Know *Myself*. What Philemon taught Jung, however, was
that there are things in the psyche that are no more 'mine' than animals
in the forest . . . or birds in the air. (*Healing Fiction*, 65)

The Catholic Church preserved the polytheism of the Greeks under
heavy disguise; the saints and martyrs and visionary prelates of the faith
adorned the walls of churches from early on; the polyphonic choral music
sung in the high vaults of the chapels produced an eerie resonance and echo
as if the human voice called forth the voice of spirits. Stained glass windows
and incense and choral voices, organ music, and steady incantatory prayer
all induced states of mind in which vision and spiritual transport occurred.
These things were borrowed out of pagan practice but given a coat of varnish to substantiate Catholic belief. But those very saints are derivatives
from the great pantheon of Mediterranean religions. The imagination was
still intact among artists given the commission to make frescoes, large mural paintings, altar inlays, and statuary for the Catholic order. The power to
see, to ferret out the divine from the landscape and to highlight it with Ja-
cob's ladders and haloes, was the original function of the imagination. But
now it was politicized and partly repressed, channeled to a specific use by an
official religion. It was not purely mystical and undirected vision, it was directed vision, and directed vision is first cousin to propaganda and its
newest relative, advertising.

To end the corrupt influences of Catholicism in Europe, the Protestant
Reformation put a ban on iconography altogether, thus ending the role of
imagination in Europe for the next four centuries. The body is no longer a
microcosm of nature and its gods. The body is no longer beautiful but dangerous, a place of instinct and lures to be primitive, unconscious. "The images which could teach the ego its limits," wrote Hillman, "as Philemon
taught Jung, having been repressed, only return unimaged as archetypal
delusions in the midst of subjective consciousness itself. The ego becomes
demonic. It fully believes in its own power" (*Healing Fiction*, 65). The body
is covered right up to the neck, and a gloomy age of sexual repression begins. Mind is all, and the powers of mind, after Descartes's paranoid essays

on the "method" of clear objective reason are published, are narrowly defined as logic and the classification of verifiable experience. Descartes saw
himself as the Aristotle of the postmedieval age, and he defined intellect as
an organ for ascertaining certainty from fixed laws and methodical empiri-
cism. He was positively afraid of imagination and its murky depths.

Homosexuality went underground as a vestige of the pagan world; it festered in dives and boys' academies, in locker rooms and among clergy and
politicians as a most secret vice. The male body was no longer acceptable as
an esthetic ideal, except among those who practiced a perversion. The
female body loses its sanctity as the handiwork of the gods and becomes
instead parts of a dislocated anatomy, breasts, genitals, buttocks for the
emerging markets in pornography and smut. The body disintegrated, and
the natural world lost its integrity as "nature" and became hinterlands of
cities, farm belts, sinister forests, and wilderness to be treated hostilely, cut
down, exploited without mercy. The industrial age was an inevitable step in
the logic of monotheism and the duality of the human being.

Romanticism was an attempt to reassert the role of imagination in European art; its allegories, parables, and visionary ballads spoke of various
gods in nature, but these spirits were fully formed and versions of the
monotheist god of Protestantism. The power to intuit natural divinity was
blunted and coarse grained. The gods were whole and removed from the
atoms of natural process; they were just sitting there on toadstools and lo-
tus blossoms, paring their nails. It was not a legitimate vision of the gods *in*
nature, but merely gods out in the woods. Nonetheless, romanticism was
here to stay; we continue to live under its bright canopy of gods and visions
and spiritual optimism. But not for too much longer. There is, according to
Morris Berman, a paradigm shift rushing upon us, sweeping the old Cartesian world away and returning us to primal Greek "holism." Here is how he
puts it in the closing pages of his book, *The Reenchantment of the World:*

> When I was a boy, the Cartesian paradigm seemed infallible to most
> Westerners, successful without parallel in the history of the human in-
> tellect. This way of life was celebrated in space programs, rapid techno-
> logical innovation of all sorts, and books with titles such as *The Endless
> Frontier* and *The Edge of Objectivity.* By the mid-1960s, it was becoming
> clear to many that science was, in fact, an ideology; and from that point
> it was a short step to the recognition that it was not a very healthy ideol-

ogy at that. It is very likely that the next few decades will involve a period
of increasing shift toward holism, Batesonian or otherwise. As scientific
civilization enters its period of decline in earnest, more and more people
will search for a new paradigm, and will undoubtedly find it in various
versions of holistic thinking. If we are lucky, by 2200 A.D. the old paradigm may well be a curiosity, a relic of a civilization that seems millennia away. Jung, Reich, and [Gregory] Bateson especially, have each
helped to point the way to a reenchanted world in which we can believe.
(296)

The "New Age" theologians are hard at work disinterring the old Greek
gods, in particular the Great Mother, as in Monica Sjöö and Barbara Mor's
influential book, *The Great Cosmic Mother: Rediscovering the Religion of the
Earth* (2nd ed., 1991), which bears these angry, but representative remarks:

The great Mother in Her many aspects—maiden, raging warrior, benev-
olent mother, death-dealing and all-wise crone, unknowable and ultimate wyrd—is now powerfully reemerging and rising again in human
consciousness as we approach the twenty-first century. . . . After thousands of years of life-denying and anti-evolutionary patriarchal cultures
that have raped, ravaged, and polluted the earth, She returns. . . . Based
in matricide, the death of all nature, and the utter exploitation of
women, Western culture had now run itself into the ground, and there is
no way but to return to the Mother who gives us life. If we are to survive
we have to attune yet again to the spirits of nature, and we must learn to
"hear" the voices of the ancestors who speak to us from their Otherworld
realms. (xviii)

The real turn toward imagination occurred in London in 1912, when the
American poet Ezra Pound scratched out some irrelevant lines from a
poem by Hilda Doolittle, a childhood sweetheart of Pound's who had come
to live in London and had passed her poem "Oread" on to him for a critique. Pound cut down to the bone what he saw as the principal image in the
poem and wrote underneath the edited result, "H. D., Imagiste." That little
epithet, *Imagiste,* was the point of renewal for imagination in poetry. The
particular poem he had edited makes a connection between pine trees and
the waves of the sea, how the pines bend and form crests and troughs under
a stiff wind:

Whirl up, sea—
whirl your pointed pines,
splash your great pines
on our rocks,
hurl your green over us,
cover us with your pools of fir. (*Selected Poems,* 26)

The idea of the poem is crucial to modern poetry: a force extraneous to either woods or sea enters and leaves its signature in the form of "waves." The
wave is not part of the material it enters, but any material can be transformed by the wave form. The imagination has identified a holistic phenomenon, a kind of macro form entering into and absorbing the smaller
phenomena of individual trees, and has perceived it spiritually as a power
that passes through any medium. This perception of nature's "ghosts" or
spirits that leave behind footprints of form plunged the twentieth century
into a new equivalent of spirit and natural events. A form is to twentieth-
century esthetics what spirit or soul was to the Middle Ages. Thus, the spirit
of waveness moves easily, like a god, through trees and through water. And
we can move the wave on into people in a stadium, who can pass the energy
and form of wave through their own bodies by standing and sitting in
unison.

That was the key to imagination: its power to discern holistic forms in
disparate events. Take Pound's famous two-line poem, "In a Station of the
Metro," and you have a wider pairing where the same form passes through.
The station platform in the Paris underground is a distinctly modern instance of random events. The commuters who have come down to await a
train could not be more unrelated to one another. And yet, under the gas
lamps they have assembled accidentally into a series of groups that the
imagination of the poet seizes upon and identifies by a most unlikely equivalent, the blossoms of a fruit tree after a rain:

The apparition of these faces in the crowd;
Petals on a wet, black bough.

Apparition is a trick word; its intended meaning is taken from French
more than English. Apparition means spirit, but it also means appearance,
"form." And the form of the crowd, even if it has come together willy-nilly,
happens to configure in the radial way petals congregate in blossoms. The

industrial world of commuters has found a direct equation with the organic world of Greek polytheism. A god resides, as form, in two disparate events, and the modern imagination has discerned its presence. The theology of imagination was back in business. Pound spent the rest of his life inspiring the use of the spiritual imagination in poetry; others discovered the same principle in painting and photography, in dance, music. The twentieth century was started on a religious imperative to bring imagination back to its original function as god sight.

Almost the moment Imagism as a movement is born, painters discover African masks and statuary as evidence of the spiritual imagination in a so-called primitive culture. Picasso's painting, *Les Desmoiselles d'Avignon* (1907), bears several Zaire masks on the faces of white women, and the Africanizing of modern art begins. Matisse, Braque, Miró, Gauguin, and later Dalí use the mask and other totems of African, Oceanic, and other cultures to document the spiritual imagination and to reassert it in themselves. And the mask is a perception of the geometry of nature also inhering in the structure of the human face: triangular eyes, rectangular mouth, cylindrical nose, and triangulated skull. Cubism would grow out of such perceptions and represent other objects strictly in terms of geometrical constants: spheres, squares, cubes, and so on.

We may say that all this is fevered romanticism cresting in the twentieth century. But look again and you will see imagination working as a faculty for observations of natural phenomena, if nothing else. Imagination as sight, as close scrutiny of nature without self-interest. The Imagist way of seeing is a mode of consciousness in which the humanist strain of manipulation, or what is sometimes called instrumental reason, is left out. The sight is that of Thoreau's or Whitman's or Emily Dickinson's in which the "image" is of a spiritual flicker in the natural world, without immediate or evident human use. The liberation of imagination from reason's daily exploitation of nature meant one could study the world again and see it fresh, see it as it might see itself.

As this new religion sweeps over the industrial West, creating an avant garde of experimental artists looking for ways to show the spiritual eye of imagination, Texas falls off the map as an artistic place. The frontier seemed to require that for culture to grow to maturity it must somehow recapitulate the history of art. So Texas was restarting European romanticism with Mirabeau Lamar's poetry, and it moved sluggishly forward until it connected with that vision of frontier experience that the historian Frederick Jackson Turner argued was a return to ultimate youth and freedom for western man. The love of youth and its ideals was a way of expressing a more deeply entrenched conception of man as an untrammeled free agent in a new world, a figure in whom nothing was obligatory but self-fulfillment. Hence, the idea that another will or spirit was greater than a human being's will was something to be ignored, avoided. Even repressed.

Dobie's sojourn in England in the mid-1940s, recorded in his memoir, *A Texan in England* (1945), is an attempt to find the roots of southwestern consciousness in the glories of English literature, especially the Romantic era. For Dobie, the greatness of poetry was more evident in Wordsworth and Coleridge than anywhere else. Wordsworth, not Whitman, was the place to start. That sentiment, while not very influential, resonated throughout the academic world as the proper relation between Texas and the outside. The revolt against Romanticism, raging among the modernists and increasingly those coming of age at midcentury, was resisted, if not wholly ignored. Texas was attaching itself to an ennobling myth of race and of religion by seeing itself as emerging from English roots.

It is worth pointing out that the southern renaissance immediately to the east, in the work of Faulkner, Flannery O'Connor, and Eudora Welty, had already severed some connections to the English tradition, and turned literature toward native materials, and native ideals. Faulkner especially depicted the South as decayed, its ideals no longer fresh or usable, but rather, like the corpse that Emily Grierson slept with forty years in the story "A Rose for Emily," a pile of bones to be discarded. Faulkner's love-hate relation to southern history made him an adversarial writer bent on exposing the wrongs of racism and the chivalric code. Other elements of southern life he loved and praised, but he was forced to reassess the Golden Age as an illusion, just as Tennessee Williams was to do in his plays at midcentury. The fury to reassess did not go west, but halted at Louisiana. Texas was still in love with its own vision of the Plains as a theater of rejuvenation and the last hurrah of European individualism. Therefore, modernism and its pagan tenets were of no use to the mainstream writers or their audience.

As a result, younger Texas artists sensing change in the air left the state for New York or Paris to find out what it was all about. Texas became a bastion of the nineteenth-century mind. And why not? Its heroic vision was the stuff of Wagnerian operas and Nietzschean supermen, and its ideals were as broadly sketched as the symphonies of Beethoven. Its graphic arts had not moved much beyond the picturesque school of the mid-nineteenth century, and its statuary was pre-Rodin monumental. It was reliving the European artistic revolution of the 1800s, but offering only pale copies of the originals. Even the independent-minded Elizabet Ney had brought over from Europe a very conventional notion of the patriarch, and her commissions were mainly to celebrate statehouse luminaries and other father figures of the Victorian era. She did not quibble, but went to work as if art had stopped before the Civil War.

The Texas imagination was caught somewhere between Dobie's version of Wordsworth and Wagner's heroic operas of the German people. The burden on art was to defend the white race and to celebrate its achievements over racial adversaries. It did that on a grand scale, and could only envision the triumph in terms of individualism and Christianity, the very elements that the modernist revolution was challenging and replacing. That is why nature is left in something of a passive state in much of southwestern painting—it is a backdrop to heroic individual deeds on horseback. "For the most part," David Teague writes in *The Southwest in American Literature and Art* (1997), "during the 1890s, that is all the desert was to Anglo-America—the backdrop for human undertakings." He goes on,

> Matthew Baigell argues that the generic quality of Remington's work arose out of a dream, one he shared in part with Frederick Jackson Turner and in whole with Theodore Roosevelt. Remington dreamed that Americans had grown into their present heroic shape through encounters with the challenging West and that he, by concentrating on its still more challenging desert portions, could through his work preserve that noble history for America's posterity. The nonhuman world is not fully articulated in his work because it does not need to be. In fact, paying great attention to details other than human ones could never have been part of Remington's project. Baigell notes that "Remington's frontier really has no location. He usually indicated landscape features with schematically rendered details—some underbrush, a distant mountain. More precise definition of background details would have imposed reality on the dream." (64)

Texas was a fussy old museum of old world clichés and discarded ideals, not because it was stupid or a backwater province of the nation, but because it was putting the twentieth century on ice. It was a dangerous and contentious age, and its new art and philosophy tore at the very roots of its faith.

The forces that should have rocked the old Texas thinking did not concentrate as they should. The University of Texas has a perverse habit of purging its faculty from time to time and sending its best talents east. Feuds broke out over the various heroic myths and their doubting Thomases on the faculty, as in the heated blood feud that developed between Walter Prescott Webb, author of *The Texas Rangers* (1935), and Américo Paredes, whose novels, *George Washington Gomez* (1990, published fifty years after it was written) and *With His Pistol in His Hand: A Border Ballad and Its Hero* (1958), are attacks on the Rangers as racial police. Leticia Garza-Falcón has followed the dispute carefully in her study of border races, *Gente Decente: A Borderlands Response to the Rhetoric of Dominance* (1998):

> While Webb all but eliminates Mexicanos from the history of the Southwest, Paredes inscribes them into that very history by means of his historical narrative; while Webb's discourse lends credence to the myth that the land is the birthright of every hardworking Anglo pioneer, Paredes focuses on what means were used to appropriate the land; while Webb glorifies the Texas Rangers, Paredes shows them to be the instruments of cruelty and injustice, usurpers of land rights. . . . Unlike Webb, Paredes was not writing for a very receptive audience, nor telling them what they wanted to hear. The reading audience of his time was not willing to applaud his efforts nor to receive his new style of writing history. After writing his classic *With His Pistol in His Hand: A Border Ballad and Its Hero* (1958), Américo Paredes was threatened by a former Texas Ranger who wanted "to pistol whip the sonofabitch who wrote that book." While Webb rose to a position of authority and power at the University of Texas at Austin, Paredes was criticized for his scholarship, was denied faculty salary raises, and was initially refused publication of his pioneering work unless he removed all negative commentary regarding the Texas Rangers and Webb. (158)

Dobie and other icons of the old guard are roundly dismissed today as purveyors of antiquated ideals and what some are calling historical illusions. They were not illusions if we consider that such writers were spokespersons for the racial majority, at a time when minority voices were silent or unheard. There simply was no discourse on the other side, among minorities. According to Garza-Falcón, "Mexican Americans have lacked, until very recent times, the moral support of Mexican intellectuals" (159), which is to say, the power to make culture lay with one race, who wrote its own history the way it chose.

Given all the hidden pressures that shaped how Texans wrote and thought, it is not surprising that the path through to the modernist era was blocked, or had a lot of rocks in the way. The strategy was to simply slow down, not grow so much until the state or the regional culture was over-whelmed by change. That meant native writers would have to repress parts of themselves, or channel creativity into accepted formulas and topics—heroics, the Alamo, the frontier West and those who broke it, and so on. Writers and painters from outside, unfettered by local restraints, have come and made great gains in expression in Texas by drawing on the modernist imagination. Consider the case of William Carlos Williams, one of the original founders of Imagism, and a close ally of Pound's.

Williams came back from a reading tour in California and stopped off in El Paso one afternoon in 1950, to see friends and meet up with dinner guests in Juárez, across the river. The experience of that day is recorded in a long meditative poem called "The Desert Music," a rare gem of modern poetry about Texas. It is venerated by local bards as one of the lyric heights of literature about the state. But what did it *do* to be so wonderful?

Williams allows himself the freedom to track the pathways of his thought without controlling them, or driving them to a specific intention, step number one in the recovery of imagination. He puts words down as they occur in his head, allowing the reader to see the formation of the language, the *form* of the words coming together. Step two: He takes us on a spiritual journey over the international bridge into Mexico, where he has a drink in a strip joint and some aging topless dancer bumps and grinds to the jukebox. He watches with his discerning imagination, and what does he see? Not just the old prostitute with her sagging breasts, but a vision of Aphrodite descending into the body of a woman to restore her divinity, her majestic role as woman in the world. He says her eyes rove over the male faces in the crowd and withhold her true self from becoming sullied by their lust; she is not fallen or disgraced, but a goddess in the flesh of an ordinary woman. He makes the Imagist connection of forms, perceiving the Greek world in the present, the goddess inside the mundane. The world is restored to its seamless continuity of spirit and matter, gods and blades of grass.

Williams showed us a textbook example of seeing through the imagination, watching the world come to life and look back as the Other, the strange, divine will of nature and the planet looking back from its own majestic vantage. The human imagination does not make things up; it perceives them acting their own roles and drama around it. The imagination is the power of the human being to see the not-not-I in the Other. That is how Dennis Tedlock, the anthropologist, put it a few years ago. Listen to the formulation carefully: the imagination sees that which is me in the not-me. By that trick of language Tedlock reverses the flow of heroic energy to the self and redistributes it back into the natural world, so that the human being is not cut off, isolated, heroically armored and alienated, but reunited to natural events and forces.

Williams's "The Desert Music" tells us in the title that the music is coming out of the desert, made by the desert's own will and energy. The poet overhears, or has the power to glimpse and understand the divine subtext, the hidden gods looking out through the cactus gardens and the wagging flesh of the old dancer. It takes great faith to give up the personal soul and see the great soul of nature. But that is what he did.

Here is another story of deserts and modern art. Georgia O'Keeffe went to New Mexico to get away from the closed New York art world. She was a fine painter, a companion of the photographer Alfred Stieglitz, himself a friend of the Imagists who articulated their esthetic in photographs. But New York is a pig's trough of fractious egos and art cliques. O'Keeffe had felt stifled by the art scene, so she went back into the hardest parts of nature, the white deserts around Taos. There, slowly, she began to create Imagist paintings of the landscape in which vital connections of *form* are lavished on her canvas. She was *seeing the landscape* and finding its multiple hidden souls.

She painted cow skulls on the desert, thigh and leg bones lying on the white sand—supposedly images of death and parched life, but she also painted flowers that celebrated the female's fertility and genitals. What we did not know until recently is that she was barren; she wanted children but could not have them. She found in the skull bones of a cow an image of her own empty pelvis, with the blue of space showing through the eye socket, a precise equation of how she saw the birth passage in herself, blue and empty as space. She painted the form of that void in the skull, withholding the other side of the equation until we found her notes and doctor's reports. The desert was a vast language of the human soul; one could find many equations between the It and the I out there. She saw its animist energies running all through the sand like invisible rivers and flowering meadows.

Behind Williams and O'Keeffe and the other modernists who came to the Southwest to do the new work are the great traditions of the Indian world in which the animistic imagination is in full flower. The drawings of the lower Pecos caves are a Sistine Chapel of the bison world, where gods and shamans and spirituality are in full array over the desert scenes. To the south lay the great polytheist cultures of the Olmecs, Mayas, and Aztecs, the Athens and Babylon of the New World. The desert has been solemnized and mythologized by great civilizations that modern Texas chose to ignore.

The imagination has no taproot into the earth when the nature around it cannot be perceived impartially. When I had been told an art fair was being held in downtown Bryan one afternoon a few months after I arrived, I made a point of strolling over to Main Street to see what the muses were up to. There were little stalls with canvases hung up on wires, the artists seated in directors' chairs nearby with a receipt book and an adding machine. The customers strolled among the stalls looking, considering. Fine, this was a promising start. When I looked, I saw the usual number-painting blotches of the amateurs; here and there a landscape seemed accurately portrayed, with an eye to poppies and bluebonnets, fleecy blue skies, a red barn. These were paintings that did not *see,* but remembered. The imposition of an organized setting bound by rules of proportion and extraneous criteria, like so much primary yellow against so much primary red. But the actuality, the subatomic flux, the image were missing. The eye had seen a few colors and patterns and made up the rest.

This is the consequence of having left the imagination in suspension, discredited from the upheavals of Christian Europe five centuries before. The world had faded to a few awkward blotches and some quick lines to hold the scene together. But the natural logic of particles and their eternal occasions had not been allowed to declare their autonomy. The painters had painted Texas mythology, the self-interested eye beholding an edible, manipulated scene. And the subjects told the rest of the story: human interest in the form of gardens, buildings, faces, domesticated animals, cute nature. These were the only vocabulary of the paintings, a world of consumable goods, not nature as it is to itself. The land had not only shriveled beyond the fringes of the city, it had gone dark in the minds of its beholders.

I came home depressed and angry that the lively, spirited forms of O'Keeffe and the mural paintings of Mexico had not had the slightest impact upon the art in Texas. There was not a single authentic work among the hundred I viewed, and yet the crowd seemed pleased. No one had expected more than this bland form of representation, and if they had seen some vivid perception of the land in itself, it would have stopped the breath, halted a passerby to stare in disbelief, in pleasure. But the day was a dismal loss; not a particle of the raw reality of life had entered into the safe, denatured compositions.

I later found the artists I had been looking for, in Austin, struggling on the far edges of the art world to make a go of it. Cecilia Bustamante and Julio Ortega had opened a gallery in Austin to show work that manifested the mural imagination of Mexico and the new spiritual avant garde coming in from south of the border; innovative work in Austin includes the paintings of Philip Trussel and the photographs of Huichol Indian life by John Christian, as well as works by a variety of artists who were once associated with Paul Foreman's Bois d'Arc Gallery. But a strong narrative base continues in the work of mainstream Texas painters, who remain rooted in a tradition of regional storytellers and local colorists.

But even the most vigilant guardians of the state's heroic self-image will acknowledge that something has changed in the regional mind since the 1960s, the watershed of change in the nation and in the western world. For one thing, power is no longer exclusively in the hands of a white majority; blacks and Hispanics now enjoy privileges that were once the preserve of white politicians and the major-party machines. Increasingly, the business and academic worlds are recruiting and promoting women to positions of power. These sea changes are still institutional and have not yet filtered down into the mind of the textbook writers, whose job it is to maintain the status quo until it is overwhelmed by contradictions. In time, perhaps, even the standard histories of Texas that schoolchildren must read will reflect the fact that the story of Texas now includes a variety of ethnic groups (and their separate histories) and both genders in the makeup of the state's identity.

But the allure of a myth of heroic selfhood vested in one ethnic group, with its elaborate story of conquest and victory over others, will die a slow death, to be sure. On it rest many other subordinate myths that glorify and elevate Texas to something above mere statehood. The ranch and oil economy on which its wealth is still largely based adorns the core mythology of a heroic and self-reliant people; the cowboy with his own brand of courage and virtues adds luster to the image of Texas as the home of champions and conquerors. With the world fascinated and still enamored with the image of the cowboy, it will be doubly hard to let go of the idea that this is *not* the home of white European heroes in the New World. But assaults are coming from all sides against this very notion of an ethnic hero, whose prowess and manhood are based on nineteenth-century ideals of race and empire and of the human being's special status in the world. We are in the midst of an intellectual civil war of sorts, with one side shoring up and protecting its claims upon a history that is largely ideological and idealistic, with another trying to import into the state notions of community, ethnic and gender diversity, and the demands for a more reciprocal relation between society and the environment. Even the architecture of contemporary Texas is adamantly "heroic" and monumental, and signifies—for the new banks of Houston and Dallas in particular—a sovereignty over the brown and relentless prairies stretching out around them.

But a region dies without strong visions and a relation to the surrounding world. A triteness and repetition take the place of inventiveness; already a fatigue has set into the way Texas does its educating and social organizing. Formulas of traditional thinking and prejudice have closed off some of the natural energies of the people to innovate, to create new social orders. The cities are segregated socially and racially, and the ratio of wealth to poverty and unemployment keeps widening. The state is needy for ideas and reforms, for liberation from its own myth, just to draw fresh breath and use the land wisely. It is in need of mystics and visionaries to tell it what the next millennium holds.

To that end, there is a significant leaning of the arts toward the south, initiated by the wellsprings of the Chicano voice in various big cities and along the border. Coming out of the writing of Sandra Cisneros, Jimmy Santiago Baca, Rolando Hinojosa-Smith, Ricardo Sánchez, and other leading writers of the Hispanic world are images of the collective human spirit of the Spanish-speaking community. The individual is not as important as the family or the community, and La Raza, the race, has its spiritual homeland in the mythical land of Aztlán, which is not so much a place as a spiritual embrace. These and other writers are raising the issue of a true counter-mythology of a united people thinking like Indian nations and collectivized tribes. The writer is not so much the voice empowered with speech as the tongue of the tribe, the means by which the group mind speaks its concerns.

For the first time in the literary history of the region there are not one but two myths being articulated continuously. A white majority continues to make writers speak for its myth of the sovereign individual while the minority populations produce writers that unify their audiences by means of chants, mythological narratives, and an array of persuasive new symbols by which to identify common cause and shared legacies. These developments are supported through financial engines like the Texas Commission on the Arts, the National Endowment for the Arts, and local and state arts support groups. The trend is not being bucked or deterred, but neither is the white audience buying up the products of minority publishers. The state is an arena of market-driven values, and the group that succeeds in selling its wares will survive. The state's managers do not meddle overmuch in the affairs of this new myth-making force in the population, but if it succeeds it will do so by reaching into the white mainstream with powerful lures and charm. Perhaps certain films are already achieving that initial interest in the Hispanic imagination, and a few Indian writers are beginning to attract white college audiences. Who knows, the next generation may be raised with dual headlights in its consciousness, a sense of balanced and opposing myths to live one's life by.

African American literature is slower to form its voice in the modern age; it is rooted in much deeper wounds and has more to do to bring itself fully to imagination. But the heritage of Africa and southern bondage are great wells of reference to the younger writers working today. Their own appeal to the audience is a call for unity and group soul, but the audience is thin and struggling to understand the difficult voice coming from its poets and novelists. It will take more time to form an audience of enlightened readers, and a large effort to educate the young and make them aware of the contentious forces of the myth world.

The imagination continues to slumber in most quarters and to remain a minor organ of thinking and practical living. Pound meant to restore imagination not only to artists but also to the public that read. The proper role of imagination is not only to see nature and to probe reality to its divine roots, but to live in the concentration imagination demands. He wanted his readers to build their own furniture, think clearly about politics and social vision, and to be forces in the shaping of the culture they lived in. That is waiting, and a great enemy of the consciousness of the public remains television and a tendency of Americans to want to live in painless security. The raw edges of life require reckless curiosity and a tolerance of discomfort, healthy bodies and active sex lives. The new literature was supposed to inspire bravery in its readers, but where the imagination is idle and repressed, life is lived vicariously and often at a comfortable perch above the fray.

Life is struggle; every creature but an air-conditioned human being knows that. Life is the free play of energies, and a swirl of atoms embracing and giving up forms, patterns, gods. When the arts do not show this fiery cauldron of energies in which the human actor is but a tongue of fire among the conflagrations, then it lies a little, and creates illusions. In a culture whose arts are not telling the whole truth and making the terms of existence plain to all, the populace rests on false assumptions, false hopes. It gives the reins of leadership to the few in power and lets them make all the decisions. The results can be catastrophic, and the public wakes to the nightmare of history and does not know what direction to take to find reality.

The imagination is thus an organ equal to logic and reason and the mathematical faculty; it is another sense telling the body how to distinguish between what is true and what is false. When the land becomes obscure because there is no clause in the social contract for active imagination or art, beware the ways in which the powerful steal the public treasure from the workers, the poor taxpayers.

The modernists opened the twentieth century by insisting that art was the threshold of social action. The new esthetic was not interested in idealizations of nature or life but rather had a kind of engineering curiosity about how things worked. There was something didactic and expository about the new arts—even Picasso's, which dismantled the instruments of Spanish music in Cubist diagrams. Why Braque and Picasso offered the public such fare, rather than, say, beautiful landscapes, opens the question of the purpose of art in the machine age. The Futurists had already shifted art away from reverie and subjective longings to a celebration of the mechanical age. Picasso was painting his own consciousness, which saw things in terms of interlocking parts and relations.

And when fascination with the functions of things wore out, objects took on new life as the ciphers and fragmentary clues to a world of myth flowing under their appearances. This is the deeper, less articulated side of the modernist spirit—the desire to see the things of contemporary western life as growing out of the primitive depths of the human imagination. Which led the painters back to Africa and to the roots of western awareness. Already the playwrights, the poet William Butler Yeats among them, were dredging up the bedrock of Irish myth and legend as the source of contemporary life. James Joyce's *Ulysses* (1922) examines a day in the life of Dublin in 1904 and shows how events on the surface of time are the reflection of Homer's *Odyssey* twenty-seven hundred years before. T. S. Eliot's reading of post–World War I London reveals an underlying "grail" legend of the early Middle Ages, and links to the vegetative deities of early Greek and Egyptian mythology.

All this energy pushed aside conventional notions of the individual, the private soul, the sovereign citizen's free will and civil rights. The ancient world revealed ties and bonds among human beings that were as strong as the bonds between atoms and the forces that governed the order of nature. The modernists were digging so deep into history that they were finding the evidence of something that preceded the notion of a "self," something akin to the tribalism that had been lost in the New World and that lingered on in African nations. The connection between a deep past and the unity of society goaded many artists to embrace forms of socialism and communism in the twentieth century. And for some, the attraction of fascism itself proved fatal and destructive. But the plunge into the dark of the past was motivated by a desire to correct, to reverse the fragmentation of modern life, as recorded in Eliot's *The Waste Land* and other mordant visions. The public grew weary of such arguments and turned instead to the diversions offered by radio, talking films, then television. It no longer required an art that attempted to involve the viewer and reader in questions of ethics, politics, and social values. It longed for escape, even as the industrial economies of the West became destructive and wasteful of natural resources.

Still, there is now an unacknowledged hunger in America for renewal and a better conscience. We are a worried people wondering what damage we are committing to our own ground with all our consumption and self-indulgence. Put another way, a change of vision opens the parts of mind that are closed, repressed by the dominance of one way of thinking. "Out there" in the world we no longer see are events and forces and mysteries that are obscured or even eclipsed by our neon and rush-hour traffic, our fifty-hour work weeks, our frantic efforts to consume the surplus goods of our overheated economy. We are like the mad hares in a race with the tortoise of nature, breathless and ill from overwork and exhausted by our need for more distraction and entertainment. We are overhyped, and there is no soothing message from any voice in the culture. Not even religion is exempt from the profit motive. We are in a sea of self-indulgence, and the arts must now get courage and open the world to us, let us see what our own obsessive consumption and zealous self-interest have been ignoring since the speed-up of life after World War II.

The gain for Texas poetry (and its readers) will be the sudden liberation of whole vocabularies locked away by one centralizing myth of the liberated and aggressive ego. To turn away from self a while, Texas poets would release a century of impacted words and ideas that have been blocked off. That process may now be under way, but readers have no idea there are worlds upon worlds poetry could enter into if the myth of the personal soul and its soldierly ego were for a while put on a hook in a dark closet. We might again hear of gentleness, patience, slow and plodding life lived at the speed of the caterpillar and the little creeks. We need a Zen garden to go to in our minds, and poetry could give us one in lyrics that turn toward the world as it is, the world that is dark and obscure, unknown to us who exert our whole energy merely trying to keep up.

Central myths, whatever their character, freeze thought, dominate it, consume it into replicas of its one or two beliefs. Must everything we do in Texas reflect our own selves and pursuits? Must all our heroes be takers and not givers? The contribution of women poets in the 1930s was to say there is another world, the victim's world, the quiet world, that is more interesting than "I." And now, in the last score of years we are hearing from the borders that even invisible republics like Aztlán are more interesting than "I." Slowly, like rain filling up a river until it swells over its banks, these other voices are dislodging that central obsession with self and offering us visions of other worlds. And until white poets consider the advantages, new language, new experience, and new visions, the mainstream of Texas lyric will continue to foul itself like one of our rivers.

But Texas was waking to the dangers of its own pollution and abuse in the first throes of the Green Revolution. A warning note to writers was sounded in a homemade manifesto out of Austin in 1987, signaling the rise of a two-man ecological movement they called "Ecotropic Poetry." The preface, mailed to two hundred poets around the country, provoked a few responses, one from Denise Levertov expressing her thanks for the good conscience of these young men. A dozen years later, the manifesto was reprinted in a new edition of essays and poems under the title *Ecotropic Works* (1999). John Campion and John Herndon open their piece with a strident, Walter Winchell–styled alarum, "This is an emergency": "[I]n this dark age poets go unheard. Or worse, seek the approval of the power elite, and validate the dangerous and obsolete myth—dominion over the earth. . . . The brain of the earth is far too complicated to isolate a single thought. The death of a species is not only sad because something beautiful has been obliterated—the death abases us all." What our poets want is nothing less than a new "myth of the planet in peril," which "must reflect accurate knowledge of nature. We must work with precision and a sense of urgency. . . . Human beings can live in the humility of the other species, or die with inherited hubris" (x, xiii–xiv).

The cover of the book reproduces a sculpture of the oroboros, the self-devouring serpent of ancient mythology, which Jung interpreted as the sign of nature as well as of the human unconscious. This is the Great Mother encircling the human world and returning creation to its own maw for rebirth. Inside *Ecotropic Works* are essays on Indian fables, Jay Peck's essay on "The Destruction of the North American Bison," another on music as environmental codes by the ethnomusicologist Steven Feld; poems by Campion, Herndon, Ken Fontenot, Bob Bonazzi, Peggy Kelly, Mel Kenne, Rachel Loden, and myself; a variety of other work touching on rock art, American Indian religion, and native astronomy. The original Ecotropic manifesto was a few years ahead of its time for the region, but the new anthology is a kind of catching up to the nation on these issues. Still, the book needles the thick hide of Texas and tries to arouse its slumbering soul to action.

Other events have corroborated the need for a new poetry to alert its readers to the dangers of ungoverned commerce. The roots of modernism have sprouted a second growth, one might say, calling for a more vigilant public and a more sensitive government to regulate industry. But Texas poetry has its own will and mind and is slow to respond to this sense of alarm churning up the rest of the nation. But little by little, there are stirrings in the arts in Texas. And certainly a new generation has taken notice of the fact that pollutants now hang above all the major cities. The great, inexhaustible aquifers of the state have shown they cannot endure the demands placed upon them by agriculture, industry, and the growth of the cities and their suburbs. Old laws permitting the withdrawal of all available water from a single well, without regard to neighboring wells, remain unchanged. The call to be vigilant is not yet heard, but some of the region's poets are at last working in the right direction and will energize poetry with a new social urgency in the years ahead.

CHAPTER 8
HOW TO READ
A POEM

Essentially, the form of the poem is composed of three elements: a speaker, a situation, and the utterance provoked. This utterance, a tricky element, is either a response to pain or a pretext for exploring the interior condition, the status of self. Most poets choose the latter, but this journey inward is perilous for all the clichés and predictable events that befall the average writer. It is hard to say anything new, unless, of course, the situation is more than just city life, more than a bad day. It has to be something so provocative that it upsets everything in the psyche at once, sending shockwaves down to the heart, the liver, and the genitals.

The poem thrives on war and plagues, depressions, and other upheavals—since the greater the shock, the deeper the journey into self. That is why we have two great movements of poetry in the twentieth century anchored on the world wars. There we find not only deep journeying but extraordinary innovations in language and form. The modernist attitude to make it new thrived in New England, in the industrial Northeast, and in California, but it was absent in the Southwest for most of the century.

The situation in Texas was extraordinarily rich and provocative: a strange terrain, much violence and bloodshed, and a natural world in ruins after the first wave of commercial exploitation. All this represents a kind of disassembled war—a disintegration of a world in slow motion over about a century of time. The poet looking at experience had every reason to feel that the times demanded a response—either to the pain or as an exploration inward. And yet, nothing happened.

Between the situation and the persona, two of the three corners of the poem, was a glass wall—some shield that prevented the poet from feeling the extent of the damage done. It did not register, or did not fully register. We have already said how the women felt, and wrote; but the majority of poets saw an imaginary Texas floating its bright gardens and cheerful towns over the devastation. Observer A is not responding to Situation B. It keeps coming out as something else, in poem after poem. The speaker's response to things is simply no response—but a projection of expectations and memories.

I have two explanations for this situation in Texas poetry—either of which will argue that the art form never matured. One is that the speaker was not really affected by the crises of the Christian religion; he or she went on believing as if there were no theological quarrels. And yet, the faith was weakening even here, in the form of fewer churchgoers, less influence of the ministers, a more self-conscious attitude of faith among the believers. The church was no longer central; it occupied a smaller place in town life, and often found itself on the bylanes and outskirts, where land was cheaper. The church simply did not set the pace for life anymore, but the *habit* of belief prevailed in the speaker's imagination. Hence, the poem did not become a search for alternate gods. It imposed an older Christian piety onto the visible world, and thus repeated the past. The second explanation has to do with the regional tendency not to look too deeply into one's self, where certainty turned to mush and vapor. The further in one goes, the more Zen you feel, until language can give out altogether, and, in the words of Emily Dickinson, you "finish knowing, then."

The regional sensibility fought for certainty, an absolute reality that introspection tended to dissolve. If the gun was the first thing you grabbed to protect yourself in a barroom a hundred years ago, now you reached for a rule or a law, a principle, a fact, a statistic to be your shield against the quagmires of the deep self. The regional self is so used to defending the settler's faith against wilderness that we find it in the poetry as a natural reflex. The land may be alien, so different it makes the mind reel out of logical orbit, which the regional poet *fights* and *refuses* to feel. I am talking about a fear of the actual that creates the glass wall between observer and nature.

The actual is blood soaked, riddled with bullets and old animosities; it is a landscape of nightmares and paranoid visions that ended in a devastation of its original appearance. None of that is allowed into consciousness as it is; it may be hinted at, and sometimes even narrated carefully, but it is never fully real, fully in the mind. That might encourage the poet to mere rant and preaching, and some few Texas poets are masters of the eco-sermon, a boring convention of regional verse. The wall is psychological and prevents too much looking into the world and too little reflection on the meaning one sees. The glass wall is a kind of consensual repressive boundary that refuses to question white history, except as triumph and victory.

Alas, that function is given to minority verse, in which we expect to find indictments and accusations and which we can dismiss as the complaint of the losing side. In Anglo poetry, we find an abundance of poetry up to our time rigidly worded and highly repressed in its emotions. Even its message is fear of the unknown, the wild, the uncontrolled, as in this poem, "Beauty Quest," by Walter Adams, which opens *New Voices of the Southwest*, published in Dallas in 1934:

> If in my quest for beauty I should find
> A berry or a grape no other poet
> Has found and nurtured, and with soul and mind
> Remove it from its wild retreat and grow it
> Where beauty-hungered multitudes pass by,—
> What priest had done a holier thing than I? (35)

The form of the poem is the tail end of a Shakespearean sonnet, the last six lines closing with a riming couplet. Shakespeare's sonnet sequence has some six or more sonnets beginning with the word "If," or starting the sestet with "If." "I" and "my" are prominent in the poem, as are "mind" and "soul." The writer has captured the essence of Shakespeare's style to articulate a major theme of Texas poetry: the taming of the landscape for human use. A berry or grape is "removed . . . from its wild retreat" and put before the public. But what is he really saying with these code words: beauty, berry, the multitudes that pass by? The berry grows out there in the wild, which is coterminous with the self's own darkness and unconscious depths; "beauty" is that transformation of the wild into the esthetic, the elevation of the primitive into the conscious. The berry is some sort of underworld fruit brought up to human subjectivity, where it can be valued, admired by passing crowds, who similarly hunger to see the wilderness devoured and made human.

The poem is not a confrontation with the not-me, but a bit of propaganda for the taming of the landscape. And taming is, in the interpretation of many women poets of the region, nothing more than the domestication and exploitation of the female. The poem is about the power of reason to uproot, interpret, and transform the alien natural world into extensions of self—to render them possessions with personal value. All this is said unwittingly, in total innocence of its ultimate meanings—but it is the faith of the region accurately captured in these words.

The process of taming wilderness has underneath it the subtle claim of making wild prairie into English green. These are the terms of domestication literature aspires to: to render the prairies into village commons and heaths, to take what is essentially New World and reformulate it into something familiarly English or at least Anglo-American. Mary Hunter Austin's poem, "Litany for New Mexico," a few pages later in *New Voices of the Southwest,* has this to say about the dry country:

> Bless God and praise Him
> For the west-sloping hour of siesta
> Under domed cottonwoods,
> That in a rainless land makes ever the sound of rain. (37)

There is a pretense of being in the rain at the heart of desert country, even though it is only the rattling of cottonwood leaves. Austin wants to escape reality and think she is somewhere else—someplace familiar to a forest dweller.

This pretending to be somewhere else runs all through the early regional poetry. It is the attempt to orient oneself to the strange by means of certain formulas of English verse language: gardens, cemetery meditations, romantic fantasy. An example is Clare MacDermott's poem "Dim Orchard," from *New Voices of the Southwest:*

> I know full well I shall find Beauty here;
>   In these green velvet ways I walk with ease,
> There lilts a robin's aria, crystal-clear,
>   Amid the branches of pale apple trees;
> Here with a vine's gay tendrils, brightly hung,
>   Plum trees pay homage with a perfumed sigh,
> And splashes of white petals deftly flung
>   A fragrant picture for my heart to hold
> So much—so much of glory I can take,
>   A fragrant picture for my heart to hold
> Of this calm glamour—that I swift forsake
>   For strange new pathways—though, so loved, the old,
> Where thoughts of that sweet passion once denied,
>   Like gleaming silver ghosts stalk by my side. (145–46)

Beauty is anything already valued and defined, the familiar, which Clare MacDermott summarizes in terms of English garden verse. We only get to the purpose near the end of the poem, when we are told such memorializing of the garden is a bulwark against taking "strange new pathways." The familiar is "so loved," a "sweet passion . . . like gleaming silver ghosts."

The key word here, as elsewhere, is garden, the enclosing of a piece of raw land to make it subjective, human. A gate will mark its entry, and walls will distinguish it from the accidental universe beyond. Inside will be those arrangements of symmetry in which flowers will abound in artificial orders, requiring daily cultivation. Raising the raw into the cooked, into a fantasy, is, subliminally, making paradise out of mere clay. The desire to reestablish the lost Eden of Christian memory is always present among pioneers and settlers, who abhor the unruliness and unpredictability of the wilderness they have entered. A few houses and a mud street will halter the wild energy, but a garden, with all its aristocratic encrustation of control, ownership, artifice, crowns the settlement with its first story. Hence, gardens abound in the nature poetry that was rampant in the decades between the world wars.

A similar sort of emotion is expressed in John McClure's poem, "Permanence," where he writes,

> Who shall remember longer than a day
> The beauty and the bloom
> Of any splendour man may snatch away
> From the quick claws of doom? (*New Voices,* 144)

These poems are in truth prayers for deliverance back to safe havens, a prayer for a return to "home." The "claws of doom" are nature's, and a natural process of regeneration is simply demonized by the poet.

When the land is the inescapable fact of reality, memories of other places are imposed on it, so that the wild prairie becomes instead a scene out of Indiana or Boston, or an "image" of what English countryside might be. The descriptive urge is filtered through an implied set of values all pointing back north or east to a land of reassuring familiarity. The poem "Brass Alarum," also by John McClure, illustrates this theme succinctly:

> I was as witless as the heathen kings
>   Whose only good was gold and minted ore,

Being too weary with too many things
    Ever to think of beauty any more.

Music was nothing, nor the sound of song.
    Beauty forsook me with no parting word.
I was a drudge who had forgotten long
    All comely tunes that I had ever heard.

Then—was it Campion or Hesperides?—
    A note of silver broke the obscene spell.
To the far chiming of old minstrelsies
    My heart responded like a brazen bell.

And there was panic in my dreams once more—
    Old tunes returning to the tocsin's beat.
The old dreams rampant at the brass fanfare
    Trampling each other under dancing feet!
Alarums of beauty made a panic there
    Like gongs of silver in a Chinese street. (*New Voices,* 144–45)

This is a more interesting version of beauty, which lies repressed behind a world of drudging work. When memory is aroused by a tune out of Thomas Campion, the "world" of Campion comes back orgiastically, and the poet takes flight.

There is little silence or any sort of wandering in the poems of *New Voices of the Southwest.* The chatter set up in these lyrics is nervously aggressive and mechanical, like the well- rehearsed words of a person defending himself from some dreaded accusation. The truth these poems try to conceal is that the land remains unwanted or unloved and the poets are at pains to find some way of concealing this fact in romantic gush. They put on the persona of English lyric poets whom we celebrate as lovers of landscape. But the guise is apparent, and the insincerity of the language comes through in clichés and exaggerations.

One may wonder if the problem writers confronted in depicting the Southwest lay partly in the fact that the poem carried with it a long history of consciousness of forests and hills and streams—all missing here. Did the habit of writing about the arboreal eastern seaboard and the island culture of England over many centuries freeze up a vocabulary for arid shimmering plains, dust storms, arroyos, and the mangy javelina scrabbling among prickly pear for its supper? We go back to Webb's *The Great Plains* to gnaw on his 98th meridian—that this stretch of dry ground with only horizons to look at is the most alien, unlikely bit of sod ever to confront a settler.

The irony of the literary situation should not escape us: a certain pride in conquering the land made it necessary to embrace it—as the spoils of victory, as the new "homeland" won by blood and violence. At the same time, those who inherited the victory were grousing privately, obscurely in their poems. How readers could square literary complaint with patriotic hurrahs is now hard to imagine. The result, most likely, is that poetry was pushed to the corner, like a pesky kid asking too many questions.

Verse seemed to have its own strategy at getting through, offering its patina of clichés, flowery adjectives, and sugary rhetoric as the coating on a bitter pill. Beneath the varnish lay certain stark admissions that went to the heart of the landscape. Julia Van der Veer writes a cautionary lyric with pagan undertones called "Little Woodland God," on the ravages of local hunters:

I think that surely there's a god
For little, hunted things;
A god whose eyes watch tenderly
The droop of dying wings.

A little woodland god, who sits
Beneath a forest tree,
With baby rabbits in his arms,
And squirrels on his knee.

And when a hunter bravely shoots
A deer with dreaming eyes,
I think that little god is there
To love it, when it dies.

But all the hungry orphan things
Who weakly call and call—
For mothers who can never come,
He loves them best of all.

He tells the breeze to softly blow,
He tells the leaves to fall;

He covers little, frightened things
When they have ceased to call.

I think his pensive, Pan-like face
Is often wet with tears;
And that his little back is bent
From all the weary years. (*New Voices,* 202)

The world belongs to men who kill, and the mothers and children are left
with the consolations of a bereaved pagan spirit. As more women wrote,
they seem to have put together a vast quilt of private symbols and designs in
which male injustices to themselves, to nature, and to the Indians are laid
out for others to decipher in another time.

Lillian White Spencer, also in *New Voices of the Southwest,* has a poem
called "Old Shaman," which opens,

My son was killed in war against the whites
My son's son starved on their way of exile
The son of my son's son is at the white school.
I would have taught him Navajo magic:
Lightnings and thunders in the medicine-house
While bright noon laughs outside;
Wonder of the holy Corn, grown from kernel to ripe ear
In a day . . .

It ends,

The son of my son's son reads a book.
He counts one and two. (*New Voices,* 199)

Eda Lou Walton, another *New Voices* poet, has a "Pima Death Chant,"
which runs along similar lines:

Pity me, and I will pity you.
Because of my sadness
This world is covered with feathers,
Because of my brother's death
The mountains are covered with soft feathers.
The sun comes over them
But it gives me no light,

Night comes over them
And has no darkness for my rest. (205)

Walton's books appeared in the late 1920s and early 1930s, when she was writing off the white-hot years of the Harlem Renaissance, issuing books with titles like *Dawn Boy: Blackfoot and Navajo Songs.* She taught at "the University of New York City," which may refer to NYU or to some earlier avatar of the CUNY system.

If a poem is an account of emotions and responses to something foreign, and the attempt to make it part of self, we may gauge just how foreign prairie and dry land were to these writers—their guard was up, and they fought their subject, most of them. They embroidered and embellished where they could, and where they were plainspoken, there is the tone of defeat or weariness, or spent anger in the language. It was a love/hate relation to the natural world, with all its quirks and pains. It was the very opposite of Eden, a place of exile where each new Adam must struggle and atone. The absence of any compelling myths about the land, any stories that would orient one's imagination to it, made it seem as if one could only fall back on description, or rhetorical formula. The titles of most books published over the decades tell us nothing. *Pageant of the Desert and Other Poems, A Cup of Thoughtfulness, Triumphant Moment, My Heart Has Wings, Images Out of the Sky,* and so on. Susan Turner Adams's master's thesis, "A Bibliography of Texas Poetry: 1945–1981," offers compelling evidence that few of the books published in those years bore significant plots or arguments for land love.

Both the local women and the outsiders were determined to voice their discontents over the hardships of ranching and rural life, and to wage literary war on the men who pressed them into hard labor, or limited their freedom. Obviously anyone taking up a pen did so out of perplexity or discontent to begin with; those that did not had a better life or were accommodated. The image we have of quiet, daunted prairie wives dying on their farms and leaving nothing but a withered homemade cross above their grave mounds is gainsaid by the poetry. The more one probes the literary subtlety of these poems, however crude their craftsmanship or morally smug their tone, we find anger, pity, simmering discontent aimed not against the land or its heritage of American Indian and Spanish roots, but against the hardness of their own husbands!

What did the men say in the same period? There lies a curious tale of par-

adox and subterfuge of its own kind. The men probe another side of character not visible in the manly culture of the times—a feminine side that
wants to love and not fight, or to admire without possessing. It is hard work
for most of them, and there is a decided retrenchment into safe romanticism. The glorying over nature is Wordsworthian, an escapism that tells you
such men wrote out of their own remorse. A curious little song entitled
"Frontier" by Benjamin Botkin, a name that almost sounds invented by
Mark Twain as a frontier joke, says more than my words could summarize
about male imagination:

> From the wind-warped trees of mothers
>   Branch tall and straight
> The dreaming sons and daughters
>   Who were born too late
>
> To tame the land or make broken
>   Bodies whole
> But will give to the land and the mothers
>   Song and a soul. (*New Voices*, 60)

The majority of men wrote around the perimeters of employment on the
ranges, narrative poems that portray cowboy life, lonesome trail songs, a
few sunset meditations, wind songs, and a variety of other stuff having to
do with men's jobs. They prefer this mask of the hard-working cowpoke or
ranch hand to the inferior role of the loafer admiring things for their own
sake. Better to pick up a rake and dream than to walk off into the dust with
a song in one's heart: "A lowering night, with muggy sultry air, / A thirsting,
restless, sullen, bawling herd . . ." (*New Voices*, 61), that sort of thing, taken
from the opening lines of "Stampede," by Earl Brininstool. Here is an
example of the Wordsworthian school on the range, a poem by Richard
Gillespie called "Up the Hills of Morning," which opens as if Dorothy
Wordsworth came tagging along, as she always did on her brother William's
jaunts around England:

> Up the hills of morning,
>   With summer in the air,
> I walked the sandy reaches
>   And you beside me there. (*New Voices*, 105)

Haniel Long is also from the English Romantic school, with his own taunting version of the "walk with me" song, "New Mexico Speaking":

You will have to go with red earth
as red earth goes with red rock
as red rock goes with red pine
before you can go with me.
You will have to go with piñones
you will have to go with bluebirds
you will have to go with the sun.
I belong to the unyielding ones—
you must yield to me first. (*New Voices*, 141–42)

The title, "New Mexico Speaking," gives away the voice of the poem, and it transposes complex emotional arguments from England to New Mexico, and nearly inverts what Wordsworth conceived as the heart of nature—a kind of motherly benevolence. Haniel Long tells us the red earth is savage, cruel, unrelenting, and will only accept those who yield to it. Long was an outsider, born in Rangoon, Burma, and educated at Exeter and Harvard before he went roaming in the Southwest. He settled in Santa Fe, New Mexico, and rubbed elbows with the remnants of the D. H. Lawrence circle, and he was writing from a very sophisticated edge of poetry. He knew the tides of modernism and was introducing its arguments to the region. Hence, "you must yield to me." This is the key to the next surge of poetry—the notion that not everything can or should be tamed. To know the land is to give in to it little by little.

Evan S. Connell, the fiction writer, writes about the Midwest from much the same point of view Texas would move to, but very slowly. Connell is a strict observer of ordinary life and its anchors in the plain, the mundane, but he observes the sparsity of his characters' lives always from a generous vision of the standards that could have been—the sensuous world that beckons from every leaf and ripple of water. The dour small-townsmen and women of Connell's world, such as the Bridges, who keep the old standards alive, slowly starve to death for lack of magic. In his most famous short story, "The Anatomy Lesson," we get something of what art could be if one were to open the heart wider, but alas, the art building in North Faber Hall remains "ashamed of its shabbiness," and the students plod along as timid amateurs with thick fingers. Andraukov, the art instructor, is a wild Slav who has a yellow moustache, reeks of cigarettes, loves life, and tries to inspire insipid students—but they dodder before the voluptuous nude model as if she were a vacuum cleaner. He finally blows up: "You do not know Clodion! You do not know Signorelli, Perugino, Hokusai, Holbein! You do not even know Da Vinci, not even Cranach or Dürer! How, then how I can teach you? Osmosis? You will look inside my head? Each day you sit before the model to draw, I watch. There is ugly model, I see on your face nothing. Not pity, not revolt, not wonder. Nothing. There is beautiful model, like today. I see nothing. Not greed, not sadness, not even fever. Students, have you love? Have you hate? Or these things are words to you? As the artist feels so does he draw. I look at you, I do not need to look at the drawing" (298).

The prairies are our nude, and the great expanse of desert lying to the southwest is another nude, and Big Bend and the Gulf Coast and the Plains cultures are other nudes demanding passion and response, but getting little of it over the decades.

The real story of Texas poetry is in the turning toward the land among a slim minority of poets from the 1930s on. The poem's hard shell had to be broken, and the land had to find its way into the small crevices of the lyric's tough English skin. The "forms" would not change because they are the architecture of race consciousness; the experimental poem will go hungry for most of the century and be the work of a handful of poets who dared to break with their own kind. The traditional or formal poem is far more than a habit of culture—it is a picture of the ground on which human beings stand.

The little wrapped poem of the eighteenth and nineteenth centuries represented the closed town or village with one road leading in. When rails and highways broke the towns open, merged them into metropolises, the poem followed close behind, dropping rime and symmetry and spreading outward into the white space around it. The poem by 1890, under the French hands of Apollinaire and Mallarmé, is a swath of Paris and its suburbs, an ooze of language outward from its own walls. And the poem has been spreading ever since, but in Texas, the neat little volume of words remains closed, tight walled, shielded—from what? Nature.

William Barney, long a postman in Fort Worth, is among the first few male writers to understand the difficulty of raising poetic standards in the region. He drew heavily upon Robert Frost to find his own voice, and he

WILLIAM BARNEY. Photograph by Paul Christensen

mirrored some of the crotchety moods of Frost as well. Frost was not an even-tempered New Hampshire man, but something of a loner, a dark soul, who found fault with much that he saw around him, and who forgave slowly. This kind of caustic, ill-humored sagacity was the right dose of wormwood for the all-too-sugary verses of Texas, with its apologies and romantic swaggering.

Barney was smart, cool blooded, and keenly alert to his circumstances. He knew his place in history, that Fort Worth was among the last little pockets of the beef industry to endure in the Southwest, after Chicago grabbed away all the meatpacking monopoly and concentrated the beef world in its own stockyards. The trail drives were ended, though Barney was old enough to have remembered some cattle drives passing by the western edge of town. The air was redolent of herds and stockyards, cowboy bars, and the sad, dark airs of the great slaughterhouses at the heart of the city. It was over, but he was the living witness of its final days. And he could look out of his western window and behold the opening to the grassland ocean in the middle of the continent.

Barney is the first writer of real size to drive the New England poem west and make it register the life of the Southwest. He won all the usual contests put on by the Poetry Society of Texas, of which he was a founding member. He appeared in the state anthologies; he was a poetry champion all the thirty-five years long he worked for the U.S. Postal Service. His achievement was to translate Frost's vision to the prairie towns without conceding anything to New England. How he did it took some hard figuring. A Texas ranch is not the same as a small New Hampshire farm, though the principles of ownership and the hard-nosed independence are kin to each other. Barney will take the woods out of New England and thin and flatten them into the Cross Timbers; the small country lanes dipping under reddened elms will become farm roads passing a few scrub oaks and some mesquite bushes.

Sometimes Barney takes his Frost whole cloth and simply remakes a poem. "Stopping By Woods" is an old standard from Frost's songbook, and under Barney's hand it becomes "Cross Timbers." The opening line of Frost's poem is "Whose woods these are I think I know." In Barney it becomes a couplet opening: "Forests of fir, and boughs bowed down with snow / I never knew; but these are woods I know . . ." (*The Killdeer Crying*, 25). The quick reader will catch Barney's wink at Frost here and elsewhere.

The achievement is not in the originality of "Cross Timbers"—there isn't much—but in the appropriation of a certain positive value for the woods that cuts across the old prejudicial attitude against "wilderness."

Barney's vision of nature is not as difficult or threatening as it can be in Frost's darker poems. Barney put more light into his landscapes, and wove in a little more of innocence and playfulness. This was sunny Texas, not moody, puritanical New Hampshire. Even death is received by nature with a certain nonchalance. Frost's attitude is a longing for easeful death, but he insinuates a love for the dark forest and the snow, which is what Barney wants to import into Texas lyric. *It is hard to love nature here, and Barney will stop at nothing to get this other attitude into words.* Frost is the guide, an affectionate, somewhat caustic lover of the natural world, but enough.

Why didn't Barney choose Whitman, then, if he was looking for a guide into the natural world? Or Thoreau? Or Emerson? Something of all of them comes through Barney, but he would only work within the disciplined measures of a poet like Frost. The others were far too controversial and *outré*, as the French say. Barney would use Frost as a sort of Trojan horse and smuggle a new attitude in under cover of conventional poetry. But, of course, Barney was an excellent craftsman, and he could manipulate the structures Frost used so well; he sometimes bettered his mentor.

I rather think Barney's strategy was the correct one: to take the standard writer of America's verse and appropriate the techniques and formalisms of the man to satisfy the entrenched conservatism of the poetry audience in Texas. Within those structures could emerge part of a new philosophy, if not the whole of it. Whitman's large, open-ended poems were bursting with the love of wilderness and of democracy writ large, but he would never catch on with the general public. He remains today a schoolbook poet, someone to be read in classes but not in the armchair. Whitman is the best of the best, the sublime master, but Frost, smaller in scale and more modest in accomplishment, hit the nerve in America's ear. He caught on. He spoke the American's taciturn, nasal speech, its clipped words, and tight vocabulary of practical terms. Frost dug deep and plied a very ambiguous subtext in his poems, but the ground, the surface of his lyrics, is as familiar as any small town square.

If Barney did not push the poem in Texas far enough, there were generations coming who would do that in weather that would allow or encourage such widening and digging down into lyric soils. Barney was writing in the nervous 1940s, and then the bland, gray fifties, and what he was saying about the wild soul of America was not heard often. The writers who joined him in his enterprise were equally cautious: Joseph Wood Krutch, Walter Prescott Webb, Lewis Mumford. None went so far as to plunge headlong into the mysteries of the New World, or to embrace the great realms of Otherness that white culture had smothered.

In "Paluxy Episode," also from *The Killdeer Crying* (Dave Oliphant's selected edition of Barney's poems, published in 1977), a man is shot and lies dying in the Paluxy River, while

> In the black-green ring of cedar now
> the Witnesses began to stir; a wren
> with a housekeeper air came brisking in;
> a khaki-hued grasshopper, thick of head
> and heavily-bechevroned, swaggered up
> from the sand bar and leapt upon a rock.
> A lizard easily scaled the black bark
> of a mesquite. A yellow butterfly
> bounced over a boot heel and sauntered off
> as in the giddy pantomime of a ballet.
> Even the Paluxy, placid though it was,
> remained a tone that came of touching stones
> a thousand times. (27)

It is enough to say Barney opened the poem up and put into it the first authentic language of landscape and local history the regional literature had seen. It brought the Texas poem up to the quality of the best southern poetry of the time, and sent poets off looking for fresh new subject matter.

Or put another way, the poem became more precise and fragile, something like a verbal sponge soaking up the trivia and the local hues, the weather passing over, the tang of the food, the slurs and drawling of local speech habits, even the quaintness of the Texian vocabulary. It became, to use Allen Ginsberg's apt phrase, "reality sandwiches," with a good hunk of the local beef and some of the salsa and lettuce, and maybe even a jalapeno pepper on it. Barney's way was to go the path of the women before him, to sympathize with the land and its cruel history, and not to ignore it by throwing on an archaic and diversionary romanticism. He went straight to the crags and the arroyos and reported on them as if he were writing newspaper articles. He even thought to address his reader as his fellow Texans, as they both pored over the sunset and the long shadows creeping over the grass. He tells us in the title poem of *Long Gone to Texas* (1986) that he bore no grudge with the land, like some settlers, and seemed to thrive in such earth:

> Some of those pioneers who came
> out of dead hopes, unevened scores,
> wrote three stark letters on their doors,
> shook disappointment off, and shame,
> and headed here to kindle a new star.
>
> At twelve I had no lasting hurt,
> no stricken heart, no dream's debris.
> Transplanted like an up-plucked tree,
> my roots caught into splendid dirt,
> and soon reset the running calendar.
>
> Whoever cultivates this patch
> earth color will stick to his hand.
> Gladly I gather from this land
> whatever harvest I can scratch. . . . (58)

A poet of Barney's caliber is not simply born into the trade; he makes himself daily through the joyous labor of observing, noting, refining his sense of what is there. He loves the land and willingly yields all or nearly all he is to it. You may view some of his homework in *Words from a Wide Land* (1993), his daybook running from New Year's Day 1936 to 1977. I am always moved by the book's close:

> 1969—Children, I will tell you another story.
>   Men are animals. The God you desire to believe in
>   is a shadow. Love between Man and Woman
>   is also animal. Men have created fiction
>   because history is unbearable.
>   Virtue, like Sin, is relative;
>   at the worst it can be extenuated.
>   The exact measurements of Science
>   contain little rotten flaws.

> Even Chance is not certain: it wavers
> between altering and not altering.
>
> Despite all these false quibbles
> and sleazy pronouncements, if you will listen
> to the rich evidence your own years will bring,
> I greet you at the door
> of your maturity. (194)

The book is sprinkled with loving detail, sweet little equations and perceptions that give you the sense that Texas is a buried paradise that only the three-eyed poets can discern, hiding under the dust and prairie winds.

> 1975—The elm trees, like a certain kind of woman,
>   shown the least bit of warmth
>   want to put out flowers
>   almost in the middle of winter. (16)

Anyone from California or New England would have said "any woman," but the cautious Texan says, "a certain kind of woman." There is a measurement of nature in this, a line drawn skillfully down through the religious consciousness that has hardened the eye against the landscape. Barney breaks through, little by little in this hornbook.

> 1976—When I dig up an earth worm
>   by accident, depriving him of life,
>   I have to reflect: I can do this
>   only because I am bigger,
>   presumably more intelligent.
>   But his title to the land is all as good
>   or better than mine—
>   he has truly invested in it. (33)

Given Barney's characteristic dryness and detachment, there is no mistaking his humor, which thrives under a solemn face. He scores all his points without so much as a wink or a nod:

> 1955—Two men engaged in a hot quarrel on the courthouse steps this
>   afternoon. One in overalls has a New Testament open, and the
>   other, plainly angry (and with spaces between his teeth) was ar-

guing vehemently. The argument apparently was going his way, for the man holding the testament seemed cowed. (33)

We may think of poetry as being "before Barney" and "after Barney." It grew up with this man's poetry, and came to sophistication in the less regionally precise poems of Vassar Miller, who was after larger, more national subjects. Miller opened the poem up psychologically by joining the regional lyric to the broad pathways of contemporary New England poetry, with its inclination toward Confessionalism, M. L. Rosenthal's epithet for the style created by Robert Lowell and Sylvia Plath.

If Barney put geography into the poem, Miller added the wounds. Her own were centered in a debilitating palsy from early youth, which eventually bound her to a wheelchair and an electric car she rode around on the streets of Houston. After her earliest book, *Adam's Footprint* (1956), which I shall discuss in some detail in a later chapter, the Texas poem ceases to hide its pains and brings them fully to the surface, in simple declarative phrases. The poem grows up under her force and becomes open and public in its searing admissions. Between these two writers, the poem in Texas filled out a vision of the land and the private soul, and was ready to take its place in the national dialog on self.

One of the strongest poets to emerge in this era was the Chicago-born Russell G. Vliet. Son of a naval medical officer, Vliet had no particular roots until his family settled in Texas City, where he attended high school. He then went on to Southwest Texas State University, where he launched himself into a career in acting and play writing. Vliet took a master's degree at Southwest with a thesis entitled "Experiment in Lyric and Dramatic Verse," after which he taught for several years in high schools in Austin and Rocksprings. He left the state and would not return except for a six-month residence at the old Dobie ranch on a Paisano writing fellowship. Vliet pursued his career as a dramatist at Yale, where he studied under Robert Penn Warren. Soon after, he began receiving important awards for his plays.

It was not until his mid-thirties that he turned to poems, and he drew upon his Texas experience to write one of the most important long poems of the time, "Clem Maverick: The Life and Death of a Country Music Singer." It appeared in his first book of poems, *Events and Celebrations* (1966); another book would come four years later, *The Man with the Black Mouth* (1970), and both won the prestigious Voertman Poetry Award from the Texas Institute of Letters. A third volume, *Water and Stone: Poems*, was published by Random House in 1980.

But it was Clem Maverick who illuminated the world of pop country music and who opened the way for poetry in Texas to escape from the narrow realm of lyric to date—those adamant categories of the psychological life, the fallen city, and the private soul begging for company. "Clem Maverick" draws on Vliet's exquisite ear for local dialect, for country humor, exaggeration, the tall tales of the cowboy songs, and for a sharp wit that zeroed in precisely to the tics and foibles of a rural crooner's personality. The poem did not exactly launch Vliet's writing career; his plays did that for him, mainly in the Northeast.

When Bill Shearer knocked on my door one afternoon in 1982 and came into my printing studio to sit a while, which he often did in those days, he had a manuscript with him that he threw into my lap. He asked me to read it and see if it was worth reprinting. Shearer had started Shearer Publishing several years before, after walking the book beat as a sales rep for Texas A&M University Press. He had learned the territory the hard way, perhaps the only way, talking to book sellers reluctant to give up an inch of shelf space for slow sellers. He knew how to pitch a book, but more importantly, how to choose which books to publish for the market. I was dubious at first, a longish poem by someone I hadn't heard of before seemed a risky venture.

But after turning page one of "Clem," I felt as if I had been swept into the world of comic theater, into a humorous realm staked out by vehicles like Meredith Wilson's *The Music Man* (1958) and Charles Strouse's *Bye Bye Birdie* (1963). The Texas twang was right, the drawl and swagger of the hero, the adoring choruses and admirers, the earthy absurdity of Erskine Caldwell's *God's Little Acre* (1933), even the exotic touches of Tennessee Williams's screenplay of *Baby Doll* (1957). It was all there, the elements of a classic. I read the rest of the poem standing up, half envious and half delirious over the poem. I called Bill later that same night to say, "Publish it! It's marvelous!" I wasn't wrong; the book took off in the reviews and the edition sold well. But Vliet was already suffering a second attack of lymphoma and died in 1984, just when his poetry career had taken off for a second time.

I am tempted to say that along with Williams's "The Desert Music," the poems of Vassar Miller and William Barney, and the gem "Clem Maverick," we may have a narrow shelf of poems we can safely say are some of the best things done in our time. To these I might add another, Albert Goldbarth's

marvelous send-up of Texas machoism, *Different Fleshes* (1979), another
Voertman Award winner, about one Vander Clyde of Round Rock, whose
early interest in circuses and his own agility on the trapeze and high wire led
him to join an all-women's circus act where he performed in drag. He
landed in Paris doing much the same thing under the name of Barbette and
was a hit. Jean Cocteau was thrilled with his performances and wrote an essay on Clyde as a figure of the artist sacrificing all for the perfection of the
art. Goldbarth's long poem pays all this back to us knowing he violates the
stereotype of the Texas he-man; a frilly drag queen swinging above a night-
club audience of the *demi-monde* was not exactly ranch material. But the
poem is funny, even hysterical in places, and puts Hemingway admiringly
on the same bed with Barbette in a bedroom rendezvous replete with
ironies to keep the Hemingway scholars scratching their heads. All in great
fun, which is, of course, Goldbarth's point in this "novel poem," as he
called it.

All these works tell us which way lies greatness in Texas poetry—a direction toward analysis and comparison of realities here and outside the state,
and a willingness to laugh where appropriate or even not. These poems lift
us above mere selfhood into the "world" where Texas is not one thing or an
absolute of anyone's partisanship, but a figure in history, foolish and brave,
important and trivial, mundane and sublime. But certainly not only local
or merely abstract in its vaunted heroics. The poems on my narrow shelf
hardly take up half a foot, but in their pages are insights into what makes
this particular patch of earth supremely human and paradoxical.

After Barney, poetry had the means for expressing the land's contradic-
tory meanings that had once been the coded secrets of female poetry. Here
is Joseph Colin Murphey's opening poem in *A Return to the Landscape,*
from 1979:

> So I have come back
> re-claiming the torn and wrinkled map
> moving onto this landscape
> and all its changeless terrain
>
> . . . .
> moving onto it
> again like cloud and sun, being
> one now only with its wind and shadow (1)

Or take this poem, by Charles Behlen, another of Dave Oliphant's favorites, writing in *Perdition's Keepsake* (1978):

After a journey
of eighty-six years
he's come home to himself.

Now he raises windows,
lies in any bed,
in fields of maize,
in the dusty grass
of his son's backyard,

crosses hands, legs
and grins in the wind. ("Grandfather William Behlen," 13)

Dave Oliphant's little book, *Taking Stock* (1973), concludes with a lyric called "Directions for Getting Here," which tells an invited guest where to find his house. It closes,

At the very next gravel drive,
sparrows there
defleaing themselves in the dust,
turn on in. Most folks
not from these parts
swear this town ain't fit for the hogs we raise,
but we've as yet to find more wrong here
than anywhere.
So come on by, bring your poems along,
we'll have the beer iced down,
the fire started,
everything ready
when ya'll arrive.

Not deathless lyric writing, but dead on in its use of the major theme Barney gave to the modern regional poem. From Robert Frost to Barney to the generation Oliphant brought to print in *The New Breed* (1973), the line has been a steady one of reconciliation with the land. It marks the descent of a poetic theme in which pioneer aggressions are counterbalanced by sympathy, identification, and with the female's capacity to merge the self with the natural world.

As an outsider, I am surprised to find myself a poet in the tradition of Barney. My own tongue has been oiled by this wise old bard's mother lode of geographical love! In a recent poem of my own called "On the Lower Brazos," from *Where Three Roads Meet* (1995), I write this little Barneyesque passage:

> The way in is a dance, a weightless
> partition of the limbs
> until the human suit of clothes
> is left on a rickety mailbox
> and you come home. The darkness
> mothers you; your father
> is the glowing sunset. You are
> mud and water with a snake
> for tongue, your hair is the drifting
> current that loves the sea. (28)

A closing poem in my third of *Where Three Roads Meet,* "Texas Field," also expresses my affection for the land, a borrowed land, to use William A. Owens's good phrase. Here is my celebration of nature's autonomy:

> Beyond the fence
> stalks of mallow
>   rattle under a norther,
>   thornberry and jack bush
> shag a dying elm, shadow world of
>   crow house, snake burrows,
> bull thistles gaping
>   like dragon mouths.
>
> The moths drift
> over the tumble-down briar
> where nothing dwells.
>
>   The wild seed creeps slowly
>   toward the grass, like lust,

> slithering over tractor ruts
>   to coil among the rusty barbs
>   hoping to lure the hybrid green
>   to droop an eager flower down,
>   partly for love, partly to save the world. (46)

But let us return to the women poets of Texas. Have contemporary women writers continued the lines drawn by their grandmothers? It is hard to say whether such sympathies as the older generation expressed for fallen nature and the vanishing Indian world are carried to any greater depth now. It is likely the trench is deeper, and that more things are being tracked in consciousness in general. We have a wide vocabulary for the natural world, thanks to five decades of ecology. We are still in the arc of the Green Revolution, so that Pattiann Rogers's work can be attached to it, and seen as one form of green celebration on the grand scale. But women are beginning to reconstruct a personal mythology with deep historic roots, leading to a vision of solidarity that goes deeper than the pop cultural sisterhoods of a few years back. Women now have the cultural means to show their traditions, and this forms a river under their poetry, songs, novels and essays—something that was not there to draw on in the early years.

Sandra Lynn comes to mind as one of the new women who entered the scene in Austin in 1980 with her book, *I Must Hold These Strangers*. A second would follow in 1989, *Where Rainbows Wait for Rain: The Big Bend Country*. The poems of *I Must Hold These Strangers* go off in different directions, trying out themes, but the real constant in the book is the body as nature, and the company of other women—as consolations for lost love, or the shock of single motherhood. "Tree" captures the theme of oneself as natural:

> . . . I green up fluid as a fountain
> but I am steady in my ground,
> my miles of roots curling
> hair by hair into the soil.
>
> My wood smells sweet
> and can be shaped into spoons or violins.
> I have my own system of writing
> and record in my body my history.
> This the saw reads as it bites. (*I Must Hold These Strangers*, 62)

SUSAN BRIGHT. Photograph by Carlos Salinas

In the poem, "Mary, Mary, quite contrary," solidarity takes the form of sympathy for the "mad woman" across the way—

From what root
does her pain
struggle to ripen
into bulbous words
only to wither
time
and again? (22)

Women have also continued the work of Vassar Miller, but not to heal the sick self or to regenerate lost bone and muscle. It would seem that the contemporary female scene is preoccupied with explorations of the female body—its sexuality, dreams, longings, the passions so long buried under Victorian politeness. The aim now is to distinguish one self from another among women, and to make various arguments by which to redefine the self as something beyond mere nurturing and nesting instincts.

Susan Bright's unending sequence of "occasional poems," begun in the 1970s, has successfully blasted through the romantic walls of conventional verse toward the heap of trivia by which we know ourselves. Her poems are laundry lists, daily menus, small details in the ongoing procession of days. She slows down poetry to an examination of overlooked particulars and places herself among a vast backdrop of the mundane. This works; it is compelling when it discovers the universal in the grain of sand. It is dull plodding when there is only the provincial world to turn over, stone by stone.

But recent work shows Bright picking up the threads of earlier women's poetry by making the identification between self and natural world, as in her book, *House of the Mother,* which won the Austin Book Award for 1994. In it is a catalog of women who have become "saints," as she writes in "Mother Saint," or more often victims of the social pressures of modern America. In "Some Women I Know," she offers a harrowing list of afflictions borne by her contemporaries, among them "child abuse," "life threats leveled / at them / for political work," schizophrenia, AIDS, "chronic depression"; another is "the child / of a rape victim." The poem concludes, "These are women / of the 20th century" (19). In "Endangered," we get the more familiar theme of nature victimized, in this case a list of animals who "drop / out of existence." They include Florida panthers, the Hawaiian monk seal, Schaus swallowtail butterflies, Laysan ducks, the thick-billed parrot, the California condor, as "one by one we go—" (21).

A new book, *Next to the Last Word* (1998), broadens its treatment of environmental abuse but is careful to distinguish this phenomenon as a symptom of corporate greed, a question of profits and exploitation of resources, rather than as an expression of male aggression. Bright's passions are to defend women's rights, but she is not an evangelist of feminist causes; she makes a clear distinction between capitalism's gross flaws and the sexual conflicts of her time. Bright's breezy style covers many subjects, but there is now a more strident tone in her poems, excoriating such groups as the Austin Planning Commission for approving building permits on flood plains and other assaults upon the will of the land. In her prose poem "Flood," she closes thus:

> For example, at a Planning Commission hearing two weeks after the great flood, mud still gleaming in summer heat all over town, bodies still being recovered from swamps and the river bottom, a developer wanted to set an eight-story apartment complex down on the top of two creek beds north of town. When asked what he was going to do about the creeks he said, *We're goin' ta move 'em.* (67)

Bright's memories of youth among polluting power plants are as lurid as Mary Karr's recollections of the refineries of the Gulf Coast in *The Liar's Club* (1996). In "Superfund," Bright recalls a beach in the late fifties where

> we played next to a tannery and a power plant
> industrial and replete with PCB's, idiot frequencies,
> next to an asbestos dump, next to a Yacht Club.
>
> Who could taste contagion in the water?
> Later we had cancer, miscarriages, retarded children,
> brain tumors. Our homes were bleached clean.
> We were children playing on a superfund site. (65)

Sandra Lynn, Naomi Shihab Nye, and Rosemary Catacolos have all written wisely about the nature of woman and the pains of maturity. Of the three, Nye is the most successful at engaging large social themes in her poetry: concern for children, preserving traditional cultures, love of the Other. She has carved out a voice and style that dwell on the lingering innocence of the female in a world of disillusionment and horror. More subtle is her ambiguous racial identity: she is Palestinian by her father, white by her mother, and brown in her sympathies with San Antonio and Central America, the loci of her poems and fiction. Books like *Sitti's Secrets* (1994) and *Habibi* (1997) explore her Palestinian roots, while *The Tree Is Older Than You Are* (1995) and *Never in a Hurry: Essays on People and Places* (1996) explore Mexico and the Southwest. She has managed to discard simple race pride to become multicultural, or protean in an age of heightened sensitivities to racial minorities. But she has skillfully controlled her voice as youthful optimism amidst the deteriorating cultural landscape of America.

Close thy Bly and open thy Nye, one wants to say—be done with mid-century atomic blues and doom and open the book of southwestern sunshine. This is her contribution to a darkening age of high school assaults, small wars that never end, and a public turned listless and banal by the corporate exploitation of every part of life. While other women write from two sides of their nature, a dark side of broken marriages and occasional hard times, Nye writes only from one, the side in which imagination rejoices in such tiny incidents as old women talking, kids romping in a play yard, sun on a windowsill.

NAOMI SHIHAB NYE. Photograph by Michael Nye

To make it all work, she takes us into the ordinary world as if we accompanied her to the corner store for sugar or a bag of flour. Instead, we are faced with a pixie with messages like this one from "Eye-to-Eye" in *Different Ways to Pray* (1980):

> We will meet at the corner,
> you with your sack lunch,
> me with my guitar.
> We will be wearing our famous street faces,

anonymous as trees.
Suddenly you will see me,
you will blink, hesitant,
then realize I have not looked away.
For one brave second
we will stare
openly
from borderless skins.
This is my salary.
There are no days off. (14)

Clear, limpid language is Nye's method of luring us away from our notion of the world. We follow her out of conventional reality into the dream
world of a new young Alice. She promises many adventures, some of them
quaint, Polyannaish, simple, a few even pointless. But what she establishes
poem by poem is a rare voice of contentment, pure, female happiness with
the world as it is. In a land of so much grim confessionalism, so much lyric
anger and disillusion, Naomi Nye has the field of optimism all to herself.
Item: "So Much Happiness," from *Hugging the Jukebox* (1982):

Since there is no place large enough
to contain so much happiness,
you shrug, you raise your hands, and it flows out of
         you
into everything you touch. You are not responsible.
You take no credit, as the night sky takes no credit
for the moon, but continues to hold it, and share it,
and in that way, be known. (61)

Nye seems to be rewriting Blake's "Book of Thel," the voice of innocence
set down in the modern city. Nye does not avoid the horrors of urban life;
she patches together the vision of simple nature struggling up through the
cracks of the city. In the title poem from *Hugging the Jukebox*, she describes
a small boy singing with large voice in front of the jukebox in a Honduran
bodega. It's not much to work with, but Nye makes it her personal anthem.
The boy is any child with a big voice singing to the world:

His voice carries out to the water where boats are tied
and sings for all of them, *a wave.*

For the hens, now roosting in trees,
for the mute boy next door, his second-best friend.
And for the hurricane, now brewing near Barbados . . . (61)

The quiet, insistent argument of Nye's various books is that she can grasp the life of ethnic minorities in America (and elsewhere) by voicing a kind of unassuming gaiety about life. She reaches out in her poems to hug the marginalized and the denied, to put everyone on an equal footing with her. She declares her democratic passions in a trance of rapturous lyricism, the kind that children know in their happiest moments. It is a fragile logic to spin out in a half dozen well-respected books, but this is Nye's strategy.

Lately she has been moving toward an adult vision, but in fits and starts. In *Yellow Glove*, the title suggests something of her turn to womanly matters; we find this new tone in "When the Flag Is Raised":

Today the vein of sadness pumps
its blue wisdom through this room and
you answer with curtains. A curtain lifts
and holds itself aloft.

Somewhere in Texas, a motel advertises
rooms for "A Day, Week, Month, or Forever."
The melancholia of this invitation
dogs me for miles. (84)

But in "Who's Who in 1941," a more familiar persona returns:

I'm being insulted in a library. The librarian thinks I'm a high school student sneaking out of class. "Who do you think you are?" she shouts. We are alone. I want to answer enigmatically. I am the ghost pressing against your window. I am the termite feasting on the secret boards of your house. She stands, she glares at me. She has a hairdo. The rest of the school is taking a test. (74)

And again in "The Brick," which begins,

Each morning in the gray margin
between sleep and rising, I find myself
on Pershing Avenue, St. Louis, examining bricks

in buildings, looking for the one I brushed
with my mitten in 1956. (30)

As she tells us later on in the poem, "the center of memory" is "the place
where I get off and on."

Naomi Nye is working to create bridges between races and offers as her
means this light-hearted, positive attitude toward multiracial life. She cele-
brates the diversity of cultures around her and does so with simple pleasure
and joy, which reverses a long history of bitterness and conflict in poetry.
She has emerged as the leading figure in southwestern poetry, and she articulates the female psyche of the region after a trying history of pioneering
on the plains and prairies and having withstood the cramping stereotypes
of schoolmarm, rancher's wife, silent guardian of household realms. Nye
brings attention to the female as a humorous, wry creature with brisk, hard
intelligence and a sense of personal freedom unheard of in the decades
before.

In that sense, Nye completes the work begun by her Texas forebears,
Lexie Dean Robertson and Vassar Miller, women who articulated the female imagination in highly disciplined lyrics. Nye goes beyond them in skill
and pixieish intelligence. She continues to grow in her work and seems now
to voice both sides of the female psyche, young and old, as in this moving
lyric, "New Year," also from *Yellow Glove:*

> Where a street might just as easily have been
> a hair ribbon in a girl's ponytail
> her first day of dance class, teacher in mauve leotard
> rising to say, We have much ahead of us,
> and the little girls following, kick, kick, kick,
> thinking what a proud sleek person she was,
> how they wanted to be like her someday,
> while she stared outside the window at the high wires
> strung with ice, the voices inside them opening out
> to every future which was not hers. (8)

In the poem "Catalogue Army," Nye manages to find the bright side of
being on mailing lists for endless junk mail. They come to her door in le-
gions, but she replies "Stay true, catalogues, protect me / from the wasteland

where whimsy and impulse / never come" (*Yellow Glove*, 75) . You get the
flavor and the stubbornness of her optimism in this passage from her essay
"Maintenance," collected in *Never in a Hurry* (1996):

> I never felt women were more doomed to housework than men; I
> thought women were lucky. Men had to maintain questionably pleasur-
> able associations with less tangible elements—mortgage payments, fan
> belts and alternators, the IRS. I preferred sinks, and the way people who
> washed dishes immediately became exempt from after-dinner conversa-
> tion. I loved to plunge my hands into tubs of scalding bubbles. Once my
> father reached in to retrieve something and reeled back, yelling, "Do you
> always have to make it this hot?" My parents got a dishwasher as soon as
> they could, but luckily I was out of college by then and never had to touch
> it. To me it only seemed to extend the task. You rinse, you bend and
> arrange, you measure soap—and it hasn't even started yet. How many
> other gratifications were as instant as the old method of washing dishes?
> (157)

In "Tomorrow We Smile," also from *Never in a Hurry*, she opens with "I
used to say to my friend Juan Felipe that I like Mexico because Mexico still
has a sense of the miraculous and he would slap me on the back and say,
'You just like the peppers, come on, be honest,' but I saw he had *milagros*,
little silver arms and legs pinned up by his bed too. . . . Juan, his mother, and
I were headed for the border that day—to eat fragrant soup with cilantro,
buy wooly ponchos and bottles of vanilla, and walk the streets of Piedras, fat
with joy" (190).

Rosemary Catacalos, by contrast, writes in the body of a woman, fully
mature, attuned to the sorrows around her. In *Again for the First Time*
(1984) she writes of her family, the women of San Antonio, and "*nuestro do-
lor,*" our sorrow. In "Katakalos," we learn of her Greek grandfather coming
to America from an island "passing from hand to hand, Greek to Turk, Turk
to Greek," to a city that had also passed from Spain to Mexico to the Texas
republic and thence to the United States, to the Confederacy, and back
again—an irony she passes up to explore the subject of her grandfather's
generosity in a world too straitened by money matters to be much welcomed. Catacalos swallows her bitterness at times—weighing the advantages of life in a wealthy country against the prejudice, abuse, and indifference suffered by immigrants and minorities alike:

The old woman spoke of harder days,
days when children flew in the windows
like flies,
eyes glued shut from hunger,
crying *Mama! Mama!*
and carrying knives with which they
threatened one another
as they all dove for the pitiful
pile of beans she had
laid out, steaming, on her belly. ("Overheard at the Basilica," 7)

Catacalos lives at the other end of San Antonio, on St. Mary's Street, far from Naomi Nye's ninety-year-old house on South Main; this is the side of town where the Dog Man walks, once a professor but now literally gone to the dogs:

bent under his tow sack,
making his daily pilgrimage
along St. Mary's Street
with his rag tied to his forehead,
with his saintly leanness
and his bunch of seven dogs
and his clothes covered with
short smelly hair ("One Man's Family," 11)

This is life under the vigilant eyes of Our Lady of Sorrows:

Good news from the town of our birth!
The Boxer remains faithful.
Every evening he gets drunk
and makes his way along the curve
of St. Mary's Street just south
of Our Lady of Sorrows,
between there and the triangle
of the Chinamen's, the J & A Ice House
and Salinas' Bonanza Club. ("Letter to a Brother in Exile," 23)

The last few lines above form the geography of *Again for the First Time,* where much of the experience of the book is contained. Like Nye, Catacalos explores the duality of her existence, the Greek roots that lead back to Odysseus and myth, and the present of San Antonio, where stories make up for a lost history. "It's why we write these poems," she tells us in "Daily Returns," to remember the stories, but also to "*relearn* faith every / day." "The trick," she says, "is not to disfigure ourselves" (67–68). Saying this brings the Texas poem a long way from its origins, and gives poetry its real function, as healing and exploration.

A new writer on the San Antonio scene, Wendy Barker, has signed up with Bryce Milligan's Wings Press there, which published her latest collection, *Way of Whiteness* (2000). Barker writes well about family and self from a long and deep-rooted love of Emily Dickinson's work. Spare, but not so austerely compressed as Dickinson's poems, Barker's lyrics flow in colloquial American in the shorter stanza forms, couplets, tercets, quatrains, and the like. These impose a certain terseness, even abruptness on the lyric voice, which in Barker's case keep the poems from devolving into chattiness. You may get a feel for her work in "Of Mice and Men," which opens

> We are setting traps, packs of D-Con. Overrun
> again by mice, rolls of paper towels chewed through,
> soft nests of leavings
> over the floor, bits of bird seed,
> clumps of the litter left after the hamster died. (11)

Her work is quiet, very low key, not quite Betty Adcock's more muscular verse line or Nye's easy magic, but sturdy, yeomanly, warm and intimate, like kitchen table talk but with a certain unmistakable verve and vinegar mixed into it.

Milligan's Wings Press is very active, perhaps the most active of the small presses after Arte Público, Nicolás Kanellos's press in Houston specializing in Chicano/a writers, and Susan Bright's Plain View Press of Austin, with about eleven titles a year. Milligan is playing it straight and making his press look around his own city for poets to publish; he is not going "national" as they say, but working the backyard, and it is paying off. His new series of Tejana writers has produced some real gems, among them Victoria García-Zapata's *Peace in the Corazón* (1999).

Slowly but surely, the poem is giving up its links to prayer. That oldest form of poem remains a haunting spirit of the contemporary lyric and draws upon very old patterns of language to appeal to God for help, conso-

BRYCE MILLIGAN

lation. The slow shift over the last few centuries toward a new god of self has now firmed its outlines and solidified its psychological content. The poets today hardly know that they open a lyric moment and begin to write from origins that go back to the temple and to the earliest forms of address. The new poet has so secularized the moment that it seems hardly more than a chance to talk aloud, to oneself, to another, to the room. And perhaps there lies something of the dangers of the modern poem: it has emptied itself of the sacred to such an extent it may allow in the merest trivia and banter, the Iowa-style "laundry list" in which the mere routines of daily life seem enough to talk about.

The poets in Texas verge close to this abyss, and some have fallen into it. The chatty poem is a waste of verbal ingenuity, and hardly seems worthy of the audience that might come around if more important matter were offered to it. Many poets have told us that the spirit still needs its voice and the poem remains the only real medium for articulating its longings. The eventual course of poetry will ultimately abandon the monolog of the self's routines and return to narrative, discovery, celebration. It must if it is to survive and nurture future audiences.

It may have to go in the direction that Dale Smith, a new poet on the scene in Austin and publisher of the quarterly *Skanky Possum,* has taken in his new book, *American Rambler,* published by Paul Foreman's Thorp Springs Press in 2000. Taking off from Cabeza de Vaca's *Relación,* the first white man's journey through Indian Texas, Smith recapitulates the lessons laid down by the poets of the Whitman tradition, the nativist avant garde in American poetry, and pushes the long poem toward a new level of social commentary. Like Olson before him, Smith has dire things to say about the corruptions of the American spirit by the profit motive and the "me-first" ethic. A bit dry at times, even a bit sermon-like, Smith is in deadly earnest to preach a gospel of giving and sharing, to turn us away from the further development of a culture of mammon. When Cabeza de Vaca tells us he reached Mexico City and found himself surrounded by Cortez's slaves and sycophants, he was sick at heart. He knew the imperial mission had already broken the spirit of the wild continent. That sentiment is uppermost in Smith's survey of the land 450 years later.

The virtue of this and other poetry being written as we speak is that it takes on subjects that are larger than self and the personal soul and engage us in debates, open forums on the future of America if left in the hands of

DALE SMITH. Photograph © John Christian

JOHN CAMPION. Photograph by Tom Ligamari

the merchants and money changers. The new generation of poets led by Smith and now John Campion will attempt to reintroduce morality into poetry, and not only a personal behavioral ideal but something approaching a morality of the community. I hope so. The trend is impressive and gives me hope. Campion's newest book, *Squaring the Circle* (1999), is also concerned with the conquest of raw America by the Europeans and the consequences of a failing culture of greed. He too pledges to continue the work of Charles Olson, and also of the botanist and historian Carl Sauer, and of Hertha von Dechend, coauthor with Giorgio de Santillana of that curious book of mythological speculations, *Hamlet's Mill* (1969).

This demanding and labyrinthine long poem moves sinuously over a lot of intellectual terrain (like his previous book, *Tongue Stones*), and if it goes dry on lyric energy at times, it pushes its own argument for a return to native ways with great determination, the fires of a true reformer and idealist. More interesting is Campion's complete breakaway from ordinary structures on the page, what critics sometimes refer to as the *mise en page* of poetry, the layout of the words. Campion's style is to sprawl, to write tiny little stanzas that seem blown about the page, or to place things in strophes as if to represent a kind of verbal shrubbery strewn across a wild hillside. At any rate, Campion is part of a process in poetry that is turning the poem into a

landscape of sorts, a pictorial motif of things not quite seen in the characters of the words but perhaps in their shapes and clusters. Ideas grow up like
thickets and windrows in this poet's technique, and part of this effort seems
to be saying, like others before him, words are no longer enough. We must
"see" what we think, or see through the letters of words into the world behind them.

CHAPTER 9
DEMOCRATIC VISTAS

The first book to be published in the New World was bilingual, a Catholic manual written in Spanish and Nahuatl, in 1539, only nineteen years after the entry of Cortez. In 1552, Fra Bartolomé de las Casas published his *Brief Relation of the Destruction of the Indies* in Seville, giving rise to the "Black Legend" about Spanish atrocities in the Americas. The two books express two sides of Spain's entry into the New World: a willingness to compromise and accept two cultures, a desire to loot and pillage the alien. Spain gave us two New World minds, that of Cortez's greed and impudence, and Cabeza de Vaca's deep affections for the Indians, as recorded in his own narrative of journeying through the Southwest, *Relación* (1542).

There were signs of a similar duality in the English invasions from the northeast, but in the clash of religions that occurred in Texas, the duality collapsed. The sides were now divided into vanquished Mexicans and Anglo victors. The Rangers were formed to protect white interests on the ranches and plantations. The Mexican border supplied migrant labor for the harvests, and other native people lived marginal lives on the farms and in small river towns. The social structure followed the lines of imperialism elsewhere, with an underdog class of deracinated natives serving the needs of white overlords.

The situation would not change until well into the twentieth century, and it collapsed when the other colonial states around the world won their independence. Slowly, imperceptibly, the Hispanic minority established a foothold in Texas and asserted its rights. But only after World War II did real change begin to take place and to set in motion the Chicano/a literary renaissance of today.

A paradox was already apparent in the state's massive sprawl over different climate zones and terrains. It was at once an extension of the Deep South of Louisiana on its eastern flank, a part of the desert Southwest on its southwestern edge, and the gateway to the High Plains on its northwestern panhandle. It was several cultures in one, with its racial tensions squeezed up into a coastal southern rim and along a river valley forming its western boundary. It was not that Texas was wholly consumed by race issues; it was undefined by virtue of its great extent and variety. There have been numerous calls in its history to break it up; annexation papers preserve the state's right to divide should its citizens so mandate. And various proposals have been put forth over the years for four or even five states to be made out of Texas.

Like the political enclaves that reside in Texas' different sections, there is a sense that different literatures are growing out of its various extremities. Is there a West Texas imagination, tinged with Hispanic, Catholic attitudes, a magical realist style of writing? It is too early to tell, but there are signs of that tendency in recent novels and poetry from El Paso. In particular the work of Cormac McCarthy, with its lush, imagistic prose and its preoccupation with the ordeals of manhood staged in the dry borderlands. Is there a correspondingly "Protestant" realism to the north and up into the Panhandle?

Perhaps so, if Walt McDonald's poetry is any gauge of the regional temper. His spare, short lyrics on the struggle to farm in hard, water-starved prairie country speak to the sense of toil and suffering as spiritual torment. Behind his vignettes of struggle and small triumphs is his Vietnam experience, a kind of masculinity that goes deep into the unconscious culture of Texas. McDonald's popularity partly lies in his drawing upon a warrior past to explain the war of man against the elements. He has spun out an important regional myth of dryland country among his many books. Here is a typical poem from *After the Noise of Saigon* (1988), "Praise":

Under the threat of summer, trees
Bring forth their fruit, here in a zone

so dry no trees grow native. The last
late killing frost was years ago.

We're overdue. Thousands of robins
dip down and believe it's spring,

listening to the tongues of sparrows
which seem to sing, bland little birds

WALT MCDONALD

that never go anywhere all winter,
and somehow survive. (8)

If we drive due north into the rolling earth of Fort Worth and Dallas, we come upon a variety of poets who feel kinship with the literature of New England, Europe, and beyond. I am thinking now of the sophisticated language to be found in the work of poets such as William Burford and Robert

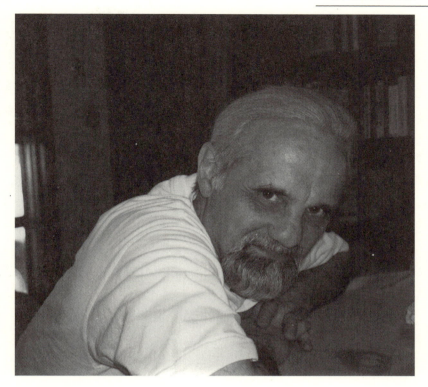

ROBERT BONAZZI

Bonazzi, who introduced French symbolism into Texas lyric. Their sense of region is muted and subtle, but detectable among the self-scrutinizing meditations they write. The soul's solitude is keenly felt in Bonazzi's *Living the Borrowed Life* (1974) and *Fictive Music* (1979), which pay homage to French masters and to Wallace Stevens.

Something else is going on in Bonazzi's poetry, in such fragile works as *Fictive Music* (1979) and *Perpetual Texts* (1986), and his newer work, which no one else was doing at the time: he was following arguments that go back to the roots of modernist experiment, in the work of Baudelaire, Mallarmé, and Flaubert—which turns on a profound distrust of words as having been appropriated for political and commercial use. Language was no longer the medium of free expression but an exploited, some might say threadbare means for showing the workings of one's consciousness. Some words simply didn't work any longer, like freedom, justice, truth, even love. They meant nothing or anything. The challenge was to not only loosen syntax from its old eloquent formulas, but to space out the words, calling attention to their peculiarities, their density and life as objects, as *things,* and not as the subservient noises by which self made its claims.

One thing you hear most insistently in Bonazzi's lyric impulse is the desire to escape from self, to liberate language from its entrapments in selfish, instrumental logic. How can one part the word from its owner, he asks in poem after poem. And this desire to deregulate language from its own corruption in the age of corporate control meant turning to odd sources for inspiration. At one extreme is the self-exploratory world of Vassar Miller's poetry, which finds a ruinous self to attend to, hardly a beautiful or enviable body to crow over and to which to call all lovers. Bonazzi was one of her inner circle, an advisor and editor, since Miller herself seemed to have no ability to make books out of her essential, overly intense lyric monadism. She could not see the whole puzzle of her scrupulous self-attention, so Bonazzi offered to do that very thing and gave her work the plot of escape, of delivery from mere selfhood into something larger, more spiritually nourishing. The result was his edition of Miller's *Selected and New: Poems 1950–1980* (1981). The poems argued for the free soul on their own, but Bonazzi's almost monkish tendencies made them say it more overtly and transparently to the stranger, the ordinary reader.

Bonazzi came to poetry partly from a love of the work of John Howard Griffin, whom he knew as a college student and who apparently took his bearings from his own spiritual journey, a path that led him not only to the Cistercian monk poet, Thomas Merton, but to a life of contemplation and spiritual rigor at various monasteries in France. The escape from self in Griffin of course led to experiments in identity that culminated in taking on the persona of a poor southern black in *Black Like Me* (1961). Long after Griffin's death, Bonazzi's interest and attraction to Griffin's solitary spiritual path crossed his own and he married Griffin's widow, took over the affairs of the literary estate, and published or reprinted a variety of Griffin's essays, the unfinished biography, *Follow the Ecstasy: Thomas Merton, The Hermitage Years, 1965–1968* (1983), and Bonazzi's companion to *Black Like Me,* called *The Man in the Mirror: John Howard Griffin and the Story of* Black Like Me (1997), for which he received rave notices in the international press.

Bonazzi is, in my estimation, the best editor in Texas, a man whose exquisite sense of timing in lyric, his nose for suggestive over flat-footed declaration, and his uncanny instinct for where the poem begins and ends have helped many a poor bard get his or her sense straight. And my own poetry was rescued many times, especially in that privileged time when he and I worked together on my own book of poems, *Signs of the Whelming* (1983), which owes much to Bonazzi's blue pencil. He was the book's publisher and made sure, as I have since found out, that the typos and the usual break-downs in manuscript were eliminated from an almost pure text.

If one were to attempt to put Bonazzi somewhere in the literary moun-tain of Texas, you would have to assign him a place near the peak, where the air is thinner and the paths are all trod by mountain goats and a few wizards and geniuses. He has taken poetry to its southwestern limits of subtlety and precipitous vagueness, where sense nearly but not quite gives out into silence and awe. But as I may have said elsewhere in this wandering memoir, he is a Yield sign to those who might otherwise want to step on it and hog the road, and declare self the triumphant virtue of Texas living. He says no, and he points to the way of Miller's own pilgrim journey in *Approaching Nada* (1977) and to Griffin's, to Merton's "seven-story mountain" toward the asce-tic life, and to his own, which is austere without being self-consciously her-metic or saintly. Among the writers I know who bring Europe and some of the best of our meditative energies to Texas, Bonazzi takes the laurel.

Burford's music is an even finer distillation of French lyric in such books as *Man Now* (1954), *A World* (1962), and *A Beginning: Poems* (1966). Densely musical lines combine to reflect not so much a region as a state of mind, a condition of the solitary imagination not giving in, attempting to transcend history and regionalism. These two writers offer a poignant atonal music to the narrative tradition; their work is important but overlooked. A kind of northern cosmopolitanism informs the writing, just as Dallas itself has a mind that looks beyond Texas—in its architecture, its banking, its notion of itself as a northern financial capital with higher ambitions. It secretly wants to be the Paris of the Southwest, and both Burford and Bonazzi seem curi-ously drawn to this worldly edge of Texas—supplying the barest outlines of that ambition on the page.

There is Barney inventing the Texas poem, and James Hoggard, the state's poet laureate for the year 2000, writing what appears to be a further extension of Barney's pastoral eclogues to include the Native American vi-sion of the prairies as sacred ground. *Two Gulls, One Hawk* (1983) has an important gestural poem in "The Tornado's Eye," in which he gives an account of his growing up—Hoggard's "Prelude," one might say. In it, a cautious unfolding of the male psyche is glimpsed in small, lyrical vignettes, where the boy learns to conceal his sensitivities, even as he proceeds toward a vision of home and community in the rough northern country, Tornado Alley, in the towns around Wichita Falls:

We lit up and smoked
and quickly turned grey,
all of us retching
or writhing in mud
sorry we couldn't even drown

except for Chuck
who couldn't get his lit

He looked like a pygmy ghost
three years old, he'd poke
a cigarette into his mouth
hold a match up at it

the wind would blow it out
or his own milk-breath

and he'd flip his weed
into the creek,
bum another one,
insisting we give him this time
a reefer that worked

little dead torpedoes
floating in the pool
by his dirty bare feet

Recovering, we tried to teach him
how to inhale

he needed to learn
to get sick, too (11)

The title poem, "Two Gulls, One Hawk" is interesting for another reason: two voices intertwine like a double helix to express the twin natures of the

Texas psyche: the one strict, orthodox, primly logical and correct, the other loose, ambling, risky, and voluptuous. Somehow these two voices seem to straddle borders and racial boundaries, as if the poet's capacity were to embrace two histories as the two facets of his imagination.

I published Hoggard's other sequential lyric book, *The Shaper Poems,* a year before, with its rustic, almost Celtic feel to the alliterative language, and its powerful rhythms bringing back the old Anglo-Saxon line of four beats and a rest. You almost feel the cold winds of Oklahoma blowing through the poems, and imagine Hoggard in his sheepskin robes wandering the cold paths of the Wichita Falls outback with a staff and a beard down to his knees. Shaper, indeed—a willful, solemn, mythological poetry of animal lusts and rages, and a human imagination caught between cities and the recent wilderness, now reduced to a mere horizon of dusty fields and a few grain silos.

Two new books published in 2000 by this prolific writer test new limits to his lyric and narrative style of verse. *Medea in Taos* points the way toward a wider sense of myth as applied to readings of southwestern life. Vassar Miller had tried her hand very deftly in this mode when she wrote one of her longest poems, *Approaching Nada* (1977), about her own pilgrimage to Taos and of her struggle to deepen her Christian faith. In this book, Hoggard explores his own peculiar frustrations with a faith that appears to inhibit or limit his capacity to embrace the land as living and changeful and even sacred. His poetry takes us another step toward questioning the roots of Anglo sensibility and faith by asking fundamental questions about the nature of nature, its potential gods, and the legacy of spirit that remains among the American Indian cultures.

This same frustration with belief and spiritual hunger pervades the prose poems of his new collection, *Rain in a Sunlit Sky.* I wrote the introduction to this book and was struck by the muted rages he is unable to repress in himself as he looks about his own region in northern Texas and again on his travels around northern Iraq and in Spain. He is looking for other gods, I noted, and seems about to leap outward from all he knows into a stranger, more compelling sense of god buried in the world before him. If so, he is taking Texas poetry somewhere it has only speculated about and dreamed of entering—the still pagan world of the prairies no amount of church building can quite destroy.

Hoggard's novel, *Trotter Ross* (1981), joins many other Texas novels on the theme of growing up. This is the major subject of male fiction writers, who are preoccupied with the dilemmas of growing up in a land that spiritualizes youth and vigor. Even without a wilderness to fight, males still gird themselves at adolescence for imaginary battle—and have their rites of passage, their ordeals of courage by which to judge themselves. Football and other sports, gangs, the armed services are the ranks of the young warriors, but there are emotional battles to fight as well, and struggles to survive the pains of high school and college, and ultimately, the arenas of mating and, then careers—all of which are difficult, soul-wearying exploits that the fiction writers record. Perhaps life is no more tough in Texas than it is elsewhere, but the frontier lingers in the mind and maturity comes at a high price. Many do not make it all the way to manhood here, and remain good old boys, perpetual hippies, drifters, and trailer-trash cowboys. The novel's theme of ripening and entry is inexhaustible.

A less strident subject of these novels is the growing attachment to the land as spiritual nurture, as "home" to the soul. Fiction writers make a distinction between the land grabbers and the land lovers; they side with the old farming communities that shared a pastoral ideal of the old ways. The novel as eclogue and idyll fills the canon of male fiction. McMurtry figures the most prominently among the fiction writers of the north country, but we should add to the list Kendall McCook's short story collection, *This Land* (1984), about three generations and their relationships to the land; the novels of Paul Foreman, *Sugarland* (1978) and *Quanah, the Serpent Eagle* (1983); and other accounts of hard scrabble on "the dryland farms."

Going to the center of the state, to literary headquarters in Austin, and its alter ego, San Antonio, we find constellations of young writers drawn to the institutional support they find there. The University of Texas occupies an important place in the making of writers in Texas. Its classes have produced several generations of writers who have gone on to become novelists, film scriptwriters, songwriters, and book publishers. One of these is Stephen Harrigan, whose retelling of the state's principal myth, the story of the Alamo, in *The Gates of the Alamo* (2000), shows the sides of the conflict, the Texan and Mexican, and spends much time on the landscape.

The city of Austin is a curiously uncomplicated place, dominated by youth and its interests. The shops, the bookstores, the music venues, the parks and jogging tracks are narrowly focused on the youthful body and its emotions, needs, desires. The adult world hardly matters, though it exists on the suburban fringes and in the complex legal community that serves and lobbies the statehouse. Austin is a distillation of certain ideals spun off of the cowboy myth and the liberation of the prairie woman. The boys in rags gliding on their skateboards over the campus streets and down the "Drag," or the women collecting to read their work or to rally their forces against another city council iniquity, are voices with long roots into the Texas past. The character of young male nonchalance has come down a long path to this moment at the turn of the twenty-first century. This shaggy, droop-shorted, feckless eighteen-year-old with digital music plugged in his ears and a shirt emblazoned with peace signs, love messages, and rock star faces, his eyes glazed and distant as he moves softly over the paved walkway of UT, is a creature much modified but indelibly raised from ingredients of the southwestern condition. The woman who saunters along on sandals, in shorts and tank top, with a tattoo on her shoulder, her hair twisted up with a rubber band, her face clear and without makeup, her mouth fixed in a sort of mildly dismissive scorn of any man's interest in her, her mind tuned to the female frequencies of feminism and ecology, is a creature born of generations of skillet-wielding farm wives, ranch women, and drudges. Her articulate angers are the liquor of a long fermentation of women's suffering, and the recent, but stubbornly blooming rose of her liberation into the mainstream.

Austin is peculiarly a woman's city, even if it is given over to a kind of youth-cult hedonism. It is the place where women have gone to redress their political grievances and found other women already there and working. I once described it as the new Island of Lesbos, a town friendly to the idea of women banding together to form art leagues, political groups, lesbian communities, and communes. Young males seem a little cowed and pushed aside by the brightness of such women, and there is a phenomenon hinted at by James Cody and other local poets of men rather forlornly living the single life amidst such powerful Amazons. Mel Kenne's book of poems, *Eating the Fruit* (1987), has a poem entitled "A Contemporary Male Story," which opens,

> Wanting
> a drink, wanting
> a woman, wanting
> to be joyful, ful-

filled, or else
only drunk, blown
away, wasted
with wanting
everything and
nothing
anything but that
which is here
now, this which is
just the reality of
an emptiness within

.   .   .   .

wanting nothing
but someone to love
or something to love
doing, and
finding no one, nothing. . . . (90)

Austin's male poets tend to dreaminess and longings of this kind, as do the songwriters, partly because they live in the city where women are amending their history and showing less interest in them. The women, on the other hand, are writing robust identity poems and political tracts, expressing love for their sisterhood, and finding an abundance of mental energy as the century closes. Betty Sue Flowers, Susan Bright, and Sandra Lynn are all movers in this world, and Bright's Plain View Press has become a very productive outlet for the gender. So has Women and Their Work, a communal work space for women artists situated prominently on Austin's Sixth Street, Austin's combination Broadway, Haight-Ashbury, and Tin Pan Alley.

Jim Cody's press, Place of Herons, the Indian name for Austin, was a valuable showcase for Hispanic and Anglo writers pursuing a vision of the ur-Texas of pre-Columbian days. The rivers and wild prairies are his subject, and writers who have excelled at a local version of Gary Snyder's "back country" exploration were always welcomed. Cody himself is a prodigious writer, and I am particularly drawn to his meditative squibs in *A Book of Wonders: Dreams, Visions, and Unusual Experiences* (1988), which takes us on a visionary tour of the city led by Jim Cody as "Moses, Coyote, and Christ

JAMES MARION CODY

and other characters." He is also "an old hag, a porcupine, . . . a monster" spinning wool and hearing the phrase, "Changing Woman, Changing Woman."

But Austin is more than its surface of youth culture. Occupying the central river valley of Texas, there is a concentration of intelligence and novelty there. The city represents a vortex of Anglo creativity and political power and draws artists and musicians to it like no other city in the state. As cities go, we might say that Austin is a kind of counterpart to San Antonio—racially and religiously. Austin is white Protestant culture, and San Antonio is Catholic brown culture. Together they represent the extremes of cultural modality in Texas. San Antonio is neighborhoods and family culture, a sultry, flowering city where poets are aware of the powerful lures of magic and miracles coming up from the southern border. The poets, male and female alike, write fables and dream narratives, and talk of mysterious transformations, and the casual sorts of magic Nye and Sandra Cisneros find in their neighborhoods. Bryce Milligan's Wings Press is now publishing a series he calls Poesía Tejana, featuring young Chicana poets from the barrios of San Antonio—sprightly, and sharp-edged lyricists with tough-love lyrics by girls who grew up too fast and are now single mothers. The Guadalupe Arts Center is the haven of writers in this literary town, with its cultural heart in the Mexican imagination.

Austin's heart is somewhere in the ether hanging over New York, Chicago, and Atlanta, which is to say, it has no municipal vision other than its broadly defined religious and racial consciousness. The poetry there is not unique to a city, or bounded in any way by the freeways wrapping the metropolis. The town is loose, open-ended, like a postmodern poem, and the poets' voices are from all over the nation and from the small towns. The magazines and books that used to cater to literature (few now survive the cuts to NEA and the Texas Arts Commission) were a little vague on what constituted capital poetry. A little nostalgia, some local color, a wide array of East and West Coast poetry styles, feminist verse, and experimental poetry—all of which seemed to say that Austin, like other big crossroads towns, was now wired to the urban network of the country, not to the little hamlets and farm towns around it.

Even so, certain movements that sprang up in Austin seem to belong just there, and no where else. Jim Cody created his own movement of nature poetry, unique to the environment around central Texas. He is especially good

JOHN HERNDON. Photograph by Carlos Salinas

at celebrating the rivers and taking us along on his walks into the hinterlands. In 1989 the Eco-Tropic movement was launched with John Campion
and John Herndon, who along with Peggy Kelly, started a reading and publication series called the Open Theater. When other movements were dying
out or already dust, the new generation had a rallying point around what
was then perceived as a war on nature by the corporations and the big cities.
Campion, a born preacher for such causes, took to his literary pulpit and in-
veighed against an insensitive, money-crazed power elite; he was from Dallas and knew of what he spoke. A lot of his jeremiads got into his first book
of poems, *Tongue Stones* (1990), for which the city gave him the Austin
Book Award, and the movement took on a certain fragile importance.

Herndon is more urban and casual in *Poems from Undertown* (1990), but
"undertown," he once told me, is the literal meaning of the word "suburb,"
a category of living he despises as wasteful materialism. The poems there
and in subsequent chapbooks monitor the degradation of the local ecosystem, but from a sharpened, precise journalistic perspective. Herndon is a
man of letters with novels, short stories, essays, and a long stint as a critic
and columnist with the *Austin American-Statesman*. In his company it is

easy to fall in with his views as he takes you for a fast walk around Town Lake, identifying the local flora and birds with casual mastery.

The city of Houston floats on a swamp, with the Gulf flowing in bayous on its edges. The underworld of Houston is difficult to access, perhaps impenetrable to writers. The concrete is a vast scab over the wetlands, as if silence and unconsciousness lay in great heaps beneath the neon-lit streets, baffling and diverting writers from its secret life. It has the face of many coastal, subtropical cities, wide and elegant with shrubbery and shade trees, large fountains, an architecture of white balconies and leisure. The throb of the ghetto is always near, and the sound of discord is faintly audible wherever one goes. The bigness has a kind of mute and incomprehensible density that makes one master a few neighborhoods but never the whole, shimmering, chaotic mass of the city.

The city is like a dynamo throwing everything outward from its furious center. The writers associated with the University of Houston's writing program are all national stars who dominate the city's literary life. Ed Hirsch, a luminary of the poetry world, writes in all directions now as critic, historian, scholar, and as lyricist. His courses at UH are accessible only through the rigorous criteria of admission to the writing program. The students there, some of the best young writers in the country, emerge with book contracts or very respectable magazine publications. Robert Phillips, once the director of the program, now a professor of poetry with an endowed chair, also has a national voice and a wide following, much of it in New York. Cynthia Macdonald, Daniel Stern, visiting poets, all make this enclave among the most revered in the wide and populous world of writing schools. And it sits modestly among the shimmering roofs of the UH campus, dwarfed by the low roar of a vast urban landscape.

Is there a Houston animus strong enough to create a municipal vision? Vassar Miller may have constructed part of that vision, but she left to others the task of completing it. One wonders what it will be like if it should ever be finished, this portrait of an oil town propped up on logy bog water and sending up massive corporate towers at its heart. It is no longer a walking town or a matrix of villages; traffic has dissolved a lot of its old southern character as a two-story old-fashioned Atlanta. It now bristles with might and money and seems too unruly, too ferocious in growth and reach to be given a character by the poets. But Lorenzo Thomas, the late Joanie Whitebird, Ahmos Zu-Bolton, Harryette Mullen, Carmen Tafolla all lived and wrote here and secreted part of that unfinished portrait of Texas' biggest town.

For ten years I made myself a catbird seat to watch the struggle of ideals in the state's literature. It was a little radio program called "Poetry Southwest," which I founded in 1977 at Texas A&M University's new radio station, KAMU-FM, an affiliate of NPR and a local sounding board for the university. My proposal for the show included a statement that I wanted to hear what the poets were thinking when they wrote about Texas. Every week I sat down in a tiny studio and welcomed my audience to another half hour of "Poetry Southwest." The format was simple enough: I would read a few books by the visitor and get up some questions to ask, have him or her read some poems, and then dig in on some issue bound to the poems. If the guest was a man, I asked what led him to write poems, and how difficult it was, emotionally, to write them. If the guest was a woman, I asked whose work she had read and what her arguments were concerning womanhood in the region. I also wanted to know what poets believed, and why they did or did not experiment with the forms they used.

The cashiers at the supermarket listened at times, and so did the pharmacist where I bought vitamins. My voice was familiar to colleagues and students, but I was only bouncing radio waves off the Brazos Valley. A few other stations signed up for a copy of the tapes and played them, but the show, like the poetry journals, attracted a small audience. Sometimes I read poems and thought out loud to myself about what they meant, or how they were composed. I conducted an informal writing workshop on the air and encouraged my listeners to support poetry, to buy a book of it now and then. Sometimes I felt as if I were only talking to myself, in a kind of electronic bathroom, humming tunes to myself in a state of near perfect solitude. When I lay in bed Saturday mornings to hear myself on the radio, I cringed at my nasal voice and the long "ers" and "ahs" I resorted to when out of words. Other times, I hid under the sheet when I began to grill a visitor too closely, a trick I had learned from my father, an investigator for the government.

Week after week the poets came in from all parts of the state, sometimes from beyond. In my roster of bards I mixed national figures like James Dickey and Gary Snyder, Donald Hall and Robert Creeley, with rising stars like Walt McDonald, James Hoggard, David Gene Fowler, and the local unknowns from around the corner. The big guns all sounded very prophetic and wonderful, with large pronouncements on the state of culture and the nation. Allen Ginsberg was my guest one afternoon, and he spoke longingly of the cadets he had seen marching about the campus; he wondered if they suffered from tight uniforms. There was Diane Wakoski, who spoke for the vision of women in the avant garde, and Susan Bright, who expressed the resilient new female of the Southwest. Nephtalí De León, Ricardo Sánchez, and Carmen Tafolla spoke on the issues of Chicano literature in the state; Harryette Mullen and Ahmos Zu-Bolton talked about African American writing in Houston.

James Cody was a favorite guest of mine, a man from the Ozark country of Missouri, a Scots-Irish descendant with a full beard and red complexion, a large head covered in wisps of thin hair, and a poetry of the wild Texas landscape that he loved. Cody was a guide to the Indian imagination, as he knew it, and a scourge of white hubris in the Southwest. He was mainly preacher and part poet, with a large social agenda of ills to discuss. His readings were always laced with social comment and an occasional improvised sermon on ecology and reverence for nature. Cody, like a handful of other Austin poets, had fully absorbed the pendulum swings of western faith, and now spoke for a return to myth and nature religion.

Grady Hillman, who worked as a poet teaching in the prisons of Huntsville and translated Quechua poetry from Peru, was another voice in the new consciousness of Texas. There was a time when Hillman teamed up with some Austin dancers in a group called PoDanSam, a compression of "Poetry and Dance at Sam Houston State University" in Huntsville, where they performed. It was mythology theater, with Hillman reciting sonorous lyrics on the mystery of the human soul while the young women in body stockings leapt across the stage performing certain ritual gestures. I was reminded of Isadora Duncan and the smoky Paris clubs where such mental theater began early in the twentieth century; it was in Texas now.

David Yates was a guest several times on "Poetry Southwest"; he was the editor of the tabloid journal *Cedar Rock,* and a good poet. He furnished the title for Dave Oliphant's influential anthology of Texas poetry, *Washing the Cow's Skull* (1981).

As a writer on avant-garde thinking, I concentrated my attention on poets who brought some of that thought to Texas now. My show was not an attempt to represent all the strains of Texas writing, but to introduce my audience to the new wave. I had a heavy hand at times, steering conventional poets to the edge, often with a shove of my hand. I cornered a few timid souls with questions they could not or refused to answer, questions about the state of nature, "alive or dead?" I would ask, like Don Imus, *Alive or dead?* It sounds like a threat now. I got blank looks sometimes, which translated into white noise over the radio. People told me the show sometimes made them sit in the parking lot until over, listening to me. I hit a nerve now and then, a literary dentist with a lyric drill in the mouth. But I was eager, full of the passions of the 1960s, intent on making real some of the things I had been writing about in my critical essays on experimental poetry.

What did I really want, I ask myself now, a dozen years later. I really wanted to know what membrane covered the state and kept out the voices of the coasts. Why didn't more information and ideas come in, illuminate the things that were so important here? How was it that such epic scenery and tragic history could be ignored for the piddling news of daily life? Was the epic dimension of Texas too much for the lyricists? What I should have asked is this: Why is it that poetry is almost always lyrical, when there are such powerful stories to tell? The cowboy poets told ballads, and the song lyricists sang ballads, but the average poet cranked out a twelve- or fifteen-line poem that sang up a few details of apartment life, lost love, lost faith, a lost nickel, a lost shoe. It would seem the muse had put blinders on the bards and given them diaries to fill. The real was so vast it demanded a new Ovid, a new Dante, and all we seemed to have about us were nickel-and-dime lyric spinners. That is a harsh judgment, but then, I am stuck with a quarter century of struggle and little achievement. And I had the microphone with which to pry into the matter, and I never went far enough. I never got a terrified confession from one of my trapped birds—a tearful admission of being lazy or superficial, or timid, or inhibited. I wanted some stark moment in which the hands went up and I could arrest the poet on the air and take the offender off to Plato's cave for a long confinement.

"Don't come out until you have written me an epic," I could hear myself say, creaking with my leather belts and holster, my Ranger hat slanted over my left eye.

No such luck. I let my birds go, one by one. Sometimes, however, things happened, the stammers quit and the talk grew intimate, and truths were spoken. At such moments I was Freud with all of Texas on the couch, and I was doing the talk cure with a vast sprawl of land and silence. Such demo-

cratic vistas gave me insight into the quiet, buried heart of literature here—
its reluctance to engage those subjects that women had dared to embrace
first, and long ago. The pain of history lay like deep sores in the chest of male
poets; they hesitated to confess them. Time and again I heard stories of innocence hardened by strict fathers, who taught their sons to "take the pain,"
to shut up and do, to go it alone, to be a man. All that is shock therapy to the
imagination, and often closes it early.

The women had no such difficulties in their childhoods; they were not
encouraged to become artists, but then, there was no strong resistance to
their reading or keeping diaries or learning how to write. The tradition
of women's literature, while unacknowledged in the region, is strong and
constant and represents a kind of hidden character of Texas. Why women
should have found writing natural to their spirits and gender, I cannot say;
it may have to do with the fact that young men had all the burdens of winning back the South put upon them, and to become poets was to dodge the
responsibility. Strong young warriors and heroes do not write, they fight. So
the women worried about voice, and caring, and learning how to be tough
on personal matters, and to open up where women had been taught to
blush. They had come a long way, and they read well on the air. I always enjoyed my talks with women; I had a sense that they lived in a normal world
and didn't need strong therapy or hard questions to get them talking.

I also had long chats with some of more professional-minded writers. I
managed to lure Paul Ruffin, from Sam Houston State University, into my
studio for chats; and Walt McDonald, fast becoming a national figure in poetry, came over once or twice. Both poets were working bravely in the seams
of the old mythology, with some twists from our time. Ruffin is a deep
southerner, with a drawl and a good sense of humor; his stories are very
popular reading now, and his poems, while conventional, are driven by the
rhythms of the pulpit and down-home colloquialism. McDonald was taciturn, measured, a shy man with an enormous passion for writing. Already
the author of some ten books of poetry, vignette, and commentary, he is
among the most sought-after poets by the magazine editors. And you find
him in every journal across the country. Seated before me with a mike in his
face, he searched for his words, and seemed more intent on listening for the
wind over the Lubbock prairies than on paying attention to the questions I
posed. Born and bred to the hard life of those arid farms around his city, he
writes about water going sour, or just going, and of old rusting pumps that

once watered cotton fields and now whistle under the northers. He described once how in flat country you can see an entire rain storm walking on water legs over the fields, the lazy gray haze that started the rain, and the big blue curtain that ended it—all in one form drifting slowly east to west at the horizon's edge. It was a powerful image and I haven't forgotten it. Water in those parched latitudes was as good as grace, I guess, and there is a lot of water sense in those small, neatly ordered stanzas of his.

There were poets I lamented not having; my efforts were diminished by not talking to them. Among those was Betsy Colquitt, who edited the journal *Descant* and was a valued source of information on the history of regional literature. I could never quite arrange to bring in Jack Myers, from Dallas, a fine writer and now a very influential one; William Virgil Davis, poet in residence at Baylor University, another poet I had neglected to my discredit. Miguel Gonzalez-Gerth, who edited the *Texas Quarterly* in its last years; Al Goldbarth, who taught at UT in the early 1980s, a brilliant poet; the poets of the UH writing school; and Willard Spiegelman, the editor of *Southwest Quarterly,* now a good friend. The list is extensive of those I had neither written about nor talked to personally. But I had read them and honored them privately: Stanley Plumly, a major figure then teaching in the creative writing program at the University of Houston, and the novelist and short story writer, and the voice of experiment in our state, Donald Barthelme. Max Apple was another fiction writer of great force, teaching at Rice University.

Jan Seale, a poet at Pan American University, eluded my grasp, as did Del Marie Rogers, and the Austin poet, Alfred Huffstickler, and a late friend, Joseph Colin Murphey, once the editor of *Stone Drum,* a remarkable journal published at Sam Houston State University in Huntsville. The list is long and painful to me, but the state is large and so is its population of poets and writers.

But one segment of "Poetry Southwest" stands out in particular in my memories. It was the day I brought in Dave Oliphant for an interview. He was down to read poems that afternoon, and I had reserved an hour or so for a radio program. I like Dave and have dealt with him on literary matters for many years. He is a fine editor and a craftsman in the designing of books; he is also a man of deep and inflexible convictions. Beneath the hard surface of his body was a furnace of raging contradictions. On the one hand he knew that the native mythology was important to the life of Texas, but on the other,

DAVE OLIPHANT. Photograph by Carlos Salinas

he saw himself as the conservator of the old Texas religion of prairie heroes
and pioneer living. He was from Fort Worth originally and told me he had
lived out on the edge of town where the Conestoga and prairie schooners
headed out into the grass seas of the open West. The vision of such brave
souls entering the void burned their footsteps into his mind.

His poetry had two or three forms, and his line, a bit slow and prosaic,
went along certain deep furrows. He wrote ballads and odes and memoirs
about the landscape, the ordinary people who grew up in the northern
towns; he had a good memory and a certain looseness of phrasing that allowed him to jaw slow, longish stories about the jazz musicians of Fort
Worth; the old swim hole and the boys who skinny-dipped there; he wrote
often about his Chilean wife, Maria, and about himself agonizing through
childhood and adolescence. The line was always literal, spare, without
strong images, without the Imagist thrust. He wrote like a yeoman Protes-

tant, with a sturdy sense of the preeminent self against a wide world of po-tential hazards, enemies, and strangers. His best book, *Lines and Mounds*, published by Paul Foreman's Thorp Springs Press, is a sensitive, bright ac-count of Indian mound buildings and their possible meanings.

Oliphant was a true man of letters, a historian, publisher of native talent, and spokesman for the literary arts. He was also a politician and knew how to get money out of the usually empty coffers of the arts foundations. His book of essays on Texas poetry, *On a High Horse* (1983), published by his own small press, Prickly Pear, is a panorama of the literary prairies. He wrote with passion and generosity about his friends in the book-length nar-rative poem, *Austin* (1985), reprinted with other poems in *Memories of Texas Towns and Cities* (2000), where I make a few cameo appearances, and with great reverence for the musical talents of the region in *Texan Jazz* (1996). He was devoted to the big voices in poetry, too, in particular Barney, whose *The Killdeer Crying* Oliphant had published.

But he did not venture beyond a certain point in his essays or his poems, the murky inner life of Texas people. There were doors one did not open in Oliphant's neighborhood. He refused to pry the heavy battens from the soul of poets. That was their secret hiding place, and what confusion reigned there or what erotic pains were heaped up, he didn't divulge. It was not his business. Oliphant tried to live as if the fluid spirit of a man or woman could not be put into verse or be subject to analysis. His art and thinking were blocked at one end, like the ordinary living one does in Texas.

Somehow Oliphant had clarified a most difficult notion in Texas belief: there was not so much a *soul* inside a human being as a self with some seeds of spiritual longing. The self, that leathery resilient organ tied by veins to the will and with a few nerve endings to the heart, was all there was of inner fur-niture. Like Cody, Oliphant was hard headed, impatient, and not given to splitting hairs over matters of psychology or of religion. There was a true and a false universe out there, and Oliphant's finger never wavered when he had to point out which was which.

It was not in Oliphant's vocabulary to say "the Soul selects her own So-ciety, then Shuts the Door," as Emily Dickinson once wrote in her house at Amherst. He would write about a man on foot in the wilderness, or a black man lifting his trumpet in a smoky dive in Fort Worth; he would show ac-tion or response, a day in a boy's life of physical events, but he wouldn't ven-ture beneath the skin.

For that matter, neither did Paul Foreman write poetry about the quick-silver of the spirit. He wrote poems like "Pecans," when Texans roll out of bed and grab up baskets to pick the fallen nuts as a rite of late summer. He wrote about redwing blackbirds and what his papa said about deer killing and snakes. He wrote love poems to his wife, but they were weather reports on the relationship, not interior voyages. The better part of the rustic po-etry of Texas, with its sensitivity to national changes, still kept to surfaces, to the outer world.

So when we sat down to my table inside the tiny studio space, with its egg-carton walls and windows looking out to production rooms, we faced off over a deep divide: a poetry of outward appearance and event, a poet-ics of mythological lava and spiritual labyrinths. I was well prepared for Oliphant; I had my strategies. He was smiling and a little nervous when the "On Air" light came on and I cranked up the show. After the usual polite chatter to warm him up, I told him I wanted to think out loud about Texas poetry a few moments. He nodded. I told him I thought that the rigors of male rearing in Texas killed off a lot of poetic sensitivity, and that only a very few boys in Texas grew up to be artists. I said I thought strong fathers and patriarchal football coaches played mischief with the growth of boys' imag-inations. That there was a macho cult in the region that pushed the femi-nine, creative side of men into an unused corner, and that the terrible story a lot of Texas poetry told was the suffering that young men endured in their childhoods. The poetry recounted in veiled lyrical imagery the torment of losing an inner voice of sweetness and curiosity, the voices of the body that longed for relation to the land and to dream worlds. The pressure to be men and heroes drove all that delicacy away and made boys think in terms of ag-gression and malice, and competition.

He listened with fidgeting fingers, and I would have gone on except there were signs of reddening in his cameo-pale face. He had strong veins in his neck, and his anger could flare up like a tornado on the plains. So I held my fire and gave him a pause in which to clear his throat and take over. He be-gan by denying everything I said; his own poetry had revealed no such suf-fering or boyhood trauma. His poetry was about the good people he had known and the brave things they had done as musicians, farmers, ranchers, and mere boys. He had folded his arms to all my inducements.

I waited for him to look up and let me speak. When he did, I said that I could find such poems in his books, if he wanted to debate the point. He wanted to debate. The smiles grew fixed. I asked him to read an excerpt from a longish poem about swimming in the Big Thicket. He began to read, but his voice wavered. He stopped and looked up in one of those rare moments when a truth will spring out of a dark place. He was an honest man, fierce in his faith, but deadly honest. He said I was right. He winced, and his voice rose a little and became very small. He read the words I had pointed to, about being a boy cut off from his own sensitivity, about being shorn of some part of himself to become a man. The pain was there; the hard outer skin of the adult male had covered the wounds. We were exposing the very cost of male transformation in the old mythology, and the hurt returned in his voice.

I had put my finger on the cost of solitude, and saw the eyes dim. It was an important moment in both our lives, with the producer looking on from his window at the two of us involved in myth talk. I don't know what we did after that. He read some more, and I pointed out, a bit callously, the other places where the trauma of isolation came into his poetry. He nodded or gave me a quick look and went on. It was enough to have struck ore once, and I suppose I shouldn't have gloated over it. But the moment sealed itself and Dave was himself again, resilient, sturdy, feet on the ground. Protected, and reconfirmed in the blood of the myth.

His very opposite is the poet Robert Bonazzi, whom I also liked immensely, still do. There was no particular Texas out there, no prairies or Indians or smoldering pioneer camp fires. Bonazzi was a spelunker of his own caverns, and a man turned almost utterly inward to himself. He had read widely in the French symbolists, the Spanish poets, had lived in Mexico for periods of time, absorbing the culture that had invented magical realism. And he was very good at writing his short, riddlesome fiction pieces, and at writing oblique symbolist lyrics. Bonazzi's realm was psychological and religious, and its peripheries were the distorted shimmering visionary world of drugs and imaginal flights.

When I wrote about Bonazzi, as I did for Tom Zigal's magazine, *Pawn Review,* I always felt his politics and historical awareness were buried deep in the silvery-smooth lyrics he wrote, often with their sense clipped off too short. You were always reading off into passages that ended in blank space or in the fingers that held the book. He loved to cut short poems that had "arguments," until the heft of a thought had barely a feather's urge to float on air. He edited other poets' work, mine included, and always the last three lines, where the "idea" took on wooden substance, got lopped.

The oblique mode had its limits, but Bob could not see them. He ventured further into that twilit horizon until his pieces began to take on the luster and fragmentation of mica chips and the sparkles of disturbed earth. The organic world had dissolved back into minerals and loose sand in some of his language. But all this obliquity is at the service of a larger, more encompassing end: the dissolution of the self, that leather-bound ego that has grown so hard and thorny in this region. He is the quiet dismantler of ego, and his inspiration comes largely from monastic life and the writers who are associated with it: Thomas Merton, John Howard Griffin. Bonazzi is a voice in the wilderness talking of redemption, esthetic and ascetic modes of recovery of spirit in an age of corporate oligarchy and epic egotism. "The Clown" is a good example of his recent work:

I feel yet disavow emotion.

Friends, neurotically complex, range
beyond any model for intellect.
Webs of thought evolve in what I read.
Mind's sensuality glows outside idea.

A mask covers the unfinished face.

The manic pursuit of the hunger traces
hysterical flights of prey. Duplicitous
inertia with its terror and paralysis.
The universe has no clutch.

Last night's ultimate drug: Space
without objects. (*Inheritance of Light*, 187–88)

Another of my close companions in the early days was William Burford, a more formal and polished individual from the higher world of Dallas society. Burford had gone to the eastern schools for his education, and carried with him the burden of a famous oil name in Texas, Skelly. (The Skelly gas stations can still be found in rural outposts of Louisiana and Texas.) His father was a formidable businessman who had married a Skelly and raised his son in a mansion on Turtle Creek. That luxurious pile of brick is now called The Mansion, a restaurant for wealthy blue-hairs and businessmen on power lunches.

One afternoon after Bill and I had got to know each other, he took me on a tour of Dallas and some of his haunts in Fort Worth, where he now lives. We stopped at The Mansion, formerly the 21 Club, and entered a crowded dining room at the lunch hour. Dressed in tweed jacket and linen pants, looking aristocratic, Bill showed me around his childhood home. Over the heads of the diners in his old bedroom, he pointed out where his bed had been, the bookcase, the toy cabinet. The diners looked up to see what manner of man had dreamed in this room where filet mignon was now being served. We left soon after, the prices on the menu being too rich for either of us.

Bill had schooled himself in the same symbolist poets Bonazzi read; there were common threads in their poetry, though Burford's was from an older school of lyric forms and language. He worked in condensed lyric phrases that reminded me a little of the work of his friend James Merrill. There were Greek allusions, and delicate frills here and there, and paraphrases of Baudelaire, Verlaine, Heine, Rilke. His study (a guest house near the main house on a hill that was once a farm but was now covered in bungalows) is crammed with beautiful art books and studies of Greek culture, histories of poetry, a large collection of magazines where his work has appeared. I was billeted there when I came to read poetry in Fort Worth. We sometimes shared the venue, or just hung out together.

Our days were often spent analyzing the skylines and curious architecture of the northern cities of Dallas and Fort Worth. Burford came from money, but it puzzled him as much as it did me. The myth of gold and power seemed odd to both of us; we were esthetes, poets, mythologists, and the money cult bore some riddle we could not quite solve. Once we stood gazing over at T. Cullen Davis's big estate, shortly after a scandalous murder had occurred, talking for an hour about the isolation, the artificial cosmos of the rich. At another time, we strolled the grounds of the Kimbell Art Museum, figuring out how Louis Kahn had imported all the details of the slaughterhouses of Fort Worth into the design of the building, to let the rich know their loot had come from the blood of animals. He had hung the French impressionists under the jagged roof lights that were modeled on the stockyard corrals, with cinders lining the garden plots, the same cinders that lay heaped on the rail beds at the stockyard entrance. Later, he wrote an essay for the *Fort Worth Star-Telegram* outlining our whole day's discussion in beautiful prose.

"Poetry Southwest" had moved me from my scholar's stool into the world

WEDDING DAY OF JAMES CODY AND JEONG JA, AT CENTER

of the writers. I spent much of my time in the apartments and small houses of Austin poets, kibitzing on literary matters, getting my nose bent in a few feuds, and eating the lean meals served by my sometimes indigent colleagues. Chuck Taylor ran a bookstore in the warehouse district of the city, and he kept one of his rooms a little more airy for readings. There, in late afternoons or on weekend mornings, someone would take to the linoleum floor and read the latest draft of a poem, or talk about the "sullen art" of poetry to which we were all wed. The faces there, bearded, slender or creased like a walnut shell, represented a cost of years and penury for the joy of writing.

Many of those faces appeared one day under a gazebo near the Colorado River to celebrate the marriage of James Cody and Jeong Ja, who had come in the full wedding regalia of her native country, Korea. The two strolled along toward us under heavy skies, Cody in dark suit and tie, wide-brimmed hat, with his wife in kimono, sash, bright colors streaming down her shoulders, her hair done up in an amazing black shape with pins and ribbons. A white shaman had come to perform an Indian ceremony in which we all partook, including the smoking of a long wooden pipe. Those many faces under the gazebo that day were captured in a photograph, preserving a moment in which the bards came together, staring out from a world the general public knows nothing about. The photograph later hung on a wall in Cody's El Paso apartment, the image remaining the same as the bards grew a little older and fatter in the gut.

On the shoulders of these and other writers, some more fashionable and successful than others, lies the burden of articulating the state's spirit. It is a heavy task, and hardly a normal soul would want to push aside his or her regular pursuits to face the terrors of the blank page. The time will come, I suspect, when more of the public will begin to take an interest in this neglected art. It is interesting on its own merits, and compelling once the basic rules of the poetry and fiction are learned. The dialog that goes on daily in the arts is fascinating and bears on the making of attitudes to come. The written word wet on the page is tomorrow's figure of speech and the next day's cliché. The formative substances of reality are first handled by the poets, and then given to the general public.

When I stayed with Cody in El Paso in 1995 to attend a memorial service for Ricardo Sánchez, I studied the photo of the bards under the gazebo at Cody's wedding. It was a funny picture, oddballs gathered together in a heap, with braids and weird hats, and floppy poor folks' clothes, and a few in white shirts and jackets, tired eyes and droopy faces, a few smiles, some children peeping out among the legs of the elders. It all seemed like a collection of Amish farmers and their wives, or Quakers meeting in the colonial days of Philadelphia. They were misfits looking out from an hour in a day in Austin. The public was jogging or working in the offices, or driving on the Mopac and I-35 freeways to malls and appointments, and the poets, beleaguered band of radicals and dreamers, were collected for the purpose of celebrating a cross-cultural marriage.

These were the forecasters, the people involved in bringing thin air and hunches into words, coining the phrases and the images that might possibly texture, complicate, balance, counterweight the monolithic structure of most thinking. When New England gave up its monopoly on culture in the United States back in the middle nineteenth century, recognizing New York and now the Middle Border as the centers of change, the poets had done their work. Emerson, Whitman, Dickinson, Thoreau, Margaret Fuller had all had their hand in shaping the air into beliefs, into visions of the American character. One might say they invented the American with their pens in Quincy, Boston, and Salem.

The writers I knew were not as fortunate as the Transcendentalists of New England. The job was not to reinvent the American character, but to react to, and sift the grains of desert sand for myths belonging to the Texas character. How this was to be done or by what new strategy of literary forms is still a matter of ongoing discussion. The grim confessional urges of a writer like Marion Winik, or the bitter satires of R. S. Gwynn, rimed and outrageous broadsides against literary liberalism and egomania, might be auguries of the future. But so might be the mythological pastiches of John Campion's poetry.

My quest for Texas bends now to three portraits of writers who have been raised in Texas from birth or who have come to the state seeking a kind of sanctuary in which to absorb old myths. The first portrait is of a white woman born and reared in Houston, witness to the growth years of Texas cities and to the power of money: Vassar Miller. The second portrait is of the African American playwright Charles Gordone, my late friend and colleague at Texas A&M University, who came west to find the cowboy myth and to revamp it to his own creative uses. My third portrait is my reading of the life and struggles of a Chicano poet from El Paso, Ricardo Sánchez.

CHAPTER 10
A PORTRAIT OF
VASSAR MILLER

For more than thirty years Vassar Miller composed poems and sorted them into various collections; nine books of poetry appeared in that time. Though she has drawn an appreciative audience to her, there has been little serious criticism of her writing. Fellow poets certainly admire her, but even so watchful a guardian of Texas poets as Dave Oliphant has been more vigilant and supportive of the work of William Barney and others than he has of Vassar Miller's. In *On a High Horse: Views Mostly of Latin American and Texas Poetry,* Oliphant counted Miller along with William Barney and William Burford as a "first generation" of Texas poets whose "poetry [is] of high seriousness and is marked by linguistic power and a mastery of traditional forms." Later in his essay "Generations of Poets," he remarked that Miller's style of the 1960s was influenced by "the confessionalists Sylvia Plath and Robert Lowell," for whom Oliphant has little enthusiasm, but he is quick to stress that all three poets "creat[ed] their styles and ideas independently, and that either they preceded certain trends in the '60s or carried on an existing tradition after a wholly regional manner" (113).

Oliphant published Miller's poetry in several of his anthologies, in *The New Breed* and again in *Washing the Cow's Skull,* but his scrupulous honesty compelled him to admit that Miller is more like the invading "émigré" poets, with whom she is frequently associated, than she is like the native bards. She has not been "concerned with region," which to Oliphant is the principal subject matter of Texas poetry. He has shown an unswerving devotion to a core of native writers who have made regional life in Texas their chief concern.

In these asides, Oliphant explains why he has not been one of her stauncher supporters. But the irony is, Miller has been passed over by critics of national literature because of her regional tendencies. She has found herself in the middle of the main extremes of literary taste; she is neither broad in her grasp of politics and social issues nor local or literal in her sense of belonging. For that reason she has eluded the attention of critics for many years and would have continued eluding them had not Larry McMurtry brought her to sudden notice in his scathing assessment of Texas literature, "Ever a Bridegroom: Reflections on the Failure of Texas Literature." Nevertheless, McMurtry made Miller important, and everyone wanted to know who had saved literature from itself.

Having castigated both the living and the dead for failing to write estimable poetry and fiction, McMurtry reserved the close of his remarks to "reverse my thrust and pay tribute . . . to the one Texas writer for whose work I have an unequivocal admiration: that is, Vassar Miller." Though his praise is indeed unequivocal, the example of Miller as the one unspoiled achiever says less about Miller's poetry than it does about McMurtry's powers of homily. Her virtues are that she works "in the hardest form—the lyric poem," where she has achieved "excellence: the product of a high gift wedded to long-sustained and exceedingly rigorous application." Her work is "hard-won, high, intelligent, felt, finished, profound." Some twelve of her poems, McMurtry says tauntingly, will "outlast all the books mentioned in this essay, plus the 50 on A. C. Greene's list as well" (*Range Wars*, 39–40).

It would not have been lost upon his stunned audience that the one figure for whom he reserved praise is a religious writer, whose work had all been in the least marketable form of writing, the "lyric poem." Though their attitudes toward Miller's work may be opposite, Oliphant and McMurtry both admire her evident craftsmanship and have used similar language to praise it: "high-seriousness," "hard-won, high, intelligent, profound." And indeed it does not take a reader long to realize that her poetry is full of lucid phrases and cleanly organized stanzas of argument. Her poems have a worked surface in which rime scheme has been rigorously tuned and sustained; her techniques are not those of surprise and finesse, but of anticipated fulfillment of pattern and function. The poems are rounded off, fitted together, sturdily joined—like that of good cabinet making. The hesitations of voice in her best poems have been removed, to leave behind a flow of precise, unwavering declaration, like that of Emily Dickinson, whose style Miller's poetry most often resembles:

Death we can manage,

. . . .

But this our mind
can scarcely handle,
too heavy even for our tongues

lacking decorum
to shape this rawness
which must make up its own words. ("Improvisation," from *If I Had
        Wheels or Love*, 253)

Silence and the unknown appealed to both Dickinson and Miller. Many
of Dickinson's poems are about falling through the final "plank" of reason
into unknown voids, to "finish knowing then," or to discover that "[m]uch
madness is divinest Sense." She describes herself as "the little tippler," and
seems to drift near the edge of consciousness for her subject matter. Indeed,
armed with the limpid grammar of neoclassical prose and the aggressive
rhythms of Charles Wesley's hymns, Dickinson felt sufficiently protected to
explore the dark fringes of rational life.

Neoclassical English, on which Dickinson's and Miller's lyric simplicity
are grounded, is a powerful instrument for articulating dilemmas and
emotional crises; its roots are in Elizabethan prose, but the Puritans had
pruned back the lavish wordplay of Shakespeare, Lyly, and Donne to create a modest though flexible medium in which to sort out the affairs of
newly urbanized English life. Its practicality and aggressive syntax
enabled Addison, Steele, Johnson, and Pope to teach their nation of villagers how to live in a city. Its simplicity and sober logic were effective
means for a woman writing in Puritan New England as it awoke to the
modern era.

Coming more than a century later, Miller's situation is less bleak, perhaps, though even here, one must pause at some intriguing parallels between the two writers. Cerebral palsy left Miller in relative isolation; society
might well seem as intimidating to her as it did to an agoraphobic Dickinson, in its intolerance of physical debility.

But the closest parallel is that both women witnessed deep shifts in their
regional cultures, as rural life gave way to urban civilization. Though attracted to its novelty and potential freedom, each had been formed in the
image of the old order and could not escape the pattern of her life to participate in the new. Their powerful energies were thwarted and driven to a
subliminal level of lyric self-analysis and reverie, to indulge in imaginary

experience that reflected the real one outside. From their private vantages, they could coolly anatomize events as they unfolded and perceive the dangers as well as the pleasures of their tumultuous eras.

Their resilience partly derived from faith in strong men, whom they found in their fathers, in potential lovers, and certainly in religion itself, with its powerful ministers and patriarchal deities. Their worship merged sexual and spiritual desires and satisfied longings for a paternal authority in their lives. In the interim of a century or more, it is possible to see in Dickinson's work a profound reflection of region and local character. Her miniature lyrics resound with the thumping meters of Sunday service hymn-sings; her common-sense logic is one with the Puritan merchant's practicality; her fascination with an "outside" world of sensations and natural phenomena was shared by her neighbors and is in thin disguise a "frontier" beckoning to her. Her primary subject, pain, was the real core of experience in her life; it gave her a body, a locus of mystery and myth, and a threshold into nature.

It remains to see how the clipped measures and the fervid religious yearnings of Miller's work reflect conditions of the Southwest and illuminate the situation of a woman writing in Houston at midcentury, just as Texas was waking from the torpors of its long neglect as an outpost of the nation. From her vantage in the 1950s, she watched the transformation of Texas from rural to urban culture, and though she disapproved of much of the hubbub and raucous wheeling and dealing, in which her father played a significant part, her observations have the same ring of truth as do Lexie Dean Robertson's poems in *Red Heels* (1928), especially the sequence "Boom Town," which chronicles the days of the wildcatters farther west.

Though never explicit, Miller's poems hint at the spread of Houston as the business center of postwar Texas. Even so, the "frontier" was a lingering presence of Texas life; as it receded into memory, its passing was loudly lamented in popular music, western painting, folkloric studies, and in fashion. The dying out of the old ways was met with sentimentality and protestation, aimed at the encroachments of the city and its leveling of such cherished ideals as self-reliance, independence, freedom to live apart. The ranch was a compact symbol of American transcendentalist notions—a unit of individual worth, a sovereign principality of the ordinary soul.

These thoughts circulate in Miller's earliest poetry and give her imagery and metaphors the tanginess of southwestern life. The very idea of movement is a struggle for her, as she remarks over and over again in early poems, such as "Epitaph for a Cripple":

Feet that, floundering, go
No way of your own will—
Numb with eternity
You now have gained your goal.

Fingers writhed from weaving
Like crabs with claws torn loose—
You mold in your unmoving
The perfect shape of peace. (*If I Had Wheels,* 15)

Clearly, motion itself, that force of migrating people, is here braked to a near halt, and her commentary on her body's disabilities is a kind of rueful twist on the heroic narrative of the westward movement. The poem concludes:

Body, wry reproach
To athlete mind, lie down—
Your lubber's limbs here couch
Graced with the state of stone. (15)

Wilderness is a pure thing diluted and corrupted by human values. To name it was equivalent to prayer; it raised the spirit of the ancient purity of America. In "Love Song for the Future,"

Deer and bear we used to stalk,
We would spend our dying pains
Nestling you with mouse and hawk
Near our warmth until it wanes.

. . . .

Loathed no longer, learn your worth,
Toad and lizard, snail and eel—
Remnants of a living earth
Cancelled by a world of steel,

Whose miasmic glitter dances
Over beast's and man's sick daze . . . (50)

Wilderness is many things to Miller, but chiefly it signifies fertility and innocence. It is the "womb's dense grove," a thing near death, since it is in jeopardy, and therefore the "whir of wings . . . called from the dusk of death"; love is "elusive like the wind," "fugitive like air," a "vitalizing breath out of nature." Loneliness is "a small beast from the woods / made a pet,"

> which, when it grew up,
> for all that they had coaxed it with words or with work,
> would turn wild again
> and tear them
>
> though it had worn
> the shape of their loves. And though they might kill it, they
>   wore
> its pelt like a mantle
> fallen upon them
> from a vanishing form . . . ("Heritage," 78)

Nature is the transcendent thing, the collective unconsciousness in many of her poems:

> The leaves blow speaking
> green, lithe words
> in no man's language.
>
> . . . .
>
> . . . the leaves
> breathe through me all men's
> in no man's language. ("Precision," 75)

Nature is, in fact, something asleep, below language and outside the range of logical category or rational grasp. It is Eden, "[w]here flesh and spirit dance, / Shadowing, bound yet free" ("Belated Lullaby," 97). Lovers take the form of "two arrows bound together / wounding no one" in "Regret" (87). It is the opposite of "the desert of the day," though she will describe urban monotony as "marshes" and "flatlands of finitude" where desultory life plods on mechanically.

Outside nature is a realm of things and ways belonging to adulthood, which Miller dismisses, except for the sexuality that is a link to nature.

Adulthood is rationality, conscious defense and aggression, an outlook altogether destructive and manipulative, opposed to the will of other things:

My flesh is
the shadow of pride
cast by my bones
at whose core lies cradled a child tender
and terrible . . . ("My Bones Being Wiser," 107)

The bones are rooted to the wilderness of the unconscious, "beneath the dark waters of my blood . . . huddled together, / rubbing themselves," to become later the "bundle of faggots / ready for burning" (106). They form a sort of cane brake in which the infant soul is hidden, though the mind elsewhere lives on in the adult world of indifference and skepticism. The bones are wiser because they live in nature, "the womb's dense grove" ("For a Christening," 46), apart from "the swirling sand dunes" ("A Dream from the Dark Heart," 108) of ordinary consciousness. "O Lord," begins "De Profundis," "defend me when I go / Through the dark in daylight . . . when snowfalls of words melt in / deserts of my deafness" (153).

In a later poem, "Seasonal Change," she calls her imaginal life a frontier between adult urbanity and primal nature: "I have built a home / On my edge of existence," having lived too long in "[t]he temperate climate of unconcern" (252). In another of her later poems, the argument against the ordinary world is put very pungently:

Light, whose limping whisper was thought,
snagged upon inertia,
knotting into lumps. ("Fall," 265)

"Light, descending from self-contemplation" becomes a heavy film over the senses, "matted to matter, clotted to shape" (265). Adulthood and its residence, the city, are the subject of "Whitewash of Houston," a breathless tirade on the city as defiled mother (based on the etymology of *metropolis*, where *metro* means mother and *polis*, city), "driving all her children dumb/down the long chute of death and safely home." In Part II, the "mother" is remembered in the pre-war days of small-town Houston, where the imagery shifts to fertility, "her apron smelling of summer" (243). A similar treatment of the city appears in "In Quiet Neighborhoods":

Now that watch fires are out, monsters tormented,
murdered, lassoed, confined to dull extinctions,
caught on our barbed wire kindness, the wild moon
Diana no longer, merely rock admired
by men who skim its surface, lumbering ghosts
found more miraculous than myth or fable—
no sheep may safely graze our savage lawns. (261)

For nine stanzas, this poem rebukes the "feast of lights" that "forbids the famished / from our tight doors," locked against a night in which "the darkness swells with grace and judgment" (262–63).

In these and many other poems, the city stands for corrupt experience and loss of vision, and nature for the "vanishing forms" of innocence and imagination, the very things McMurtry roundly denounces other writers for saying. As he remarked in "Ever a Bridegroom," "virtually the whole of modern literature has been a city literature. From the time of Baudelaire and James, the dense, intricate social networks that cities create have stimulated artists and sustained them. No reason it should be any different in Texas, since we now have at least one or two cities which offer the competitions of manners upon which the modern novel feeds. [But] where has this experience gone? Where are the novels, stories, poems, and plays that ought to be using it? Why are there still cows to be milked and chickens to be fed in every other Texas book that comes along? When is enough going to be allowed to be enough?" (*Range Wars*, 19).

As if to rebut all this, Miller's poem "Liebestod" opens,

If I could merge myself into the country
Of trees and shrubs and where the air flows pure
Over my head, so battered by the sentry
of fixed identity,

.   .   .   .   .   .

But steel-gilt buildings, hidden less each mile,
Sprout blooming pallid hues of the horizon,
Tall toadstools delicate with dawn—and poison. (*Wheels*, 275)

McMurtry's essay is interesting not for damning with faint praise, but for confronting the most basic issue of Texas writing: its passion for nature and rural life. In this, Miller would appear to be the more sure and correct of her position as a writer in renouncing the city and embracing agrestic values, and for encrusting her arguments with symbols of primal nature.

McMurtry appears to fumble the question and turns against his own readers as retrograde in their tastes and expectations of literature. "Part of the trouble I am afraid, lies with Texas readers, who, if my experience is any indication, remain actively hostile to the mere idea of urban fiction," he writes. Artists who succumb to their demands show "intellectual laziness." "The result," McMurtry concludes, "is a limited, shallow, self-repetitious literature which has so far failed completely to do justice to the complexities of life in the state" (*Range Wars*, 19, 21).

But Miller's poetry suggests that nature and rural life are, in fact, a response to the city, though in ways less demonstratively overt than McMurtry recommends. Her poems are in line with the major post-Romantic tradition in rejecting industrial urban culture and in finding vitality in things belonging to an undefined prior world. Her equation of nature with the unconscious, with primal instincts, with freedom of emotion goes back to Blake, Coleridge, and Wordsworth; nature and the old ways are the source of youth and strength. Debility and corruption lay in the city, in commerce and competition. The ideal of purity is a young man or woman raised close to nature, and who thinks like an animal, with cunning, shrewdness, and keen senses.

The "city" stands for the thinning of blood. The separation of man from nature withers vitality; like the myth of Antaeus, whose mother was earth and whose touch revived his powers, man is strong only in the presence of natural things, and he is vitiated by their absence. The "tenderfoot," "greenhorn," "easterner," and "city slicker," "the man in the three-piece suit," the dandy, are images of desiccating urban life, the diminished powers of the human spirit when sequestered in artificiality. These caricatures populate the satiric fiction of southwestern literature from Mark Twain to Sam Shepard. Miller's canon is steeped in these prejudices and idealizations common to southwestern art. Indeed, her views of the city are reinforced by much popular culture, particularly western music, with its laments over lost customs.

Though the image of cowboy has long been cheapened and exploited by the nostalgia merchants, beneath the tawdriness of the "urban cowboy" and the dance halls, the dude ranches and western wear outfitters, is a heartfelt conviction that one is rejuvenated by symbols of Old West days, and a grain of youth is imparted to the person who retains some small part of its memory. But it is the youth longed for that makes these fragments of the western past cohere to express a regional ethos. There is a richly developed myth of youth invested in the image of pioneering on the western plains, of living on small holdings, driving cattle, and camping in the wilds. As cities spread, they compelled a more emphatic expression of this myth—as a means of coping with and accepting the losses and changes that accompany the transformation of southwestern life.

The almost universal preoccupation of writers and artists with the passing of the old ways, notably in the plays of Sam Shepard, involves more than artists bending to the will of their audience. Such artists not only have a compelling subject matter but also a pretext for exploring a psychological landscape, a mythic sense of place. The dissolution of nature in everyday life is a commentary on aging and on death itself. The city's inorganic symmetry and amorality are features of a counter-mythology of age and experience. The "urban cowboy" is a figure who has joined the ends of paradox in himself, and his decadent and erotic nature are signs of ruined youth, squandered energies.

Miller's poetry ignores obvious southwestern symbolism and goes to the issue behind it, youth itself. Freedom and creativity are deeply felt when she slips into the voice of a child, to relive a memory of her childhood. The "child" in her poetry is the most insistent of her repertoire of voices. "Once as a child I loved to hop," from "Adam's Footprint," and so on through the years. Her affectionate addresses to her father are from the child: "to my comfort as my father's stir / In sleep once solaced my child's heart" ("Though He Slay Me, *Wheels*, 66).

> . . . you cheat me of my anger
> with your gentleness,
> making my thoughts children
> that sit around you,
> flowers wilting and waiting
> the dews of your attention. . . . ("Conquered," *Wheels*, 69)

Hence, the bones "at whose core lies cradled a child tender and terrible," and the merry child's voice in "And":

> and poems sprouted out of my skin
> that slap-happy time when I dreamed love growing
> on trees as money doesn't . . . (176)

In "Cycle," one has the theme of rejuvenation pure and simple:

Never love went

more naked to bed than when
my body shrugs off
logic's gold sheath

in the black irrational . . . (185)

Youth returns in "Lying in Bed Late," when

I keep the darkness locked behind my lashes
To seed my flesh with sleep, my head with dreams,
Pulsing to melody within my blood,
Making my stiff bones burgeon like green branches. (189)

In "Insomniac's Prayer," "dreams jump out of my skull / like pictures in a child's pop-up book" (188). In "Transmogrification," renewal lies in being a thing of nature:

I am rooted
into rocks that lie
in cool absolutes of sleep.

I stare puzzling
over the difference
between my feet and this earth. (217)

"I grow from my poems / in a green world," she writes in "Raison d'Etre" (224). Poetry and youth are one in her work. To think is to return to youth; the natural state of childhood is that pre-logical awareness where purest freedom is, but for the last time. Awakening to this freedom occurs when her father brings home a typewriter, remembered in "Subterfuge":

. . . bearing it in his arms like an awkward bouquet

for his spastic child who sits down
on the floor, one knee on the frame
of the typewriter, and holding her left wrist

with her right hand. . . . (289)

"Wild Child" is her equivalent of "cowboy," with whom "we shoo death away" (293). The child's realm is furnished with a mythic tiger, a luxurious forest, and other reminders of the wild origins of the species, when life was undivided from nature. In "Summation," she describes aging as

> . . . loneliness
> being the dew that melts
> in solitude's sun,
> since I have discovered
> the court of my childhood
> burned down, the halls of its
> approval collapsed, and
> have come home to myself
> here in my homemade world. (294)

The relation of poetry to youth is summed up in "When the Living Is Easy," where she notes "the poem is outside me, . . . like a child tugging me out of my sleep" (303). Of death, Miller says in "Prayer to My Muse,"

> I'm none too sorry,
> longing to be back
> coiled in my wombworld,
>
> too smug and small, I know,
> no wider than my bed
> where no one sleeps but me. (308)

Religion in Miller's poetry has deterred some readers from a full appreciation of her work. But its theme is inextricably bound to her vision, and to dismiss it is to misjudge the complexity of her thought, or the breadth of her sensuality. Close readings of her meditations reveal an unorthodox, even problematic relation to Christian belief. Miller's faith, like that of other artists of strong belief, is passionate and creative, again, like Emily Dickinson's, who once wryly asserted,

> Some keep the Sabbath going to Church—
> I keep it, staying at Home—
> With a Bobolink for a Chorister—
> And an Orchard for a Dome—(Poem 334)

and like Flannery O'Connor's, with whom Miller also identifies herself (compare "Affinity," *Wheels,* 254). Her tradition of writers includes Thomas Merton, Teresa of Avila, and E. B. Browning; there are tributes and dedications to Mary Magdalene, the Virgin Mary, Joan of Arc on the one hand, and to Helen Keller, Anne Sexton, Marianne Moore, and even Sophie Tucker on the other. It would stretch things to say there is a common denominator here, except for the obvious one that all have strong convictions and talents. But this tradition suggests the idiosyncratic nature of her awareness; her faith is neither institutional nor casual, but a root of her creativity.

Her faith can be simple at times, as in the poem "Morning Person," which opens "God, best at making in the morning, tossed / stars and planets, singing and dancing" (250). It is a child's vision, but it holds a clue to her other uses of religion. In "Exorcism," Miller makes a connection between her father and religion:

Father, glum ghost of Christmas Past,
if you are anywhere around,
I hope you are propitiated,
old Christmas-hater! (256)

The identification of parent with God occurs whenever she puts on her child-persona, where innocence permits her to voice all manner of thought, especially sexual longings. Combining hints of incestuous devotion with religious ecstasy, she reveals an uncensored craving for love voiced in religious images:

My tears at Silent Night smoke upward,
orgasmic shivers

along the spine of Midnight Mass . . . ("Exorcism," 256)

"Rest, rest," she tells her father, "ghost, childhood's god" (256). Christ and her father are interchangeable suitors in her dreamscapes, and redemption can be confounded with rape, seduction, with "the dream of being broken into": "come, Savior of / us, the ungentle, Holy Thief of night!" ("In Quiet Neighborhoods," 263).

Her father is "a second sun" ("Against Daylight Savings Time," 264), and "Light," in the next poem, is "God's pseudonym, / ground from the guts of sun" ("Fall," 265). Even Eucharist has sexual connotation; it is a primal act, the taking of a divine lover. The usual decorum attendant upon communion "would distract / From this resplendence of the naked act" ("Dining Room Eucharist," 267). The "mystery" of Christian revelation is "over our heads and hearts," she writes in "The Inescapable Day," "like a child's pajamas" (269). Faith is a path back to youth; its figures and principals form a landscape of the memory of childhood; to enter one is to enter the other, where she is blamelessly whole and primitive.

In an impressive sonnet sequence entitled "Love's Bitten Tongue," which closes *Struggling to Swim on Concrete* (1984), she remarks on her faith:

> Of praying may (in mercy become prayer)
>
> My backward journey be—Christ, teach me this!
> This trek begun and left when, hope to spare
> I saw ahead a new metropolis
> All burnished brightly with an innocence
> Now peeled the same as paint from ancient houses . . . (*Wheels*, 276)

Religion's "backward journey" is psychological, a descent to the preconscious where holistic thought is once more possible. Religion is her childhood vision of the world; hence, the male gods who crowd her thought and desires become one with her father, "[a]s His old daughter toddles safely home to God" (276). Though religious eroticism is nothing new to poetry, Miller's devotions capture the polymorphous eroticism of adolescence, one of the depths of religious ecstasy:

> Here where these white-headed trees
> blanched by the cold desert sun
> open upon rosy rock
> nippled and cocked toward the sky
> stabbing my eye with its gaze. ("Approaching Nada," 229)

In sonnet 22 of "Love's Bitten Tongue," her frankness is keen and earthy:

> So You have opened me to woe and wonder
> Much sharper than woe, far keener than pain
> Pitching the techniques of thought that might pander
> To the gimmicks of mind, but split open mine
> That prays, "What shall I do, Jesus? How deal

With those flesh-splitting throbs, pain, dread, rapture
Which rupture my being drooping and dull
To the literal Word, ecstatic scripture?" . . . (284–85)

Though Miller has changed denominations, she has stayed within the
Protestant faith, which is itself a bond with her region. The Protestant
denominations swept over Texas even before it separated from Mexico.
Protestantism broke the Spanish Catholic stronghold on the region and interrupted a long reign of medieval absolutism and aristocratic social control. The evangelical churches that first penetrated the territory were mobile,
autonomous, and appealed to the free-thinking pioneers. The earliest con-
gregations were the first townships, villages, social units on the empty landscape. Religion is profoundly wedded to the rural past of the state; the
revival of Christian religion since World War II goes hand in hand with renewed interest in early southwestern life. Religion and the old ways possess
the same attractions to the urban Texan: through faith, one literally revives
the past and the youth that clings to its memory. The very term "reborn"
suggests this rejuvenating thrust in southern and southwestern religion.

The modern church, though vastly different in style and attitude from
the way it was in its rural beginnings, can still recreate the village atmosphere of early Texas through church suppers, socials, baptisms, and other
unifying events. For Miller and for many others, religion is a "backward
journey" to a mythic origin. Miller's vision is wider and more daring than
that of the ordinary believer's, but she has not departed from the concept all
share alike: that in religion, one makes the descent to innocence and youth
and submits willingly to being a child again within a congregation, as a minister assumes the role of father. She enriched the vision by adding to it the
rest of the pristine landscape of adolescence that Henri Rousseau, Blake,
and Wordsworth earlier celebrated, and that Dickinson voiced:

"We'll talk all night until we swoon away," you promised,
friend of my innocence and of no more than that,
the only rule allowing for such talk. ("Eden Revisited," *Wheels,* 266)

Miller is bound to her region and transcends it; she shares the fears and
prejudices of her countrymen, and her artistry bears the same careful
craftsmanship to be found in country quilts and ranch-house carpentry.
But there is a knowing sophistication in her use of her materials; she orders

them with a wise simplicity and a grasp of their importance. Her body was her instrument for perceiving the reality around her; if it caused her pain and unbearable loneliness, it stood for the land around her as much as it was the covering of her bones and soul. She could read Texas through each effort it took to move or to stand, or to speak. Somehow that encoiling of a sick body around her tongue gave her the insight into the land's inertia and slowness to respond, as well as how human beings can cause such pain by their reckless disregard.

She joins other poets who have been posted at the border between country ways and the rise of cities; her themes are the losses involved in change and how one copes with them. But her greatest achievement seems to be that she gave the women who wrote before her their triumphant moment of clarity—she articulates their pains and consolidates them in a body of elegant, flawless statements, leaving nothing or hardly anything unsaid to the world.

CHAPTER 11
A PORTRAIT OF
CHARLES GORDONE

Charles Gordone, a playwright I knew, died in 1995 of liver cancer. He was seventy years old, a black man with a little Cherokee and some Irish and Cajun in him, and the first black playwright to receive a Pulitzer Prize for drama, in 1970. In 1987, he came south after a wandering life in film, television, and laboratory theater, sick from alcoholism, and beaten by his own early success. He had won big on his first play and then felt himself lifted off the ground into stardom, where he dried up, recoiled on himself, grew fearful that he was only a Johnny-one-note. He was a born actor and had appeared in notable films, among them *Street Fight* (1975), a hard look at ghetto violence and gangs, and a slew of TV serials, where he had talking parts, sometimes more than that.

He headed to the Southwest after stints in New York and California, dried out several times, a wandering sort of Bojangles of the boards and a man who turned deeply inward and quiet after shooting his wad. He brought along his white girlfriend, Susan Kouyomjian, a black-haired woman from an old line of Armenian people, whom he had met at a theater in Berkeley. They laid low at first; the university he landed in was an old military school on the central Texas prairies, with values buried deep in the cotton bottoms of the Brazos River and attitudes honed and fierce as flint chips and Confederate swords.

He was a man of polished skills; his smile was direct and open, with a certain theatrical ease about it. He had several personalities, each devised over years of working in white theater communities on both coasts. He knew how to get along, how to play the game, how to step around the heavier egos in his path, and still achieve something of the broad, unsculpted vision he carried in himself.

It was not until his death, when the obituaries appeared in the papers, and some conversations I had with his companion, his "life-mate," as he called Susan, that I learned some of the details of his early life. He grew up in farm courntry around Elkhart, Indiana, home of Steinway pianos, and early on took after his cowboy grandfather by wearing Stetson hats and boots to high school. When told there were no more black cowboys in America, he replied, "Well, there is now."

He was a track and field man for his high school, and he knew all about having to stay out of restaurants while his teammates went in to eat lunch on their road trips. He was given a different hotel if they stayed overnight. He knew he belonged at one level of society, the level that used his running skills, and did not belong at another. The other, the disconnected level, left him solitary and rejected, and he learned much about human nature in those hours when he was told to stay outside while his teammates enjoyed their meal.

Gordone was neither black nor white, but a man at the center of all the races in America, in whom Europe, Africa, and Native America merged. He *was* the melting pot, if indeed the country ever actually was one. But Charles found out that America was fearful of mixed races, and imagined itself as white; the truth said otherwise, but American values rested on the culture of England, and on a religion of the personal soul bathed in rationality and self-interest. It had no use for groups, or the tribal religions of Africa and Latin America.

He bore the same ingredients "Injin Charlie" possessed in the story "Belles Demoiselles Plantation" by George Washington Cable. This old man is related to the Creole family of the de Charleus, but he is a "dark white man," in Cable's words. His animal cunning triumphs in the end, and the pure-blooded Creoles lose their place with the fall of slavery. Gordone was also from Louisiana Cajun blood; his relatives "turned left," he said, when they headed north, winding up in Indiana. But he had his blood mixed in the Deep South and carried that with him into the polarized world of Indiana, where he discovered you needed pure racial credentials to get ahead. If you were black, you should act white. But Gordone refused and found himself shut out of everything but sports.

The unfinished democracy of America covers only part of the population; if you are not of the accepted majority, you get torn on the jagged edges of a half-created country, like the characters in his play, *No Place to Be Somebody* (1969). There was simply no room, no structure to include "the others." They stood outside, having been told there was "no room," "no seats," or simply "no service." In the land of plenty, the "other" was subjected to hidden scarcities—and was told to go away. The play's protagonist, Gabe, recites a poem on negritude at the start of act 3, which ends,

Bein' black has a way'a makin' ya mad mos'
Of the time, hurt all the time an' havin'
So many hangups, the problem'a soo-side
Don't even enter yo' min'! It's buyin'
What you don't want, beggin' what you don't
Need! An' stealin' what is yo's by rights!
Yes! They's mo' to bein' black than meets the
Eye!
It's all the stuff that nobody wants but
Cain't live without! (80)

His dramatic skills developed in high school, since he lived two lives growing up. An outer one smiled, adjusted, competed, tolerated the injustices that sprang up at him on the road, or when he entered town. He met the calm, half-hidden anger of racism in the slowness with which he was served or given his change. He knew enough to stay in his own neighborhood and to go to certain restaurants and stores where he could expect to be treated decently. The inner man smoldered, had already a certain reckless anger and resentment. Where it could go to get out of his system, he did not know. He chose instead to disguise the real Charles behind that lucky smile, the becoming, easygoing personality he was perfecting.

Another side was forming in secret, and it was like the private personality many black men in America have, a covert self that spoke rarely, never showed its true will or mind to outsiders, and either fueled a powerful imagination or talent, or became pure grief and violence. It is a dangerous self, volatile and yet fragile, easily wounded or smothered. It is like an Achilles' heel, a soft place that, once exposed by some setback or difficulty, could become a thirst for self-annihilation. Charles would stumble into alcoholism, eventually, when things got over his head; it would eventually kill him, since death came through his liver.

But in setting out, he had ambition. He must have felt that a highly coordinated body had given him confidence—he could move gracefully, he knew how to use his body to express thoughts otherwise inexpressible: forms of joy, forms of rage that words only distorted. He was light, very tightly strung to his bones, and therefore almost without gravity when he moved. He seemed to balance on a high wire when he walked, placing his feet evenly on an invisible axis that took him where he thought he wanted to go. New York was waiting for him. He found himself there, almost too quickly. He was pursuing a dream; he knew he was not the first black man to come to New York in search of a stage, a role, a power to move audiences. He was part of some procession of people who could not be deterred. Farming was dead, so there was no going back if he failed. He had to lay everything he was on the table, one big wager on the future.

He studied acting with Lee Strasberg and Elia Kazan, and writing with Langston Hughes, he told me, though the fact did not show up in any of the biographical accounts. He said Hughes was a stern teacher, and taught only by the principle of his own hard work, which the young writer took to mean endless hours of rewriting. Hughes was not only a perfectionist of the line and phrase but also a man trying to convert a white literary tradition into black jazz. How to skew the language so that it became all flats and sharps, and sounded black—in the rhythm of the phrase. That was Hughes's lesson to younger writers who knew about the Harlem Renaissance only from books and courses on the subject. The real work of poetry was taking Shakespeare's sonnet and twisting it into a trumpet solo, in order to "explain and illuminate the Negro condition in America," he once wrote. Hughes's manifesto is contained in his 1926 essay, "The Negro Artist and the Racial Mountain," where he wrote that the burden of every black writer is to explore the "soul-world" of his own people. Hughes would tolerate nothing less than a complete inventory of American negritude, and Charles was his stubborn apprentice.

Hughes's principles were hard to accept, especially for a young man who never quite saw himself as a volunteer in the racial wars in America. Charles was a man of crossed bloods, and he thought he could live a sort of unbounded principle of equality as a man between races. When success stormed him after the opening of *No Place to Be Somebody* in 1969, he began to fight the critics who wanted to lump him in with the Black Panthers, the Black Power movement. Gordone quoted contemporary slogans of the civil rights era in the play, but he also mocked the protests and picketers—they merely polarized the races by demonstrating. What lies under the racial anger of the play is a desire to erase the false or imaginary differences between blacks and whites. He did not believe in "black culture," or any ethnic culture; these were illusions of a weakened people looking for pride in any form. There was culture, and it cut across color and religious lines; either something was humanly interesting, or it was not.

Gordone wanted to explore the "American chemistry" of race, its slow, almost immeasurable blending process, more akin to events in geology than to sociology. Any population was a kind of meltdown of differences cultivated elsewhere; America was an open arena, a force field where the human atoms clustered, combined, radiated energy, fought, but could not invent a way of being that was significantly different from other ways of being. That was Charles's belief; he was a dogged preacher of it. He scoffed at O. J. Simpson's pleas for sympathy because he came from the ghetto. He had little interest in those playwrights who wrote only for white audiences, and assumed only white middle-class people came to plays. When he was with Susan in Berkeley, their projects were to stage old Shakespeare classics with people from various races in the leads. A black Hamlet, a white Othello. Why not? Susan was artistic director and watched with a kind of awe as Gordone swept through old formulaic dramas and unzipped them racially—he let fly. He wanted to blow up the old race myths embedded in such fortified dramas as the Greek tragedies, the Elizabethans. If he could pry them open, he would be continuing the work of *No Place,* in spite of the blockheaded critics who read the play as race anger and race pride.

The critics of his play kept working the theme that *No Place* was a glimpse into black rage from a disaffected black man with a machete for a pen. That critical reception forced Gordone to speak his views more plainly, as in his article in the *New York Times,* "Yes, I Am a Black Playwright, But . . ." (January 25, 1970), in which he wrote, "In the last analysis, I do believe there never has been such a thing as 'black theater.' What is called black theater has, as it should, come out of the civil rights movement. . . . The commercial theater—the Broadway stage—has depicted blacks in sensational and stereotypical ways [without] showing any interest in the black experience. Not yet, in my time, and it is my time that I am most vitally interested in." He was just as adamant twenty-five years later in interviews, such as the one conducted by Susan Harris Smith, included in *Speaking on Stage: Interviews with Contemporary American Playwrights* (1996): "Because I'm a playwright of color who does not write black plays, I've experienced some isolation. I don't write exclusively for blacks. The scholars who put together anthologies don't know what to call me, but that's their quandary, not mine. I personally see that not to be categorized is an advantage for any playwright. If I've been made to pay a price or experienced any negative consequences, I must also say there is a tradeoff in not belonging to either that makes it possible for me to talk to all. As a consequence I'm able to create characters from a whole spectrum of American people. It's been an essential part of my work" (170). But did that mean the theater was open to "American chemistry" and that black playwrights were now free to engage in a racial dialog? Gordone's answer: "We are still bound up in a racist tradition. Many folks in the theatre have seen things a certain way for so many years that it's difficult to integrate a lot of my thoughts and ideas because traditions are in the way. It's very slow. I know there are many parts of the country that are behind, behind socially, and the children did not experience any of the civil rights movement or know much about it—they're just ignorant no matter what color they are. The answer lies with the playwright: every problem does not have to be a Caucasian one." As for regional theater, it "isn't doing much of anything," either, he observed in 1995, the last year of his life (170).

Charles was essentially an actor, later a director. It was while he was performing in Jean Genet's *The Blacks: A Clown Show* (1960), first Off-Broadway and then on the road for six years, with a cast that once included James Earl Jones and Maya Angelou, that he conceived the idea for a play. Genet's "ritual" theater portrayed the inner and outer life of black people through the metaphor of a circus, with magic tricks, surrealistic events, a kind of "mind" theater, if you like. Gordone's participation in this nightly ritual hatched a sequel, a more earth-bound rendering of American black consciousness, with its seas of anger boiling up and over the seawalls of the plot. The play went through innumerable drafts, after Hughes's example; when he finished it, or thought he had, he was invited to a party in Greenwich Village and left the manuscript on the subway. It would take him another year to reconstruct *No Place,* but in the process, he learned compression, simplicity, the direct line. It was a better play, and eventually found its way to Joseph Papp's Public Experimental Theater, a kind of laboratory with only 109 seats. Papp gave the play to a twenty-four-year-old "very WASP director," Ted Cornell, a Yale Drama School student, the very opposite of Gordone, whom Papp described as "barefoot, bare-chested and pigtailed, looking more Iroquois-Chinese than African" (*No Place to Be*

Somebody, ix). He paid Gordone one hundred dollars for production rights and put him to work as an assistant director.

When rehearsals were over, something magical had overcome the cast; the play was hard-edged, the talk snaking out of controlled fury; the subject was blackness in all its forms, overlapping and including the white world surrounding it, and the suffering, the rage, the frustration underlying every black man's existence. The white college girl comes in for a drubbing; she is sensitive, a liberal, but she is unlived, an innocent tied to high crimes and political corruption through her father, Judge Bolton. "Chemistry" is everywhere; Shanty is white, and works for Johnny, a tough black bar owner, who in turn has connections with white mafiosi. The prostitutes are white and black, and take their tricks over the race line. Everything is mixed up in the play, and yet blackness remains a constant, a measure of racial unhappiness in New York, and America. The play sets out to teach the audience, which was also mixed at each performance.

When the play debuted, the house was packed and the response brought the critics around. Usually "experimental" theater means amateur, wispy sorts of expressionism with lots of soggy monologs; this play erased the distinctions between drama and the conflicts out on the streets. The play was moved to the Public Theater complex, with a much larger seating capacity, where it ran for two years before going on the road with different companies. Gordone directed the play on three national tours over a period of seven years (1970–77), then it was translated into several languages and went abroad. It got mixed results, but in Italy, France, and South America it went over big. "It's a question of mixed bloods—a problem of mixed bloods," Gordone said. "In France they're up on Franz Fanon and Genet," by way of explanation of its success there (*Speaking on Stage,* 169).

The form of *No Place* was born in a mixed-blood Algerian-French homosexual ex-con's mind, that of Jean Genet, whom Jean-Paul Sartre subjected to minute scrutiny in his biographical epic, *Saint Genet: Actor and Martyr* (1963). Sartre was looking for the threads of criminal genius that would explain the workings of unconscious civilization undergirding France and western civilization. Genet's homosexuality and colonial blood gave him a nuanced second identity as the "dark man" of Europe, which in turn made Genet a special interpreter of the American black—the bona fide dark man of the New World. Gordone: "Genet's *The Blacks,* which I acted in for six years during the sixties, created on stage the reality that was beginning to alter America outside the stage door. So as we performed this ritual each night, it became a way of comprehending through drama the rapid changes" (*Speaking on Stage,* 169).

No Place to Be Somebody takes place in Johnny's Bar in New York City, where a young playwright, Gabe Gabriel, Gordone's alter ego, introduces himself to the audience by balling up another page of his troubled play, which he is typing at a table in the bar. He is in the company of prostitutes, a destitute drummer working part-time in the bar, a short-order cook named Mel who was studying dance, and a few other hangers-on in a dead-end world. Gabe is slowly drawn into the criminal depths of Johnny's life and ultimately has to kill him. In the course of the play, Gabe sings, harangues, orates, and recites poems to the audience in long preambles to each act. He has the final lines in the epilogue as well, where he stands wearing black mourning drag, a widow's black shawl slung over his shoulders, as he sums up a dismal history of blacks in America, which he hopes is coming to an end, "a dying into that new life."

The play is at once old-fashioned thriller, minstrel comedy, slang, jive talk, a procession of prostitutes and gangsters, Mamet-style bullet-fire dialog, and bits of sentiment all draped over a plot of degraded life under the iron heel of racism. Strains of the current world come into the play from Black Panther slogans to the chants of Vietnam peaceniks and civil rights protesters, white girls hoisting pickets, and crooked judges making deals with the local mafia. Gordone threw into the mix everything he had observed in New York over the ten years he had been living there—a microcosm of races and money lust and violence, churning at the heart of the most powerful city on earth. His reading of the social order? That it was deeply blighted by the failures of the social experiment in equality—but that something would come of it, if idealists like Gabe could live long enough to act, write, and preach the gospel of hope—as Gordone himself set out to do.

Walter Kerr hailed Gordone in the *New York Times* as the best playwright since Edward Albee. The plaudits were overripe and were squandered in an attempt to link this play with the cresting of black liberation movements. But the text does not align well with the age or the social context; it has to do with a sort of cowboy mystique of the independent spirit set against the feudalism of American money. *Midnight Cowboy* owes an unconscious debt to its vision.

From that vantage point America was a visible landscape of terrors and craggy deeps, where the old spiritual energies of the New World were being incinerated. But the success of this first entry into the big time caused my friend Charles to go blind and stagger back wondering where his voice had gone. He had awakened the giants to the smell of money and the demand went out for another big hit. But the birth of a man's sense of himself had been fully stated, and the story, at least for now, was over.

I don't think Charles knew the full burden of his situation until much later; he must have felt that a play would form in him if he were patient with his energies. He waited, and I have to say something else took over: the need to fill out the personality of a winner others expected to find in him. The actor came out; the energy to write got channeled back into the energy to perform. The play became his daily life, and the sequel everyone waited for was being premiered in private apartments, bars, receptions, speaking gigs, director jobs, as the path outward into the world kept opening under his feet.

As the story goes, and there are several versions passing around, he wandered out of New York to California to try Hollywood, and the result, while not a complete flop, got him up to the bar too often. He became a lush and a hack TV writer, and the punishment of those years writing piece work put the seed of death in his body. He redeemed himself by going into the provinces to direct small theater productions, always with the intention of promoting multicultural, intercultural, cross-cultural visions for the audiences of inner America.

Charles had walked away from the New York theater world at a time when, according to his own statement on the matter, theater was becoming factionalized, turning into a Bosnia of ethnically pure domains of white gay theater, feminist theater, black radical theater, feminist black theater. He would have none of it, but a man who walks away from the roilings of his own society to keep to a vision, is doing lonely work. The world does not come with you. Walter Kerr is reported to have put his hand up to his eye to scan the horizon, asking in his column one Sunday, where has Charles Gordone gone after such a bright beginning? The *Times* obit recalled this ironic salute and kiss farewell from America's critic, as if to suggest the cause of death was artistic failure.

Charles wandered America like a modern Ishmael in search of his patrimony, his real home. There is the stuff of myth in his life, but he was not conscious enough, he did not do Langston's homework sufficiently to piece together the odds and ends of a personal myth story. But it was there, latent, buried, half revealed in his wandering footsteps and lonely childhood. "Well, there is now."

There is a book on Dogon statuary, *Art of the Dogon: Selections from the Lester Wunderman Collection* (1988), showing the reaches of the black mind into the depths of human vision. Among the figurines photographed in lush brown tones are men on the backs of various horse-like animals, from herding days on the African plains. The little terra cotta and wooden effigies are cowboy amulets, and Charles needed one back in Elkhart. There were lots of black cowboys in Africa, and the truth about cowboys in the Old West, as everyone now knows, is that the job was so dreadful, dark, painful, and lonely, only the bottom dogs of America flocked to the ranches and signed on with the outfits. The job fell to the mixed bloods and the free blacks and renegades and white fugitives. The trade was rough and without heroes, and short-lived, but came of an old tradition belonging to ancient African gods and some extraordinary bull gods out of Mediterranean culture.

If you are looking for manhood and your place in life, a four-legged animal and the prairies are the instruments by which men across time have found them. A black man from Elkhart, Indiana, was on the right track, grabbing at the vestiges of an archetype from the deep layers of male history; he just didn't have the right sources to instruct him in the rituals. But he was hurting, and his imagination had been wounded by a success that had come too easily. If Charles had not found this basic myth of the masculine psyche, he would have died earlier.

Charles knew that a man's redemption lay in finding the pieces by which he becomes whole and ordered in himself, and the gist of the rite involves a beast as magic and soul work. The beast is his own desire, his rages, his revenge against the elders who would crush the life out of him. The rage of *No Place to Be Somebody* is that of a young brave attacking bears in the guise of old spiteful fathers. The fathers are always trying to kill the sons, and the brave proves himself by striking some fierce equation of the father in the wild, with his bow and a quiver and nothing more. Kill something big and you have moved onto your own ground, defeating the first fear of men in the world, their own sires.

The father is not well defined in Gordone's writing; we have the son in fury, the son in flames, the son cursing and kicking his way against invisible enemies, against the odds. Johnny comes close to a father image by always flinging dollar bills at Gabe, and at Mel, too. Sometimes Shanty gets money from the till. And it is Johnny whom Gabe will eventually shoot—out of love, as well as anger. The next step is the turning of anger into creative force, the mounting and gentling of a creature that is the animal mask of the rider's soul. And for Charles, the task was daunting and unfinished. He seems to have lost the second stage of male deliverance, the mounting of the beast, and let himself go to seed instead.

For the rest of his life he wandered around trying to get to the second phase of the myth of deliverance. He had to find his steed, and the barstool was no substitute. Nor was a director's chair, though it came closer to the idea, if only in the form of making other actors project *his* energy, *his* vision of a set of events. The actors became a combined beast prowling a stage, moaning, emoting, meeting up with the small gods that theater brings down out of the flies to modern audiences. It gave him solace to direct, to act, and then to teach.

The play is the oldest religion; it has to do with waking up out of the animal spirit and becoming human. It has to do with severing from the mother and taking on the burdens of the man to come. Its purest emanation is that of Oedipus, who solves the riddle of the sphinx by saying it is man that is mortal and fated to die. He leaves the animal dream world and the gods are angry at his pride, his desire to be free of the natural world. He breaks out, the first fugitive, the first humanist.

Gordone wrote his own Oedipus, someone who had not killed the father but only a substitute, and not a very good one at that. Gordone also depicts a black man who has come out of the woods to be a man in the city. He almost makes it, if he isn't caught first and thrown into prison. That was Charles's read on America, and it went the opposite way of most readings by black writers. The more common view was that the black man suffered in nature; he was the victim of agriculture, which made the city an artificial place where day and night merged and seasons disappeared. The black man looked to the city as salvation from the taint of being the "natural man," but

Gordone saw the city as poison and death. As the cowboy poet Buck Ramsey recalled in an article entitled "A Revival Meeting and Its Missionaries: The Cowboy Poetry Gathering":

> Charles frequently discussed with his new companion [Susan] his belief that the aspirations and happiness of black Americans would remain trampled and shattered as long as they continued to be caught up in urban chaos with its utter degradation of soul and psyche, that a people could not endure as a viable American tribe if they remained packed a way in city ghettoes. He told a friend in the autumn of 1995, "The notion that black people are at their roots country people really raised hackles when I talked about it with my old friends in the civil rights movement. Now, as a Westerner, I believe the thwarted instinct of African Americans for a dignified involvement with nature is the biggest cause of their problems. Making them realize their heart's true habitation is not urban is a simple idea, radical in the true sense of the word, and seminal to everything I have become as a thinker and artist in the last decade of my life."

The West was the land of redemption, the place where the Mithraic myth of riding the beast was the older and deeper form of deliverance, the archetype of male becoming. Gordone's vision lay at the edge of Hemingway's, though they were at different ends of the racial spectrum. But because Gordone did not mount the beast and engage the next step of the myth of himself, he did not know who he was. The bull had become a minotaur in the labyrinth. The descent to find him came in the form in which many writers engage the beast below, through the bottle. I don't know how severe his problem was; it was serious enough that once he renounced it, he never went back. And he returned to New York to start over again, according to his own statement, recorded in 1995 at the Gene Autry Museum in Los Angeles. He says he went back to Harlem to pick up the pieces, to find the path.

It didn't work, and when there was a chance to go west once more, not to the coast but to the West of myth, he took it. He found himself in 1987 a resident writer on a D. H. Lawrence fellowship near Taos, New Mexico, with nothing to write but with everything to consider. He was shaken down to his essence once more, a man exposed. Susan was with him and they spent the time walking, looking at sunsets, fussing at the typewriter. He was stalled, but he was not idle. He was working, but the work went on in the depths. He was dredging up the second stage of himself, and the part that he had to accomplish to get on with it. He would never finish the task, but the sheer immensity of the act of a man at sixty-two preparing to chase down the beast and climb onto its back for the ride of his life drew all the courage and resolve he had.

When he came to Texas A&M, in our sprawling prairie campus, he came quietly, settled into teaching in the Theater Arts program, and came up to see the rest of us in English. We occupied different floors of a large building then dominated by the business college. He was working his magic on the students; the plays were better performed and he was getting his farm kids and city girls to forget their southern manners and get down. They got down. They got so fundamental at times he ran into the Christian orthodoxy of his department. They balked and thwarted his plans, and finally he gave up and came over to us full time.

That's when I met Charles, when he moved into an office across the wall from me. I could hear him through the thin partition laughing up gales with his students. He was the original anti-intellectual teacher/writer, and he put students on a raw edge of their lives. He dared them to open up, and he had the brass, the strategies, the raw nerve of New York acting days to get them to come half way. They peeled open like ripe fruit. He had a way with them that was so potent and instinctual, only the hardest refused to burst forth like yaupon after a spring drench. I didn't realize at the time that he was opening himself through the process, writing his own redemption, you might say, through these young actors, who were, in effect, playing parts of his life. The playwright never stopped composing.

He created an atmosphere of loud talk and laughter that is the mark of actors, the sign of having passed through the repression of America into the emotional open. They were very loud, the kids in his office, howling unnaturally at his jokes, emoting with so much energy and force that it all seemed faked, theatrical. But he approved, and the magic, if that is the word for such difficult cases, seemed to work in them. They carried themselves differently as creatures coauthored by Gordone. The rest of us carried on in whispers and sober looks, while Gordone ranted and told jokes and cursed and threw his boots up onto his desk and told his admirers to get loose.

They did. He did. And the professors around him frowned a little in disapproval. Somehow the liberation he was performing for students ran counter to orthodoxy, and though it was a mark of one's liberalism to nod appreciatively, secretly, discreetly, a disapproval had begun. Gordone probably didn't notice, or if he did, he chose to ignore it. The more important thing was this slow procedure of unlocking the boy in Elkhart and doing it through the very tight, locked-in young white students who melted when they were around him.

Repression is an odd and pervasive disease in America. It comes of being young as a country, with an uncertain and explosive mix of human beings from five continents living together in an uneasy truce of religions, races, and sexes. The tension is everywhere, and the truest theater lies in the streets where cars bully and overtake each other, run stop signs, speed up behind slow movers, and blast horns and shine bright beams, all to vent frustrations of a repressive, overly docile population. The street is where the strains are let out and people become anonymous boors. Against such pent-up energies and passions Gordone moved carefully, keeping to himself, choosing his friends from outside the department and the community.

Gordone was a study in powerful talents and an unfinished intellect, a man who seemed caught between the demands of the physical body and its needs, languages, symbolism, and racial history, and the mind, with its remote worlds of moonlit thought, its silence, its labyrinths. He was dubious about the mind; he tended to express a low humor and a sense of utter disregard for the intellectual pride of people around him. He doubted the intentions of intellect, especially among black writers and activists. His anger came out at the mention of people like Henry Louis Gates, Jr., Imamu Baraka, Malcolm X. These were writers who fought back against racism with race pride, reversing the labels but not the logic of eugenics arguments, claims to racial purity, and the like.

As the mixed man of his times, Gordone seemed to think that any argument about race would end in disastrous extremism. The mind was sick, or an undependable voice inside the body. The body spoke through dance, gesture, laughter, crying, shouts, but not through the high-falutin' structures of argument. Arguing provoked fictitious landscapes and invented cases in order to win; the body seemed to loom out of nature and could speak only of the organic world—of what held people together as animals in a food chain. Myths were important, but humor was the most crucial aspect of Gordone's tradition, the one he saw himself continuing through his own work. The laugh I heard through the thin walls was in part a denunciation of the falsehoods of learning itself, and a way of venting the body's heat and emotion. The laugh is our equivalent of a bray, or a hoot, or a howl.

Laughing joined us to the carnival world of Rabelais and Chaucer, Aristophanes, and the antics of crows and mockingbirds. The laugh leveled pride and posing; to laugh was to express the nonracial, universally animal dimension of human existence. And he laughed a lot.

This is the Charles who showed up in the department in his cowboy regalia, half boots and western shirt, a wide-brimmed hat raked low across his forehead. He was show biz on the outside, even if he knew what he was about in private. Susan certainly did; she applied her energies toward helping him to discover the various cowboy poets now performing to huge audiences in Amarillo and Dalhart, and in Elko. She got him interested in their work, made sure the poets knew who Charles was. She cleared out the underbrush between an urban Charles rusticating in central Texas and the last of the prairie bards working ranch jobs in the Panhandle and out on the great western plains. They met, talked, saw their common ground, and after a time, though still cautious with his friendships, Charles let down his guard and began to see a connection between his own work and what these men were trying to save of the old mythology.

We are talking about a process of bridge building in which one part of the span juts out from Elkhart, Indiana, sixty-odd years ago, and the other begins in Elko, Nevada, in about 1990, when Charles and Susan drove out to a cowboy poetry gathering. At that point, according to a biographical statement he wrote himself, Charles had completed drafts of a new play, "Roan Browne and Cherry," about a bankrupt rancher and his half-Indian daughter, and two black ranch hands. Red, white, and black. It was the essential three-way channel of blood lines in America, the ultimate colors of the republic. Charles Olson, the poet on whom I have shed much ink in my professional career, a founding spirit of postmodern poetry in America, once received a Guggenheim for a project he called, "Red, White, and Black," the story of race and diversity in America and how they were poisoned. He never wrote it; it was an epic requiring another Melville, some new American Homer to complete.

Gordone was fitting together his bits and bobs of the epic in his own way, with redundant coloration in Roan Browne and his bright red Cherry. They were, in truth, the colors of his own pulse; he had found characters at last in whom to discover his own makeup. What happened to them would be the riddle of what he was making of himself now. He went out to Elko to learn more about his characters, he said. He didn't know enough about how they thought, or felt, or acted to be sure which way to put them through strife and resolve it.

If Charles could have broken from the whole of western drama's tradition of conflict as the expression of character, he might have liberated himself from the impasse he was in. He needed some primordial rites to guide him into the recreation of self. He needed black religion out of Africa, and Indian religion out of America, to write the play of characters representing parts of a man coming back together without violence or tears. Was it not Alfred Adler who said the soul can only speak through the wounds of the heart? It seems to say of western people that they have so buried their gods in the earth and so removed their hearts from daily life they must bleed first to become forthright and passionate. Charles Gordone needed to reinvent drama from its roots in religious ritual, and to eliminate from its structure the archetype of conflict as the path of renewal. Something as fundamental as love and desire for unity must replace the heart of drama if he was to succeed in expressing his soul. But he could not imagine it; drama was life, and life was bitterness and conflict and, ultimately, despairing resolutions.

What Charles heard at the cowboy readings was a kind of men's choir singing to honor a way of life in the grasslands, among the jayhawks and coyotes and the spiritual winds that blew down out of the vanished Indian world. The poetry spoke to an order of relations between human beings and the mystery of an unknown continent lying under its veneer of settlement. They were laments, and poems of praise, and ballads of ordinary heroes set to a cantering meter with a little male sweetness in the language, some nostalgia, a code of loyalties and affections for a life apart from the hard glare of Amerika. The Indians call their chants good medicine, and Charles, after a long life of questions and blind ends, got some good medicine from the boys in Elko.

Charles was hatching a new play to be called "Ghost Riders" behind the unrealized potentials of "Roan Browne and Cherry." It was only an idea sketched in the roughest form out of materials that Robert Downey worked with in *Putney Swope* and Mel Brooks spoofed in *Blazing Saddles* two decades before, only now Charles was going to merge both into *High Noon,* and cut deep into a myth world of film stories. Somehow a black man on the run would show up in the corrupted center of a western town and confront the greed, sloth, and degradation of its white lords and do it all in a gun duel on Main Street. The black man had taken all the blame for the dark side of

America long enough; Charles wanted to write his play, across the very same screen that had projected white redemption in the western wilderness. He would design a hero to go right into the cut-out of Gary Cooper in the movie posters. His hero would be the black man come of age, a free spirit in the same basic wilderness in which white men had shown their mastery of instinct. Legendary western heroes from all races and all periods would join him, the "Ghost Riders," and cheer him on to free the town of its own degradation. This new Charles, the name of his protagonist, would give us the next stage of Charles Gordone as the black man in possession of himself.

When Charles asked me into his office one day to show me the paragraph he had written about this project, I was intrigued but doubtful. It was only a paragraph, an idea, but a good one, a hook into something. I wish I had known then what I am writing about him now, for I would have embraced him on his victory. He had locked onto the myth of himself at last. He was going to write in the black man who mastered himself through the horse he rode and who manifested his personal order by ridding the town of its corruption. If a black man could redeem white society, the race story in America could come to a close and a new story would begin. It would be the "dying into the new life" Gabe had predicted.

The western film, the horse opera, the oater, cheap as it is, doggedly repetitive and formulaic for an intolerable number of decades, strewn with phony heroes and villains, is one of the deepest registers of the American psyche. It gives us the two tests by which a man can be said to have entered the world: self-discipline and protection of the community. So far only a white man had played the role.

Now Charles wanted to cast a black man in the starring role. It would be Africa that came into the New World to declare that nature was not the enemy, nor was the dark skin of human nature; the real enemy was the mind's fabrications. A black man's natural passion would liberate the body in the New World, and restore the community that once existed between indigenous life and wild America. This was what the cowboy poets sang about, a male despair over the wasted blood and passion that ended in the loss of natural wonders. Gordone's idea was the sequel Walter Kerr had been anticipating. It was twenty-five years late in coming, but it was coming if Charles could live long enough to write it.

The poignant downbeat of his last few months is his attempt to rally from a sickbed to get to the airport and out to Dalhart, on the Texas Panhandle, where the cowboy poets had arranged for his use of a ranch house on part of the XIT ranch, a legendary spread in which to write of the black man as a hero. Friends rallied to him and drove him to Easterwood Airport in College Station, propped him up to wait for the boarding call, only to find Gordone fading again, asking to be taken home. The flights were canceled several times in succession, and Gordone would sit in his house wondering where the next chance would come from. He was determined, but failing. Susan kept him alive and goaded him gently. "The woman is driving me crazy," he told me pathetically in his hospital bed one afternoon, when I had come to visit.

I visited him several times, each time having to draw a deep breath and steel myself at the sight of a man shriveled to the ghost of his former sinewy body. The athlete had faded away, and a kind of Gandhi emerged, bones and skin, a face of shadows and caves, loose eyes, wandering mouth. The style had lifted, and behind it, under the façade and the bravura, under the hundred layers of masked identity and soul, was the only man left. Illness and impending death revealed what appeared to me as my brother, who had died similarly twenty-six years before. Illness exposes the common underlying humanity in each of us, and in the rubble of Gordone's dying body lay the very bones and skin, the innocence, the lamb-like Christ suffering alone. For once, Gordone seemed someone I knew, or could know. He was vulnerable to my questions, and I felt for a moment the man was me.

Charles was smaller, weaker, frailer, less imposing than the actor, the sexy, driven, hard-edged, weary Gordone of better days. He was a deeper self, and I cannot help but think his urgent, impassioned quest for self was perhaps a blind alley for him. The real man lay in a kind of giving up, surrendering to illness and to the America that seemed to have killed him off at his prime. If he had given in earlier, put down his powerful pride and anger and allowed the worst to happen to him, perhaps he would have disappeared into oblivion. Then again, he may have found a more simple and natural conduct, and a voice to embody it, one that would have seared our hearts. Instead, we fought him because he was fighting so hard himself.

At the memorial service on campus held a few days after his death, a gathering of faculty and students filled a good part of the chapel. A long list of speakers with formal statements got up to show their love, admiration, and friendship for this very private man. I sat in the back listening to these words on his behalf and had the uncomfortable feeling that Charles had fooled them all. They each boasted of a different Charles and thought of him in the very clichés in which he had styled his masks. It was laughter from Paradise to hear such groping and desperate eulogies.

With the formalities over, the audience was invited to speak in its own turn. After some rustling in the seats, one of Charles's former students got up to say she had been touched deeply by a man who gave her confidence to write. She labored for her words, her face soft and tear-stained. Her voice broke several times, but she got out her testimonial of a man who had awakened some sleeping soul within. She felt his honesty, she said, and it made her come to her own senses. She felt passion for the first time, the thrill of her own honesty. Other students said as much, as twenty more rose and spoke their brief, tearful thanks.

They made an unwitting chorus of straggling voices, but their text was not about art and making, but about the loneliness of their lives. Charles had probed down under the glitter of the average Texan, with his or her new clothes and bright smiles, the clean, abrupt thought, the varnished sense of God each carried around as the sign of ultimate individuality. Perhaps Charles challenged the very notion of what it is be a self, or the costs of individuality to these lonely, empty youths. They were told an education and a job were the ends of life, and Charles had showed them this was not enough. The heart went begging in such meager aspirations, and the love of others was denied by the man or woman who aspired only to a suburban ranch house with a two-car garage. It was not enough, not sufficient for the making of America. And certainly not a wise trade for the loss of the primal land and its call to the soul.

The man had left his legacy in the form of these young whites coming forth to speak without shyness about their need for spirit and creative acts. They had been transformed from mere grasping middle-class kids into something like wakers from a dream. Charles had shot his cap gun in the air and challenged his followers to join him in the great drive west. How far they will go to reach their own grassland visions is a hard guess. Most will wander away into the jobs that swallow up the imagination in America. A few will persist, get down about their lives, straggle along; a few will die hoping. Maybe one of them will get as close as Charles did, with a paragraph in which the germ of the answer lies in opaque syllables, a few lines of prose where the mythological moment holds its fire.

The day of his death, Susan told me, Buck Ramsey (who has since passed away) called and asked if Charles needed anything. Charles was quiet, and Ramsey sang him a song of the river, the water flowing down to the sea and dissolving into its great depths. Charles listened quietly to this voice singing to him over the telephone. In the afternoon, with the sun slanting through the bedroom windows, he let go at last.

Afterward, Susan dressed Charles in his ordinary cowboy clothes, a frayed shirt and his old jeans, and put a black Stetson on his chest. In his pocket she put a sea bean that grows in South America, she told me, and must travel the whole course of the Amazon down to the sea before its tough jacket opens and a seedling springs forth. The men from the funeral home were both cowboys and promised Susan they would honor him as a fallen brother. They folded him in an Indian blanket and took him away. When his ashes were given to Susan, she went out to the Panhandle for the burial service. The poets were there and brought a riderless horse with Charles's boots turned backward in the stirrups; his ashes were scattered in an arroyo, and in the soft windless evening, with the sun pink in the amber sky, the ashes lifted like a ghost into the grasslands.

CHAPTER 12
A PORTRAIT OF
RICARDO SÁNCHEZ

Ricardo Sánchez came into my life in the mid-1980s. Gravel voice, a beard scraggled on his cheeks, receding brow with thin dark eyebrows and heavy, deep-set eyes, their gaze penetrating and powerful. He bore with him the aggressions of a man who had served time in both the California and Texas state prisons for various felonies; he knew his enemies, he sized up strangers quickly. His mouth was large, expressive, with a look hovering uncertainly between a scowl and a smile. He was powerfully built and heavy in the chest, with a stance that came of long years growing up tough in a border town. He was not easily fooled. But he was vulnerable, and he was hurt deep down. He was a man who could never spit up all the anger in his belly, and he would die of abdominal cancer, a terrifying analog to the rage that swirled in his soul.

Sánchez's poetry is a study in the salvaging of two broken languages. The English of his day was a medium for expressing the empty generalities of government ideology and the disillusionment of writers. Rosmarie Waldrop, a poet of considerable daring and experiment, began her career by declaring that "the poets who are seriously dissatisfied with our conventions of language (and do not just take this attitude as an excuse or because it is fashionable) are working at the borders of the unsayable and unknowable. They are trying to explore the areas bordering pure spirit or the void, unformed matter or energy, and their realm of 'things' considered as having a self-sufficient being alien to man." Her manifesto, called *Against Language?* (1971), is a diatribe against the exhausted state of English in the early 1970s, just about the time Sánchez came onto the literary scene. Waldrop was sounding the call for a new poetry, soon to be called "Language" poetry, which promised to blow up the orders of English and to start over again, from the rubble and "border" states of a new language.

Spanish at the time was the medium of sentimental histories and political accommodation to the ruling elites, or the soured and disenfranchised tongues of the poor and outcast. Dwelling in both languages, mixing them according to a formula of hot Spanish and cold, polysyllabic English, Sánchez extended the powers of a regional patois, but his was a dialect of paradox and of internal fractures; its diction bore all the ruinous potholes and fissures of a disintegrating social discourse.

Sánchez was at the threshold of a shifting center of gravity in the United States, an era in which minorities were rising to create their own forums in the Watergate era, and a time of doubt, self-accusation, and disillusion among the leaders of the white majority. He knew this and tried to exploit its vulnerabilities, and yet his own hopes and fears created complex emotional ambiguities in his use of English, which he both loathed and admired. In effect, Sánchez was a poet overwhelmed by the historical and psychological conflicts of the languages he tried to craft into an epic on equality. It couldn't be done.

His situation is not unlike that of Chaucer's in the fourteenth century, or Dante's in the thirteenth, when the ruling languages were in decay and new regional dialects of Italian and English were forming. Each writer threw in with the new vulgate and drew on the energy of a people liberated from imperial oppression. The Italian of Dante's time was sweet and clear, rich in the odors and sounds of Florentine Italy, logical and sturdy without the stiff formality of imperial Latin. Chaucer's English, born of Norman French and Latin roots, was fertile in the rough Anglo-Saxon monosyllables adopted by Celtic tribes. For both writers, the dialects were speech held in trust by native peoples. But Sánchez found himself an epic poet without a new dialect in which to articulate the common faith and trust. There was none.

Instead, the raw border Spanish he used growing up in the barrios of El Paso and later in prison bore the character of a rootless, excluded migrant world. The condition of that limbo was not unlike the situation of the Roma in Hungary and Romania, a people driven away, disenfranchised, denied their civil freedoms or the simple dignities of a place and a right to work. The Palestinians have suffered a similar fate; so have the Irish under nine hundred years of spiteful British rule. There was something worldwide and archetypal about the border Spanish underclass of the American Southwest, something epical and tragic, with roots in the origins of racism and human territoriality. And yet the blunt, colorful speech of this peasant dialect, ground down by a century of poverty and social rejection, had not flowered into a wild shrub. It had remained in the shadows of a larger Spanish of more settled culture to the south. This was *pachuco* Spanish, a tongue spoken at the fringes of white civilization, slurred, harsh, acrid in its humor and cynicism, fatalistic in its outlook.

It would take enormous affection and courage to lift such a tongue out of its despair and make it flexible, expansive, intellectually brave. Sánchez chose instead to use that raw nerve in the Chicano Spanish tongue to tap the emotions at the bottom of his soul, the harder feelings against an unfair society, the morbid doldrums he accumulated from a life of hardscrabble in and out of penal institutions.

The English Sánchez would master bore all the angularity and weight of a tradition of individualism long in the making in Europe and given its final luster of ego-philia in America. It was the tongue of the separated, the distinct, the cunning and merciless. It was the world's own tongue of commerce and competition; it was spoken by diplomats representing state interests and aggressions, by rock musicians and media-saturated youth worldwide. It was a language of raw power, with its oppressive control over nature and the "new world order" of commerce. English would soon become the tongue of the militaristic west, with its small strategic wars and its NATO forces bombing Kosovo, an English spoken by the jet pilots over Iraq, by troops intervening in Somalia, Sudan, Haiti, and other chaotic, repressive states. It was the tongue of the conquerors, of world-gripping corporations, and of world culture.

Spanish, at the other extreme, carried the community's common soul into the words, and merged self with an immediate, sensuous world. The body was alive still, the elbows and legs and feet of a man were parts of speech, and the woman or man desired by a lover was a landscape, a garden, a paradisaical place in the verbs and adjectives of a lyric poem. The denigrated peasant tongue of border Spanish, stubby and unevolved, was nonetheless a powerful raw material of tribal thinking barely marked with the ravages of European Enlightenment, the Inquisition, the Industrial Revolution, or any of the other social burdens placed on English. And yet, for all that it proffered in the way of a new speech like the new Italian or the new English of Chaucer's era, it was not a new seed in the ground, ready to sprout. It was an old turnip.

Finding himself between two such languages forced Sánchez to express the dualistic nature of his own identity. He was, on the Spanish side, a pachuco from the El Diablo barrio of El Paso, a rough, unfinished border tough. In English, he became a man with a Ph.D., at home in the world of government programs and bureaucratic procedures, a man of letters, one of the educated in a time when literacy and academic credentials were a ticket into white society. He was a creature formed by both languages, half and half, but his entire struggle as a writer was to forge these halves of citizenship into a new postapartheid American. But in the end, his cultural moment blocked the clear flow of such absolute faith, except in asides, in fragments, and under the flow of a lava-hot political argument with the age.

English had begun to unravel in the postcolonial era. The death of western empires caused other cultures to reassert their primacy in the world. But the loss of London as the capital of western authority meant English had lost its true home. It was now the medium of banking and transport, of stock exchanges and international trade. It was no longer a language of truth and experience but a tool of manipulation in the hands of merchants and politicians. Sánchez records his own disillusionment with English in a style that both condemns and parodies the faults of the language. In his preface to *Canto y grito mi liberación* he writes,

> Other—and more serious—demands for conformity came not from the readily recognizable establishment, but from a neo-oligarquía—the poverty pimps in charge of most (95% or so) federally funded programs. Now these pendejos are the dangerous ones, for they have lulled the community and co-opted the movement (to them it is movidas, not movimiento, ¡y que si las mueven!), and they will not hesitate to destroy if it means their newly acquired status and high salaries (color them pastel-brownie and very much self-aggrandizing coconuts). This group has it down pat . . . they have even adopted an almost barrio patois which they use very emotionally when they rappingly weep out about what it feels to be desmadrado (deracinated), and they laugh on their way to the bank. (13–14)

English as used by experts and extremists on all sides of social questions raised discourse to a technical jargon, and in stretching it to accommodate so many ideological lobbies and their agendas, it ceased to be the tongue of the working class. By 1970, when Sánchez began publishing poetry, English was the medium of the ruling class; other languages and subdialects of English were discourses without power.

The subdialects were heard on the country's regional radio stations and in country and western music, in the town halls and communities where it was used to air the complaints of citizens no longer in touch with government or with the fine arts and higher culture. One heard it in the Tim McVeigh trial for the Oklahoma City bombing, in the rebuttals to government raids on Ruby Ridge and the Branch Davidian compound, in defense of private militias and gun laws. Otherwise, the regional discourse and the classes that use it are invisible.

The situation was ripe for politicians to exploit, and it has been done merely by turning against the liberalism that had mouthed a technical discourse of freedom and equality while shutting out the mainstream of white America.

Sánchez's English is a satire of the ruling tongue; he forces his diction to the extreme of academic polysyllabia, to expose the abuses made of the common tongue by the various privileged enclaves who thought they represented the conscience of the left. But Sánchez implies throughout his poetry that such a tongue, obscure, high-falutin', Tristram-Shandyish in its convolutions, served itself first and dealt out the morsels of public aid in a haze of impenetrable gibberish. Sánchez's anger never abated; writing in 1990 on the same cultural castration of minorities in his foreword to *Eagle-Visioned/Feathered Adobes,* he noted that "[t]he promise of the movement had been subverted, its values perverted, and its future almost cast asunder." He goes on:

> Perhaps those poets who value their words and who are willing and determined to create from their own visions a better world will ultimately topple those [government] programs now manned by self-serving opportunists. Artists and poets should realize that assistance with strings attached is no assistance, for it is a trap which robs one of integrity and meaning. In toppling city and state-sponsored cultural programs, we might just do away with parasitic patronage. There can be no autonomy when one is forced to submit to authorities for one's livelihood, and the Guakamolee Theater [Guadalupe Cultural Arts Center] in La Oreja [San Antonio] is an example of a gutted process which could have made a difference for the people. (11)

By now the epic on equality Sánchez had set out to write was as thwarted and "gutted" by the expropriating energies of the government as were all the so-called multicultural agencies set up to improve minority life. Sánchez's epic had turned into a Rabelaisian satire on white liberalism:

yes, santa fé,
republic
of shoddy, tourist pleasing replications,
much
has died
    and been left
to fester
    upon your features;
invaded,
    you seem to have acquiesced,
and, like the serpent,
devoured yourself
within
the brine
of self-disdain (58)

The Santa Fe of his month-long visit in October of 1981 is a landscape of cultural euphemisms, a kind of Disney theme park in which the wild original landscape has been tamed, muted, decorated with the varnished semblances of native life. It is a deceitful text of adulterated native culture, an anglicized version of the once primordial homeland where some of Sánchez's bloodline originated. The condition of towns like Santa Fe, cultural centers of native life in general, are the condition of language: a doctored and highly manufactured government prose obscuring the truth from all but the most probing minds.

Not only has Sánchez found the languages of his time unworkable, irreparable instruments for projecting the mind/soul of a people, they are now the objects of his scorn. He is a visionary without allies or cohorts, except for those few brave souls he honors in his preface: Nephtalí De León, Dolores Huerta, Abelardo Delgado, Zarco Guerrero, Carmen de Novalis, Carlos Rosas, Bert Corona, César Chávez. Otherwise, the Southwest of the Indians has decayed into a "garish pastiche . . . for preening tourists" in a city that could "well accommodate / a thousand taco-bell buildings, / and the tourists would all / probably feel / that they had had / authentic-genuwhine/ cuisine a la mexique" (63).

The satiric edge and the acid tone of his poetry take us back to the early days of Ginsberg's declamatory style in "Howl" and "Kaddish," the poems of *The Fall of America* (1972). There is something inchoate and desperate in such tirades, a "back-against-the-wall" rhetoric that lashes out at enemies high and low, in the disguise of one's own color and speech. Ginsberg's rages touched the boundary of paranoia, in honor of his mother's rages and of his own persecution as a Jew and homosexual in Cold War America. Sánchez has brought Chicano poetry up to the edges of this preliminary anger against a "system," a "combine," in the coinage Ken Kesey makes in *One Flew over the Cuckoo's Nest* (1962). It would seem that Sánchez had hit upon a way of maturing Chicano lyric to this point of white anger and discrimination, a Chicano Beat poetry, perhaps, loud, heavy in the bass, large in vocabulary, and in deadly earnest against the same forces the Beat poets had railed against.

Behind the failed epic Sánchez tried to write is a second text, a strategy to raise the level of racial anger and resilience by tapping into the revolution that stimulated white writers to separate from the academic tradition and construct the postmodern alternative.

English was a ruined language, and while it served him well as a satirist of the ruling class in America, it also prevented him from becoming a great poet. He could not use it to express his true feelings. The distortions and biases of the language made him express anger, disillusionment, scathing denials, but rarely the creative vision of the races transcending the prejudices of the white majority.

What Sánchez records when he writes in English is the condition of the language itself, its enormous vocabulary of inaneness trapping the conscious mind in its own wasteland:

yes, write
that position paper
which shall explain
in quantum terminology
the exquisiteness
of culturalist expressionists
re-inventing the cultura wheel,
let that wheel turn and turn and turn,
let it roll over the brain and soul,

and, as it rolls,
do let it leave
its tracks upon
blood, history, and placid flaccidity ("Sentiments hacia Belén," *Eagle-*
      Visioned, 16–17)

But no sooner is this satiric passage established than Sánchez tries to
wring sincerity from it by offering a literal, that is, a serious statement of
Chicano needs:

we have become inured to feeling pain/truth,
let there be an abstract of it
upon the breezes amidst canyon lands,
let it be atole, chaquehue, and
sentimientos refritos,
a conceptual paper
girded by enchanted and mysterious
chants
bouncing off the sangre de cristo mountains,
it can well be an academic bit
which skims off
the chaos of the moment
or an elated sense of senselessness,
whatever,
as long as it complies
with nothing and everything
      simultaneously,
displeasing while appeasing,
a sobriquet
of maundering words,
some sibilant
and others sybaritic,
neoteric posterings
or resurrected fables,
as long as the writing reflects
a Nuevo Mexico
that can either be real
or feelingly imagined . . . (17)

The passage does not reverse the satiric edge of the earlier language; the same high-pitched discourse pours down the page, mixing sobriquet with maundering, sibilant and sybaritic, neoteric posterings (posturings?) conveying the detached, intellectualized remoteness that Sánchez otherwise rejects. But he would now have us believe that such barbarous speech can "reflect a Nuevo Mexico that can either be real / or feelingly imagined." The truth is, given such terminology and the botched character of English in the era of small wars, it cannot reflect anything but its own threadbare rationalizations.

Sánchez must argue his cause by repetition and insistence, to push a perspective through the ruinous channels of an English he scorns. He cannot turn off the shrill rhetoric of the learned classes to speak in some unsullied form of common speech; it does not exist except in forms that are for various reasons equally suspect or denigrated, such as southern dialect or Tex-Mex speech. None of these works because they are tongues that can only express the limited goals of a small, beleaguered group. The tongue of the tribe no longer exists, and one can write in the language of the master class only so long before hypocrisy or forced eloquence set in. Sánchez writes in jags of English and then drops off into peasant Spanish for a while, the hard-knocks Pachucoese of the barrios, before zooming up into Pentagonese or government gobbledygook again. His poems are linguistic roller coasters, and his readers feel their necks jerking as he whiplashes through the turns of a class system gone to extremes, with all the gaps sending the coaster cars clanging.

I remember once raising the name of Sánchez in a conversation with Rolando Hinojosa-Smith, the novelist of the Rio Grande Valley. "He's all anger," he said; "there's only one note in his songbook."

"At least he's honest," I said.

"Honest? Just by being angry he's honest? What about those who are doing the work of making a life? Aren't they honest, too? A lot of writers come out of poverty or misery and don't fall into the trap of accusing everyone."

Maybe so. Maybe Sánchez was crazy, a used-up man by the time he emerged from Huntsville and started publishing his writings. He must have absorbed a vast mosaic of broken languages in jail, hearing the boys in their neighboring cells cooking up tattoo dye over a candle, whispering their curses and rage in the middle of night. Anyone who has done time in the prison system comes back a kind of polylinguist, with a headful of dark im-

ages and spells hurled against the master class. Prison is a bit like Ahab's
ship, the *Pequod,* where you hear the language of the indentured, the poor,
the desperate—all speaking polyglot English, and none of it suitable for
sweet song. Sánchez is the measure of that, but his achievement, broken and
bunged up as it may seem at times, was to raise peasant Spanish out of
its doldrums and give it the breadth of a new language—partly English,
but partly Indian and racially undifferentiated working-class jive. Sánchez played his homemade patois on Dizzy Gillespie's trumpet, and it all
sounded like some endless riff, some brilliant but drunken solo in the midst
of an otherwise conventional song.

If we interpret Sánchez's work as a whole, a span of eight books ranging
from his first and in some ways his best book, *Canto y grito mi liberación*
(1973) to his *Selected Poems* of 1985, and most recently, the *Loves of Ricardo*
(1997), it is the statement of a social activist whose political and social ideals
go back to the liberalism of the Roosevelt era. Sánchez's political life began
shortly after his release from the Texas prison system, when he was appointed director of the Itinerant Migrant Health Project, an agency of the
Colorado Migrant Council, which disbursed federal funds to families of
migrant farm workers. Sánchez's orientation to the dispossessed follows the
lines of federally mandated social programs. He believed ardently and fully
in the powers of central government to right the wrongs of regional people.
He appealed directly to those powers in its own bureaucratic and technical
jargon. Much of his anger against the ills of society arose from a sense that
it was the local government and the local conditions that victimized him.

Despite the fervor of his identity as an outcast and as a man descended
from a mixture of heritages on the border, he was a traditional liberal. He
distrusted the means by which the federal government translated its social
programs at the local level, but the mind at the center was more enlightened, more compassionate, less contaminated by local hatred and ignorance. The core of government preserved for Sánchez the tatters of the
American dream; there, at least, the ideals of a fair and open society lingered
among a few policy makers and planners, even if the purity of the message
got lost on its way down to the grass roots. That faith in government as the
moral and ethical center of American life was perhaps the only untarnished
aspect left for Sánchez to believe—the rest of the experiment in New World
democracy was a tragic failure.

His poetry, he wrote in a preface to *Canto y grito,* "is my song of love for the valleys, mountains, cities, plazas, women, children, carnales, carnalas, gentes, and entirety of the earth," but it is also "[a song] of anger at our failing to create a society of caring, our failing to attain humanness . . . it is thus an indictment mixed with a hopeful plea that the unsanity of this manmade idiocy be righted—for our morality demands it, for our humanity commands it, for without a change in course we are damned all the way to hell" (15).

Sánchez's poetry is complicated by the double nature of his relation to the social whole. And by his own double nature. To look at him in his little bookstore in San Antonio, where he eked out a living in the early 1990s, was to feel the extraordinary enigma of the poor man. He was broke usually, and the bookstore was no more kind to his purse than it had been to Paul Foreman's. But he floated on strange seas of thought, to borrow a line from Wordsworth; he traveled the fiery edges of the linguistic universe trying to reach the power elite through words. He was a politician first and last, a man in his bully pulpit, railing at injustice, using the poem as a hustings in the middle of an imaginary campaign for president.

The times I invited him to College Station to read poems, to tape a few shows for "Poetry Southwest," he came in his ironed guayabera shirt and sandals, his face large and his eyes slitted into an expression of deep suspicion of the people I introduced him to. But his handshake was so engulfing and warm that people would forget their intimidation and begin to smile and banter. The women loved him; he was irresistible to them. They leaned against him, they flirted, they found some dark but potent energy in him that made a few go quite limp before him. He would shoot me a wink at such times, and let me know who was in charge of the proceedings.

I played Gene Wilder to this heap of masculine energy, this Zero Mostel of the Hispanic down under. And what a wonderful show he gave. He would throw out his hands to sweep the horizon as his reference, and lower his already gravelly voice to grind out the word "governor" or "House of Representatives." He would sneer, and make your chin snap at his sudden shout in the midst of conversation. He talked as if the cell block were still gabbling away at a roar. He had to cut through the confusion, and he did so with his wide, lascivious mouth and cavernous voice.

He drank a little, never to excess in my presence. He was gentle with people, though he had a look of utter ferocity. He was a bulldog with a kind of spaniel's heart inside him. But his mind was deadly, both in earnest and in focus. He meant what he said, and he would fight, perhaps even die for the sense of freedom he demanded from America. His poems followed the oldest American tradition—the sense that what one said in art was to be used by the readers to improve their lives. He came from Whitman's sources and followed the activist line of poetry from William Carlos Williams to Pablo Neruda, with stops along the way for Charles Olson, García Lorca, and Rimbaud. He was cruder than these brilliant masters, but he was someone who could claim his place among them.

You couldn't take Sánchez by halves; he was a whole man and you could hear him eating in his poems, making love, arguing, fighting his enemies. He lived in his words, and he sometimes slept in them. When we sat once in a little diner having coffee, he passed his notebook to me to write down what I was thinking. I jotted a few marginal thoughts, nothing of any passion. He looked, sniffed, turned his nose up at me as if I had sneezed on the page. He wrote something and passed it back—and lo, it was poetry, the spigot of words that he turned on at will and that filled his many books. He actually lived one poem all his life, a kind of chant and grunt, a rumble of the guts, both brilliant and pure animal.

Sánchez was the last Roosevelt liberal in Texas, and he mocked the evils of corrupt government in the nasal English of the bureaucrats. He fashioned his utopian social vision of fairness and equality out of the same corrupted speech. He was a poet who tried to reach the average citizen in a time when the common tongue no longer existed; his laughter and bitterness rang out louder than his hopes and dreams. The result is the gorgeous wreckage of an epic poetry written in the age of impeachment politics, and in the teeth of high school massacres and little wars in Kosovo. He was trying to tell us to stop, reconsider our path, not to forget the poor bedraggled common folk, each alone in his or her corner.

CHAPTER 13
"THE SIMPLE BITTER SAP"

Living here as long as I have, a quarter century now since I came down the east side of Texas in my Ryder truck, I have wondered why the poets chose to ignore the very myths that made the state world famous. If they could have jumped on the cowboy myth, would they not also be world famous? As minstrels of the lasso and corral? As the carolers of the Plains Indian wars and the little micromyths of horse breaking and the rest? Poetry never really made it big in Texas; it has had a few stars and some successful books, but in the main, it is a region that is still not known through its poetry.

The world knows Texas through films and television dramas, and largely through fiction, and one play—*The Best Little Whorehouse in Texas.* But even the origins of that particular plot came originally from television, from roving reporter Marvin Zindler's sin-busting exposé of central Texas life. The poets have not defined Texas the way T. S. Eliot, Wallace Stevens, Robert Frost, and Edwin Arlington Robinson defined New England, and the way Robert Lowell and Sylvia Plath redefined it. Walt Whitman and Allen Ginsberg captured New York. The Midwest was given a literary consecration through Carl Sandburg, Edgar Lee Masters, Theodore Roethke, and James Wright; and the South, the glorious South had Edgar Allan Poe and Vachel Lindsay, a host of Agrarian poets like Robert Penn Warren, John Crowe Ransom, and Allen Tate. James Dickey revived southern poetry in the 1960s, and a new generation is writing up the post-Vietnam urban South, poets like Dave Smith, David Bottoms, Bin Ramke, and Betty Adcock.

But the Southwest had poets who chose not to engage the principal myths, the ones on which the meaning of the Southwest was based, or fixed in the national imagination. It fell to novelists to seize and conceptualize the Southwest, as if story were the true medium of southwestern life. Perhaps it was. Dobie was a great storyteller, and I have often told my students that the real possessors of wealth and power in America are the storytellers. The story is perhaps more natural to a place that has never quite extinguished its frontier; it lies here as mere land along the highways, as chaparral and brushy hills, as dry land gone bankrupt, as oil fields gone dry. The land remains unconquered, and anyone who ventures into it is almost immediately drawn into myth and fable.

Even during the 1920s when poetry was hot, the fiction writers were making their mark on the national scene. Mary Austin, Willa Cather, and Dorothy Scarborough were publishing novels that would endure. Mary Austin's Indian folk tales, her "One-Smoke Stories," were widely popular, and her novel, *Starry Adventure* (1931) established her reputation. Cather's *Death Comes for the Archbishop* (1927) is the first psychological study of a man's transformation after coming into contact with southwestern Indians. Scarborough's *The Wind* (1925), a kind of Brontë sisters' rendering of wind as sexual torment, opened the way to symbolist fiction in Texas. Oliver La Farge's *Laughing Boy* (1929), which won the Pulitzer Prize, is a serious study of Navajo culture. Perhaps it was more a New Mexico fiction renaissance than it was a Texas movement. Paul Horgan's *No Quarter Given* (1935) is a sophisticated satire on the well-to-do of Santa Fe, and his *Figures in a Landscape* (1940), about ordinary small-town New Mexicans, was sorely needed in Texas as an antidote to the dime westerns and cheap romanticism attracting the pulp fiction crowd. Conrad Richter narrated the passing of the New Mexican cattle kings in *The Sea of Grass* (1937), which Dobie's *The Cow People* (1964) retells in a Texas context, but as documentary portrait, not fiction. No one had yet taken up the smaller subjects of Texas; to allow readers elsewhere to experience simple daily life here. Texas was daunting, an epic place demanding epic means, like Edna Ferber's efforts in her novel, *Giant* (1952), and the triple-decker sagas of McMurtry. By the end of the 1940s, writers were beginning to piece out the meaning of life on the lower Plains, little by little, from Oklahoma, New Mexico, Arizona, and California, with Texas providing less than its fair share of fictional realism.

Dobie's assessment of the local fiction was dismal; he noted that "fiction that appeared before World War I can hardly be called modern," and he conceded that Bret Harte had cornered the market on fictional cowboys for a long time to come. He was writing this in 1941 (*Guide to Life and Literature,* 179–80). He cites Austin and Cather, of course, as eminent neighbors, and Horgan and La Farge, and George Sessions Perry's *Hold Autumn in Your Hand* (1941), and a Brazos River tale by James Stephens, *Crock of Gold*

(1940) as noteworthy. Then, of course, the real eminence of Texas writers, and one who could not seem to escape from her Texas roots, Katherine Anne Porter, whom he finds psychologically compelling, but perhaps a little too esthetic. Dobie compares her to A. E. Housman! But most of the fiction about the Southwest "has betrayed rather than revealed life, though not with the contemptible contempt for both audience and subject that characterizes most of Hollywood's pictures on the same times, people, and places" (*Guide to Life and Literature,* 178). So much for fiction by the start of World War II, as Dobie canvassed the field in the 1943 edition of *Guide to Life and Literature of the Southwest;* the accent of his title is on the life and its factual portrayals in memoirs, research, and first-hand accounts, rather than on the literature, which he found woefully lacking in substance or fact.

If you were to squint an eye at the literary situation I have been sketching in these last few chapters, you would see on the one hand a poetry of personal and figurative suffering largely written by women, and fables of triumph and conquest written largely by men. Between these stools fell the real Texas, all its truth and sorrows, which few writers had grasped in words. Was Dobie right, that the real Texas lay in nonfiction classics like *The Great Plains, Goodbye to a River,* and William Owens's memoir of growing up in Pin Hook, *This Stubborn Soil* (1966)? I'm on to something here, to judge by the editors of *The Texas Literary Tradition: Fiction, Folklore, History,* whose selective bibliography from 1900 to 1983 has its longest category of books on "The Vanishing Frontier," some fifty-four titles in all. This is a Texas according to journalists, historians, sociologists, geographers, naturalists, and personal observers, as opposed to the lesser groups of novelists, the "Old Order," women writers, and writers on the "Texas mystique."

Apply this same standard to other regions, asking if the journalists and essayists captured New England or California, and you would scratch your head. Ultimately, they did not, at least not as surely, or as durably, as did the poets and fiction writers. These are the ones who combine the substance of experience with the spirit of place, its myths and ideals, its intangibles, and its unconscious culture.

Perhaps the literary process in Texas is a little like an oyster with a pearl, and the writing has gone on in secret for a long time, in a corner of the cultural mind—too murky and remote for any but the most curious to look into. This is more like the truth of what has been going on for much of the twentieth century. The critics of *Texas Women Writers* seem to think that because women were writing much of the state's literature, gender alone explains some of the neglect literature has received. But there is also a distinctive, deeply rooted distrust of the very act of reading in the region. For many here, the Bible is the only legitimate text to read for instruction. The secular tradition has never enjoyed wide popular appeal, and perhaps never will. Its character has been maligned as frivolous and distorted, or merely corrupt. Even Dobie's dismissal of fiction and poetry in his time conveys something of a moral disapproval of secular writing as a kind of foolish make-believe, especially when, as he argued vigorously, "the actualities of southwestern life" are begging to be recorded accurately.

The myths and "Texas mystique" not only cover over some of the region's darker history but also serve as a kind of therapy for losses suffered in the Civil War. I choose the pearl as my metaphor of the writing process because a grain of sand is an irritant deep in the core of an oyster's life, and the nacre that it secretes is the gleaming surface put around this irritant. It must be that the literary process of a century or more is a kind of layering of nacreous words around some essential irritant, an issue buried at the heart of the state's identity. Maybe the oyster image is wrong—maybe it's the myths that are the nacre, and the writers are more like dentists, drilling down through the pearly luster to this ineffable core where some kind of spiritual feud is at work.

And the state's really serious literature has more to do with pain than with pleasure. The women wrote of pain in the landscape, and the new generations after the Vietnam War wrote of guilt, shame, humiliation, disorientation. In between was a generation of realists both in fiction and in poetry who described the awkward transition from rural to urban culture, the losses involved in leaving Pin Hook and Archer City behind for the expansive urban worlds of Dallas and Houston, or L.A. and New York. The literature is about loss of innocence, the loss of the ranch as the measure of someone's liberty and self-possession, the loss of wild earth and the beginnings of a national culture seeping in through the phone wires, the television transmitters, the interstates. The local literature, humble as it often is, served as a kind of collective diary of a state that wanted to see itself as a republic, a sovereign, inviolable place in America, with its own fought-for origins and traditions. The writers said otherwise, and doggedly drilled down to the quick of experience where the pain festered unattended.

The opening poem of Vassar Miller's collected work, *If I Had Wheels or Love* (1991) begins with an image of pain, a child's "crooked step wrenched straight," a "child scrabbling in the dark" (3). The poem is called "Adam's Footprint," as if to say that the beginning of life in Texas was this twisted print in the ground of someone struggling to walk. The last poem of the book is almost too cannily placed, with its closing line, "If I had wheels or love, I would be gone" (341). I am reminded of John Howard Griffin's relentless suffering in *Black Like Me* (1961), taking the racial abuse of white men directed at what they thought was a Negro shining their shoes. The humiliation, the descent to the racial underclass of the Deep South, seemed to clarify the literary gesture of the state—a pure, even borrowed pain as the source of inspiration. The ritual gesture of Texas literature seems to be to put oneself in a place or situation in which the myth doesn't operate, but rather mere human suffering is the experience. Not that all literature is only about failure and disappointment; far from it, some of the best writing is about triumph and ecstasy, but always at a time in which the body is the evidence, the truth-teller.

I do not think Dobie quite understood this principle when he waved away the body of writing up to the midcentury. It was a truth that did not engage the boastful side of regional culture; it quietly murmured its own testimony and built up a reality out of sensations, minor setbacks, the fine-grained disappointments of daily life that did not square up with the region's status as a great arena of initiative and self-drive. In his title poem, "After the Noise of Saigon," Walt McDonald deals with the pain of his Vietnam experience during a hunt, when "here I am, alone / with a cougar I've stalked for hours, / climbing until I'm dizzy." The closing stanzas show us how even this fine, prolific poet reaches down to the quick of real pain as the key motif of his poetry:

These blue trees have nothing
and all to do with what I'm here for
after the noise of Saigon,

the simple bitter sap that rises in me
like bad blood I need to spill
out here alone in the silence

of deep woods, far from people I know
who see me as a friend, not some damned
madman stumbling for his life. (*After the Noise of Saigon*, 65)

Is it intentional, a knowing confirmation of the theme of pain by the poets as they write? Almost everywhere you look, once you have the theme in mind, you see it—glaring back with its red flag, its dim eyes? Peter Wild's selection of poems in Oliphant's *The New Breed* opens on the theme, and the poem, "Thinking on the Plains," is worth quoting in part:

When a storm comes here
    it comes in a great bruise,
a black prairie fire
    raging from the Llano Estacado

. . . .

thank God, it's no worse
    than having a tooth pulled,
in the numbness of lights
    the sound of roots tearing loose,
of a carcass being split
    up the middle;
and just as quickly
    it's over . . .

people who love me
    don't seem to understand
    what parts I leave and what I take,
what muscle they strip
    from my bones. . . . (188–89)

Is it Wild's contention that to think is to dwell on the pain within? Then consciousness in Texas poetry is essentially awareness brought on by pain, a memory, or a direct sensation as one writes. Pain—whether in the form of loneliness, Bob Bonazzi's specialty, or pains of memory, the province of Walt McDonald's imagination, or the pains of disease, as in the world of Vassar Miller, or the pains of racial rejection, as in the poetry of Ricardo Sánchez.

My own poems now seem to me a diary of painful longings and aches for love, a pain to belong, to be rooted, to be home in the world—and always failing. The opening poem of my book, *Signs of the Whelming* (1983), is "Pangs of Sleep," about a Hyperion-like lover who cannot reach the beloved, no matter how hard he tries, for she is both woman and the moon:

I hear you dreaming at night,
aloof in sleep; sweeping the light
from your skin until you are as clean
as the moon. I come from the bottom
of the world, mudlark of night,
streaking up the sky to you.
You above, a white idea,
cleaning the space around you
with your breath, as I lunge on
snoring feet from crack to crevice
of evening, driving you higher. (7)

If pain is at the heart of poetic vision in the state, pain as news, pain as declaration of the self, pain as consciousness, pain as the roots of history, then what makes poets, myself included, work at its articulation as if there were hardly another subject in our imaginations? This is the imponderable at the heart of literature, for it spills into the fiction, it spills into the non-fiction as well—the revelation that under the surface lives a kind of river of pain coursing through all of us. And any poem is an excavation of the sur-face, the nacreous outer layer of neutrality, boastfulness, optimism, to this river. The poem knows when it is framed, fully formed, when it can make pain its epiphany, its brief lyric perception of the self. The self as pain.

Any literature that will dwell so hard upon a subject must be counter-pointing another force going in an opposite direction. Is there a pervasive pleasure principle out there that poetry has staked out as the opposition? What is poetry defending as reality, if it can be found only in the torments of the body, in the negative self? Perhaps the answer lies in the nature of the successes on which the cowboy myths are based. The taming of wild nature and the mastery of the horse have to do with equilibrium, a security against a foreign will—expressed in nature's power over human life. Maybe Peter Wild's note to his poems, reprinted in *The New Breed,* is instructive: "The border is different from the rest of the country. A huge isolated land, a land apart, a country unto itself; and despite the great deserts, floating peaks, temperate forests, marshes, badlands where everything organic eventually turns to bone, then stone, despite the dramatic shifts the travelogues tell about and which are true, it is most of all a land of dullness, persistent dull-ness; because man cannot fit into the dimensions, at least he cannot fit with any harmony or dignity unless he is willing to make himself small, very small" (188).

The mastery of the one set of myths is here opposed by the desire to concede and grow small in the literature. Mastery might well be a disguised form of repression, for the breaking of the horse to obey a human being means the wildness has gone underground, sublimated by the horse in its willingness to carry a human on its back. The stubbornness has not disappeared; it has gone into the unconscious of the horse, just as the sense of a universal mastery of nature in Texas may well have repressed the body into numbness, or into a neutrality that material rewards, comfort, security, money in the bank, a big car sustain—without allowing one to feel the immediacy, the impingement of the world around us.

Does poetry then excavate the neutralized body of a materialistic culture to find the pain of being itself? The myths of mastery derive from the cowboy's life on the ranches and cattle drives, but that very figure is actually a form of repressed individuality, a team player's life—someone who willingly submitted to the frequently quixotic rules of a foreman or straw boss, and whose job could easily be terminated by the slightest sign of disobedience. It was a paramilitary life drawing its work force from veterans of the Confederate army, from slavery, and from Indian tribes, and it became explicitly military when cowboys signed up to be Rangers or joined the local militias. By a curious stroke, men coming into the new post–Civil War Southwest were not so much individualists—a few were and would become entrepreneurs and big ranchers—but men who surrendered their autonomy to authoritarian forms of work. A certain annihilation of sensibility, of resistance, was necessary to fit in—to become good at one's calling, a fact often overlooked in studies of the popular mythology of the region. The cowboy wore an elaborate uniform, could be recognized in his calling by chaps, brimmed hat, boots, a pistol, and his horse. He represented a fixed set of attitudes and values, part of some larger movement of men who went together toward some common, unstated goal in life—their escape from the constraints of ordinary culture. To do so meant tolerating the discomforts and deprivations of life on the road, or under the thumb of a trail boss. It was as if the herds dictated the anonymous functionality of the cowboys, the one mirroring the order of the other. The western film tried to ignore this side of ranch life, to concentrate on the image of the heroic loner following his Emersonian inner voice on the frontier, rendering justice with his gun. Two traditions seem to have collided in the films: New England transcendentalism and southwestern authoritarianism, with the result that we lose the authenticity of the actual conditions that Dobie demanded from fiction.

The cowboy did, however, lay down a vision of young manhood that stuck, that seeped down into the masculine bedrock to form what is expected of male youth. Out of the cowboy comes the image of a powerful, aggressive physicality that can be broken like the mustang—and made to serve an authority or elder. That image of taming the wild male spirit by annihilating the body's powers to resist fed into the passion for football, which operates at a profound level in the regional psyche. Every junior high and high school, no matter how humble its circumstances, has its football stadium night lights and bleachers, and the name of the team emblazoned on the wall facing the road. The boys work under a paternal, often ruthless sort of coach demanding complete obedience to his wishes, and they are inculcated with a tolerance for pain and discomfort in the game. The boys are powerful, trained for aggression, and sent out to do battle on the football field in an atmosphere that is uncannily parallel to the rodeo arena next door—where animals are similarly driven to aggression and then restrained by a more cunning, it not more powerful will.

Both forms of entertainment are explorations of control—in football, the control of brute physical aggression for the possession of symbolic territory, and the attempt to control the vagaries of a ball tossed into the melee. And in the arena, the capacity to control a desperately struggling animal bucking off its rider while trying to escape the cords that eat into its skin. In both, nature tries to win back its freedom and to overthrow the human estate. But the theater of symbols is rigged to show human transcendence most of the time.

That is why the idea of unions is anathema in the Southwest; Texas will not tolerate them. The concept of a group imposing its own countering will on management goes against the grain of southwestern ideals. Authority is too important to be challenged, especially on grounds of physical complaint or remuneration. The group is a source of energy to be used as an implement of some higher intelligence, a more enlightened will. The group's will is subordinate, an undirected and possibly feral will that would undo the victories over wild nature won by the conquest over wilderness. Hence the universal vigilance against autonomy, against the flow of complaining energies from below. Control is the poetics of a people who have broken the will of nature and now rule precariously over its various forces. Religion reinforces the rights of authority and preaches a tolerance for the pains of this world, to gain the rewards of the next. The body is numbed from the head down, from faith or fear down to the hands and legs.

You can sense the passive accommodation to power that flows through poetry; it drops out of sight when power is consolidated, as in times of war or insecurity. At other times, when forces call such authority into question, an outpouring of poetry is the first response from the grass roots of society. It comes out of nowhere and imposes itself in oddly pervasive ways—in ephemeral magazines, broadsides, in newspapers, on walls, in reading halls. It happened, just as we might expect, in the throes of the South's defeat, when women organized themselves into clubs and professional associations, and used the poem as a kind of open diary. Men followed, because they too were affected by the loosening reins of power over them.

Poetry had a second renaissance at the end of the 1920s, when Wall Street and the economic powers of the country began to fail; it opened the channels of the body once more, and the poetry of consciousness, the language of pain and sensation, arose once more and became a flood of passion and emotion in all those publishing houses in Dallas and among all those hundreds, if not thousands, of reading and writing clubs meeting in small-town libraries and civic centers. It died out where we would want it to on our historical graph, as the Second World War gathers its furies again, and authority is once more imposed by men from the top down. Now rationing, doing without, offering one's services, yielding to contingency made the body go numb once more, and poetry slowed to a trickle, and then to an arroyo's dry sand.

Poetry was gone from the 1950s, a decade of naked power in the Cold War, the era of William H. Whyte's organization man and the gray flannel suit. It was a time of flattops, melodramas on TV, films about power struggles in the corporations, and toward the end of the decade, films about youth revolting from the parents, finding their own way. When the 1960s came, a youth culture sprang up, and with it a renaissance of poetry on the national scene: Beat poetry in New York and San Francisco; the New York School; Black Mountain poetry, Deep Image, and myriad splinter groups. The common ingredient in all of these movements was disenchantment with authority—a need to talk back at the militarized ruling classes with their armament of corporate money and government power, generally known as the military-industrial complex. It gave us what we now call post-modernism, with all its upheavals of form and value.

The postmodern urge to challenge power would have abated of its own, with the aging of its first generation of poets, but the Vietnam War burst upon the middle-1960s and energized a new wave of poets to make louder protests, and to spread their opposition against the war to the political parties supporting it. The rallying cries of the movement were many, but not lost among them was the warning, "Don't trust anyone over thirty." If the war had been won, authority would have been restored and questions would have died away. But the failure of the war awoke outrage and skepticism, and a renewed sense that power was not expressing the common will. The defeat in Vietnam awakened a much deeper sense of anti-authoritarianism in the South not felt since Reconstruction.

Poetry in Texas began to flow again, from many channels: from women, who were influenced by the national liberation movements, and from white males looking for ways to express their own new sensitivity to pain and doubt. It was natural, inevitable, that men should take the primary metaphor of the abused land as the means by which to record the pains of their own resurgent bodily consciousness. Poetry flowed into the capillaries under the skin, became the measure of one's personal agony and despair, a medium in which to record the de-numbing, the reawakening of the self's boundary. Soon enough, the African American liberation struggle had its effect on Texas as well, under the leadership of poets like Ahmos Zu-Bolton and Harryette Mullen, who together organized the Voodoo Festivals in Houston. The Chicano movement was gathering momentum in California, Arizona, and in the border counties of Texas, and finding venues for publication in a new Houston press, Arte Público.

The tides of poetry are linked directly to the state of power and its prestige; when power is consolidated and defending the state or the nation, poetry subsides, evaporates. When power is called into question, poetry flows with its adversarial language of the awakened body. Poetry is about resurgence, recovery from suppression or willing submission. It is the language of the body's return to nature, with all its old unwillingness to be bullied or shoved aside by utilitarian arguments. Poetry is not just the song of protest in times of instability or unrest, but a celebration of nature's separate universe of forces that wriggle out of human control. And because the body is so intimately bound up with the idea of nature, it too becomes wild again, liberated, recalcitrant, bitter, awake, refreshed, returned to the wild, where it sings of its renewed beast nature and happiness. Or maunders and weeps over its sufferings, and appeals to the reader for pity or understanding.

But poetry's moment is usually not very long, eight or ten years at the most. After that things get stale, the anger threadbare, the similes and metaphors of outrage timid from overuse. It may be that when I arrived in 1974 and found myself in the first torrents of poetry in the state, I was amazed at the energy, its array and variety, its depth. It was everywhere, like great gobbets of rain in a very long storm. The rivers were rising with it, the desert was green with it. But now, some quarter century later, with the almost steady onslaught of intrigues, scandals, crises in Washington, and the investigative passions of independent counsels vetting Nixon, Reagan, Bush, and Clinton, the moment of poetry has become elongated, kept alive by the crumbling of monuments and certainties from above, and by poets grown old in their angers and resentments. A new generation is taking over, and more magazines are filling their pages, but the quality of articulation is inferior, a sign that things have gotten stale again, that poetry's crest is over for now. Good poets everywhere, in and out of state, have complained that poetry has been tamed, made safe, even prophylactic, against real esthetic experience. A toothless old hag has replaced the muse, or better, a toothless old gent has taken over inspiring—and alas, so much of new poetry is of the "Iowa school" variety, squibs of confession in a jaunty, colloquial style. Charles Bernstein makes my point more pungently in his assault upon National Poetry Month, a device of the Academy of American Poetry to popularize the art, which unwittingly links it to other overlooked things needing recognition for a day or a month. His comments appeared recently in "Against National Poetry Month as Such," a brief online essay for the University of Chicago Press's website: "The reinvention, the making of a poetry for our time, is the only thing that makes poetry matter. And that means, literally, making poetry *matter,* that is making poetry that intensifies the matter or materiality of poetry—acoustic, visual, syntactic, semantic. Poetry is very much alive when it finds ways of doing things in a media-saturated environment that only poetry can do, but very much dead when it just retreads the same old same old."

What is needed by my own generation and by younger poets is a determination to seize this period of relative calm, not to say indifference, in poetry as a time for reassessment, a time to reflect upon where poetry should flow as the new millennium opens. Already there are signs of where things might go to attain that elusive sense of greatness or of definition by which a region comes of age esthetically. The minor status of poetry in the state's relatively short literary history is a challenge to writers now, who must guard against the general tendency to simplify the poem, to make it palatable to a mass audience. The new poetry must push aside the documentarians of life and begin the imaginative work of reinterpreting the natural world to urban dwellers, of relating the story of the Plains and its epic past in language that is utterly, daringly fresh, contemporary, and believable. What is needed, in short, is a poetry of expanded vision. Let me explain.

It was never enough to project one's alienation or repression onto the landscape as a vision of where one lived. That left the land in a negative state, as a mere victim of wrongs that existed only within the human sphere. The land was impassive, aloof, in another dimension. Rendering the landscape as wounded, exploited, or ruined by greed and malice robbed the Plains and the black prairies of their own authenticity, their own proper estrangement from human concerns. It did not advance a reader's understanding to resort to a subtle form of pathetic fallacy, the projection of one's private emotion onto the world. While it was necessary to excavate a veiled or even repressed inner life, to vent the anger at being second-class citizens or rejected minorities, it was quite another to transcend the immediate grievances of life to grasp some larger, enriching relation that would liberate the writer—and begin the process of naming, relating, envisioning a region as home. The currents of poetry for a hundred years have been inward, self-oriented, leaving the outside world sketchy at best. And the message has nearly always been of the ailing self, the unhappy soul longing for a home.

What is missing in most poetry is an affirmation of place—an affirmation of its own existence, and its inexhaustible mysteries and powers. I do not mean a new romanticism of place, but a simpler, more penetrating vision of the land as the great Otherness to be watched, heeded, pursued for its own strange reality. The conditions under which we live now beg poets to teach us what the land means, and how it works, why it is important to us, how our lives depend upon it. Where it comes from and how it was made. The land is the province of geologists and petroleum engineers, specialists in a world of isolated, and partially related facts—instrumental facts to be used for the enrichment of private commerce. Not for the edification of an illiterate citizenry, bereft of even the simplest names of plants and without a sense of geography beyond the map and the highway sign. Asked where people came from in an audience attending Gary Snyder's poetry reading in Austin a few years back, the answers were names of towns. Snyder smiled, and politely reminded his listeners that that is only a name, a human name to be found on maps, but had nothing whatever to do with the real sense of home in the natural world. What rivers, species of trees, grass, what animals inhabited this space with you, he asked? What winds cool it, and what forces water and pollinate your fields? All that drew a blank.

The job of the poets is to reeducate the public about their own soils and natural history, and to liberate the land from its burden of human associations. The land must be separated by the poets so that it stands on its own and becomes a frontier of knowledge again, a frontier to be entered as a garden of natural wonders. What does the average Texan know about the Plains, their origins and evolution into present-day grain and sorghum farms, cattle ranches and oil leases? What lived here ten thousand years before, and how did the first human hunters arrive, by what means did they first survive? Who or what told them they could dine forever on the flesh of the buffalo, and give up all forms of sedentary community—and join the other plains-dwelling humans of the world in perpetual nomadism? Do we know these things well? Do they help us to venerate what is out there on the blurred horizons? Have the poets worked on the problem of our natural ignorance?

Homer's gift to the Greeks were two epics that were like encyclopedic geographies of the known Aegean and Mediterranean worlds—the allegories, the heroic exploits, the monsters and gods, were all thinly fleshed pretexts for explaining the variety and depths of the known world. The average listener of *The Iliad* and *The Odyssey* had never left his or her village or read a book. That kind of pure and surrounding ignorance was broken down by poetry; a similar kind of pure and surrounding ignorance has grown up around ourselves, and we have no poets who are willing to begin the practical instruction needed to relate us to our own natural habitats. We do not monitor government policies, the work of the Corps of Engineers, the river authorities, the Department of Agriculture, or the extension agencies when they alter the conditions of the environment. We are too ignorant to ask about consequences, or to defend the estuaries, the coastal wetlands, the nesting grounds of the cattle egret and other herons, the rights of rattlesnakes and prairie dogs. We do not have fables to explain their worth to us; we lack stories to unite these things to a common home. A few interest groups and watchdogs make a noise, and sometimes halt work on highways cutting into animal reserves or fragile ecosystems, and we learn a little about how one link connects another in the life chain. But the information comes to us in boring ways, and it is hard to pay attention. We do not sense the magic of nature, or its powers to transform us. When the biota is interrupted, we depend upon our specialists to tell us what it means. The common citizen is not concerned, because he or she is uninformed.

The way to open the subject circuitry of poetry and force language into an engagement with the world is first to remove human pain from the landscape. Let it go. Pain should be confined to purely human confessions, and the limitations on that theme will discourage poets from writing too much of it. A few poets began working in that direction back in the early 1970s. They combined humor with a bit of whimsy, a sardonic tone that told you they were not going to talk about themselves. They had other subjects to develop. Their strategy was to use personal charm to draw in a reader, and to promise to tell stories that were slightly magical in tone or plot, or they would poke fun at themselves, or see the brighter side of life. Naomi Shihab Nye, Betty Adcock, and Leon Stokesbury were in the forefront of these younger poets, and they knew they were going against the grain. They were *laughing*, not grousing.

That was a fresh start, and all three had reputations that soon leapt beyond their regional audiences. They offered something new in the world, a lighter relation to the Southwest, a willingness to suspend old themes and histories and assume that what occurred around them was interesting for its own humorous reasons. "The True Meaning of Life Revealed" is fairly typical Stokesbury, from his book, *Often in Different Landscapes* (1976):

Some personage is at this very minute driving across
the well-worn plains. Who do you suppose it is?
He arrives, smiling; making awkward apologies
for his Ford's disarray. Do you think this means
you're to join him in his travels? He doesn't say.
Oh, and you were just getting ready to think about
your first love for the first time in years.
Here come five clouds, shrugging along. Notice

how they hover and begin to rain. This all seems
connected, but he continues simply smiling, his moustache
aquiver, and hands you the envelope, that you cannot open,
in which, he claims, is concealed his mission and name. (13)

This is the same "cowboy" who appears in the Coen brothers' film, *The Big Lebowski,* a demythologized old cowpoke wearing his symbols but hardly taking himself seriously. He is a cut-out, like a cigar-store Indian, refreshingly dismissed as nothing more than an old creaking bit of *deus ex machina.* And the speaker is no more worried about his own life than he is about the weather. We are free of the old entrapments, the encumbrances that once made up the sole tradition of poetry. The land has been taken off its humanistic leash.

Betty Adcock's book, *The Difficult Wheel* (1995), opens on a promising note, in the poem "Prophecy":

The poets have gone out looking for God again,
having no choice,
disguising as typeface, mirror, theory's fretful counterturn
the old search in the voice.

The trees still wave, green as a summer sea.
The grain still makes in the ear
a richness we can almost hear.
And the world still comes to be. And not to be.

Nothing has changed, really, we whisper,
though all we trumpet is the changing stir.
And the air is emptied where they were:
spirits, gods, demons, with whatever

named them gone like fallen wind. . . .

The poem closes on an intriguing note: What will the poets do now? As they search farther afield, will the poets fall as well, with a trajectory matching the descent of those ancient spirits they still seek?

What we do have is light. See how they are still burning—
all those classical noses, Coyote's laughing muzzle,

Shiva's raised foot, Christ's cheek, the dazzle
of leafy-armed women darkening, ashy-turning.

With this candle to see by, the poets are calling
and calling, much further out than they thought,
not kneeling but falling. (4–5)

The poem longs for the return of story, the story of land and animals, which the poets cannot quite bring back. But the job to do has been stated. And a wealth of lore exists already in the oral traditions of folk tales among the Hispanic and African American regional cultures, some of it collected and published already—for use by all poets in the region. Tales of Coyote and his innumerable permutations, the dog tales of the border counties, the Plains Indian fables and myths, akin to aborigine song-lines for another flat country. There is a great wealth of storytelling that has not circulated through white poetry, male or female, and begs to be rediscovered and put to use.

But the poets have other work to do that will draw audiences back to reading and appreciating this neglected art. The work includes weather lore, and tales of the farmers and ranchers, the real life of the cowboy in all its humble calling, and the vast kingdoms of plant and animal life that remain provinces of scholarship and specialized disciplines, which should pour their immense learning into poems, for common use.

There is not enough breadth and mastery of the local realities in Texas poetry. That is the chief reason few beyond the poets read or listen to it. If poetry were to explain again, in clear and vivid words, the history of the Permian Sea, and the evolution of the soils, grasses, and ungulate populations of the Plains, people would read again. And if poets were to trek with me and John Campion down to the Lower Pecos River Valley to observe, venerate, and study the great cave art that preponderates in those sandstone vaults and overhangs, and try to decipher their meanings—people would scramble to buy the poems, and keep them near at hand. The wonders of the great bison herds are left unsaid in Texas poetry—and this was the final turnaround of the southern herd, before it went north again to follow the cool weather and the last grama shoots before winter set in.

Do we know anything at all about the early cultures of this old mythical place the Spanish called Gran Quivira? Ringing the grazing grounds all

through the south terminus of the grasslands are caves with their encryp-
tions and figures, their stalk-like shamans floating above the campfires and
tripods, with dream animals hovering over. Has any poet strived to interpret and retell the stories of the original dwellers here? The evidence of bull
worship and buffalo gods is enormous; the atmosphere of an epic story
lingers over these dry plains and crumbling cave walls.

The land is epic in all senses, with ancient kingdoms lying south of us in
Mexico, old enough to be declared a second Egypt. And yet, only a handful
of poems have dealt with this imposing subject matter. Poetry will live when
new young Homers come along to tell the larger story to readers who are
simply unaware of what they live among. Naturalist poets, historical poets,
mythological poets, religious poets are all needed to fill the pages of books
no one dared to write before. While some poets felt the postmodern urge to
rip up the past and reassess western experience, their mistake was to embrace too many fragments of old religions without making them personal,
local, to be shared. Their visions were exotic and bookish and did not move
an audience to come again.

The real lore of Texas is not its feverish rehearsals of conquest over Mexico, or its patently masculine myths of breaking the spirit of wilderness.
Rather, the tales to be told are simple ones in which the land is rediscovered
and appreciated as different from human affairs, a new universe where petty
human concerns vanish as triviality. The reader in Texas will come back if
the dreams are strong enough and the stories so compelling that they teach
us something. And this, poets have not done adequately. And many writers
do know the stories, or some of them; I have whiled away many evenings
with Paul Foreman, Dave Oliphant, Robert Bonazzi, John Campion, Joseph
Colin Murphey, David Yates, and Susan Bright, all of whom had much to
relate about their knowledge of the region and its long history.

But the majority of poets have come to believe that poetry wanted something else, a self foremost, the poet's own body as the text of reality. That was
a necessary evolution of the word here, but once done, the situation demanded a deeper grasp of fact and actuality—and a power to make mere
fact come alive and to reflesh the oldest myths of the earth. What is needed
now is an imagination that knows no race or religion, no color lines of any
kind, when it tells its stories. There should be no dividing line between
white tales and black tales, red tales or brown ones. The mind should be as
borderless as the original grasslands, and tell the story of the land, all of it.

Poetry, regional and national, reflects the isolation of the middle class from both the rich and the very poor. The national diary of poetry is about middle-class angst, loneliness, marital problems, children's alienation from adults, institutional fatigue, and a glut of other anxieties. In the 1950s, the brand-new postwar movement known as Confessionalism swept over the literary landscape as a revival of verse energies. But look closer and you find that it is all about the educated and professional class feeling empty, suffering existential nausea and claustrophobia in Boston, New York, Iowa City, and London. The poets were ill, and their x-rays were poems showing how cancerous and tubercular was the human body. It was a sad poetry, lustrous in technique and dead in content.

"I myself am hell," said Robert Lowell, echoing Satan's words from *Paradise Lost,* in "Skunk Hour," the anthem of midcentury poetry, with its maudlin theme of lovesickness and its eerie vision of skunks:

They march up Main Street:
white stripes, moonstruck eyes' red fire
under the chalk-dry and spar spire
of the Trinitarian Church. (*Life Studies,* 89)

I have shocked more than one audience by observing that these so-called skunks seem a thinly veiled reference to a civil rights march of about the same time. I may be wrong, but except for the poems of John Berryman, this distinguished movement of university poets hardly ever mentioned an African American or a poor man or woman, in its voluminous outpouring of grief and anguish. I rather think part or all of the illness recorded there is not war guilt or angst over the new prosperity of Cold War America. It was an illness of being separated, rootless, cut off from whatever is the diversity and vitality of actual America. Boston was and is a mixed city of all races and classes, not a melting pot, a pressure cooker, a cyclotron, a labyrinth of realities. And one hears only of bad marriages, tranquilizers, bouts of madness, sterility, the boredom of academic careers—nothing of the dark, moist, vibrating extremes of a crowded city. It is all in the head, you might say, a middle-class disease of thinking too much, brooding over issues nourished by being out of touch.

Poetry in Texas is grafted onto part of this Confessionalism, as I have said in regard to the work of Vassar Miller. The inwardness is there, the emphasis on private suffering. She was cut off by illness from general commerce with Houston, but enjoyed the company of writers, a wide circle of friends, her editors and publishers. But she did not know Houston, which throbs with the energies of other races and a great galaxy of social classes. She couldn't break through to it—she wrote from the isolated heart, pining for the company of real lovers and true friends. She speaks unwittingly of the condition of poetry as an art of ethnic and social desertification, lovely and moving as her words are. Perhaps they are more poignant because of this isolation, which she faithfully records in her work.

Other poets are variations, suffering degrees of her isolation, and write accordingly. The classes are just as stratified and polarized in Texas as in Boston, and poets write from an imploding frame of social consciousness. Even the most passionate proletarians, such as Jim Cody, Alfred Huffstickler, Judson Crews, and David Yates, could not bring into poetry the reality of people outside the narrow confines of the educated middle class. Some would defend the right to do so, and Texas poets are heeding the advice to write about what they know. My advice is, know more. If the landscape has removed its secrets from an ecologically illiterate people, society has also vanished from our minds. The media attend to stories about those with purchasing power, and solve their crises with a little romance and fantasy. We do not know the really hardscrabble of the urban poor, the truly down and out. We do not know the rigors of being black or brown in Houston and Dallas since Griffin's day; we don't have Griffins anymore to tell us what it is like to be black or brown from a white perspective.

The narcissism runs deep, and the melancholy seems more a symptom of isolation than it does of real metaphysical problems. Poetry could cleanse itself with information about the workings of the whole human society of a city, as much as it could cleanse the soul by knowing nature again. As James Dickey once told me, poets in America are satisfied to master a postage-stamp bit of technique and stay with it their whole lives. I would say that the same postage stamp holds their consciousness of society as well, a cramped and tiny space of middle-class conflicts that are so often repeated we know them all by heart and can finish almost any lyric we see in print. The first line is enough, like the first few notes of a pop song. You know where it's going, and it is dull.

The man or woman who crosses over to know the misery of the poor, or the true estrangements of ethnicity, the beauty and the eccentricity of other ways of life—from gay marriages to communes, to revival tents and religious cults, from lives of the obese and the deformed to those who live in Edens of luxury and money—all this is news and it isn't coming from the poets. We need compassion and curiosity about people as much as we need the self-exploring contemporary lyric. I do not fault the novel or the short story as much for being socially thin; they venture more into the pockets of urban life. The film is catching up to the social realism of the twenty-first century. Only poetry remains a cloistered art set deep inside the realms of middle-class refinement.

Whitman said all this in 1860 in "To You," a poem I quote in full from *Leaves of Grass:*

> STRANGER! if you, passing, meet me, and desire to speak to me,
> why should you not speak to me?
> And why should I not speak to you?

In this moment of the last year of the twentieth century, everything is estranged but the personal soul. The suburbs insulate, the job is cushioned against the shocks of urban reality; the car buffers out the noise and confusion of reality, and lulls us with plush stereo music. The TV holds back the tedious and particular reality of daily life. Everything is filtered and controlled, from the computer to the day care center's brand of foster parenting. The food we eat is processed, rearranged, no longer garden fresh but factory fresh. And the poem, tired old dog that it is, records this overcooked spaghetti of a life in its own limp phrasing, its lack of daring or exposure to the world about us.

I started this book with a walk through the poorer stretches of my own town of Bryan and found myself alone—a quarter century ago. Nothing has changed; if anything, the isolation has gotten worse among my own kind. Even my students, who keep me informed of the world they are bringing into being, seem less aware of the street life I know. I have to tell them things about their own cities, and they listen with a bemused interest. They haven't heard. They are surprised when I tell them they are too sheltered, have not beat their soles on the street enough, and hardly know a thing about slums, barrios, the working-class districts. They know all about the Target store, nothing about the Salvation Army thrift shop, or the St. Vincent de Paul store with its old, worn-out suits and run-down shoes. They haven't been down to the night town, the pawn-shop rows, the mission houses, the public emergency wards. They may never go. They may never know, but they are also learning to write poetry in my classrooms. I try to open them, but it is slow work.

Poetry needs a new consciousness, and it is time we gave it one. When that happens, the Southwest will get written down as it deserves to be, and the poets can take the credit for having made Texas poetry great—finally. The fullness of reality demands its delivery in the poem, and to teach the country and the world what life is like west of the American dream, in a country part imaginary and part real, part myth and part sorrow, part sun and part darkness of memory.

EPILOGUE

On a hot May morning in 1996, I flew out to Amarillo to conduct workshops in poetry and fiction for a group calling itself the Panhandle Professional Writers. It is an old writing club from back in the days when women first banded together. The ground lay in vast checkerboards of brown and light green below the airplane as we lowered down into the landing path. A sinister-looking earthworks grew up suddenly with bunkers and guard towers, marking the site of the notorious Pantex bomb factory, where nuclear warheads are assembled. Some of the buildings had been dismantled, the metal bones left to bake in the sun. The debate now is whether to convert the dying factory into a repository for nuclear waste. But the factory is built over the Ogallala Aquifer, whose waters are drawn on by seven states. The governor wanted the income and jobs the repository would bring, but others were against it. The writers told me later that the town was divided; they said it as if it didn't matter, that the repository or something like it would go in anyway.

Once on the ground, I was taken to my hotel, a Holiday Inn on the side of a fierce highway of racing trucks and cars heading into the vast openness of the plains. Amarillo was not much different from other small towns across the deserts and plains: Wal-Mart stores, an IHOP, a Denny's on the frontage road, Toys-R-Us in a strip mall. The houses were a hodge-podge of ranch styles, bungalows, and Cape Cods. No sign of the work of Frank Lloyd Wright anywhere to be found. The trees were all planted since the war, low, bushy-crowned shade trees for the little side streets. A drought had been grinding along since last September, and the talk around town was about El Niño and hard times. The farmers had plowed under their wheat and corn crops.

My host toured the city with me, driving me along Route 66, taking me past the big helium reserve, a federal boondoggle, and stopping at the famous Cadillac Ranch to admire the rusty hulks buried up to their front doors in a wheat field. Stanley Marsh, the town millionaire, commissioned this work and a few dozen fake road signs bearing such things as a pair of scissors or a fox, with the words "Foxy Lady" stenciled above and below. It was his brand of humor, and he could afford to indulge it. I'm told you could order your own sign for about five hundred dollars and a road crew would install it. I looked for the fake signs, but the roads were a blur of signs to begin with. Marsh drove a pink Cadillac around town. He was one of seven landed families forming the upper gentry of Amarillo. But like a lot of people at this edge of Texas, Marsh was a nomad—his entire world seemed to float on tires.

We drove out to Palo Duro Canyon to admire the little Prairie Dog Fork that had cut so deeply into the red, iron-rich earth, and to walk over the various creek crossings where bright yellow water moved sluggishly through the weeds. The yellow water gave the town its name. The canyon was a forlorn old temple of raw, flaking stone, and deep, silent earth. A particularly vaginal looking cave overlooked one small inlet of eaten rock, where tourists would go as if to pay homage to a source of life and leave after a few snapshots. Some Indians may have camped here and found shelter. Otherwise, Boy Scouts had the run of the place, and an outdoor theater cranked up a Paul Green–type of outdoor drama called *Texas* each summer, with cowboys carrying six flags over the canyon wall beyond, to the gasps of the audience. Quanah Parker, Charles Goodnight's Comanche friend, makes a cameo appearance each evening to the tom-toms, as a crowd of pioneers mill about on stage, most of them amateur actors from around the area.

I photographed Goodnight's cabin, which was made of crude timbers and rough mortar; it had weathered the century well. Solid house, with thick lintel and window frame, too small to be more than a camp house. This is where he first sheltered with his herd, with buffalo at one end and Comanches coming and going from the other entry. He had lowered his wagons and gear by rope from a sheer cliff and led the herd down a switchback trail. The gorge was cut out of red jagged rock and was warm where we stood. At night it would be very cool in here, under the arid floor of the desert. The creeks whispered, and the trees that grew here were very tall, bushy willows, elms, and fat oaks. It was good earth.

This is where Georgia O'Keeffe came to renew herself. I could well imagine Indians coming back from a life of hunting to find this gorge a solace

and reassurance. It told you nature was good, that it had a heart. The bright
burning heat above us was one sort of nature; this was another. It was re-
markably quiet, a kind of monk's retreat. It seemed we were treading sacred
ground to walk here. This was part of that great structure Jay Peck talked
about as the wonder of a twenty-five-million-year-old geological process
that also created the Great Plains. The Rockies burst up and parched the
ground beneath, and slowly, imperceptibly, fed the bitter earth with minerals and sparse rain—enough to lure the migrant grazers onto it. Then it
became a vast ecosystem in which human, beast, dog, and insect lived
undisturbed for ten thousand or twelve thousand years.

At the Big Texan Steak Ranch restaurant, where our workshop was held,
a raised platform featured a table and chair, napkin and plate, waiting for
the next customer who dared to eat a 72-ounce steak, plus salad, potato, and
roll, in one hour, without assistance from anyone. The talk is that a woman
of 108 pounds did it, and an eight-year-old boy did it. And several customers asked for a second helping of these enormous planks of beef and ate
it down as well. The steak, the size of a large phone book, is on ice in the
lobby. A chair in the lounge where we met is fashioned entirely of cow horns
and looks like Attila the Hun's easy chair. Stuffed bears, buffalo heads, deer,
coyotes, birds, Indian weapons, and all sorts of guns adorned the interiors.

The writers were mostly older, in retirement, schoolteachers and a few
ranchers and farmers, some middle-aged and younger women, but they
were few. The original group formed in 1920 and called itself the Panhandle
Penwomen; men came much later. The women still dominated, and they
were clear, bright, prairie-hardened females whose voices rang with authority and who chided the men around them with humorous looks. The
old ranchers who had spent their lives in the sun had eyes that were crinkled
shut; they smiled like men unused to being indoors.

Getting things going was slow work; something like seventy-six years of
such meetings had gone before me. I was participating in that very ritual by
which women first invented local poetry. They had worn away all consciousness about the act of gathering to discuss writing. They behaved as if
they had heard most of what I had to say before, many times. Other writers
had come here with ideas, a few strategies to share, and left with a check, a
round of handshakes.

I gave my two workshops and left to a chorus of appreciative thanks; few
bought my books. The air outside was merciless with hot winds and feedlot

odors, with the dust rising to put a glare on the sunshine. So little is asked for, and the modest give of nature was enough, or almost enough. The women seemed drained by the harshness of climate and terrain, but hearty, stubbornly made. They were like the sage grass and saguaro, inured.

I told them to heed the little voices in the back of their minds; those were the ones that teachers killed off early by making kids sit up straight, pay attention. A young boy or girl is a wild animal and all those chattering voices inside are the body talking, instinct telling the mind its desires. To be a writer is to reawaken these natural whispers and to let them take over. That's what writing really is—a way of listening to voices that we thought we had lost.

Several women told me they had been schoolteachers and had broken the wild spirits of many children over the years. They winced at my criticisms and agreed now, after thinking it over, with what I said. But the rest reserved their opinions until later. They were schooled in the angers of a distant God, whose will was translated by formidable preachers and carried out by harsh justice, and a plain, uncomfortable education. My words were like a brief spring rain on the dust of a garden plot, but the green I provided would be short-lived and undefended against the powers of the sun.

They wore thick skin around their child-like spirits, and I had found a way to tease the child back into their faces. The women, especially, felt I was honest with them. They chose to believe me, but in that Texan way of keeping the eyes down, the lips skeptical. I could have wished for more approval or signs of emotion; I settled for what I got.

But it wasn't really enough. I didn't shake anyone's roots, I didn't recreate the world for them, and I should have. I had come a long way from one side of Texas to this one, a distance measured by miles and a lot of years. I came with a little of the knowledge of this landscape and with a sense of tragedy inside me—tragedy that what seemed so hardy and stubborn, so rooted and implacable in its determination, was still not enough. Anglo culture here was woefully inadequate to the land, and to its past. These were people who gathered to hear what someone from elsewhere had to say, but in their hearts they were satisfied with a way of life, a faith in themselves. They didn't need me as a way out or as a path.

But the race that perished here at the hands of the westward push of Europeans had not tried to break the land. It was understood thousands of years before that the land was eternal, unchangeable. You pitched a frail little tipi here and moved on when the summer raged, or the droughts killed off the ephemeral life. You didn't try to farm such land; it was beyond farming. But from above, in the plane coming in, you could see these vast circles of mild green where irrigating machines had gone round and round spraying moisture into the desert floor, feeding the seeds. It was an eerie sight, vast numbers of these circles floating uneasily over the red earth, as if Mark Rothko had come here to paint a few of his abstract compositions, a few more *Earth and Green* paintings. It was that attempt to change the will of the earth and humanize it, make it work.

But this was earth that didn't do human bidding. And the cultures that once walked here knew that—you accepted the rule of some ferocious animal called the sun and the wild, hard, unyielding beast of the land. Between them you were that bug that crawled around, pursuing a little meat for the day, a little fire for the cold of night. And all the while, you tried to reach out with your wizards and shamans to talk to these powers of myth and religion, to offer them little appeasements in the form of beaded pouches, a carved stick, a tale at night around the fires. You had so little human will to assert over what was a living landscape.

Amarillo lived in a cramped and suffocating vision that humans prevailed and that they were alone and without a living landscape to fit into. The town was a closed mind, adamant about following procedures and habits that could only work by daily battle and adversity, by excessive amounts of water and pesticide and waste to sustain the life that was not meant to grow this way. It was a forced and artificial culture, and clearly a lesser civilization than the one it had vanquished. Amarillo was America in miniature, the cultural realm that had put all its faith in machinery and artificial solutions and now lived in an uneasy, expensive, and utterly blind relation to nature. Everywhere you looked, things were arbitrary, indifferently made or thrown together, as if deliberately made temporary while these good Christians eked out a survival in the wilderness of the New World.

But the women I met *did know something,* or they wouldn't have listened at all. They knew something was vitally and profoundly wrong with a culture that didn't grow or open itself fundamentally to the powers around it. The regime they lived under was simple enough—a desire to contain the human world within a few artificial amenities like air conditioning and plumbing, a system of roads and the comforts of television. But the price was to be deaf and blind to the truth of this brilliant, difficult, alien terrain, with its own laws and its own powerful myths. All that was beyond the reach of their imaginations, and still they strived to write and tell stories to one another, to connect themselves to something beyond their own lives.

The truth was, Amarillo seemed poised on the very edge of the New World, as if it were about to open the last door to what was primal and everlasting in this country. But a certain definition of god and heaven and biblical injunction said not to, and the people went on living in the old ways, with the nuclear weapons plant nearby, the irrigators throwing their white spray into the wind, and the wind blowing down on those hot little streets with the moans of eternity. It was Texas, and it had its rules to live by, some of which refused to let the heart know this land in a way that would have dissolved some of the boundaries between what is human and what isn't. A sense of wonder might have been a new language for the writers I was now leaving behind. But they would go on with the vocabulary they had, and the parched vision they were given, and make do, abide, and go on.

It was a harsh sentence, unnecessary. The imagination starved under its tyranny, but that made for tougher spirits and leaner lives and was the law they accepted. I could no more convert a hard Christian out here than I could a snake. Literature might never water the desert of the heart in this curious land, so long as it came from sources alien to the desert and from other worlds. Until someone crossed over and said to Texas that a new faith was needed, things would go on as they had for a century and a half—with a hard logic and a determination not to give in to the voices that spoke through the ground and the weather.

South of us, in Mexico, the land had already entered into human vision; and before this town was built, straggling nomads carried with them gods and feathered charms that not only connected them with the spirits here but with the gods elsewhere, in Australia, Africa, the mountain deities of Tibet, and the voices of the mist in the hills of southern China, in the depths of the Nile Valley. The native world was once entirely unified by the same gods and folk tales, and there was no such thing as isolation or disconnection from the ground you trod upon with your relatives and dogs and your travois heaped with skins and poles. It is gone now, uprooted and discarded, and only the dry ground remains, with a people determined to live out their isolation as best they can. I am reminded of what Robert Frost said at John Kennedy's inauguration back in 1961, in his poem, "The Gift Outright":

> The land was ours before we were the land's.
> She was our land more than a hundred years
> Before we were her people. She was ours
> In Massachusetts, in Virginia,
> But we were England's, still colonials,
> Possessing what we still were unpossessed by,
> Possessed by what we now no more possessed.
> Something we were withholding made us weak
> Until we found out that it was ourselves
> We were withholding from our land of living,
> And forthwith found salvation in our surrender. (*Modern American Poets*, 225)

There has been no surrender in Texas, only cultural warfare against what still remained the alien will of things—needing to be broken. The great circles of artificial moisture and green in this desert was such a war. The Pantex plant was another war, aimed at all we distrust in the world, perhaps for good reason. But distrust it was. A distrust of the things as they are. No question that the Anglos were and are the interlopers on the land, and the idea of surrender was alien to the very bedrock of imagination among these people. The boys at school fought on the gridiron, fought for their girls, fought to get jobs, and fought the termites and fire ants and the hot weather as long as they could draw breath.

Surrender began, I suppose, in listening to the body's murmurs and echoes, those distant, discarded voices exorcised in cramped desks at school, to the crack of a ruler or a scolding voice. The little voices that roam in the body are the spirits of nature, calling to us to surrender, to give in, yield a little. In a poem of my own, "Dying Mole," written some years ago and recited once in the company of Paul Foreman, who singled it out as among his favorites from my work, I wrote that this modest tunnel-digger was now dying above ground, and has one last thought to give to the world:

> Beware, beware cries the dying mole
> with the buzzard loafing overhead,
> give in, yield thyself, conquer selfishness.

The land was a text, a biblical scripture waiting to be read by anyone open enough to translate its wisdom: the land demanded surrender, a chance to possess those who nursed from it. But it was so alien, so distant, so remote from anything in the roots of western thinking, how could one yield ego and passion, self and religion to such a threat, such a difficult mother? That was the question. That is the question lying at the heart of Texas itself—this land in which the first generations took what they could from nature and gave back little. The next century will demand surrender, repayment, veneration in a form that will humble the human dwellers. "People shape, or at least re-arrange, the land," wrote Tom Pilkington in his own orienteering book, *State of Mind*. "But reciprocally the land shapes people; sometimes the shaping even seems like vengeance for sins against the environment. 'The spirit of place,' in prophetic Lawrentian terminology, *will* be 'atoned for'" (51).

We were all of us west of the American dream, still carrying those immigrant passions to advance and enrich ourselves, only to face land that denied this easy wealth or satisfaction. It was not quiet, passive earth; it was vast epic nature, powerful beyond our wildest estimates and fears. It was a nature that would always humble those who attempted to wrest anything much from it. Our heroes had made it big, but that was then. The bounty of water and petroleum resources that once made it seem a paradise for easy plucking have all dwindled; thick smog hangs over Big Bend National Park, one of the great treasure houses of nature. Houston is now the nation's most polluted city. Smog has crept over the coastal plains to hang its thin, gray, death-colored veils over little Bryan, where the trees are no longer as fresh or vigorous as they were when I arrived. The great sepia-dark Brazos is corrupted with every sort of agricultural excess. The new Texas is a lesser place than it was even a century ago; what remains is this rocky, twisted, thorn-laced, difficult face of another god—whose demands for atonement after pillage and waste are very clear.

The Comanches learned a way to walk in the high grass in which no stem was broken or bent for long; the way closed behind you as you crept forth over the face of earth without a trace. That should tell us something about the modesty of human participation—take, but leave no trace. And after eating, give thanks. And return what is not consumed to its place where it may regenerate. These are simple virtues, but good ones, solid ones for making the earth yield its fruits forever. There are some here who believe, and believe deeply, that they are punished by this earth, and must take up the struggle for life where Cain left off.

NOTES

These notes provide bibliographical information about works discussed at the chapter and page locations indicated in the column at left.

PREFACE

xii   D. W. Meinig, *Imperial Texas: An Interpretive Essay in Cultural Geography* (Austin: University of Texas Press, 1969).

xv   Dave Oliphant, *On a High Horse: Views Mostly of Latin American and Texan Poetry* (Fort Worth, Tex.: Prickly Pear Press, 1983).

xv   Tom Pilkington, *State of Mind: Texas Literature and Culture* (College Station: Texas A&M University Press, 1998).

CHAPTER 1. FIRST THINGS

11   Herman Melville, *Moby Dick,* ed. Harrison Hayford and Hershel Parker (New York: Norton, 1967), 169.

12   Walter Prescott Webb, *The Great Plains* (Boston: Houghton Mifflin, 1931).

19   Geographical details are gleaned from Carle C. Zimmerman, "The Great Plains as a Region," in *Symposium on the Great Plains of North America,* ed. Carle C. Zimmerman and Seth Russell (Fargo: North Dakota Institute for Regional Studies, 1967), 3–9.

25   Especially helpful in understanding the Anglo culture of independent Texas is Meinig, *Imperial Texas,* 38–62. Also useful is *The Anglo-American Texans* (San Antonio: University of Texas at San Antonio, Institute of Texan Cultures, 1975).

CHAPTER 2. OF UNDERWORLDS

39   John Graves, *Goodbye to a River* (New York: Knopf, 1960).

40   Larry McMurtry, "Ever a Bridegroom: Reflections on the Failure of Texas Literature," *Texas Observer,* Oct. 23, 1981, 1, 8–18; rpt. in *Range Wars: Heated Debates, Sober Reflections, and Other Assessments of Texas Writing,* ed. Craig Clifford and Tom Pilkington (Dallas: Southern Methodist University Press, 1989), 13–41.

CHAPTER 3. POETRY READINGS

51   Richard Poirier, *Robert Frost: The Work of Knowing* (New York: Oxford
       University Press, 1977).

51   E. D. H. Johnson, *The Alien Vision of Victorian Poetry* (Hamden, Conn.:
       Anchor, 1963).

52   Leonidas Payne, Jr., *A Survey of Texas Literature* (New York: Rand
       McNally and Co., 1928). See also Mary Tucker's *Books of the Southwest: A
       General Bibliography* (New York: J. J. Augustin, 1937), which she
       describes as "the first complete list of the 'Books of the Southwest.'" Of
       the forty-eight books listed under the rubric "Verse and Songs," few
       contain original poetry.

52   *Texas: A Guide to the Lone Star State, Compiled by Workers of the Writers'
       Program of the Work Projects Administration in the State of Texas* (New
       York: Hastings House, 1940). See the chapter entitled "Literature,"
       124–32.

52   Hilton Ross Greer, ed., *Voices of the Southwest: A Book of Texan Verse*
       (New York: Macmillan, 1923); Greer and Florence Elberta Barnes, eds.,
       New Voices of the Southwest (Dallas: Tardy Publishing, 1934).

53   Paul Christensen, "The Buried Life: Texas Women Poets: 1920–1960," in
       Texas Women Writers, ed. Sylvia Ann Grider and Lou Halsell
       Rodenberger (College Station: Texas A&M University Press, 1997),
       287–93.

55   Billy Bob Hill, ed., *Texas in Poetry: A 150-Year Anthology* (Denton:
       Center for Texas Studies, Texas Studies Association, 1994).

56   Ray Gonzalez, ed., *Inheritance of Light* (Denton: University of North
       Texas Press, 1996).

59   William Carlos Williams, *In the American Grain* (Norfolk, Conn.: New
       Directions, 1925).

65   Annette Kolodny, *The Lay of the Land: Metaphor as Experience in
       American Life and Letters* (Chapel Hill: University of North Carolina
       Press, 1975); *The Land before Her: Fantasy and Experience of the American
       Frontiers: 1630–1860* (Chapel Hill: University of North Carolina Press,
       1984).

65   *A Book of the Year* (Dallas: Poetry Society of Texas, 1951).

66   John Graves, "The Old Guard: Dobie, Webb, and Bedichek," in *The
       Texas Literary Tradition: Fiction, Folklore, History,* ed. Don Graham,
       James W. Lee, William T. Pilkington (Austin: College of Liberal Arts,
       University of Texas at Austin, Texas State Historical Association, 1983),
       16–25.

66   Cecil Robinson, *Mexico and the Hispanic Southwest in American
       Literature,* rev. ed. of *With the Ears of Strangers,* 1963 (Tucson: University
       of Arizona Press, 1977), 339.

66   J. Frank Dobie, *Coronado's Children: Tales of Lost Mines and Buried Treasures of the Southwest* (Dallas: Southwest Press, 1930).

67   Walter Prescott Webb, *The Great Frontier* (Boston: Houghton Mifflin, 1952); *Texas Rangers: A Century of Frontier Defense* (Boston: Houghton Mifflin, 1935); *Divided We Stand: The Crisis of a Frontierless Democracy* (New York and Toronto: Farrar and Rinehart, 1937).

67   Roy Bedichek, *Adventures with a Texas Naturalist* (Garden City, N.J.: Doubleday, 1947).

67   Webb, *History as High Adventure*, ed. E. C. Barksdale (Austin, Tex.: Jenkins Garrett Foundation/Pemberton Press, 1969).

67   Larry McMurtry, "Southwestern Literature?" *In a Narrow Grave: Essays on Texas* (Austin, Tex.: Encino Press, 1968; rpt., Albuquerque: University of New Mexico Press, 1983).

67   A. C. Greene, "The Texas Literati: Whose Home Is This Range, Anyhow?" *New York Times Book Review*, Sept. 15, 1985, 3, passim.

68   Christine Pickering Ford, "Sign Language in *Lonesome Dove*," in *Myth and Voice of Texas Writers*, ed. William E. Tanner (Arlington, Tex.: Liberal Arts Press, 1991), 15–28. Quotation from Don Graham, "Regionalism on the Ramparts: The Texas Literary Tradition," *USA Today*, July, 1986, 74–76.

68   Larry McMurtry, *Lonesome Dove: A Novel* (New York: Simon and Schuster, 1985).

CHAPTER 4. I AND THOU

71   Davis Foute Eagleton, ed., *Texas Literature Reader* (Dallas: Southern Publishing, 1916).

71   John L. McCarly, *Wind in the Cottonwoods* (Dalhart, Tex.: Dalhart Publishing, 1936); *Prairie Nights and Yucca* (Dalhart, Tex.: Dalhart Publishing, 1934).

71   Anna J. Pennybacker, *A History of Texas: For Schools*, rev. ed. (Austin, Texas: Mr. Percy V. Pennybacker, Publisher, 1912).

75   David W. Teague, *The Southwest in American Literature and Art: The Rise of a Desert Aesthetic* (Tucson: University of Arizona Press, 1997).

79   Webb, "The Approach to the Great Plains," in *The Great Plains*, 140–204; see esp. 184–200.

80   Eleanor James, "Martha White McWhirter (1827–1904)," in *Women in Early Texas*, ed. Evelyn M. Carrington (Austin: Texas State Historical Association, 1994), 180–90.

81   J. Frank Dobie, *Guide to Life and Literature of the Southwest, with a Few Observations* (Dallas: Southern Methodist University Press, 1943); *Guide to Life and Literature of the Southwest, Revised and Enlarged in Both Knowledge and Wisdom* (Dallas: Southern Methodist University Press, 1952).

82   Steven Ford Brown, ed., *Heart's Invention: On the Poetry of Vassar Miller* (Houston: Ford-Brown and Co., 1988).

84   John Howard Griffin, *Black Like Me* (Boston: Houghton Mifflin, 1961).

84   Paul Christensen, "From Cowboys to Curanderas: The Cycle of Texas Literature," *Southwest Review* 73, no.1 (winter, 1988): 10–29.

86   Dave Oliphant, ed., *The New Breed: An Anthology of Texas Poets* (Austin, Tex.: Prickly Pear Press, 1973).

88   Paul Foreman and Joanie Whitebird, eds. *Travois: An Anthology of Texas Poetry* (Berkeley, Calif.: Contemporary Arts Museum of Houston, [1976]).

93   Gary Snyder, *The Back Country* (New York: New Directions, 1968, 1971).

94   Robert Bonazzi, *Living the Borrowed Life* (New York: New Rivers Press, 1974); *Fictive Music* (Houston: Wings Press, 1979); *Perpetual Texts* (Mansfield, Tex.: Latitudes Press, 1986).

95   John Campion, *Tongue Stones* (Austin, Tex.: Eco-Tropic Books, 1990).

95   Giorgio de Santillana and Hertha von Dechend, *Hamlet's Mill: An Essay on Myth and the Frame of Time* (Boston: Gambit Press, 1969).

CHAPTER 5. "GOOD-BY, YOU BIG LUMMAX, I'M GLAD YOU BACKED OUT"

102   Michael Rice, *The Power of the Bull* (London and New York: Routledge, 1998).

103   Jay Peck, "The Destruction of the North American Bison," in *Ecotropic Works,* ed. John Campion (Berkeley, Calif.: Ecotropic Books, 1999), 37–44.

103   Charles Olson, *Call Me Ishmael* (New York: Reynal and Hitchcock, 1947; rpt., San Francisco: City Lights Books, n.d.).

106   John A. Lomax and Alan Lomax, *Cowboy Songs and Other Frontier Ballads,* rev. ed. (New York: Macmillan, 1938), xviii.

107   William Cronon, George Miles, and Jay Gitlin, eds., *Under an Open Sky: Rethinking America's Western Past* (New York: Norton, 1992).

110   Jacqueline Jones Royster, *Traces of a Stream: Literacy and Social Change among African American Women* (Pittsburgh: University of Pittsburgh Press, 2000).

111   Betty Wiespape, "Literary Societies and Writing Clubs in Texas, 1890–1940: Their Role in the Development of Regional Literature" (Ph.D. diss., University of Texas at Dallas, 1998).

112   *Dallas Morning News,* Mar. 31, 1999, 4C.

112   Cronon, Miles, and Gitlin, eds., "Becoming West: Toward a New Meaning for Western History," in *Under an Open Sky,* 18–19.

CHAPTER 6. A PHOTO ALBUM

125   Mary Louise Ferguson, *When We Speak of Mysteries* (Bryan, Tex.: Cedarshouse Press, 1986).

142   Paul Foreman, *Redwing Blackbird* (San Francisco: Headstone Press, 1973).

144   George Sessions Perry, *Hold Autumn in Your Hand* (New York: Viking Press, 1941); *Walls Rise Up* (Garden City, N.Y.: Doubleday, 1959).

CHAPTER 7. THE IMAGINATION

148   Alfred North Whitehead, *Process and Reality: An Essay in Cosmology* (New York: Macmillan, 1929).

149   Whitehead and Bertrand Russell, *Principia Mathematica,* 2nd ed., 3 vols. (Cambridge: Cambridge University Press, 1925–27).

150   Fritjof Capra, *The Tao of Physics: An Exploration of the Parallels between Modern Physics and Eastern Mysticism,* 3rd ed. (Boston: Shambhala, 1991).

151   Jane Ellen Harrison, *Themis: A Study of the Social Origins of Greek Religion* (Cambridge: Cambridge University Press, 1912).

151   David Miller, *The New Polytheism: Rebirth of the Gods and Goddesses* (New York: Harper and Row, 1974; rpt. Dallas: Spring Publications, 1981).

151   James Hillman, *Healing Fiction* (Barrytown, N.Y.: Station Hill Press, 1983).

153   Morris Berman, *The Reenchantment of the World* (Ithaca, N.Y.: Cornell University Press, 1981).

154   Monica Sjöö and Barbara Mor, *The Great Cosmic Mother: Rediscovering the Religion of the Earth,* 2nd ed. (San Francisco: Harper San Francisco, 1991).

154   Hilda Doolittle, *Selected Poems* (New York: Grove Press, 1957).

157   J. Frank Dobie, *A Texan in England* (Boston: Little, Brown, 1945).

159   Américo Paredes, *George Washington Gomez: A Mexicotexan Novel* (Houston: Arte Público Press, 1990); *With His Pistol in His Hand: A Border Ballad and Its Hero* (Austin: University of Texas Press, 1958).

159   Leticia Garza-Falcón, *Gente Decente: A Borderlands Response to the Rhetoric of Dominance* (Austin: University of Texas Press, 1998).

160   William Carlos Williams, *The Desert Music and Other Poems* (New York: Random House, 1954).

161   See, e.g., Dennis Tedlock, "The Analogical Tradition and the Emergence of a Dialogical Anthropology," in *The Spoken Word and the World of Interpretation* (Philadelphia: University of Pennsylvania Press, 1983), 321–28).

161   For the skull imagery, see Laurie Lisle, *Portrait of an Artist: A Biography of Georgia O'Keeffe* (New York: Washington Square Press, 1980), 322–23.

CHAPTER 8. HOW TO READ A POEM

179   Susan Turner Adams, "A Bibliography of Texas Poetry, 1945–1981" (M. A. thesis, Texas A&M University, 1982).

181   Evan S. Connell, "The Anatomy Lesson," in *The Short Story*, ed.
       Willoughby Johnson and William C. Hamlin (New York: American
       Book Company, 1966), 289–303.

184   William Barney, *The Killdeer Crying*, ed. Dave Oliphant (Austin, Tex.:
       Prickly Pear Press, 1977; rev. ed., 1983).

187   Barney, *Long Gone to Texas* (Austin, Tex.: Nortex Press, 1986); *Words
       from a Wide Land* (Denton: University of North Texas Press, 1993).

189   Vassar Miller, *Adam's Footprint* (New Orleans: New Orleans Poetry
       Journal, 1956).

189   R. G. Vliet, *Events and Celebrations: Poems* (New York: Viking Press,
       1966); *The Man with the Black Mouth* (Santa Cruz, Calif.: Kayak Books,
       1970); Albert Goldbarth, *Different Fleshes* (Geneva, N.Y.: Williams and
       Hobart Smith Colleges Press, 1979).

191   Joseph Colin Murphey, *A Return to the Landscape* (Fort Worth, Tex.:
       Prickly Pear Press, 1979).

192   Charles Behlen, *Perdition's Keepsake* (Fort Worth, Tex.: Prickly Pear
       Press, 1978).

192   Dave Oliphant, *Taking Stock* (Dallas: Prickly Pear Press, 1973).

193   John Campion, Paul Christensen, and John Herndon, *Where Three
       Roads Meet* (Bryan and Austin, Tex.: Cedarshouse/Open Theater, 1995).

194   Sandra Lynn, *I Must Hold These Strangers: Poems* (Austin, Tex.: Prickly
       Pear Press, 1980); *Where Rainbows Wait for Rain: The Big Bend Country*
       (Granbury, Tex.: Tangram Press, 1989).

196   Susan Bright, *House of the Mother* (Austin, Tex.: Plain View Press, 1995);
       Next to the Last Word (Austin, Tex.: Plain View Press, 1998).

197   Naomi Shihab Nye, *Sitti's Secrets* (New York: Four Winds Press, Maxwell
       Macmillan International, 1994); *Habibi* (New York: Simon and Schuster
       Books for Young Readers, 1997); *The Tree Is Older Than You Are: A Bilingual
       Gathering of Poems and Stories from Mexico with Paintings by Mexican Artists*
       (New York: Simon and Schuster Books for Young Readers, 1995); *Never in a
       Hurry: Essays on People and Places* (Columbia: University of South Carolina
       Press, 1996); *Different Ways to Pray: Poems* (Portland, Ore.: Breitenbush
       Publications, 1980); *Hugging the Jukebox* (New York: Dutton, 1982); *Yellow
       Glove* (Portland, Ore.: Breitenbush Publications, 1986).

202   Rosemary Catacalos, *Again for the First Time* (Santa Fe, N.Mex.: Tooth of
       Time Books, 1984).

208   John Campion, *Squaring the Circle* (Berkeley, Calif.: Ecotropic Works, 1994).

CHAPTER 9. DEMOCRATIC VISTAS

210   David Arias, *Spanish Roots in America* (Huntington, Ind.: Our Sunday
       Visitor Publishing Division, 1992), 121.

211   Walt McDonald, "Praise," in *After the Noise of Saigon* (Amherst:
       University of Massachusetts Press, 1988).

213 Robert Bonazzi, *Living the Borrowed Life* (New York: New Rivers Press, 1974), and *Fictive Music* (Houston: Wings Press, 1979); *Perpetual Texas* (Mansfield, Tex.: Latitudes Press, 1986); Bonazzi, ed., *Selected and New Poems, 1950–1980* by Vassar Miller (Austin, Tex.: Latitudes Press, 1981); *The Man in the Mirror: John Howard Griffin and the Story of* Black Like Me (Maryknoll, N.Y.: Orbis Books, 1997).

215 William Burford, *Man Now* (Dallas: Southern Methodist University Press, 1954); *A World* (Austin: University of Texas Press, 1962); *A Beginning: Poems* (New York: Norton, 1966).

215 James Hoggard, *Two Gulls, One Hawk* (Austin, Tex.: Prickly Pear Press, 1983); *The Shaper Poems* (Bryan, Tex.: Cedarshouse Press, 1982); *Trotter Ross* (Austin, Tex.: Thorp Springs Press, 1981); *Medea in Taos* (San Antonio: Pecan Grove Press, 2000); *Rain in a Sunlit Sky* (Houston: Page One, 2000).

218 Kendall McCook, *This Land* (Austin, Tex.: Eakin Press, 1984).

218 Paul Foreman, *Sugarland* (Berkeley, Calif.: Thorp Springs Press, 1978), and *Quanah, the Serpent Eagle* (Flagstaff, Ariz.: Northland Press, 1983).

219 Mel Kenne, *Eating the Fruit* (Kuala Lumpur, Malaysia: Cedarshouse Press, 1987).

220 James Marion Cody, *A Book of Wonders: Dreams, Visions, and Unusual Experiences* (Bryan, Tex.: Cedarshouse Press, 1988).

223 John Campion, *Tongue Stones* (Austin, Tex.: Eco-Tropic Books, 1990).

223 John Herndon, *Poems from Undertown* (Austin, Tex.: Eco-Tropic Books, 1990); *Proof That the World Is Real* (Austin, Tex.: Tantra Press, 1999).

226 Dave Oliphant and Luis Ramos-Garcia, eds., *Washing the Cow's Skull: Texas Poetry in Translation/Lavando la calavera de vaca: poesía texana en traduccion* (Fort Worth, Tex.: Prickly Pear Press, 1981).

231 Dave Oliphant, *Lines and Mounds* (Berkeley, Calif.: Thorp Springs Press, 1976); *Austin* (Austin, Tex.: Prickly Pear Press, 1985); *Texan Jazz* (Austin: University of Texas Press, 1996).

232 Paul Foreman, "Pecans," in *Redwing Blackbird*.

CHAPTER 10. A PORTRAIT OF VASSAR MILLER

241 Vassar Miller, *If I Had Wheels or Love* (Dallas: Southern Methodist University Press, 1991).

242 Lexie Dean Robertson, *Red Heels* (Dallas: P. L. Turner, [1928]; rpt., Dallas: Kaleidograph Press, 1939).

252 Vassar Miller, *Struggling to Swim on Concrete* (New Orleans: New Orleans Poetry Journal Press, 1984).

CHAPTER 11. A PORTRAIT OF CHARLES GORDONE

256 George Washington Cable, *The Creoles of Louisiana,* ed. Arlin Turner. (Rpt., New York: Garnett Press, 1970).

256   Charles Gordone, *No Place to Be Somebody: A Black Black Comedy in Three Acts,* intro. by Joseph Papp (Indianapolis: Bobbs-Merrill, 1969).

258   Langston Hughes, "The Negro Artist and the Racial Mountain," *The Nation,* June 23, 1926, 692–94.

259   Philip C. Kolin and Colby H. Kullman, eds. *Speaking on Stage: Interviews with Contemporary American Playwrights* (Tuscaloosa: University of Alabama Press, 1996).

260   Jean Genet, *The Blacks: A Clown Show* (New York: Grove Press, 1960).

261   Jean-Paul Sartre, *Saint Genet: Actor and Martyr* (New York: Pantheon Books, 1963).

264   Kate Ezra, *Art of the Dogon: Selections from the Lester Wunderman Collection* (New York: Metropolitan Museum of Art/H. N. Abrams, 1988).

266   Charles Gordone quoted in Buck Ramsey, "A Revival Meeting and Its Missionaries: The Cowboy Poetry Gathering," in *The Changing Faces of Tradition : A Report on the Folk and Traditional Arts in the United States,* ed. Elizabeth Peterson (Washington, D.C.: National Endowment for the Arts, 1996), 44.

CHAPTER 12. A PORTRAIT OF RICARDO SÁNCHEZ

275   Rosmarie Waldrop, *Against Language? Dissatisfaction with Language as Theme and as Impulse towards Experiments in Twentieth Century Poetry* (The Hague: Mouton, 1971), 121.

278   Ricardo Sánchez, *Canto y grito mi liberación (y lloro mis desmadrazgos . . .): pensamientos, gritos, angustias, orgullos, penumbras poéticas, ensayos, historietas, hechizos almales del son de mi existencia* (Garden City, N.Y.: Doubleday, 1973).

279   Sánchez, *Eagle-Visioned/Feathered Adobes: Manito Sojourns and Pachuco Ramblings, October 4th to 24th, 1981* (El Paso, Tex.: Cinco Puntos Press, 1990).

281   Allen Ginsberg, *Fall of America: Poems of These States* (San Francisco: City Lights, 1972).

281   Ken Kesey, *One Flew over the Cuckoo's Nest* (New York: Viking Press, 1962).

284   Sánchez, *Selected Poems* (Houston: Arte Público Press, 1985); *Loves of Ricardo* (Chicago: Tia Chucha Press/Northwestern University Press, 1990).

CHAPTER 13. "THE SIMPLE BITTER SAP"

288   Mary Austin, *Starry Adventure* (Boston: Houghton Mifflin, 1931).

288   Willa Cather, *Death Comes for the Archbishop* (New York: Knopf, 1927).

288   Dorothy Scarborough, *The Wind* (New York: Harper and Brothers, 1925).

288   Oliver La Farge, *Laughing Boy* (New York: Literary Guild of America, 1929).

288   Paul Horgan, *No Quarter Given* (New York: Harper, 1935); *Figures in a Landscape* (New York: Harper, 1940).

288   Conrad Richter, *The Sea of Grass* (New York: Knopf, 1937).

288   J. Frank Dobie, *The Cow People* (Boston: Little, Brown, 1964).

288   Edna Ferber, *Giant* (Garden City, N.Y.: Doubleday, 1952); *Crock of Gold* (1939).

288   James Stephens, *Crock of Gold* (New York: Macmillan, 1940).

289   William A. Owens, *This Stubborn Soil: A Frontier Boyhood* (New York: Scribner, 1966).

292   Paul Christensen, *Signs of the Whelming* (Fort Worth, Tex.: Latitudes Press, 1983).

293   Wild's poems first appeared in Doug Flaherty, ed., *Their Place in the Heat* (Albuquerque, N.Mex.: Road Runner Press, 1971).

298   Charles Bernstein, "Against National Poetry Month as Such," an essay commissioned for the University of Chicago Press website, <www.press.uchicago.edu>, May, 1999, in conjunction with the publication of his book *My Way: Speeches and Poems* (Chicago: University of Chicago Press, 1999).

301   Leon Stokesbury, *Often in Different Landscapes* (Austin: University of Texas Press, 1976).

302   Betty Adcock, *The Difficult Wheel: Poems* (Baton Rouge: Louisiana State University Press, 1995).

305   Robert Lowell, "Skunk Hour," in *Life Studies* (New York: Farrar, Straus, and Cudahy, 1959).

EPILOGUE

315   Robert Frost, "The Gift Outright," in *Modern American Poets: Their Voices and Visions,* ed. Robert DiYanni (New York: Random House, 1987).

INDEX

Gordone, Charles, xiii, 238, 255–74;
background, 256–59; and Dogan
effigies, 264; "Ghost Riders," 270–
71, 272; last days, 271–74; *No Place to
Be Somebody,* 256–57, 258–59, 260–
63, 264–65; and race, 255–57, 258–
59, 260–61, 262, 263, 265, 268, 269,
271; "Roan Browne and Cherry,"
269–70; and Susan Kouyomjian,
255–56, 266, 269, 273–74; as teacher,
267–68, 273; "Yes, I am a Black
Playwright," 259
Graham, Don, 68
Graves, John, 39, 66, 145; *Goodbye to a
River,* 39, 145; in *The Texas Literary
Tradition,* 66
Great Plains, The (Webb), 12, 67, 79,
177, 289
Greene, A. C., 67, 240
Greer, Hilton Ross: *New Voices of the
Southwest,* 52, 54, 75–78; *Voices of
the Southwest,* 52
Griesser, Charles, 135–39; Ellie-Mae
(wife), 139
Griffin, John Howard, 84, 306; *Black
Like Me,* 84, 214, 291; and Bonazzi,
214; *Follow the Ecstasy: Thomas
Merton, The Heritage Years 1965–
1968,* 214; and Merton, 214
Guadalupe Arts Center, xv, 279
Gulf of Mexico, 10, 20, 26; coast, 10
Gulf Stream, 5, 10
Gwynn, R. S., 94, 238

Hall, Donald, 225
hands, 37–39
Hannah, James, xv
Harrigan, Stephen: *The Gates of the
Alamo,* 218
Harrison, Jane Ellen: *Themis: A Study
of the Social Origins of Greek
Religion,* 151
Harte, Bret, 110, 288

Hartmann, Evalyn: "Olmec," 92
*Heart's Invention: On the Poetry of
Vassar Miller,* 82–83
Heine, Heinrich, 143, 235
Hemingway, Ernest, 66, 191, 266
Heraclitus, 143, 147
Herndon, John, xv, 145; discussed,
223–24; *Ecotropic Works,* 168–69,
223; and Open Theater, 223; photo,
233; *Poems from Undertown,* 223
heroes, ix, 70, 131; cowboy, 55; white
European, 164
Hill, Billy Bob: *Texas in Poetry: A 150-
Year Anthology,* 55–56
Hillman, Grady, 226
Hillman, James, 151–53; on demonology,
151–52; *Healing Fiction,* 151–52
Hinojosa-Smith, Rolando, 164, 283
Hirsch, Ed, 224
Hispanics, 14, 16, 84, 163, 211, 303;
imagination of, 165; magic healers,
211; poetry, 95; Tió Tom, 24; writers,
220. *See also* race
Hoggard, James, xiv, 92, 94, 225;
analysis of, 215–18; *Medea in Taos,*
217; *Rain in the Sunlit Sky,* 217; *The
Shaper Poems,* 217; "The Tornado's
Eye," 215–17; *Trotter Ross,* 217–18;
Two Gulls, One Hawk, 215
Holocaust, 84, 106
"Home on the Range," 105
Homer, 300, 304
Horgan, Paul, 288
Horse, 100–102, 105, 106
Houston, Tex., 224–25
Howells, William Dean, 51
Huffstickler, Alfred, 94–95, 229, 306
Hughes, Langston: and Gordone, 258;
and Harlem Renaissance, 258; "The
Negro Artist and the Racial
Mountain," 258
humanism, viii, 156
Hurst, Jennifer, 91

PAUL CHRISTENSEN earned his Ph.D. at the University of Pennsylvania and has been a professor of English at Texas A&M University since 1974. He is a poet and essayist who lives part of the year in France, where he is a contributing editor to *France Today*.